Children's Social Worlds in

Tiia Tulviste · Deborah L. Best ·
Judith L. Gibbons
Editors

Children's Social Worlds
in Cultural Context

 Springer

Editors
Tiia Tulviste
Department of Psychology
University of Tartu
Tartu, Estonia

Deborah L. Best
Department of Psychology
Wake Forest University
Winston-Salem, NC, USA

Judith L. Gibbons
Department of Psychology
Saint Louis University
Saint Louis, MO, USA

ISBN 978-3-030-27035-3   ISBN 978-3-030-27033-9   (eBook)
https://doi.org/10.1007/978-3-030-27033-9

This Springer imprint is published by the registered company Springer Nature Switzerland AG
The registered company address is: Gewerbestrasse 11, 6330 Cham, Switzerland

This book is dedicated to our children, our biological ones, as well as the many we have "adopted" as mentees and special friends. Also, included in this dedication are the numerous children who have participated in our research projects over the years. As we learned about aspects of their social and cognitive development, we grew to understand the essential role that culture plays in their ever-expanding worlds. We have learned so much from all of the children in our lives, and we thank you.

Foreword

*The boys and girls of the world enter many different
childhoods and depart them through many different doors.*
Göran Therborn (2009 p. 338)

Imagine a child around age 3 or so, a period in early childhood that features often in
this important book you have before you. Bring that child up in your mind. If you
could do one thing to influence the life of that child, what would that be—the most
important influence in that child's development? Some of the most common
answers to this question, at least in the developed, Western world, include stimulating the child, talking to the child a lot, touching and holding the child, nutrition
and health care, being sure the child is securely attached to the parent, providing
peers and friends, good schools, and perhaps a trust fund for financial security!
Now all of these are important influences on a child's development, but this book
invites us to consider another way to think about this question. The most important
thing we could do that would influence the developmental path of that imagined
child is to decide where on earth—in what family, in what community, in what
nation state and political economy—that child and its family are going to grow up!
When you brought up that image of a 3 year old in your mind—was it of a child sort
of floating in space? Was the child in someone's living room, in a family and
neighborhood and culture somewhere? Were there other people around in your
thoughts?

Of course, all the things that we often mention as important things in a child's
development—holding the child, attachment, peers and so forth—matter for every
child in every family. Yet all of them happen somewhere on earth in a specific
family situation, in some cultural learning environment. What nutrition and health
care is available and how secure is it? Who goes to schools, how long can they stay,
how are lessons taught and how are children expected to learn, and what is taught?
Who cares for children, what does "security" and social trust mean and how is it
displayed? What are the religious traditions in that community or family and what
moral direction for a good life motivates parents and their children? *Children's
Social Worlds in Cultural Context* focuses on important topics in what children
learn and how they do so in communities around the world, how children are
parented and socialized, and children in difficult, risky circumstances. The book

balances features that may be common everywhere, those that differ across cultures and nations, and those that vary even within a community. Important features of development are put into family and cultural context. As the book you are about to read promises and delivers on: "... [each author] highlights their culture-specific social relationships that are important for successful adaptation in their societies and social worlds."

The assumption that might be made when we think of what would be important features of development all too often presumes an autonomous individual child, in a specific dyadic relationship with another person, in which specific actions of that other person impact the child, thereby producing a (hopefully) positive outcome for the child. But the chapters in *Children's Social Worlds in Cultural Context* do not make that implicit assumption. The frame is of an *interdependent* child embedded in a rich social world consisting of material resources in an ecology, a complex world of shared social supports for parents and children and peers.

Children's Social Worlds in Cultural Context covers many important topics that are found all over the world—topics of universal human concern, but typically with widely different ways of responding, different ecocultural patterns of beliefs, scripts and schemas, and varied outcomes for children and families. These include sibling relationships, peer relationships, multiple caretaking of children, prosocial behaviors, peer conflicts, collective conflict resolution, gender, joint social tasks, learning styles—especially collaborative learning in groups, sociolinguistics of family and community conversations, grandparenting, the circumstances of immigrant children and children in institutional care, children's awareness of risk and protection from risk, and cognitive and emotional development. If you bring that child up in your mind again, and think of the child's tasks and chores, or sibling relations, or all these other aspects of the child's life—you will have the chapters in this book to help put that child into social context in many places around the world!

There are many factors that go into the varieties of family structures and family formation around the world described in this volume, including inheritance and family ownership laws, descent laws and norms, marriage customs, residence and household formation patterns (including the availability of joint or extended family), gender role beliefs and practices, religious and spiritual beliefs about family, and many others. The same is true for parenting, socialization and child care. Of course in all communities, there are fundamental parenting and family care expectations for insuring child safety, provision of food, shelter, clothing and other subsistence needs, maintaining direct care and the provision of a care system, providing emotional and other support, training children for social competence and the ability to be adaptively competent in the economic and material world around the family, and others. Parents, other kin, and community supports and institutions all share these essential functions. This volume explores many of these topics.

Last but not least, these chapters are not methodocentric. That is, they are not narrowly limited to only experimental research designs, only quantitative ways of representing family and child life, and narrow sampling from single cultures or relatively wealthy and advantaged groups. These chapters incorporate mixed methods, with pluralistic conceptual frameworks, designs, and samples.

The chapters include rich qualitative data, ethnographic data, and varied cultural experiences, as well as quantitative data and carefully designed studies. Social development in cultural context requires these kinds of pluralistic, integrated kinds of methods.

In addition to the intellectual richness of the concepts and topics throughout this book, you will find important messages about how to use these perspectives to consider improvements in policies and practices to hopefully improve the lives of children. For example, the chapter on institutional care by Julian, Li, Wright, & Jimenez-Etcheverria describe this for Russia, China, Ghana, and Chile. Interventions must take account, in deep ways, of the local goals, practices and beliefs of the community they are intending to change. This paper makes a point that applies to many of the topics in this volume: "… given the unique challenges and social climates within institutions in various regions of the world, the nature of the most effective and sustainable intervention in one region may be very different than that of another region, and approaches that seek to identify and support effective and locally sustainable practices may be most advantageous." This is an important lesson for every well-intentioned effort to intervene to improve children's and families' circumstances in every local context.

Los Angeles, CA, USA   Thomas S. Weisner
                                                                                              UCLA

Reference

Therborn, G. (2009). Family. In R. A. Shweder, T. R. Bidell, A. C. Dailey, S. Dixon, P. J. Miller, & J. Modell (Eds.), *The child: An encyclopedic companion* (pp. 333–338). Chicago, IL: University of Chicago Press.

Preface

This book grew from two symposia presented at the 24th Biennial Meeting of the International Society for the Study of Behavioural Development (ISSBD), Vilnius, Lithuania, July, 2016. A Springer Editor contacted Tiia Tulviste, who had organized the symposia, and asked if the presenters would like to write a book about the topics that had been discussed. Debbie Best and Judy Gibbons agreed to be co-editors of the book with Tiia Tulviste. Several of the authors of the book chapters—Debbie Best, Heidi Keller, Anni Tamm, and Barbara Rogoff—participated in the conference and gave presentations about how children's development is embedded within their cultural contexts. Other distinguished researchers from different parts of the world whose research had explored children's social development in cultural context were invited to write chapters. We were delighted that they agreed to join our book project, expanding the scope of the book. With this book, we would like to introduce the interested reader to the variability of children's social worlds and the important roles that culture plays in their development.

Tartu, Estonia   Tiia Tulviste
Winston-Salem, USA   Deborah L. Best
Saint Louis, USA   Judith L. Gibbons

Acknowledgements We are exceedingly grateful to Katelyn E. Poelker who contributed to our book beyond her contribution of an excellent chapter. We would like to acknowledge our great appreciation of Heidi Keller for her encouragement throughout the development of the book and her many valuable suggestions. Our greatest thanks go to our colleagues who contributed fascinating chapters to the book. We have truly enjoyed reading the chapters and working with our colleagues throughout the process.

Contents

1   **An Introduction to the Role of Culture in Children's
    Social World**   1
    Tiia Tulviste, Deborah L. Best and Judith L. Gibbons

Part I   What Children Learn

2   **Children's Social Development: Developing Selves
    and Expanding Social Worlds**   9
    Pirko Tõugu

3   **Children's Management of Attention as Cultural Practice**   23
    Rebeca Mejía Arauz, Amy L. Dexter, Barbara Rogoff
    and Itzel Aceves-Azuara

4   **Culture, Communication and Socio-cognitive Development:
    Understanding the Minds of Others**   41
    Mele Taumoepeau

5   **Emotional Development: Cultural Influences on Young
    Children's Emotional Competence**   55
    Nicole B. Capobianco, Caitlin D. Bush and Deborah L. Best

6   **Young Children's Gender Development**   75
    Deborah L. Best and Judith L. Gibbons

7   **Sharing and Caring: Prosocial Behavior in Young Children
    Around the World**   89
    Katelyn E. Poelker and Judith L. Gibbons

8   **Peer Interactions: Culture and Peer Conflict
    During Preschool Years**   103
    Anni Tamm

9   Together or Better Singular? German Middle Class Children's
     Problem Solving in Dyads and Triads 117
     Heidi Keller, Swantje Decker and Paula Döge

Part II   Socialization of Young Children

10   Parenting: Talking with Children Across Cultural Contexts...... 135
     Tiia Tulviste

11   The Sibling Relationship in Ecocultural Context............... 149
     Ashley E. Maynard

12   The Roles of Grandparents in Child Development:
     A Cultural Approach 161
     David W. Shwalb, Ziarat Hossain and Giovanna Eisberg

13   Japanese Preschool Approaches to Supporting Young Children's
     Social-Emotional Development 173
     Akiko Hayashi

Part III   Children in Unique and Challenging Circumstances

14   Socialization and Development of Refugee Children:
     Chances of Childcare 187
     Julian Busch and Birgit Leyendecker

15   Children's Perspectives of Risk and Protection............... 201
     Yael (Julia) Ponizovsky-Bergelson, Dorit Roer-Strier, Yael Dayan
     and Nira Wahle

16   Young Children in Institutional Care: Characteristics
     of Institutions, Children's Development, and Interventions
     in Institutions 217
     Megan M. Julian, Junlei Li, Annie Wright
     and Pamela A. Jimenez-Etcheverria

Part IV   Conclusions

17   Children's Culturally Enriched Social Development 233
     Tiia Tulviste, Deborah L. Best and Judith L. Gibbons

Index 241

Editors and Contributors

About the Editors

Tiia Tulviste, Ph.D. is a professor of developmental psychology at the University of Tartu, Estonia. In her research on child cognitive and social development, she has paid special attention to the developmental contexts in which children grow. At the beginning of her scientific career, Dr. Tulviste was involved in studies trying to detect the role of schooling in the development of verbal thinking by comparing thinking processes of adults with and without school education in Soviet Central Asia and in West Siberia. During recent decades, she has been interested in the question to what extent changes in developmental context (e.g., return to the Western world in Estonia) reflect changes in cultural meanings and practices of child socialization as well as their effects over time on child development and adjustment. Dr. Tulviste has acted as project leader in several comparative research projects related to child socialization and development dealing with cultures around the Baltic Sea, such as Estonia, Finland, Latvia, Germany, and Sweden, as well as the U.S.A. She has written numerous journal articles and book chapters in this field. She is the former president of Estonian Union of Psychologists and is a member of the editorial board of the *European Psychologist*, *International Journal of Behavioural Development* (1998–2002), *and Estonian Papers in Applied Linguistics*.

Deborah L. Best, Ph.D. is the William L. Poteat Professor of Psychology at Wake Forest University, USA, where she previously served as Chair of the Psychology Department and was the first woman to serve as Dean of the College of Arts and Sciences. She is active in the International Association for Cross-Cultural Psychology as an Honorary Fellow, President (2000–2002), and Treasurer (1988–1997), and in the Society for Cross-Cultural Research as President (2011–2012). She has served as Associate Editor (1996–2012) and Editor (2012 to present) of the flagship journal of IACCP, *Journal of Cross-Cultural Psychology*. She has written and edited five books as well as numerous book chapters and research articles; her work includes landmark studies of gender stereotypes in 30 nations. Her research has focused on children's cognitive and social development, primarily examining gender-related concepts among young children in the United States and other countries.

Judith L. Gibbons, Ph.D. is Professor Emerita of Psychology at Saint Louis University, USA. She is the founding editor of the American Psychological Association Division 52 journal, *International Perspectives in Psychology: Research, Practice, Consultation*, former president of the Society for Cross-Cultural Research and the Interamerican Society of Psychology (SIP), a former Fulbright scholar at the Universidad del Valle de Guatemala, and an Associate Editor of the *Journal of Cross-Cultural Psychology*. Her research includes the study of the development of adolescents, especially girls and at-risk youth, in the majority world, intercountry adoption, and gender roles. With many collaborators, local and international, she has published numerous journal articles on those topics. She has written or edited three books including *The Thoughts of Youth: An International Perspective on Adolescents' Ideal Persons, Intercountry Adoption: Policies, Practices, and Outcomes*, and *Women's Evolving Lives: Global and Psychosocial Perspectives*.

Contributors

Itzel Aceves-Azuara University of California Santa Cruz, Santa Cruz, CA, USA

Rebeca Mejía Arauz ITESO University, Guadalajara, Mexico

Deborah L. Best Wake Forest University, Winston-Salem, NC, USA

Julian Busch Ruhr University, Bochum, Germany

Caitlin D. Bush Wake Forest University, Winston-Salem, NC, USA

Nicole B. Capobianco University of Virginia, Charlottesville, VA, USA

Yael Dayan Hebrew University of Jerusalem, Jerusalem, Israel

Swantje Decker AWO Münsterland-Recklinghausen, Recklinghausen, Germany

Amy L. Dexter University of California Santa Cruz, Santa Cruz, USA

Paula Döge Diakonie Deutschland, Berlin, Germany

Giovanna Eisberg University of New Mexico, Albuquerque, NM, USA

Judith L. Gibbons Saint Louis University, St. Louis, MO, USA

Akiko Hayashi Meiji University, Tokyo, Japan

Ziarat Hossain University of New Mexico, Albuquerque, NM, USA

Pamela A. Jimenez-Etcheverria Universidad de La Frontera, Temuco, Chile

Megan M. Julian University of Michigan, Ann Arbor, MI, USA

Heidi Keller Osnabrück University, Osnabrück, Germany

Birgit Leyendecker Ruhr University, Bochum, Germany

Junlei Li Harvard University, Cambridge, MA, USA

Ashley E. Maynard University of Hawai'i at Mānoa, Honolulu, USA

Katelyn E. Poelker Hope College, Holland, MI, USA

Yael (Julia) Ponizovsky-Bergelson Ruppin Academic Center, Hadera, Israel; Hebrew University of Jerusalem, Jerusalem, Israel

Dorit Roer-Strier Hebrew University of Jerusalem, Jerusalem, Israel

Barbara Rogoff University of California Santa Cruz, Santa Cruz, CA, USA

David W. Shwalb Southern Utah University, Cedar City, UT, USA

Anni Tamm University of Tartu, Tartu, Estonia

Mele Taumoepeau University of Otago, Dunedin, New Zealand

Pirko Tõugu University of Tartu, Tartu, Estonia

Tiia Tulviste University of Tartu, Tartu, Estonia

Nira Wahle Kibbutzim College of Education, Technology and the Arts, Tel Aviv-Yafo, Israel

Annie Wright Virginia Commonwealth University, Richmond, VA, USA

Chapter 1
An Introduction to the Role of Culture in Children's Social World

Tiia Tulviste, Deborah L. Best and Judith L. Gibbons

Abstract Over the years, children's social development has generated much research interest, beginning with the early twentieth-century observational studies of children in nursery school settings. However, examination of those studies, and later ones, indicates that most research has focused upon children in the Western English-speaking world. Much less is known about children's social development in other settings. The research presented in these chapters takes an expanded culture-specific view of children's social development over the preschool years. By focusing on the significant role that the cultural context plays in shaping children's social and emotional behaviors, a more representative picture of children's adaptation to their social worlds is evident. What young children learn, how they are socialized, and how they navigate challenging circumstances are explored.

This book is about children's social worlds. The focus is on social development—on children's social interactions and relationships that evolve in different cultural contexts. Although social development has been the most popular research topic in developmental psychology since the 1980s, there is still little known about the varied social worlds in which children live, and their impact on the course and outcome of social development. Social development more often has been studied experimentally in the Western English-speaking world. The current book aims to fill the gap by taking a cultural perspective, with special attention to the contexts in which social development occurs. We invited distinguished researchers from different parts of the world to write about children's social worlds and to discuss the possible impact context may have on their social development. The authors review the latest scholarly research and they offer their own empirical findings about various aspects of social

T. Tulviste (✉)
University of Tartu, Tartu, Estonia
e-mail: tiia.tulviste@ut.ee

D. L. Best
Wake Forest University, Winston-Salem, USA

J. L. Gibbons
Saint Louis University, Saint Louis, USA
e-mail: judith.gibbons@slu.edu

© Springer Nature Switzerland AG 2019
T. Tulviste et al. (eds.), *Children's Social Worlds in Cultural Context*,
https://doi.org/10.1007/978-3-030-27033-9_1

development. The book does not address developmental or behavioral problems. It is about typically developing children growing up in various developmental contexts. It highlights their culture-specific social relationships that are important for successful adaptation in their societies and social worlds. The focus is on cultural aspects of social development over the preschool years. This is a period of significant growth in different facets of the child's social development, beginning in toddlerhood and extending into the time when children are ready to go to school.

The chapters in this book revolve around the following three overlapping and interrelated topics: (1) what children learn, (2) socialization of young children; (3) children in unique and challenging circumstances. Based on these topics, the book is divided into three parts.

Part I: What Children Learn

The first part of the book deals with the question of what children within different sociocultural backgrounds are expected to learn. It identifies topics related to the acquisition, development, and use of the social skills that are valued in children's specific sociocultural contexts. These skills are culture-specific skills, and they allow children to create and maintain relationships, communicate with others, and to get along with children and adults at home as well as outside of family. Children must learn social rules, conversational styles, attentional strategies, prosocial behavior, social understanding of mental states, and also recognize and regulate emotions within their cultural setting.

In Chap. 2, Pirko Tõugu describes how children's social worlds expand during the preschool years by their having more contact with other children. She identifies how children's culture- and gender-specific understanding of social rules and of themselves and other people in the world around them develop though play interactions with peers. She describes gender differences in social rules that boys and girls consider most important to follow while playing. She also describes the development of gender- and culture-specific understanding of self and others found in children's recounting of their experiences.

In Chap. 3, Rebeca Mejía Arauz, Amy L. Dexter, Barbara Rogoff and Itzel Aceves-Azuara present data on contrasting types of attentional strategies used by children from 5 communities—two from Indigenous-heritage communities of the Americas and three with extensive Western schooling experience. They argue that children's cultural practices in everyday life, rather than children's national belonging, underlie the development of distinctive attentional strategies.

Mele Taumoepeau's Chap. 4 examines the development of children's psychological understanding of themselves and others through their interactions with parents about their own and others' mental states. Her review focuses primarily on the relationship between the frequency of making references to mental states and using mental state language in such interactions. She considers children's understanding of inner states across cultures and provides a foundation for the following chapter.

Chapter 5, written by Nicole B. Capobianco, Caitlin D. Bush, and Deborah L. Best reviews evidence from a large body of comparative studies documenting cultural variability in children's emotional development. Children's emotional expressiveness, emotion regulation, and emotion knowledge are considered. The authors discuss the role of interactions with different socialization agents in children's learning to recognize, regulate, and understand their own and others' emotions.

Chapter 6, by Deborah L. Best and Judith L. Gibbons, deals with the question of how children's gender identities, roles, stereotypes, social interactions, and other aspects of gender develop within the cultural expectations of what it means to be a boy or girl. The authors discuss the role that parents, peers, and children themselves play in gender socialization, and children's gendered behavior and beliefs within various cultural contexts.

In Chap. 7, Katelyn E. Poelker and Judith L. Gibbons review studies about the development of children's prosocial behavior. They describe instrumental, empathic, and altruistic helping, and they point out cultural differences in what constitutes helping, the available opportunities to help, and whether self-recognition is a prerequisite for prosocial behavior.

In Chap. 8, Anni Tamm reviews studies of children's conflicts and the emotionally laden peer relationships that provide the backdrop for the initiation and the course of those conflicts. She focuses on cultural differences in the causes of conflicts, the strategies used to settle them, and the eventual outcomes that occur. For children as young as three years of age, cultural values shape the ways they balance autonomy and relatedness in the context of their peer conflicts.

In Chap. 9, Heidi Keller, Swantje Decker, and Paula Döge are particularly concerned with children's cooperative problem solving in dyads and triads. They found that German children have difficulties cooperating in situations other than dyadic settings or when working in isolation. Many German children fail to cooperate in triads, a finding which the authors attribute to the autonomous German educational orientation and the dyadic one-to-one interaction style common to Western families.

Part II: Socialization of Young Children

Developmentally, children learn appropriate social skills through their interactions with different agents of socialization—parents, siblings, peers, day-care teachers, and other significant others. These socialization agents help shape children's skills, and these skills are necessary for communicating with these important others and for forming and maintaining relationships with them. This part of book contains chapters that deal with socialization of children by different socialization agents.

Tiia Tulviste's Chap. 10 is about family—the initial and primary setting of child socialization. The focus of the chapter is on cultural variability in ways of talking with children, in the cultural meaning of talk addressed to children, and in the extent to which parents encourage children's conversational participation. She points out that through participation in such conversations children acquire language and its culture-specific use, as well as values deemed important in their specific culture.

In Chap. 11, Ashley Maynard describes siblings' relationships across cultures and the ways in which they contribute to children's socio-emotional and cognitive development. Most children grow up with siblings who usually differ from them in age, sometimes in gender, and in their familial roles. She notes that the care, obedience, helpfulness, and rivalry between siblings vary across cultures as do expectations about the sibling roles after childhood.

The theme of Chap. 12 by David W. Shwalb, Ziarat Hossain, and Giovanna Eisberg is the role of grandparents in children's social development. Although parents are usually the most import adults in children's lives, the parents of children's parents may also play a crucial role. Grandparents of preschool-age children make important contributions to grandchildren's care and socialization, and they also contribute emotional and sometimes financial support to their parents. Moreover, in high-risk families or in stressful circumstances, such as having a parent with serious health problems, grandparents can serve as protective factors.

Akiko Hayashi's Chap. 13 describes Japanese preschool teachers' pedagogical strategies of minimal intervention in children's disputes. This practice scaffolds a collective locus of control, allows the children involved in the conflict to experience strong emotions and to learn independent conflict resolution strategies. Knowing that they are being observed by the teacher who is present, children involved and those watching learn conflict resolution strategies in a safe but emotionally laden situation.

Part III: Children in Unique and Challenging Circumstances

The last section is comprised of three chapters about social development in special circumstances. Children described in these chapters find themselves in circumstances that are usually stressful and difficult, often upsetting, and not of their own choosing.

In Chap. 14, Julian Busch and Birgit Leyendecker provide important background information about recent immigration into Europe, especially into Germany, focusing on immigrant and refugee families with preschool-age children. They emphasize the role of culture-sensitive childcare in supporting refugee children's development, preparing them for German schools as well as facilitating family adjustment to the new living situation after immigration.

In Chap. 15, Yael (Julia) Ponizovsky-Bergelson, Dorit Roer-Strier, Yael Dayan, and Nira Wahle discuss the question of cultural variability in what is regarded by children as risk and what makes them feel protected. They illustrate these risk concepts with Israeli data gathered by children from diverse populations. The chapter looks at children's perspectives about risky and safe places expressed during children's group discussions about photos and drawings that they made themselves.

Children in institutional care is the topic of Chap. 16, where Megan M. Julian, Junlei Li, Annie Wright, and Pamela A. Jimenez-Etcheverria characterize children's experiences in institutions in Russia, China, Ghana, and Chile. They discuss the circumstances that lead to children's placement in residential care facilities. They also discuss how growing up in such settings place children at risk for later social, emotional, and behavioral difficulties. They emphasize the need for culture-sensitive interventions to improve social-emotional care for institutionalized children.

Part IV: Conclusions

In the final chapter of the book, Tiia Tulviste, Deborah Best, and Judith Gibbons provide some conclusions about the importance of examining and understanding children's social development within their sociocultural context. Children's social development is an amazingly complex process that is flavored in various ways by the developmental mechanisms within the specific cultural context in which they grow up. The culturally enriched experiences and people children encounter along this journey help shape their cognitive and social behaviors, enhancing their learning within the developmental process.

Part I
What Children Learn

Chapter 2
Children's Social Development: Developing Selves and Expanding Social Worlds

Pirko Tõugu

Abstract During the preschool years children become more independent in talking about their experiences and expressing their ideas. They also start to spend more time outside the immediate family circle and engage more with their peers. Play becomes an important activity and a significant socialization context among peers. The chapter focuses on children's peer interactions and socialization in play and the development of self, as it is expressed in children's stories about the events experienced. It highlights the changes in social cognition and in the experiences of boys and girls as conveyed in their accounts of experienced events. Cultural differences observed in these aspects of children's lives are also discussed.

During the preschool years, children start to spend more time outside the immediate family circle and become more knowledgeable members of their respective social and cultural group. This is a time when there is heightened stress on them to organize their relationships and activities with other children in a culturally and socially appropriate way and to form a basic understanding of their own identity. The construction of children's social identity already begins in infancy (Ochs 1993), but continues throughout childhood and adolescence. In this chapter I will describe how preschool children act as socialization agents for their peers and how children's representations of their experiences and themselves and others develop during that time. First, I will focus on how children organize their play interactions with other children in different cultural contexts. Second, I will turn to examples of children's talk about their experiences with the focus on how these accounts are tied to the cultural context and become more gender-typical and how they reflect children's developments in social cognition.

As children's social circles widen in the preschool years, they often come into contact with peers. In most parts of the world, preschool children are in regular contact with other children, be it in the form of institutionalized child-care or sibling supervision (Edwards 2000). There is a longstanding understanding that peer company and peer interaction is beneficial for children's development. The positive

P. Tõugu (✉)
University of Tartu, Tartu, Estonia
e-mail: pirko.tougu@ut.ee

effect of peer interaction can be observed in the moral (Piaget 1950; Turiel 1983), cognitive (Singer et al. 2006), and social domain of development (Blum-Kulka and Snow 2004). At the same time, peer interaction is closely tied to the cultural context that guides the social processes in peer relationships and interactions (Chen 2012). Peer interaction is influenced by the cultural and social values and is, therefore, an important context of socialization.

Play in Different Cultural Contexts

Peer interaction often involves play. Play has been defined as a child-lead activity that is voluntary, enjoyable, and has no clear purpose (Weisberg et al. 2013). Such an activity has been seen as developmentally beneficial in most of the Western world (Singer et al. 2006; but see also Lillard et al. 2013, for review). At the same time, play can be considered a cultural construct and the amount of adult engagement in and support for children's play varies in different cultural contexts (Göncü et al. 2007; Haight et al. 1999). For example, Göncü and colleagues (2007) describe that while in the Western world children play with both peers and adults, in the more traditional societies play is seen as a child activity without adult involvement. Yet, despite the fact that different cultural contexts see the value and purpose of play differently, children in very different settings do engage in play with their peers (Edwards 2000; Gaskins et al. 2007). Gaskins et al. (2007) point out that even in societies where play is discouraged, children do engage in playful interactions with peers and use play to entertain younger siblings.

In addition to variations in adult support for play, children's play activities in different cultural contexts also differ (Farver et al. 1995; Göncü et al. 2000). The cultural milieu, the prominent values in the context, and the immediate setting all affect children's play activities (Farver et al. 1995). Farver et al. (1995) show that the pretend play interactions of Korean and Anglo-American preschool children differ as the play behavior is influenced by the socialization practices of the respective contexts. In providing a model for the children, the cultural context supplies the input for the content of children's play: Corsaro and Eder (1990) have argued that children appropriate information from the adult world to create their own peer culture and activities. Corsaro and colleagues (Corsaro 1988; Corsaro and Rizzo 1988; Corsaro and Schwarz 1991) have shown how this peer culture involves routines appropriated from the respective adult culture and have claimed this to be an important socialization mechanism in peer interaction. For example, Corsaro and Rizzo (1988) demonstrated how kindergarten children use the *discussione*, a verbal routine of public debate in Italian with a predictable style and structure. Kindergarten children used the stylistic devices characteristic of a *discussione* in a discussion-debate in play and by doing so they both participated in and created a specific peer culture and practiced cultural routines of the adult society.

The effects of cultural values, beliefs, and socialization norms are also seen in the way children interact with each other. Farver and Shin (1997) have shown that Korean-American and Anglo-American preschoolers use different communicative strategies in organizing pretend play. Korean-American preschoolers use polite requests, tag questions, and statements of agreement in engaging with their peers more often than Anglo-Americans. At the same time, the Anglo-American preschoolers more often than Korean-Americans rejected their partners' suggestions and used directives. Another study has contrasted peer interaction in Estonian, Swedish, and Finnish preschools (Tulviste et al. 2010). The authors of this study also showed how children in these cultural contexts communicated with their peers in a different manner: of the three groups, the Estonian children were the most directive when talking to their peers and the Swedish children the least directive. Authors of both studies point out that the differences in peer interaction can be reflective of the socialization norms and values in the societies.

Gender Difference in Play

Along with the above-mentioned cultural differences, there are gender differences in children's companions and activities. In the Western world, studies have shown that during free play children segregate themselves according to gender, especially in middle-childhood (Maccoby and Jacklin 1987), but also at earlier ages (Fabes et al. 2003). There is some indication that spontaneous same-sex segregation is also characteristic of other contexts besides the Anglo-American context (Farver and Howes 1988; Fouts et al. 2013) and among children with a different cultural background (e.g., Mexican; Martin et al. 2013). Farver and Howes have observed spontaneous play in Jakarta, Indonesia, and America, and report gender segregation in both locations. Fouts et al. (2013) investigated Bofi foragers and Bofi farmers in Central Africa and showed that gender segregation could be more pronounced in less egalitarian societies with clear adult gender roles. As for the activities that the children engage in, Fabes et al. (2003) point out that play in boys' groups is more active and forceful than in girls' groups. Martin et al. (2013) show that common interest in the (gender-typical) activity could partially explain the preference for same-sex play mates. In traditional societies the activities expected of children of different sexes also affect their play behavior: boys often have more leisure time for play while girls are more engaged in household chores (Edwards 2000). Therefore, play seems to be both culturally and socially constructed.

The evidence reviewed so far suggests that peer interaction is affected by the cultural context and the norms and values of the society are reflected in peer play and peer interaction. This means that the company of peers could be a very important socialization context already for preschool children. When children try to organize their activities, they have to set up the rules of the activity and make sure that they are upheld. In some cultural contexts, there is clear hierarchy in peer and sibling relations with the older children looking after the younger ones. In these cases, the older children are also in charge of the play interactions that have to make allowances in order for the younger children to participate (Gaskins et al. 2007). Other contexts do not have such clear hierarchies and peer groups are formed on the bases of likability and friendships among same-age peers. In these cases, there is more leeway in how children organize and negotiate their activities. We will now turn to look at an example of how 3–7-year-old children organize their play.

Socialization of Social Rules in Peer Play

Tõugu and Tulviste (2010) investigated what kinds of rules are upheld in Estonian kindergarten peer groups and which children are the ones to assert the rules. We observed 3–7-year-old children play for twenty minutes in self-selected groups of three. The groups played in their everyday day-care setting and they were free to select and organize their own activities within the limits of the space.

Before describing the findings, a short description of the context where the study was carried out is relevant. The study was carried out in Tartu, Estonia. Estonia is a small country with the population of 1.4 million people in the North-Eastern part of Europe. Tartu is a university city and the second largest town in Estonia with about 100,000 inhabitants. Estonia was part of the Soviet Union, but has since its collapse undergone several political, economic and societal reforms. Since 2004 Estonia is a member of the European Union. Nowadays Estonia is a developed country with a high-income economy. At the same time, studies have shown that the values held in the society are more traditional than in the neighboring Nordic counties (Tulviste et al. 2012, 2017).

In order to understand how the Estonian children organize their activities, we examined two kinds of rules that have been identified: (1) conventional rules, and (2) moral rules (Nucci and Turiel 1978; Turiel 1983). Conventional rules refer to general conventions of appropriate behavior and language, politeness, cleanliness and order of things, and rules of a structured game (e.g., "You have to put it back where it belongs.", "The one who rolls a six, starts the game."). Moral rules are references to what is fair and good and include statements about possessions, harming others, and equity (e.g., "You can't take it, I had it first!", "Don't hit!"). Children's comments about these different types of rules were identified (Piotrowski 1997). We also calculated children's talkativeness and noted their gender to see how these aspects affect children's references to social norms.

Gender was an important predictor of references to moral norms with boys commenting on moral rules more often than girls. Consider the following examples:

A group of two girls and a boy are playing house. The boy parks his toy car, the girl goes to re-park it in a different place.
Ella: So let's do it so that all the cars are parked.
Henry: This is my car!
Henry grabs the car from Ella.
Henry: It is! This is my car! I started playing with it first.
(Conflict over the rule of possession; moral domain.)

A group of boys is running around playing an imaginary shooting game. One boy grabs hold of the other's shirt.
Ryan: Don't!
Michael: Ryan. I'm pulling.
Ryan: Stop! It hurts!
Michael: I'm pulling this way. Let's play monsters.
(*Conflict over the rule of hurting others; moral domain.*)

A group of three boys is playing cards. One of them is about to pick up a card.
Alec: Matt! It's wrong! It's my turn, Matt!
Matt: No, it's his turn. Kenneth's.
Alec: It is?
Matt: It's your turn.
Kenneth: Mine?
(*Conflict over the rule of turn-taking; moral domain.*)

It is important to note that seniority among children does not seem to be a factor when the general rules of good and fair are in question. It does seem that whenever the rules of fairness or possession are broken, or someone is hurt, the injured party is quick to speak up and enforce the rules. Now the question remains whether these transgressions are more likely to happen in boys' groups (like examples 2 and 3) or whether the boys are just more likely to speak up in such cases (example 1).

The conventional rules are more often noted by older and also more talkative children. For example, consider the following example when a group of girls was trying to figure out what to do.

Mia threw a ball.
Bridget: Mia, you shouldn't throw a ball. Let's play volley ball.
Mia: Okay. I'll catch.
Bridget: Actually, no Mia, you can't throw a ball. It might fall out of the window.
Mia is still about to throw the ball.
Bridget: No, Mia! You can't!
(*Conflict over the rule of appropriate behavior; conventional domain.*)

After a while the same group decides to play hide-and-seek.

Mia is reciting a counting-out rhyme to decide who will be the seeker. The rhyme ends at Bridget.
Bridget: When the rhyme ends at me, this means that I am hiding.

Mia recites again, the rhyme ends at Marta.
Bridget: Mia is seeking, we are hiding.
Mia: How long do I have to wait?
Martha: Because, when the rhyme ends at you, you are free.
Bridget: We'll call when you can start.
Bridget: Who is found first, is the next seeker.

They play for a while; Bridget is to be the next seeker.

Bridget: I don't want to be the seeker.
Bridget: But you can't hide in the front room.
Martha: Count until ten.
Bridget: Let's not play hide-and-seek any more.
(*Examples of rules of a structured game; conventional domain.*)

In this group, Bridget often draws on the conventional rules that are set in the day-care environment (as in the first example), that are well-known among children in general (as in the counting-out rhyme), and that can be established by children themselves to ensure a smooth game (as in "You can't hide in the front room"). In these examples, only Martha chimes in once to repeat a convention about the counting-out rhymes that Bridget has already alluded to. Throughout the play session, Bridget is also talkative in general and speaks more than her playmates. Therefore, she embodies a nice example of how the more talkative children are more likely to establish and enforce the conventional rules in a peer group during play.

Here again, the cultural context could define what are the distinct rules, norms, and conventions that children refer to in their interaction. The older and more talkative children seem to have a special role to play in guiding the play interactions and enforcing the social norms based on these examples. It would be particularly interesting to know if the finding that the age and talkativeness do not make a difference in upholding moral rules is culturally universal, especially considering that what is considered moral is dependent on the cultural context (Shweder et al. 1987). Yet, even with these few examples, we can see how the children state and enforce the rules accepted in the society and act as socialization agents for their peers.

Alongside the developments in peer interaction and the expanding social world, children's understanding and representation of their experience also develops. I will now turn to children's personal narratives or recounts of their experience to highlight the developmental changes in children's social cognition and social identity as observed in these recounts during the preschool years.

Reminiscing and Personal Recollections

Several authors argue that personal narratives and autobiographical memories are the base for the development and maintenance of self (Conway et al. 2004; McLean et al. 2007; Pasupathi et al. 2007). At the same time, both are to a certain extent affected by cultural socialization (Nelson and Fivush 2004; Wang and Brockmeier 2002). In early childhood, most of children's experiences are reflected upon and recollected with the help of a parent in the form of reminiscing. Such shared reminiscing supports children's emerging sense of self and provides structure for recounting personal narratives (Fivush et al. 2011). Sometimes studies of mother-child reminiscing point to gender differences in memory socialization. Parents have been shown to have more detailed reminiscing conversations with daughters than with sons and daughters display more detailed (Reese et al. 1996; Reese and Fivush 1993) and better formulated recollections (Haden et al. 1997) than sons at an early age. Parents also discuss emotions in a more detailed manner with daughters as compared to sons (Fivush et al. 2000).

At the same time, mother-child reminiscing reflects the cultural context and values in the style of reminiscing used and the content discussed (Schröder et al. 2013; Tõugu et al. 2011; Tulviste et al. 2016; Wang 2007; Wang et al. 2000). (Some of these differences are further discussed by Tulviste in the same volume.) Authors of these cross-cultural investigations tie the differences in the content and volume of children's memories to the culture-specific way of reminiscing and the value of autonomy and relatedness in the particular context. In autonomy-oriented contexts where a child's uniqueness and initiative is valued, reminiscing conversations tend to be longer and more detailed and center more on the child. In relatedness-oriented contexts, the conversations are more skeletal and the social world is often the focus of these talks. These differences in mother-child reminiscing conversations could have implications for children's social-emotional development (discussed in more detail by Capobianco, Bush, and Best in the same volume), social cognitions (see also Taumoepeau in the same volume), and the development of self.

As children grow older, they become more competent in representing their experiences and their self in independent recollections. There is reason to believe that these recollections also reflect the cultural context and the values socialized in earlier reminiscing conversations. Wang (2004) analyzed interviews with 180 preschool to second-grade children from the USA and China. The children recounted four past events and provided a description of themselves. The results revealed that Chinese children were more likely than their US counterparts to provide brief accounts that focused on social interactions and their everyday experiences. The US children, instead, provided elaborate accounts of past experiences that focused on their own part in it. The author suggests that the results reflect the different value attached to a distinct and autonomous self in the two cultural contexts.

Besides reflecting the cultural milieu, children's recollections can also display differences in the social identity based on their gender. A few studies have indicated that recollections display gender-specific styles and point out how boys and girls focus on different aspects of their experiences in their personal narratives. For example, Buckner and Fivush (1998) have shown that 8-year-old girls provide more socially oriented recollections of their past experiences and mention more people than 8-year-old boys.

The above-mentioned studies indicate that children's social identity is reflected in the accounts of their past experiences. The same accounts also illustrate children's understanding of themselves and the social world around them and the developments in their social cognition. I will now turn to examples of how children's recollections begin to display the gender-specific nature during the preschool years and how their representations of themselves and others change during that time.

Gender Differences in the Development of Recollections

Tõugu et al. (2014) carried out a longitudinal investigation of children's recollections of their experiences. We had 275 Estonian children provide recollections of their last birthday and the past weekend on two occasions almost two years apart. At the beginning of the study children were 4 years old on the average, and during the second wave of the study the average age was 6. The personal narratives that the children provided were studied for content, i.e., utterances by children were coded as they referred to either (a) themselves as the agent, (b) themselves together with someone (co-agency), (c) the social context, or (d) the nonsocial context.

During the first wave the stories provided by the children were brief in nature, with most utterances referring to the nonsocial context. In addition, there were small gender differences in the content of the accounts, with boys talking more about the nonsocial context than the girls. Here are two examples from the first wave, the first is from a 4-year-old boy and the second from a 4-year-old girl, both providing an account of their weekend:

Research assistant:	But what did you do at home with mom and dad over the weekend?
Boy:	Our computer broke, the one upstairs, not mom's.
RA:	Mhmh.
Boy:	And Mark took out the letter "k" and "j" with his teeth.
RA:	Took out "k" and "j" with his teeth?
Boy:	Yes, but then put them back luckily.
RA:	Mhmh. But tell me what else did you do?
Boy:	Well, Legos and then mommy made a hut for us of an old broken box. So there was no exit on this side, only here there was a small hole to get out.

Research assistant: What did you do at home over the weekend?

Girl: I was ill. …I played with dolls. Dressed the dolls in the computer.

(*unrelated talk*)

RA: What else did you do at home over the weekend?
Girl: I played in my room with my other toys.
RA: What else did you do with mom and dad?
Girl: Yes. When we were, mom cooked, and then we made a big house. Mom helped me make it. We played with mom.

In these examples, we can see how the boy includes details about the broken computer and the hut in his recollection of the weekend. The girl, unlike the boy, does not focus on the nonsocial world as much, but rather talks about her play and how mom was involved in it.

During the second wave when the children were older, the recollections were a bit longer with more references to all the content categories. Also, gender differences had significantly increased. Boys talked more about themselves than girls, and girls mentioned other people and themselves together with someone else more than boys. Here are two examples from the second wave, the first one is from a 6-year-old boy and the second from a 6-year-old girl, again both of them talking about their weekend.

Research assistant:	But tell me then what did you do at home with mom and dad over the weekend?
Boy:	On Sunday I took a bath and on Sunday I ate at McDonald's. And then when it's Saturday I am at my grandma's and grandpa's.
RA:	Mhmh.
Boy:	And then at grandpa's I just started playing with the cars and they have some animals there too and. I have a rabbit there and when the rabbit got cold then it always comes to grandma's lap and then we brought it inside. At the moment it lives in the shed, but in the summer it is outside.
RA:	Mhmh.
Boy:	And then I don't remember anything else.

Research assistant:	But tell me what did you do at home with mom and dad over the weekend?
Girl:	They were washing, they were doing, they were working and sometimes they clean at home.
RA:	They clean the house. But what did you do together over the weekend?
Girl:	I played tag with my dog.
RA:	Mhmh. What else?
Girl:	I was in my room and played with Barbies.
RA:	Mhmh.
Girl:	And then I helped mom water the flowers and then we went for a walk all together. And that's it.

Here we can see that although both children mention other people, the girl talks more about what the other people were doing and also mentions what they were doing together. The boy is more focused on what he was doing and also provides details about the rabbit. This shows that experience, although it may be similar in nature, comes to be represented or presented differently by boys and girls.

In a different analyses of the development of social cognition, the same recollections were analyzed for how children referred to themselves and others and how the developmental changes in these references reflected children's changing social cognition (Tõugu et al. 2018). Here, children's utterances about themselves and others were categorized as (a) only mentioning themselves/the other, (b) referring to one's actions, (c) referring to one's inner states (emotions, preferences, etc.). During the first wave, when the children were on average 4 years old, they generally talked about their own actions, and only mentioned other people. When they were around 6 years old, they talked more about their inner states than before, and also described others by the actions that they undertook during the described events. Consider the two examples:

A 4-year-old girl's recollection of her birthday during the first wave.

Research assistant:	Alright, tell me about your birthday!
Girl:	Grandma was at my birthday.
RA:	Grandma was.
Girl:	My grandma. And Lily.
RA:	Lily.
Girl:	And George. And Bridget. And no-one else.
RA:	What else do you remember?
Girl:	Daddy brought me a jumping ball.

A 5-year-old girl's recollection during the second wave:

Research assistant:	What do you remember about your last birthday?
Girl:	I remember I wanted Pipi Longstocking at my birthday. And we played a game where we put newspapers on the ground and had to make them smaller and stay on them.
RA:	Mhmh. What else?
Girl:	And then there was a game where we had to run around the chairs and the other children who lost, took them away one by one. Everyone who lost the chair had to leave the game.
RA:	Mhmh. What else do you remember?
Girl:	I wanted to show Pipi how fast I run. And then Pipi and other children also raced. And I was the one to make it first.

In the first example provided by a 4-year-old girl, the child mainly lists the participants in the event (in this case, who was at the birthday party). Only on one occasion does the girl mention what someone else did. The second example provided by a 5-year-old girl is much more detailed about what other people did at the party. It also provides examples of the use of inner state talk. The girl refers to what she had desired for the birthday party ("wanted Pipi") and what she wanted to do at the birthday party ("wanted to show Pipi"). She also describes what the other participants at the event were doing.

As personal recollections form the basis of self, the results outline how children's social identity becomes more gendered during preschool years. The examples provided here dovetail with the work of Buckner and Fivush (1998) showing that girls' recollections have a more social focus than boys' recollections. They also complement and append the reminiscing work that has shown that the socialization of autobiographical memory can be a somewhat different experience for boys and girls. At the same time, again, it would be particularly interesting to see if the appearance of gender-typical accounts is a universal development or socialized differently in the various social or cultural contexts. The examples also show how children's social cognition changes and their representation and understanding of themselves and others develop. This inquiry would also benefit from a more culturally diverse approach.

Conclusion

This chapter has provided a glimpse into the development of children's social identity and the expansion of their social world and social knowledge. First, I showed how play is a culture-specific activity and discussed how children as socialization agents help peers become competent members of the cultural group in the context of peer play. Second, I turned to reminiscing and recollections that have both been shown to reflect cultural values and beliefs. I used children's developing recollections of their experiences to show how their social cognition develops and how they themselves develop gender-typical representations of their experiences during the preschool years. These are just some of the important social developments of preschool years that can be related to children's expanding social worlds and social and cultural experiences.

Acknowledgements The writing of this chapter was supported by the Estonian Research Council (grant no. PSG296).

References

Blum-Kulka, S., & Snow, C. E. (2004). Introduction: The potential of peer talk. *Discourse Studies, 6*(3), 291–306.

Buckner, J. P., & Fivush, R. (1998). Gender and self in children's autobiographical narratives. *Applied Cognitive Psychology, 12*(4), 407–429. https://doi.org/10.1002/(SICI)1099-0720(199808)12:4%3c407:AID-ACP575%3e3.0.CO;2-7.

Chen, X. (2012). Culture, peer interaction, and socioemotional development. *Child Development Perspectives, 6*(1), 27–34.

Conway, M. A., Singer, J. A., & Tagini, A. (2004). The self and autobiographical memory: Correspondence and coherence. *Social Cognition, 22*(5), 491–529.

Corsaro, W. A. (1988). Routines in the peer culture of American and Italian nursery school children. *Sociology of Education, 61*, 1–14.

Corsaro, W. A., & Eder, D. (1990). Children's peer cultures. *Annual Review of Sociology, 16*(1), 197–220.

Corsaro, W. A., & Rizzo, T. A. (1988). Discussione and friendship: Socialization processes in the peer culture of Italian nursery school children. *American Sociological Review, 53*, 879–894.

Corsaro, W. A., & Schwarz, K. (1991). Peer play and socialization in two cultures: Implications for research and practice. In B. Scales, M. Almy, A. Nicolopoulou, & S. Ervin-Tripp (Eds.), *Early childhood education series. Play and the social context of development in early care and education* (pp. 234–254). New York: Teachers College Press.

Edwards, C. P. (2000). Children's play in cross-cultural perspective: A new look at the six cultures study. *Cross-Cultural Research, 34*(4), 318–338.

Fabes, R. A., Martin, C. L., & Hanish, L. D. (2003). Young children's play qualities in same-, other-, and mixed-sex peer groups. *Child Development, 74*(3), 921–932.

Farver, J. A. M., & Howes, C. (1988). Cross-cultural differences in social interaction: A comparison of American and Indonesian children. *Journal of Cross-Cultural Psychology, 19*(2), 203–215.

Farver, J. A. M., Kim, Y. K., & Lee, Y. (1995). Cultural differences in Korean-and Anglo-American preschoolers' social interaction and play behaviors. *Child Development, 66*(4), 1088–1099.

Farver, J. A. M., & Shin, Y. L. (1997). Social pretend play in Korean-and Anglo-American preschoolers. *Child Development, 68*(3), 544–556.

Fivush, R., Brotman, M. A., Buckner, J. P., & Goodman, S. H. (2000). Gender differences in parent–child emotion narratives. *Sex Roles, 42*(3–4), 233–253.

Fivush, R., Habermas, T., Waters, T. E. A., & Zaman, W. (2011). The making of autobiographical memory: Intersections of culture, narratives and identity. *International Journal of Psychology, 46*(5), 321–345. https://doi.org/10.1080/00207594.2011.596541.

Fouts, H. N., Hallam, R. A., & Purandare, S. (2013). Gender segregation in early-childhood social play among the Bofi foragers and Bofi farmers in Central Africa. *American Journal of Play, 5*(3), 333–356.

Gaskins, S., Haight, W., & Lancy, D. F. (2007). The cultural construction of play. In A. Göncü & S. Gaskins (Eds.), *Play and development: Evolutionary, sociocultural, and functional perspectives* (pp. 179–202). New York: Lawrence Erlbaum Associates.

Göncü, A., Jain, J., & Tuermer, U. (2007). Children's play as cultural interpretation. In A. Göncü & S. Gaskins (Eds.), *Play and development: Evolutionary, sociocultural, and functional perspectives* (pp. 155–178). New York: Lawrence Erlbaum Associates.

Göncü, A., Mistry, J., & Mosier, C. (2000). Cultural variations in the play of toddlers. *International Journal of Behavioral Development, 24*(3), 321–329.

Haden, C. A., Haine, R. A., & Fivush, R. (1997). Developig narrative structure in parent-child reminiscing across the preschool years. *Developmental Psychology, 33*(2), 295–307.

Haight, W. L., Wang, X. L., Fung, H. H. T., Williams, K., & Mintz, J. (1999). Universal, developmental, and variable aspects of young children's play: A cross-cultural comparison of pretending at home. *Child Development, 70*(6), 1477–1488.

Lillard, A. S., Lerner, M. D., Hopkins, E. J., Dore, R. A., Smith, E. D., & Palmquist, C. M. (2013). The impact of pretend play on children's development: A review of the evidence. *Psychological Bulletin, 139*(1), 1–34. https://doi.org/10.1037/a0029321.

Maccoby, E. E., & Jacklin, C. N. (1987). Gender segregation in childhood. *Advances in Child Development and Behavior, 20*, 239–287.

Martin, C. L., Kornienko, O., Schaefer, D. R., Hanish, L. D., Fabes, R. A., & Goble, P. (2013). The role of sex of peers and gender-typed activities in young children's peer affiliative networks: A longitudinal analysis of selection and influence. *Child Development, 84*(3), 921–937.

McLean, K. C., Pasupathi, M., & Pals, J. L. (2007). Selves creating stories creating selves: A process model of self-development. *Personality and social psychology review, 11*(3), 262–278.

Nelson, K., & Fivush, R. (2004). The emergence of autobiographical memory: A social cultural developmental theory. *Psychological Review, 111*(2), 486–511.

Nucci, L. P., & Turiel, E. (1978). Social interactions and the development of social concepts in preschool children. *Child Development, 49*, 400–407.

Ochs, E. (1993). Constructing social identity: A language socialization perspective. *Research on Language and Social Interaction, 26*(3), 287–306.

Pasupathi, M., Mansour, E., & Brubaker, J. R. (2007). Developing a life story: Constructing relations between self and experience in autobiographical narratives. *Human Development, 50*(2–3), 85–110.

Piaget, J. (1950). Cooperation and the moral development of the idea of justice (M. Gabain, Trans.). In *The moral judgement of the child* (pp. 195–326). London: Routledge & Kegan Paul Ltd.

Piotrowski, C. (1997). Rules of everyday family life: The development of social rules in mother-child and sibling relationships. *International Journal of Behavioral Development, 21*(3), 571–598.

Reese, E., & Fivush, R. (1993). Parental styles of talking about the past. *Developmental Psychology, 29*(3), 596–606.

Reese, E., Haden, C. A., & Fivush, R. (1996). Mothers, fathers, daughters, sons: Gender differences in autobiographical reminiscing. *Research on Language and Social Interaction, 29*(1), 27–56.

Shweder, R. A., Mahapatra, M., & Miller, J. G. (1987). Culture and moral development. In J. Kagan & S. Lamb (Eds.), *The emergence of morality in young children* (pp. 1–83). Chicago: University of Chicago Press.

Schröder, L., Keller, H., Kärtner, J., Kleis, A., Abels, M., Yovsi, R. D., et al. (2013). Early reminiscing in cultural contexts: Cultural models, maternal reminiscing styles, and children's memories. *Journal of Cognition and Development, 14*(1), 10–34.

Singer, D. G., Golinkoff, R. M., & Hirsh-Pasek, K. (Eds.). (2006). *Play = learning: How play motivates and enhances children's cognitive and social-emotional growth.* New York: Oxford University Press.

Tulviste, T., Kall, K., & Rämmer, A. (2017). Value priorities of younger and older adults in seven European countries. *Social Indicators Research, 133*(3), 931–942.

Tulviste, T., Mizera, L., & De Geer, B. (2012). Socialization values in stable and changing societies: A comparative study of Estonian, Swedish, and Russian Estonian mothers. *Journal of Cross-Cultural Psychology, 43*(3), 480–497.

Tulviste, T., Mizera, L., De Geer, B., & Tryggvason, M.-T. (2010). Cultural, contextual, and gender differences in peer talk: A comparative study. *Scandinavian Journal of Psychology, 51,* 319–325.

Tulviste, T., Tõugu, P., Keller, H., Schröder, L., & De Geer, B. (2016). Children's and mothers' contribution to joint reminiscing in different sociocultural contexts: who speaks and what is said. *Infant and Child Development, 25*(1), 43–63.

Turiel, E. (1983). *The development of social knowledge: Morality and convention.* New York: Cambridge University Press.

Tõugu, P., Suits, K., Tulviste, T. (2018). Developmental changes in children's references to self and others in their recollections of past events: A longitudinal study. *European Journal of Developmental Psychology, 15*(5), 565–579.

Tõugu, P., & Tulviste, T. (2010). References to social norms by preschool children and their linguistic expression. *European Journal of Developmental Psychology, 7*(2), 249–264.

Tõugu, P., Tulviste, T., Schröder, L., Keller, H., & De Geer, B. (2011). Socialization of past event talk: Cultural differences in maternal elaborative reminiscing. *Cognitive Development, 26,* 142–154. https://doi.org/10.1016/j.cogdev.2010.12.004.

Tõugu, P., Tulviste, T., & Suits, K. (2014). Gender differences in the content of preschool children's recollections: A longitudinal study. *International Journal of Behavioral Development, 38*(6), 563–569. https://doi.org/10.1177/0165025414537922.

Wang, Q. (2007). "Remember when you got the big, big bulldozer?" Mother-child reminiscing over time and across cultures. *Social Cognition, 25*(4), 455–471.

Wang, Q. (2004). The emergence of cultural self-constructs: Autobiographical memory and self-descriptions in European American and Chinese children. *Developmental Psychology, 40*(1), 3–15. https://doi.org/10.1037/0012-1649.40.1.3.

Wang, Q., Leichtman, M. D., & Davies, K. I. (2000). Sharing memories and telling stories: American and Chinese mothers and their 3-year-olds. *Memory, 8*(3), 159–177.

Wang, Q., & Brockmeier, J. (2002). Autobiographical remembering as cultural practice: Understanding the interplay between memory, self and culture. *Culture and Psychology, 8*(1), 45–64.

Weisberg, D. S., Zosh, J. M., Hirsh-Pasek, K., & Golinkoff, R. M. (2013). Talking it up: Play, language development, and the role of adult support. *American Journal of Play, 6*(1), 39–54.

Chapter 3
Children's Management of Attention as Cultural Practice

Rebeca Mejía Arauz, Amy L. Dexter, Barbara Rogoff
and Itzel Aceves-Azuara

Abstract This chapter addresses the idea that a focus on participation in cultural practices is more productive for understanding cultural aspects of young children's learning than comparing membership in racial or national identities. We illustrate this idea with observations of contrasting attentional strategies used by children from 5 communities varying in cultural experience as well as nationality. Children from two communities with Indigenous experience—one in the USA and one in Mexico— skillfully attended simultaneously to multiple events more often than children from three Western schooled communities in the USA and Mexico. In turn, children from the three highly schooled communities more often alternated their attention between multiple events, with attention to one event interrupting attention to another. We argue that both patterns of attention relate to participation in broader constellations of cultural practices and histories of ways of organizing learning in children's communities. We situate the children's attentional approaches in community practices organizing learning, especially connecting simultaneous attention with *Learning by Observing and Pitching in* to family and community endeavors (LOPI), which appears to be common in many Indigenous communities of the Americas.

We greatly appreciate the participation of the children and the permission for their involvement from their parents and teachers and the children's schools in Guadalajara, México, and Santa Cruz, CA. Thanks to Sofia Jiménez Mejía, Karime Infante, Isaac Andreu, and Julia García Mejía and the team of research assistants and coders at ITESO in Guadalajara for their contributions to this project. This project has been made possible through the support of the Center for Informal Learning and Schools, UC/MEXUS-CONACYT (Grant No. CN-02-68), the National Institutes of Health and Human Development (Grant No. T32 HD046423), and the National Science Foundation (Grant No. 0837898). Please address correspondence to: Rebeca Mejía-Arauz rebmejia@iteso.mx. Amy L. Dexter is now at California State University San Marcos.

R. M. Arauz (✉)
ITESO University, Guadalajara, Mexico
e-mail: rebmejia@iteso.mx

A. L. Dexter · B. Rogoff · I. Aceves-Azuara
University of California Santa Cruz, Santa Cruz, USA

© Springer Nature Switzerland AG 2019
T. Tulviste et al. (eds.), *Children's Social Worlds in Cultural Context*,
https://doi.org/10.1007/978-3-030-27033-9_3

23

Children's Management of Attention as Cultural Practice

The study of cognition often assumes that the ways that middle-class European American people manage their attention reflect human attentional management universally, as pointed out by Chavajay and Rogoff (1999). To counter such overgeneralization, research sometimes examines attention within distinct social categories such as race, ethnicity, or nationality, but often overgeneralization still occurs within these broad social categories. As argued in Rogoff (2003, 2011), we do not believe that the answer lies in making smaller and smaller membership category distinctions, but in focusing instead on people's participation in *cultural practices*. We draw attention to children's lived experience with cultural practices, in which they develop their familiar repertoires of ways of doing things (Gutiérrez and Rogoff 2003; Rogoff et al. 2014a, 2018).

Cultural practices are the ways that communities of people live, including their routines and norms, which vary across (and within) cultural communities. Cultural practices contribute to the regular patterns of daily life for children and families (Rogoff et al. 2014a). For example, in families where reading is a common and valued activity, preliterate children may "read" a book by speaking a few remembered phrases, imitating how the book is held, the pace at which pages are turned, and the intonations of reading aloud. Likewise, in communities where everyone pitches into help in household activities, babies observe how the family coordinates to clean the house, prepare a meal, or do laundry, and young children are often eager to contribute to the shared endeavor, learning both the skills and the expectation of helpfulness (Alcalá et al. 2014; Coppens et al. 2014, 2016; López et al. 2012). When included in everyday mature activities, young children learn by observing and pitching in; they manage ceremonies, cultivate plants, or even butcher a pig (Gutiérrez et al. 2015; Mejía-Arauz et al. 2015; Rogoff 2014). Thus, family and community practices contribute to children's lived experience and their repertoires of practice.

A focus on participation in cultural practices examines how children engage in and learn from the activities of their families and communities (Goodnow et al. 1995; Whiting 1976). In contrast, attempts to examine cultural variability by contrasting isolated behaviors across discrete, static demographic categories may provide a misleading understanding of human development (Gutiérrez and Rogoff 2003; Rogoff 2003, 2011). Demographic labels such as "Mexican" or even more specific labels such as "Mayan" or "Nahua" are often treated as indexing homogeneous characteristics of these groups. In a cultural practices approach, research *empirically* investigates the variations of practices within and across communities and examines changes over time, rather than making assumptions about people's skills or characteristics on the basis of their membership in static social categories such as race, ethnicity, or nationality (e.g., Rogoff 2003, 2011; Rogoff and Angelillo 2002; Rogoff et al. 2014b).

In this chapter, we investigate distinct ways that children manage their attention that correspond with cultural practices embedded in their communities' ways of living. Building on the perspective that understanding cultural variability in cognitive development requires attending to the socially and historically situated cultural practices in which children participate, we examine children's attention to multiple ongoing events in five communities spanning two nations. We expect attentional practices to be similar in two communities with Indigenous-heritage practices—one in the USA and one in Mexico. And we expect their form of attention to contrast with that of three communities with long-term extensive experience in Western schooling—one in the USA and two in Mexico.

We are particularly interested in open, broadly focused simultaneous attention to multiple ongoing events, which does not neglect one focus in favor of others, even momentarily. Children's simultaneous attention to nearby activities and to their own activity may facilitate learning in communities where they are generally included in community events; they thus have many opportunities to learn by observing that they might miss if they only focused on one event at a time (Rogoff et al. 1993; Silva et al. 2015). The inclusion of children in the range of mature community activities is a common cultural practice in Indigenous communities of Mexico and Central America, contrasting with the segregation of children that is common in communities with extensive Western schooling experience (Gaskins 1999; Morelli et al. 2003; Rogoff 1990, 2003). Gaskins and Paradise (2010, p. 100) suggest that in communities where children are present and expected to learn from observing the daily activities of the community, their attention is "on duty" at all times and becomes second nature.

In this chapter, we first describe research indicating that children from Indigenous-heritage communities of the Americas more often simultaneously attend to ongoing events and pay attention to events that are not directed to them, compared with children in highly schooled Western communities. We then describe how ways of attending appear to be a key feature of different ways of organizing learning in distinct cultural communities. We then present a study of patterns of attention across five communities which found that how children attend to multiple ongoing events relates more closely to communities' cultural practices (such as broadly including children in mature activities) than to nationality or ethnicity. Next, we discuss how these findings contribute to understanding distinct ways of managing attention that are embedded within different constellations of cultural practices that form paradigms organizing learning. Finally, we argue that understanding processes of culture change is aided by taking a focus on cultural practices rather than static demographic labels.

Cultural Differences in Attention to Surrounding Events

Research on cultural differences in attention has challenged a line of research based mostly in European American middle-class communities suggest that individuals can focus on only one event at a time (Broadbent 1957; Pashler 1994). However, research with people from Indigenous communities of the Americas has noted skilled use of simultaneous attention, as well as attentiveness in situations in which children are not directly addressed (Chavajay and Rogoff 1999; Correa-Chávez and Rogoff 2009;

Rogoff et al. 1993). Rogoff and colleagues have referred to such broad attention and alertness to ongoing events as wide, keen attention (Rogoff 2003; Rogoff et al. 2003), and Gaskins and Paradise have called it "open" attention that is "both wide angled and abiding" (Gaskins and Paradise 2010, p. 99). Such attentiveness is seen as a Mapuche (Indigenous Chilean) grandmother reminds her 4-year-old granddaughter to be aware of her little sister: "You must always be aware, be present for her" (Murray et al. 2017, p. 374). Similarly, in a Zinacantec Maya community a competent person is one having *ch'ulel*—"paying attention with eyes, ears, and spirit" (de León 2017, p. 56).

> This competence is the power to be mindful, by paying attention to what is happening in the environment and to others. [Zinacantec Maya] expect children to observe, pay attention, and be ready to collaborate by his or her own initiative without being told. In sum, the Zinacantec Mayan socialization ideology of child development as reflected in the expression "oy xo xch'ulel" ["she already has a spirit"] assumes mastery of focused attention, awareness of others, and the surrounding environment. (de León 2017, p. 49)

This attentiveness is an active process of being alert, noticing what is happening, and also making sense of it, as understood in Maya communities in Quintana Roo, Mexico (Rosado May et al. in prep; see also Lenkersdorf 2008). This active process is marked in Mexican communities by the common use of the word "fíjarse" ("to notice") in relation to paying attention. It is a call for keen, careful, focused attention that implies more than looking. It also implies understanding or figuring something out, with the intention to "fix it in the mind" for later responsible use. Such attention is apparent in accounts of learning in a Yucatec Maya community, where people refer to observing closely and pitching in as "settling in the eyes." An interviewee recalled, "So I, since I was 10 years old it had already been settled in my eye like that, it had already been settled in eye" (Cervera 2019 year).

The next sections describe comparative research that indicates that people from some Indigenous and Indigenous-heritage communities of the Americas are more likely to pay keen attention than middle-class people of several national backgrounds. The research examines (1) third-party attention to ongoing events in which children are not directly addressed and (2) skillful attention to several events at once without interrupting attention to competing events.

Cultural Differences in Third-Party Attention

Children from Indigenous-heritage communities of the Americas seem to be especially attentive to surrounding activities that are not addressed to them, showing "third-party attention." For example, in a demonstration of origami paper folding, triads of Mexican-heritage children from families with limited Western schooling were more likely to observe each other folding, compared with European American middle-class children (Mejía-Arauz et al. 2005).

A series of studies has examined children's third-party attentiveness and learning when waiting nearby as an adult showed their sibling how to make a toy. Indigenous

Guatemalan Mayan children whose parents had little Western schooling carefully attended to the demonstration provided for their sibling, despite being given no indication that they would later have use of the information. They showed sustained attention most of the time, twice as much as European American children whose parents had extensive Western schooling experience (Correa-Chávez and Rogoff 2009; for a video showing these contrasts, see http://videohall.com/p/693). Similarly, in the same situation, children from US families that had immigrated from Indigenous regions of Mexico (with only basic Western schooling) showed sustained attention more often than children from Mexican immigrant families with extensive Western schooling experience (López et al. 2010; Silva et al. 2010).

In all three of these studies, the children's third-party attentiveness resulted in greater learning. The children from families with closer involvement in Indigenous practices of Mexico or Guatemala, and less experience in Western schooling, needed significantly less help to build the toy they had observed their sibling making than peers from highly schooled backgrounds (Correa-Chávez and Rogoff 2009; López et al. 2010; Silva et al. 2010).

Similar contrasts appeared in a more naturalistic study during a home visit in which 3- to 5-year-old children were present when their toddler sibling and mother were operating novel objects. Mayan 3- to 5-year-olds spent most of the visit attentive to the mother-toddler interactions or other interactions that were not directly addressed to them—more than twice as much as European American middle-class children in the same situation (Silva et al. 2015). The European American middle-class children more commonly just paid attention to their own activity, unrelated to the activities of others, or seemingly demanded attention by fussing or showing off. Third-party attention like that observed among the Mayan children may be related to children's simultaneous attention to several events at once.

Cultural Differences in Simultaneous Attention

Attention to multiple ongoing events entails seamless broad attention without sacrificing attention to one focus in favor of another. This may be helpful for learning by observing the everyday life of the community (Chavajay and Rogoff 1999; Correa-Chávez et al. 2005, 2011; Rogoff et al. 1993). In the first study examining cultural differences in simultaneous attention, Rogoff and colleagues (1993) found that Guatemalan Mayan toddlers used simultaneous attention as they manipulated a novel toy while attending to ongoing conversation and surrounding events. In contrast, middle-class European American toddlers seldom attended to events simultaneously. Instead, they frequently alternated their attention between multiple foci or seemed unaware of other events of likely interest. This cultural variation in attention to multiple ongoing events was replicated in a study in which all children from both backgrounds had a similar family size (Chavajay and Rogoff 1999).

In both studies, the Mayan toddlers simultaneously attended to multiple ongoing episodes more often even than the *mothers* in European American middle-class families, and Mayan mothers used simultaneous attention in most of the session (Chavajay and Rogoff 1999; Rogoff et al. 2003). The authors suggested that there is a Mayan cultural preference for being attentive to surrounding events, related to the opportunities available to learn by observing and local values prioritizing children's involvement.

Children's use of simultaneous attention also differs between cultural communities within the USA. Cultural variation in simultaneous attention to multiple events was observed among 6- to 10-year-olds as they engaged in an origami paper folding demonstration (Correa-Chávez et al. 2005). US Mexican-heritage children whose parents had only basic schooling managed their attention simultaneously to multiple foci such as their own folding, the folding of their peers, the completed origami figures on the table, and the research assistant who provided the origami demonstration. They attended simultaneously more than US European-heritage children or US Mexican-heritage children whose parents had extensive schooling experience, who often quickly alternated their attention between foci.

Both third-party attention and simultaneous attention to ongoing activities may foster children's learning from opportunities to be present in the valued activities of their families and communities. These practices are aspects of a paradigm for organizing learning that seems to be more prevalent in Indigenous-heritage communities of the Americas in which Western practices have limited hold than in communities with extensive experience with the practices of Western schooling and related ways of organizing learning.

Attentiveness Is an Aspect of How Learning Is Organized

Wide, keen attention is one of the features that define a paradigm for organizing learning that seems to be widespread in Indigenous communities of the Americas: *Learning by Observing and Pitching in* to family and community endeavors ("LOPI," previously called *Intent Community Participation*; Paradise and Rogoff 2009; Rogoff 2003, 2014; Rogoff et al. 2003, 2015). Other features of the LOPI paradigm include children being involved in the wide range of family and community endeavors, pitching in with solidarity to help (like everyone else), taking initiative in collaboration with other children and with adults, and learning to contribute responsibly to the productive and social activities of their family and the community. The importance of children's presence and engagement in the daily work of Mesoamerican communities appears in Aztec documents from almost 500 years ago (Chamoux 2015).

The LOPI paradigm contrasts with a way of organizing learning that is common in Western schooling, which Rogoff and colleagues (2003, 2007a) refer to as *Assembly-Line Instruction*. Among the features of Assembly-Line Instruction are segregation of children from many family and community endeavors, instruction in exercises out of the context of productive activity, unilateral control of children by adults, and encouragement of a singular focus of attention that is managed by adults (Rogoff 2003; Rogoff et al. 2007). Teachers are charged with drawing children's attention to key aspects of a lesson, requiring children to maintain this focus, and monitoring whether they are successfully controlling the child's attention (Paradise et al. 2014). This may be done explicitly by requesting children's attention, "One, two, three, eyes on me!" or by using gestures or an exaggerated tone of voice.

The practices that organize learning in Western schools are often mirrored in the practices used by highly schooled parents to engage children in the home. In families with several generations of formal schooling, which includes most European-heritage US families (according to Bronfenbrenner et al. 1996), parents often interact with children in school-like learning scripts (Laosa 1982; Morelli et al. 2003). For example, they commonly ask assessment questions such as "where is your nose?" (Rogoff et al. 2015). In the study that we present below, we predicted that family histories connecting families with Indigenous American practices and/or with Western schooling (and related practices) would distinguish the attention management of their children, irrespective of nationality or ethnicity.

Patterns of Attention Across Five Communities in Two Nations

Our study examined the use of simultaneous attention by children whose parents and communities differed in experience with distinct cultural paradigms for organizing learning. Regardless of nationality (US or Mexican), we expected that children from communities with historical connections to Indigenous communities (which often include children in community life, as in LOPI) to be more likely to focus skillfully on several events at once. In contrast, regardless of nationality (USA or Mexican), we expected children of parents with extensive Western schooling experience to be more likely to attend narrowly, on one focus at a time, as is often encouraged in schooling and related practices of middle-class life (Chavajay and Rogoff 2002; Rogoff 2003). We expected nationality (USA or Mexican) to play little role; we placed our bets on children's family historical and ongoing experience of Indigenous Mexican or Western schooling (and related) practices.

The Five Communities

Two communities with Indigenous practices. Two of the five participating communities likely maintain involvement in practices of Indigenous peoples of Mexico, whether residing in Mexico or the USA. In both the *Indigenous-heritage town* and the *Pueblo US immigrant* communities, it was common for parents to have only basic schooling, consistent with the historically restricted access to schooling in Mexican Indigenous and Indigenous-heritage communities (Bonfil-Batalla 1987; López et al. 2010; Silva et al. 2010). Although discrimination and Mexican policies have led people not to claim an Indigenous identity, Indigenous practices remain part of the diversity of many Mexican communities (Bonfil-Batalla 1987; Rogoff et al. 2014b). Many Mexican immigrants to the United States come from Indigenous-heritage communities and retain some Indigenous practices (Fox and Rivera-Salgado 2004).

Indigenous-heritage Mexican town. This was a small town with pre-Colombian Indigenous roots that is now encompassed in the periphery of Guadalajara. At the time of this study, the inhabitants of the *Indigenous-heritage Mexican town* and other related towns continued some traditional Indigenous practices (e.g., for pregnancy, birth, weddings; Lorente Fernández 2006; Nájera-Ramirez 1998; Rogoff et al. 2014b). Many fathers were employed in construction or at local factories; grandfathers and great-grandfathers had farmed or had done day labor. Mothers usually worked in their own or others' homes and some were market vendors, similar to the grandmothers and great-grandmothers. The average schooling of mothers was elementary school ($M = 5$ grades, range $= 0$–9), similar to fathers, and both grandparents and great-grandparents averaged about 1 grade (Rogoff et al. 2014b). Children had an average of 4 siblings.

Pueblo US immigrant families were also likely to have historical connections to Indigenous practices (Mejía-Arauz et al. 2007; Rogoff et al. 2014b). They were immigrants to a town on the central coast of California from similar communities in Mexico as the *Indigenous-heritage Mexican town*, largely from rural parts of Michoacán as well as from Jalisco (Fox and Rivera-Salgado 2004; Passel et al. 2004). Mothers had less than 12 grades of schooling, probably an average of 6 or 7 grades according to community averages. Children had an average of 1.6 siblings.

Three extensively schooled communities. Parents in the three other communities had extensive Western schooling experience (12 or more grades), 1 in the USA, 2 in Mexico:

European American middle-class families on California's central coast usually had several generations with extensive schooling; their mothers had at least 12 and usually about 14-16 grades of schooling. The children attended the same school as the children from the *Pueblo US immigrant* community. These children had an average of 1.2 siblings.

Cosmopolitan Mexican families, in Guadalajara, had generally lived in major cities of Mexico for several generations and had professional occupations and extensive schooling over at least 2 generations. Mothers had an average of 15 grades (range $= 12$–18, like fathers), and grandparents averaged almost 10 grades; greatgrandmothers averaged 2 grades and great-grandfathers averaged 10 grades (Rogoff et al. 2014b). Children had an average of 1.4 siblings.

Nouveau Cosmopolitan Mexican parents, in Guadalajara, were often the first generation to live in a city and to engage in extensive schooling; they often were owners of small businesses or employees in professional service companies. Mothers averaged 14 grades of schooling (range 8–18, like fathers), and grandparents averaged 7 grades; great-grandmothers averaged almost 6 grades and great-grandfathers 4 grades (Rogoff et al. 2014b). Children had an average of 1.3 siblings.

Children's Attention During an Informal Demonstration

We recruited 111 triads of 6–9-year-olds from schools serving the 5 communities for an origami paper folding demonstration, held in a spare room at their school. The children in each triad shared the same community background and the same gender (with approximately equal numbers of boy and girl triads), with an approximate one-year spread in age.

The children each folded their own figure, sitting next to each other at a table. After a brief warm-up, a female bilingual Mexican research assistant (blind to the research hypothesis) showed the triad how to fold a simple pig and then a more difficult jumping frog, using their preferred language. She followed a script that dictated her pace, amount of instruction, and an informal style of interaction; a procedural check showed that she followed the script similarly for all triads.

We focused on the child who was seated in the middle in front of the camera, to make sure we had visibility of the child's face to code attention with precision. We coded the episodes with multiple ongoing events that occurred during the first five minutes of the demonstration of the second origami figure. (The episodes involving multiple events comprised approximately a quarter of the time.) The multiple events almost always involved children attending to their own folding (96% of the time) and often the folding of the woman providing the demonstration (69%), with occasional attention to other children's folding (15%) or studying the model figures that were on the table (6% of the time).

A bilingual college student native to México (blind to the questions of the study) examined the children's gaze, posture, and responses to available information to code the number of seconds that children spent in any of four mutually exclusive categories of attention during episodes with multiple ongoing events: Simultaneous attention, Alternating, Shift of Attention and Apparently Unaware. The first author (RM-A) coded 30% of the sessions to check for reliability: Simultaneous attention (Pearson correlation, $r = 0.80$), Alternating attention ($r = 0.82$), Shift of attention ($r = 0.96$); Apparently unaware ($r = 0.92$): reliability for existence of multiple events was $r = 0.83$.

Our primary interest was whether the child's form of attention during multiple events was either simultaneous or alternating. The other two attentional categories— shifting attention from one event to another and not returning, and apparently being unaware of an ongoing event—were infrequent, occurring less than 1 and 7% of the time, respectively. These did not differ across the 5 communities. There were no significant differences by gender in any attentional approaches.

Simultaneous attention was when the child attended actively to two events at once, without pausing or interrupting their attention to either event. Attention to each event was as fluid as if there were no other focus of attention, such as when a child attended to the research assistant's demonstration while skillfully continuing work on her own figure. Simultaneous attention does not involve a break in attention to track several ongoing events, *unlike* what is often referred to as multitasking, in which attention is "pulled, stretched, split, and scattered" with "rapid task switching" and "switching attention… toggling between tasks" (Wallis 2010, pp. 4, 6, 8).

As expected, children from two Indigenous-heritage communities attended simultaneously during a higher average percentage of the time in which multiple events occurred than children from the three extensively schooled communities (planned comparison $t = 2.38$, $p < 0.02$). Children from the Indigenous-heritage Mexican and the Pueblo US immigrant communities attended simultaneously an average of 48 and 39% of the multiple events time (SDs $= 22$ and 17%, respectively). In contrast, children from the European American middle-class, Cosmopolitan Mexican, and Nouveau Cosmopolitan Mexican communities attended simultaneously in only 31, 36, and 32% of the multiple events time (SDs $= 16$, 16, 18%).

An example of simultaneous attention comes from a child from the Indigenous-heritage Mexican community, who alertly followed the exchanges between the other two girls while she also paid attention to completing her own fold. One of the other girls silently asked the third girl for help; when the third girl tried unsuccessfully to fix the figure, the watching girl intervened to help, at the precise moment that the other two seemed lost with the folding, while she simultaneously took care of folding her own figure.

Alternating attention was when a child attended to two ongoing events by alternating between them. This involved halting attention to one focus of attention in order to attend to another, such as stopping folding their own figure for an instant, in order to watch the folding of another child. (This may be a skilled form of "multitasking.")

Children from the three communities where extensive schooling was common usually alternated their attention to multiple events. They did so in a significantly higher percent of the multiple events time (European American middle-class 57%, SD $= 19$%; Cosmopolitan Mexican 56%, SD $= 18$%; Nouveau Cosmopolitan Mexican 62%, SD $= 20$%) than children from the Indigenous-heritage Mexican and the Pueblo US immigrant communities, who alternated their attention an average of 45 and 46% of the multiple events time (SDs $= 22$, 17%; planned comparison $t = 2.77$, $p < 0.01$).

An example of alternating attention comes from a triad from the Cosmopolitan Mexican community. A child who was having difficulty with her folding looked over to her companion's figure while momentarily pausing her own folding, and after this glance she turned her attention back to her own figure.

Conclusions

The children's patterns of attention were distinguished by whether their family likely had experience with Indigenous Mexican practices or with Western schooling and related practices, regardless of whether they were in the USA or Mexico. Children whose families likely had experience with Indigenous Mexican practices more often attended simultaneously when multiple events occurred at once, whereas children whose families had extensive experience with Western schooling were more likely to alternate their attention between ongoing events, with a brief interruption of one event to attend to the other.

Our findings of skilled simultaneous attention to multiple ongoing events among children from communities with Indigenous Mexican histories join a few other studies in challenging prevailing theories of bottlenecks in attention (Chavajay and Rogoff 1999; Correa-Chávez et al. 2005; Rogoff et al. 1993). The results contribute to showing how the narrow attentional strategies of a particular cultural group (largely middle-class European American) cannot be assumed to represent the ways that human attention works.

Further, the findings of this study support the idea that children's attentional strategies fit with the practices common in their communities, irrespective of nationality and ethnicity. In this study, both simultaneous attention and alternating attention to ongoing events were prevalent within communities of one Mexican city; both attentional strategies were also found in communities within one US town.

Focusing on demographic categories such as race or nationality may provide a first glance at cultural differences, but it does not improve the acuity of our insights about culture very much. In addition, a focus on race or nationality to represent culture presents the risk of essentializing or using deficit perspectives to describe the ways of life of nondominant groups (Gutiérrez and Rogoff 2003). Examining people's experience with distinct cultural practices provides a correction to the common overgeneralizations based on membership in national and ethnic groups (and even residence in whole hemispheres, such as research contrasting East and West, or Us and The Rest).

The findings point to the importance of understanding the cultural practices of children's everyday lives (Rogoff et al. 2014a, 2018). Children's attentional strategies relate to their participation in the broader cultural practices of their communities. The next section posits that these forms of attention management are embedded in cultural practices organizing children's learning, such as being involved in adult-managed lessons or in ongoing community activities.

Attention Management Is Embedded in Cultural Practices Organizing Children's Learning

Our finding that children from three highly schooled communities commonly focused attention narrowly and alternated attention between competing events adds to previous research among children from communities with extensive experience in Western schooling and related practices (Chavajay and Rogoff 1999; Correa-Chávez et al. 2005; Rogoff et al. 1993). Narrow focus on one event at a time fits with a learning paradigm that often organizes instruction in Western schools, where teachers attempt to focus children's attention narrowly and control their engagement in lessons (Paradise et al. 2014).

Our findings also add to a growing body of research on children's simultaneous attention to multiple events in communities with historical connections to practices of Mesoamerican Indigenous communities (Chavajay and Rogoff 1999; Correa-Chávez et al. 2005; Rogoff et al. 1993). Children with family histories of engagement in Indigenous Mexican communities are likely to have experience of practices involved in the paradigm organizing children's *Learning by Observing and Pitching in* to family and community endeavors (*LOPI*; Paradise and Rogoff 2009; Rogoff 2003, 2014; Rogoff et al. 2015), which appears to be common in Indigenous communities of the Americas.

The practice of wide-angled simultaneous attention to multiple events, without sacrificing attention to one for the sake of another, is likely to facilitate learning by observing and contributing to the wide range of important activities of their community. Observing and contributing are key features of LOPI. With simultaneous attention, a person can carry on with what they are doing at the same time as being aware of surrounding events that may hold importance, as the Indigenous-heritage children in our study often did.

Simultaneous attention may be encouraged by cultural values and expectations emphasizing observation and participation. In communities where people are expected to be aware of what is going on with the group and ready to pitch in, simultaneous attention supports the maintenance of awareness of the direction of the group and relevant events that may need action. In Mexico and among immigrants from Mexico, a valued practice is being *acomedido/a*—a cultural practice without a direct English translation, which means being alert to what is going on and pitching in without being asked (López et al. 2012).

Indeed, previous studies in the same communities that we studied have also found evidence along the lines of other features of LOPI, including being *acomedido/a*. For example, children of the two Indigenous-heritage communities of the present study often show initiative in helping at home, and often collaborate through considerate and articulate nonverbal communication (Alcalá et al. 2014; Coppens et al. 2014; Mejía-Arauz et al. 2012). In other Indigenous-heritage communities, studies likewise have found an emphasis on children's engagement in learning through observation, third-party attention, collaboration, and articulate nonverbal conversation (Chavajay and Rogoff 2002; Correa-Chávez et al. 2005; Correa-Chávez and Rogoff 2009; Mejía Arauz et al. 2007).

Focusing on children's involvement in everyday cultural practices aids researchers' and practitioners' becoming aware of important skills that could otherwise be overlooked, such as simultaneous attention. This focus also facilitates a strengths-based approach (González et al. 2005; Rogoff et al. 2017). Awareness of cultural variation in strategies of attention is important for institutions serving children from distinct cultural backgrounds. Such awareness would help ensure that the skill of children who simultaneously attend to more than one event is recognized, rather than seen as an attentional deficit in school settings that assume that attention should be singular and narrow. Research has generally defined productive attention as having a single focus, often branding other types of attention as "unfocused" (Ruff and Rothbart 1996). This definition may contribute to the disparities in the diagnosis of Attention Deficit Disorder in the USA across cultural groups (Schmitz et al. 2003) and expansion of this diagnosis all over the world without consideration of cultural variations in attention management (Smith 2017).

Schools and other institutions serving children would do well to change by building on the familiar practices and strengths of the students who now attend them. To conclude this chapter, we argue that a focus on cultural practices aids in understanding cultural changes and continuities.

A Focus on Practices Facilitates Studying Dynamic Cultural Processes

A focus on cultural practices aids in understanding cultural changes as well as continuities in children's and families' lives. In contrast, conceptualizing cultural groups in demographic terms (such as race or nationality) often assumes that characteristics of groups are static.

Future research should examine which practices are maintained and which transformed or discarded when people experience the practices of several cultural communities. To what extent and under what circumstances do Indigenous-heritage families of the Americas extend familiar practices to new situations or maintain cultural practices of Indigenous communities when they move away, or when they experience foreign cultural practices such as extensive Western schooling? For example, Indigenous-heritage Mexican children who routinely contributed voluntarily and collaboratively in their household were also more likely to collaborate in a school-like game or instructional activity (Alcalá et al. 2018; López Fraire et al. 2019).

Alternatively, people may switch to new practices, as has been observed among Indigenous parents who became teachers educated in Western schooling approaches. They interacted with their own children in school-like ways—including trying to manage children's attention—in contrast to other Indigenous parents who did not have much experience with Western schooling (Chavajay and Rogoff 2002; Mejía-Arauz et al. 2013).

Other possible cultural dynamics include combining practices from different cultural traditions or using different approaches in different contexts, such as home and school. Several studies find that children from Indigenous-heritage families of the Americas with extensive family schooling engage in attentional practices and collaboration in ways that either mix the two cultural systems in intermediate approaches or distinguish which contexts to use different practices (Chavajay and Rogoff 2002; Correa-Chávez et al. 2005, 2016; Correa-Chávez and Rogoff 2009; López et al. in preparation; Mejía-Arauz et al. 2013; Rogoff et al. 1993).

A focus on cultural practices as a way to understand attention not only helps to broaden understanding of how humans use their attention. It also can encourage learning how to use attention in more than one way, which would help children navigate the different contexts of their lives. The children from all 5 communities in our study attend school and are likely learning to use the kind of narrowly focused attention that is often required of schoolchildren. In addition, the children from all 5 communities can benefit from learning to attend to several events simultaneously, in a skillful alertness that is likely to help them learn from what is going on around them.

References

Alcalá, L., Rogoff, B., & López Fraire, A. (2018). Sophisticated collaboration is common among Mexican-heritage US children. *Proceedings of the National Academy of Sciences, 115*(45), 11377–11384.

Alcalá, L., Rogoff, B., Mejía-Arauz, R., Coppens, A. D., & Dexter, A. L. (2014). Children's initiative in contributions to family work in Indigenous-heritage and cosmopolitan communities in Mexico. *Human Development, 57,* 96–115.

Bonfil-Batalla, G. (1987). *México profundo: Una civilización negada [Deep Mexico: A civilization denied]*. México: Grijalbo.

Broadbent, D. E. (1957). A mechanical model for human attention and immediate memory. *Psychological Review, 64*(3), 205–215. https://doi.org/10.1037/h0047313.

Bronfenbrenner, U., McClelland, P., Wethington, E., Moen, P., & Ceci, S. J. (1996). *The state of Americans*. NY: Free Press.

Cervera, D. (2019). Maya children´s learning to be vernacular architects. Manuscript submitted for publication.

Chamoux, M. N. (2015). Conceptions of educational practices among the Nahuas of Mexico: Past and present. In M. Correa-Chávez, R. Mejía-Arauz, & B. Rogoff, (Eds.), *Children learn by observing and contributing to family and community endeavors: A cultural paradigm. Advances in child development and behavior* (Vol. 49, pp. 253–271).

Chavajay, P., & Rogoff, B. (1999). Cultural variation in management of attention by children and their caregivers. *Developmental Psychology, 35*(4), 1079–1091. https://doi.org/10.1037/0012-1649.35.4.1079.

Chavajay, P., & Rogoff, B. (2002). Schooling and traditional collaborative social organization of problem solving by Mayan mothers and children. *Developmental Psychology, 38,* 55–66. https://doi.org/10.1037/0012-1649.38.1.55.

Coppens, A. D., Alcalá, L., Mejía-Arauz, R., & Rogoff, B. (2014). Children's initiative in family household work in Mexico. *Human Development, 57,* 116–130.

Coppens, A. D., Alcalá, L., Rogoff, B., & Mejía-Arauz, R. (2016). Children's contributions in family work: Two cultural paradigms. In S. Punch, & R. M. Vanderbeck & T. Skelton (Eds.), *Familial and friendship relations and spatial socialities, Vol. 5*. Heidelberg, Germany: Springer. https://doi.org/10.1007/978-981-4585-92-7_11-1.

Correa-Chávez, M., Mejía-Arauz, R., & Keyser, U. (2016). Schooling and changes in child and family life in indigenous communities of Mesoamerica. In D. Silva Guimarães (Ed.), *Amerindian paths* (pp. 107–132). Charlotte, NC: Information Age Publishing Inc.

Correa-Chávez, M., Roberts, A. L. D., & Martínez Pérez, M. (2011). Cultural patterns in children's learning through keen observation and participation in their communities. In J. Benson (Ed.), *Advances in child behavior and development* (Vol. 40, pp. 209–241). Burlington: Academic Press.

Correa-Chávez, M., & Rogoff, B. (2009). Children's attention to interactions directed to others: Guatemalan Mayan and European American patterns. *Developmental Psychology, 45,* 630–641. https://doi.org/10.1037/a0014144.

Chávez, M., Rogoff, B., & Mejía-Arauz, R. (2005). Cultural patterns in attending to two events at once. *Child Development, 76*(3), 664–678. https://doi.org/10.1111/j.1467-8624.2005.00870.x.

de León, L. (2017). Emerging learning ecologies. *Linguistics and Education, 41,* 47–58. https://doi.org/10.1016/j.linged.2017.07.003.

Fox, J., & Rivera-Salgado, G. (2004). *Indigenous Mexican immigrants in the US.* La Jolla, CA: Center for U.S.-Mexican Studies, UCSD/Center for Comparative Immigration Studies, UCSD.

Gaskins, S. (1999). Children's daily lives in a Mayan village: A case study of culturally constructed roles and activities. In A. Goncu (Ed.), *Children's engagement in the world: Sociocultural perspectives* (pp. 25-60). Cambridge, MA: Cambridge University Press.

Gaskins, S., & Paradise, R. (2010). Learning through observation in daily life. In D. Lancy, J. Bock, & S. Gaskins (Eds.), *The anthropology of learning in childhood* (pp. 85–117). Lanham, MD: Altamira.

González, N., Moll, L. C., & Amanti, C. (2005). *Funds of knowledge.* Mahwah, N.J: Erlbaum.

Goodnow, J. J., Miller, P. J., & Kessel, F. (1995). Editors' preface to "Development through participation in sociocultural activity. In J. J. Goodnew, P. J. Miller, & F. Kessel (Eds.), *Cultural practices as contexts for development* (pp. 45–65). San Francisco, CA: Jossey-Bass.

Gutiérrez, I. T., Rosengren, K. S., & Miller, P. J. (2015). Día de los Muertos: Learning about death by observing and pitching in. *Advances in Child Development and Behavior, 49,* 229–249. https://doi.org/10.1016/bs.acdb.2015.08.004.

Gutiérrez, K., & Rogoff, B. (2003). Cultural ways of learning. *Educational Researcher, 32,* 19–25. https://www.researchgate.net/publication/233895989_Cultural_ways_of_learning.

Laosa, L. M. (1982). School, occupation, culture, and family: The impact of parental schooling on the parent–child relationship. *Journal of Educational Psychology, 74*(6), 791–827. https://doi.org/10.1037/0022-0663.74.6.791.

Lenkersdorf, C. (2008). *Aprender a escuchar [Learning to listen].* Mexico DR: Plaza y Valdés Editores.

López, A., Correa-Chávez, M., Rogoff, B., & Gutiérrez, K. (2010). Attention to instruction directed to another by U.S. Mexican-heritage children of varying cultural backgrounds. *Developmental Psychology, 46,* 593–601. https://doi.org/10.1037/a0018157.

López, A., Najafi, B., Rogoff, B., & Mejía Arauz, R. (2012). Collaboration and helping as cultural practices. In J. Valsiner (Ed.), *Oxford handbook of culture and psychology* (pp. 869–884). Oxford: New York, NY.

López Fraire, A., Rogoff, B., & Alcalá, L. (2019). *Cultural differences in helping without being asked.* University of California, Santa Cruz, Manuscript in preparation.

Lorente Fernández, D. (2006). Infancia Nahua y transmisión de la cosmovisión: Los ahuaques o espíritus pluviales en la sierra de Texcoco (México) [Nahua childhood and transmission of the cosmovision: The Ahuaques or rain spirits in the mountains of Texcoco Mexico]. *Boletín de Antropología, 20,* 152–168.

Mejía-Arauz, R., Correa-Chávez, M., Keyser Ohrt, U., & Aceves-Azuara, I. (2015). Collaborative work or individual chores. In M. Correa-Chávez, R. Mejía-Arauz, & B. Rogoff, Children learn by observing and contributing to family and community endeavors: A cultural paradigm. *Advances in Child Development and Behavior 49,* 25–51.

Mejía-Arauz, R., Keyser Ohrt, U., & Correa-Chávez, M. (2013). Transformaciones culturales y generacionales en la participación colaborativa de niñas y niños de una comunidad púrhépecha. *Revista Mexicana de Investigación Educativa, 18*(59), 1019–1104.

Mejía-Arauz, R., Roberts, A. L. D., & Rogoff, B. (2012). Cultural variation in balance of nonverbal conversation and talk. *International Perspectives in Psychology: Research, Practice, Consultation, 1,* 207–220. https://doi.org/10.1037/a0030961.

Mejía-Arauz, R., Rogoff, B., Dexter, A. L., & Najafi, B. (2007). Cultural variation in children's structures of participation in a shared activity. *Child Development, 78,* 1001–1014. https://doi.org/10.1111/j.1467-8624.2007.01046.x.

Mejía-Arauz, R., Rogoff, B., & Paradise, R. (2005). Cultural variation in children's observation during a demonstration. *International Journal of Behavioral Development, 29,* 282–291. https://doi.org/10.1111/j.1467-8624.2007.01046.x.

Morelli, G., Rogoff, B., & Angelillo, C. (2003). Cultural variation in young children's access to work or involvement in specialized child-focused activities. *International Journal of Behavioral Development, 27,* 264–274. https://journals.sagepub.com/doi/10.1080/01650250244000335

Murray, M., Bowen, S., Verdugo, M., & Holtmannspötter, J. (2017). Care and relatedness among rural Mapuche women: Issues of cariño and empathy. *Ethos, 45*(3), 367–385.

Nájera-Ramirez, O. (1998). *La fiesta de los Tastoanes: Critical encounters in Mexican festival performance.* New Mexico: New Mexico University Press.

Paradise, R., Mejía-Arauz, R., Silva, K. G., Dexter, A. L., & Rogoff, B. (2014). One, two, three, Eeyes on me! *Human Development, 57,* 131–149.

Paradise, R., & Rogoff, B. (2009). Side by side. *Ethos, 37,* 102–138. https://doi.org/10.1111/j.1548-1352.2009.01033.x.

Pashler, H. (1994). Dual-task interference in simple tasks. *Psychological Bulletin, 116,* 220–244. https://doi.org/10.1037/0033-2909.116.2.220.

Passel, J., Capps, R., & Fix, M. (2004). *Undocumented immigrants: facts and figures.* Unpublished manuscript. Urban Institute, Washington, DC.

Rogoff, B. (1990). *Apprenticeship in thinking: Cognitive development in social context.* Oxford: New York, NY.

Rogoff, B. (2003). *The cultural nature of human development.* NY: Oxford.

Rogoff, B. (2011). *Developing destinies: A Mayan midwife and town.* NY: Oxford.

Rogoff, B. (2014). Learning by observing and pitching into family and community endeavors. *Human Development, 57,* 69–81.

Rogoff, B., Moore, L., Najafi, B., Dexter, A., Correa-Chávez, M., & Solís, J. (2007). Children's development of cultural repertoires through participation in everyday routines and practices. In J. E. Grusec & P. D. Hastings (Eds.), *Handbook of socialization: Theory and research* (pp. 490–515). New York, NY: Guilford Press.

Rogoff, B., & Angelillo, C. (2002). Investigating the coordinated functioning of multifaceted cultural practices in human development. *Human Development, 45,* 211–225.

Rogoff, B., Coppens, A., Alcalá, L., Aceves-Azuara, I., Ruvalcaba, O., López, A., et al. (2017). Noticing learners' strengths through cultural research. *Perspectives on Psychological Science, 12,* 876–888. https://doi.org/10.1177/1745691617718355.

Rogoff, B., Dahl, A., & Callanan, M. (2018). The importance of understanding children's liveexperience. *Developmental Review, 50,* 5–15. https://doi.org/10.1016/j.dr.2018.05.006.

Rogoff, B., Mejía-Arauz, R., & Correa-Chávez, M. (2015). A cultural paradigm—Learning by observing and pitching in. In M. Correa-Chávez, R. Mejía-Arauz, & Rogoff, B. (Eds.), Children learn by observing and contributing to family and community endeavors: A cultural paradigm. *Advances in Child Development and Behavior, 49,* 1–22.

Rogoff, B., Mistry, J.J., Göncü, A., & Mosier, C. (1993). Guided participation in cultural activity by toddlers and caregivers. *Monographs of the Society for Research in Child Development, 58* (7, Serial No. 236).

Rogoff, B., Moore, L., Correa-Chávez, M., & Dexter, A. L. (2014a). Children develop cultural repertoires through engaging in everyday routines and practices. In J. Grusec & P. Hastings (Eds.), *Handbook of socialization: Theory and research* (pp. 472–498). NY: Guilford Press.

Rogoff, B., Najafi, B., & Mejía-Arauz, R. (2014b). Constellations of cultural practices across generations. *Human Development, 57,* 82–95.

Rogoff, B., Moore, L., Najafi, B., Dexter, A., Correa-Chávez, M., & Solis, J. (2007b). Children's development of cultural repertoires through participation in everyday routines and practices. In J. Grusec & P. D. Hastings (Eds.), *Handbook of socialization: Theory and research* (pp. 490–515). New York, NY: Guilford Press.

Rogoff, B., Paradise, R., Mejía-Arauz, R., Correa-Chávez, M., & Angelillo, C. (2003). Firsthand learning through intent participation. *Annual Review of Psychology, 54,* 175–203. https://doi.org/10.1146/annurev.psych.54.101601.145118.

Rosado-May, F. J., Urrieta, L. Jr., Dayton, A., & Rogoff, B. (in press). Learning and innovation in indigenous knowledge systems. In N. S. Nasir, C. D. Lee, & R. Pea (Eds.), *Handbook of the cultural foundations of learning*. London, UK: Routledge.

Ruff, H. A., & Rothbart, M. K. (1996). *Attention in early development*. Oxford: New York, NY.

Schmitz, M. F., Fillipone, P., & Edelman, E. M. (2003). Social representations of attention deficit/hyperactivity disorder 1988–1997. *Culture and Psychology, 9,* 383–406. https://doi.org/10.1177/1354067X0394004.

Silva, K., Correa-Chávez, M., & Rogoff, B. (2010). Mexican heritage children's attention and learning from interactions directed to others. *Child Development, 81,* 898–912. https://doi.org/10.1111/j.1467-8624.2010.01441.x.

Silva, K. G., Shimpi, P. M., & Rogoff, B. (2015). Young children's attention to what's going on. In M. Correa-Chávez, R. Mejía-Arauz, & B. Rogoff (Eds.), Children learn by observing and contributing to family and community endeavors. In *Advances in Child Development and Behavior, 49,* 207–227.

Smith, M. (2017). Hyperactive around the world? The history of ADHD in global perspective. *Social History of Medicine, 30,* 767–787. https://doi.org/10.1093/shm/hkw127.

Wallis, C. (2010). *The impacts of media multitasking on children's learning and development*. New York, NY: The Joan Ganz Cooney Center at Sesame Workshop.

Whiting, B. B. (1976). The problem of the packaged variable. In K. F. Riegel & J. A. Meacham (Eds.), *The developing individual in a changing world* (Vol. 1, pp. 303–309). Chicago, IL: Aldine.

Chapter 4
Culture, Communication and Socio-cognitive Development: Understanding the Minds of Others

Mele Taumoepeau

Abstract This chapter reviews the literature on the role of children's social experience in promoting cognitive development. During early childhood, children develop a psychological understanding of others, in which they become increasingly skilled at recognising and identifying the internal states that motivate behaviour. This development does not take place in a vacuum, however, with robust evidence that the interactions children engage in with their caregivers—particularly discussion about their own and others' mental states—predict children's socio-cognitive development. Such discussions reflect the cultural milieu and thus vary significantly across cultural groups. The focus of this chapter is on cultural differences in the style and content of parent–child language interactions, and the significance of these differences for the development of a psychological understanding of others. In integrating previous findings across a range of cultural groups, I hope to advance our theoretical understanding of socio-cognitive development.

A child (aged 4) asks her mother, "What are you doing, Mummy?" "I'm thinking", responds the mother. "Your brain has gone to Christchurch for a holiday", replies the child. Her older sister (aged 6) retorts, "If her brain has gone to Christchurch for a holiday, how can she think?"

This conversation between the author's two daughters while she was deep in the throes of studying for her Ph.D. is particularly illuminating because it illustrates the particular focus of these two children on the workings of a mind—as a disembodied entity. How children arrive at this level of insight remains a source of interest to developmental psychologists. This interest is foundational to developmental psychology because reflecting on the mind, and ascribing mental states to others, has been viewed as essential for interpreting behaviour.

One of the foundational experimental tasks that tested this mentalistic stance was established by Wimmer and Perner (1983). In this task, a doll (Maxi) and his mother placed some chocolate in a cupboard (location 1). Maxi then leaves the room and the

M. Taumoepeau (✉)
Department of Psychology, University of Otago, Dunedin, New Zealand
e-mail: mele@psy.otago.ac.nz

© Springer Nature Switzerland AG 2019
T. Tulviste et al. (eds.), *Children's Social Worlds in Cultural Context*,
https://doi.org/10.1007/978-3-030-27033-9_4

chocolate is moved to a different cupboard (location 2). The child is then asked where Maxi will look or search for the chocolate on his return. The correct answer is that Maxi will search where the chocolate was originally placed, and that this response reflects the child's understanding that one can hold a false-belief about the state of affairs of the world. Although much of the focus has been on children's false-belief understanding, knowledge of false-belief is part of a staged developmental process towards mind understanding in which children first demonstrate an understanding of desire and emotion states, which forms the foundation of later knowledge about thoughts and knowledge as underpinning behavioural motivation. Empirical data support a specific developmental timetable of belief-desire reasoning, with tasks that measure the diversity of desires as a motivator for behaviour acquired earlier than tasks which measure children's understanding of the source of knowledge, diversity of belief, and false-belief. More specific scaling of these tasks in order of conceptual difficulty reflects qualitative changes (paradigm shifts) in children's representational systems, namely, with the trajectory beginning with an understanding of diversity of desires, followed by diversity of belief, the source of knowledge, false-belief, and hidden emotion (Wellman and Liu 2004). More recently, however, the universal trajectory of development has been challenged when examined in non-Western groups. I start by reviewing the growing body of studies that has identified differences in developmental milestones and trajectories of social understanding between nation groups. I then focus on the social and cultural framework that drives this development variation and the implications of these findings for a theory of social understanding.

Theory-of-Mind Understanding Across Cultures

The developmental timetable of belief-desire reasoning was, until recently, reinforced cross-culturally, with an article by Avis and Harris (1991) describing the belief-desire reasoning of 34 Baka hunter-gathering people of southeast Cameroon. In this study, children's performance on the change of location false-belief task (highly adapted to the cultural context) demonstrated the predicted pattern that older children (mean age of 5 years) would do better than younger children (mean age of 3.5 years) in predicting where the protagonist would look for his corn kernels on return, namely in the location that he had left them. In fact, the authors suggest that the age of acquisition might have been underestimated in some cases. The highly adapted nature of the task, making it a more naturalistic test—children could choose where the corn kernels could be transferred too, which ranged considerably—may have influenced how children responded, with the alternative location one that would be contextually completely unreasonable to search for (e.g., in the protagonist's clothes, the child's hand, in a basket, in a nearly pot). Nonetheless, this age-related change in performance was further analysed cross-culturally in a larger study conducted by Callaghan and colleagues (2005), again using similar "naturalistic" versions of the task. The general finding was that across 5 diverse nation groups—Canada, India, Peru, Samoa and Thailand—the developmental trajectory endorsed younger failure with the task and older success. The implication of these findings was that theory-of-mind ability is served by a universal theory of development.

Cross-Cultural Variation in Theory-of-Mind (ToM) Performance

Despite this cross-cultural concordance, other studies have documented across a variety of nation and cultural groups discrepancies in the ages at which children reliably pass different social cognition tasks (Callaghan et al. 2005; Hughes et al. 2014; Lecce and Hughes 2010; Liu et al. 2008; Mayer and Träuble 2013; Shahaeian et al. 2011; Wellman et al. 2001). In these studies, the findings have questioned the specific shift to above chance performance in older children relative to 3-year-old peers as well as the expected age at which children reliably pass false-belief tasks. For example, Filipino children demonstrate a "later than expected" age at which children pass false-belief tasks, with only 15% of 5-year-olds passing (De Gracia et al. 2016) and Pakistani 4-year-olds show similar at-chance performance compared to their 3-year-old counterparts (Nawaz et al. 2015). Other studies, particularly from the Pacific, indicate that even quite old children still find certain false-belief tasks difficult, such as 8-year-olds in Samoa (Mayer and Träuble 2013), and 38% of 12- to 14-year-old children of ni-Vanuatu children from Nguna island (Dixson et al. 2017).

Moreover, expected sequences that appear more culture-specific are emerging. The Western sequence described above, in which Diverse Belief is understood earlier than Knowledge Access, shows a reverse trend in children from China and Iran. A comprehensive study of ni-Vanuatu children's performance on social understanding tasks across a range of language groupings offers a sequence that follows neither the Western, nor Chinese/Iranian sequence, with understanding Diverse Desires not conforming to an early acquisition pattern. Within-culture analysis has revealed some important insights regarding within-culture sequence variation, such as in the analysis of Indonesian children which showed no difference in false-belief understanding between two socio-economically distinct Indonesian groups (middle-class versus trash-picker, *pemulung*), and an Australian middle-class group, whilst demonstrating delays in knowledge access and emotion concealment for the Indonesian trash-picker, *pemulung* group (Kuntoro et al. 2013).

Early work documenting differences in developmental trajectories has revealed important procedural differences that might explain differences in performance, but also get to the heart of what we mean when someone passes a false-belief task. In Vinden's (1999) study of children from three non-Western cultures (Mofu of Cameroon, Tolai and Tainae of Papua New Guinea), performance on a false-belief test was around 2 years later than Western children, particularly if they were asked where they "thought" the person would look. In contrast, when they were simply asked where the protagonist would look for the object, more children passed at an earlier age. Thus, all children seemed to respond differently when asked where someone would "look" for an object compared to where they "think" they will look. The latter question uses a mentalistic stance whereas the former avoids situating the children in that frame. An important distinction this study reveals is how the use of mental state terms can cause problems for interpretation. We will address this later when we consider the socialisation of mental state talk. Moreover, there appeared to be an effect of schooling on all children's performance, which suggests that the "decontextualisation" of mental states can develop through the process of schooling, and is consistent with Hughes and colleagues (2014) contention that schooling plays a significant role in orienting children towards a mentalistic stance.

Theories of Social Understanding

Cross-cultural work thus presents a challenge to current theories of how children develop an understanding of the minds of others. In particular, theories that favour a nativist viewpoint struggle to explain why such variation in developmental trajectories should occur. Such a viewpoint posits that children are endowed with core concepts, and that development reflects general conceptual changes which are driven by systematic maturational change and are largely independent of the socio-cultural milieu (Leslie et al. 2004; Leslie and Thaiss 1992). But how does one then explain increasing evidence of variation in social understanding across cultural groups? Researchers have looked to alternative theoretical perspectives that remove the onus of development on child-driven cognitive developments, and focus on how children arrive at shared meaning through their socio-cultural experience. Ochs and Schieffelin (1984) proposed that "Culture encompasses variation in knowledge between individuals but such variation, although crucial to what an individual may know and to the social dynamic between individuals, does not have its locus within the individual" (p. 284). Known as social-constructivist approaches, such perspectives place investigative value on how we talk to our children because it is a reflection of our social and cultural goals, and language as a cultural tool is central to this transmission (Lillard 1998). Thus, how we use language with our children is embedded in a system of meaning that is culturally based, and consequently interactions between children and caregivers are culturally organised. This theoretical emphasis reflects Vygotsky's and Mead's position that meaning is created through the cultural and social interactions in which we engage, and is endorsed in a range of theoretical positions (Mead 1934; Vygotsky 1978). Carpendale and Lewis (2015), in proposing a relational systems model, argued that the social interactions and scripts that infants and children are exposed to serve to co-create meaning and understanding. Budwig (2002) proposed that children do not passively adapt to adult systems of meaning, but are active participants in creating meaning. The common thread is that understanding the mind as a cognitive function is inseparable from the socio-cultural context in which it emerges, a position that is exemplified in Nelson's (2003) "community of minds" analogy—that children are enculturated to enter into a system of shared meaning.

Social Correlates of Theory-of-Mind

Variation between cultures refocuses our research attention on potential differences in cultural milieu that might determine why such differences exist. Importantly, however, if adequate explanations are not forthcoming, cross-cultural variation may also force us to challenge the adequacy of current explanatory frameworks. Empirically, there is evidence that children's socio-cultural experiences are highly varied, and that these experiences have a direct impact on children's socio-cognitive milestones. Recent meta-analyses of the social correlates of social understanding report robust, yet highly heterogeneous effects of social correlates of mental state understanding, including socio-economic status, sibling number, parenting style, parental discussions about mental states and mind-mindedness—the trait capacity to treat children as agents with minds (Devine and Hughes 2018; Tompkins et al. 2018). Given that the style and quality of language interactions strongly reflect cultural imperatives, our focus will be on the effects of talking about mind for social understanding.

Talking About the Child's and Others' Minds

There is now substantial research demonstrating these effects across a range of contexts, including naturalistic observations, wordless picture-book descriptions and reminiscing narratives. In Euro-American cultures, parents who make more references to children's mental states have children who pass social cognition tasks at younger ages. The change in parents' use of mental state language from the early toddlerhood period to early preschool years also has an effect on early evidence of social understanding. Reflecting a belief-desire reasoning theory, parents' references to desires are initially more important for developing very young children's mental state vocabulary and emotion understanding than talking about thoughts and beliefs (Taumoepeau and Ruffman 2006, 2016). Moreover, referring to the *child's* desires is especially important for scaffolding an understanding of mind. Satisfying one's desire is a feature of early social interactions and young children regularly act to make their desires known and to fulfil these desires. As articulated by several researchers, the initial use of mental state words may not refer to mental states themselves, and that over time children's functional use of desire terms begins to develop and change to reflect a better understanding of the connection of these terms to mental states (or functionally referring to an internal state; Budwig 1999; Nelson 1996). Varying the contexts under which "want" is referred to helps children increase their mental state vocabulary (Ruffman et al. 2018). Budwig (1999) presented a nuanced analysis of children's development of the pragmatic or functional use of desire terms, in which children initially use the term "want" to refer to an assertion of desire, which is to be acted upon immediately [I want nuts], as well as obtaining objects of desire. Later uses encompass permission requests, which Budwig (1999) suggested indicates an awareness of the socially mediated aspects of language function. In other words, in successfully realising desire, terms need to be used in a permission sense.

In older preschool children, variation in maternal use of mental state terms predicts children's subsequent passing of theory-of-mind tasks (Adrián et al. 2007; Ruffman et al. 2002; Taumoepeau and Ruffman 2008). This is especially true when mothers use cognitive terms in ways that clarify, explain or make explicit the mental state [She *thought* she would visit her mother; she *knows* it's in the box because she saw it] (Slaughter et al. 2007), and in cognitive utterances that are semantically connected to the interlocuter's previous turn [c: it's a doggy!; m: yes, it is a doggie, where do you *think* it's going] (Ensor and Hughes 2008). Some of the earlier work establishing these effects in cross-sectional designs was later extended using longitudinal designs that showed that mothers' talk was driving children's later understanding rather than the other way around (Ruffman et al. 2002).

Reminiscing and Mental State Understanding

Most of the analyses of mental state language interactions described above have elicited these conversations through naturalistic (mealtimes) or picture-book description tasks that refer to here-and-now contexts. Reminiscing conversations—referring to autobiographical events in the past—have provided an important perspective on the effects of parental discussions about mental states and children's later theory-of-mind. Reminiscing is qualitatively different from here-and-now contexts because it is necessarily a decontextualized event. Thus, analyses of reminiscing conversations are effectively analyses of the co-construction of a mental state. Reminiscing allows children to engage in self-reflection, through which they develop an understanding that there are contrasting perspectives on an event (Fivush et al. 2006; Reese and Cleveland 2006). Caregivers have at their disposal many stylistic ways in which the past shared mental state can be constructed, and analyses have revealed that highly elaborative references to the past event—open-ended questions and statements that provide new pieces of information—foster earlier children's autobiographical memory recall, as well as performance on theory-of-mind tasks (Doan et al. 2019; Doan and Wang 2010; Fivush et al. 2006; Reese and Cleveland 2006; Taumoepeau and Reese 2013; Welch-Ross 1997).

Cross-Cultural Differences in Parental Interaction Style

Given the significance of language socialisation for theory-of-mind development, it is striking that few studies exist outside of English speaking contexts. In this section, we first address non-Western studies of parental use of mental state talk, followed by studies of elaborative reminiscing style.

The theme that connects the few non-Western studies that have examined maternal use of mental state language is the scarcity of use relative to Western counterparts. In an analysis of Pakistani mother-child dyads engaged in their normal everyday home activities, Nawaz and Lewis (2018) demonstrated that over a 60-minute period at two time points (mean ages 48 months and 56 months), both maternal and child total references to mental states were 2 and 1% at each time point. This is low when compared to a British study, in which over a 30-min dinnertime session, total mental state talk for mothers was 24% and children 10% (Ensor and Hughes 2008). Other studies have also found similar differences in the propensity to use mental state language. Using a picture description task, in an analysis of caregiver-toddler inter-actions of New Zealand (NZ) families that self-identified as Pacific Island over five time points between 15 months and 39 months, Taumoepeau (2015) demonstrated that the strength of identification within this ethnic grouping determined the extent to which mothers talked about mental states with their children. Specifically, moth-ers who identified more strongly with their Pacific ethnicity were less likely to talk about mental states. In addition, the overall percentage of mental state language was low for this cohort, compared to a predominantly New Zealand European samples (using the same picture materials) who in place of which used up to six times more the amount of desire talk with the 15- to 26-month age grouping (Taumoepeau and Ruffman 2006). In contrast, emotion discussions, although initially low when the children were 15 months, showed greater acceleration over the preschool years for the Pacific group.

Similarly, in a study comparing 4.5-year-old Iranian and New Zealand children's socialisation experiences, both a picture description task and a "describe your child" narrative (Taumoepeau et al. 2019) showed that Iranian mothers (compared to the New Zealand mothers) were much more likely to talk about behavioural rules and explanations for behaviour rather than the internal states underlying behaviour. The Iranian mothers were also much less likely to talk about cognitive states. When asked to describe their child to the experimenter, overall the NZ European mothers talked more about their child, yet there was no difference in the proportion of mind-minded attributes (she's a *happy* child, she *wants* to be a doctor, she's *clever*) between the two groups. This difference in emphasis on the individual versus other is also evident in a study of Chinese immigrant and American parent-child dyads, in which Chinese immigrant parents talked more about behavioural aspects/actions in a story telling task, whereas the European Americans referred more to internal states (Doan et al. 2019).

Are Conversations About Mental States Important for Social Understanding Across Cultures?

Generally, studies to date demonstrate a ToM advantage conferred for children whose parents use more mental state talk or show more trait mind-mindedness, regardless of culture. In a recent study by Hughes and colleagues (2018), which compared Hong Kong and British parents' tendency to talk about their children in a mind-minded way, British parents were much more likely to refer to attributes of the child that reflect an internal state or motivation. Mind-minded talk was correlated with theory-of-mind, and differences in mind-mindedness predicted nation differences on the theory-of-mind tasks.

In the Iranian-New Zealand comparison described above, talking about behavioural rules and norms was not predictive of Iranian children's ToM; rather, the extent to which mothers referred to internal states accounted for the disparity in the two countries' performance on the social understanding tasks. In the Pacific study, caregiver mental state talk still appeared to predict children's scores on social understanding tasks, and in particular, the extent to which Pacific mothers increased their use of cognitive terms over time predicted children's later emotion situation understanding and knowledge ignorance. Similarly, in the Doan and colleagues study (2019) maternal references to mental states predicted children's concurrent emotion situation knowledge for the Euro-American children, and growth in knowledge for the Chinese immigrant children, whereas references to physical behaviours, including behaviours underlying mental states (e.g., crying) were negatively associated with emotion situation knowledge for both groups of children.

There are, however, exceptions. In the Pakistani study described above, only children's use of cognitive terms (and not mothers' references to mental states) was uniquely associated with children's performance on social understanding tasks, after controlling for age. Nawaz and Lewis (2017) suggested that "Children's construction of mental state terms serves as a route into grasping the mind in a culture with very little conversation about thoughts and feelings" (p. 7). Thus, what this reflects is a stronger emphasis on the child's rather than the mothers' use of mental state terms in the construction of mental state understanding.

Lu and colleagues (2008) also proposed a different socialisation pathway towards understanding others' minds in Chinese culture. In this cultural context, where children are exposed to and use very few mental state terms, talking about other people more generally, not specifically about their mental states, reflects a practice that is consistent with the cultural imperatives that privilege others' roles and the importance of social relatedness. In their analysis of children's autobiographical memories, children's references to others more generally, rather than specifically to their mental states, were associated with their performance on false-belief tasks. Indeed, if children were then trained to attend to the characters in a story, without specific references to their mental states, these children performed better on ToM tasks than if they were trained to attend to physical characteristics of the story.

Broadening Our Conceptualisation of Social Understanding

This brief review draws our attention to the pre-eminence of discussions about mental states, but also to potential differences in the socialisation mechanisms that drive children's understanding of mind. There is little dispute as to the importance of language socialisation; however, the extent to which it is the major contributor remains an area of dispute. On the one hand, the evidence suggests that for Western groups, at least, references to mental states and mental state terms are robustly predictive of children's later theory-of-mind. The explanations for why this is effective are multifaceted: children benefit from hearing terms that underlie a range of internal states (Ruffman et al. 2018); referring to mental states also helps draw children's attention to the workings of the mind, and children are thus able to refer to their own internal states and the states of others in learning these terms. These explanations, however, favour a locus of control that is central to the child and are largely consistent with current theory that favours the *intentional stance*, which posits that for children to understand social behaviour they must learn about others' minds or mental states and view behaviour as intentional, shaped by their knowledge, beliefs and desires. This account emphasises an individual orientation toward the mind and psychological explanations for behaviour. This theory neglects, however, the *normative stance*— consideration of children's deontic reasoning, in which they appeal to norms, obligations or permissions when explaining behaviour (Clement et al. 2011; Kalish and Cornelius 2007; Rakoczy and Schmidt 2013; Wellman and Brandone 2009; Wellman and Miller 2008). In this account, the emphasis is not on autonomous internal states of the individual, but rather on collective, normative explanations (Ames et al. 2001). In interpreting why a person is happy to keep a sick relative company for several hours, a child might reason that the person is *obliged* to, rather than the person especially *wanting* to. Evidence for this type of reasoning is found in Japanese children's justifications for behaviour in false-belief tasks. These explanations focus much more on children's actual behaviour as well as social norms and rules and are much less likely to refer to mental or internal state motivations (Naito and Koyama 2006). Similar evidence is found in other interdependent cultures, where the focus on causes of behaviour is more likely to rest on situational or contextual effects rather than the individual's disposition—which is more likely in an independent context.

Explanations for these differences in attributions appeal to different constructions of self (Miller 1986). For instance, in independent-oriented cultures, the concept of personhood is viewed as independent of the context and reflects the person's notion of individual autonomy over their actions. In interdependent cultures, self-concept comprises a greater sense of relatedness or connectedness to others in social relationships (Markus and Kitayama 1991). But it is not just the child's explanations or justifications for behaviour that reflect this stance. As described above, the types of interactions that certain cultural groups favour also reflect a stance that is focused much more on normative and rule-based explanations for behaviour. The value of the reminiscing literature is that it has sampled across a wide variety of cultural contexts ways in which mothers talk about the past. Children's understanding that their experiences reflect a unique perspective lead to the development of a subjective self (Fivush and Haden 2002; Fivush and Nelson 2004). In developing this subjective perspective, children learn that others also have a unique perspective on the event. The development of a subjective self, however, is also influenced by culture; notions of self will thus be socialised in ways that facilitate the creation of the culturally meaningful sense of self. Cross-cultural analysis of autobiographical memories and the extent to which mothers refer to internal states during these discussions reveal clear differences in style that are consistent with cultural definitions of self (Wang 2013).

But what does this mean for the notion of a theory-of-mind? Children the world over function effectively in their social worlds. Paradoxically, as Dunn (1988) pointed out, younger children's difficulty with false-belief tasks belies their competence in navigating their social world as young infants. The supposed delays in non-Western children's theory-of-mind performance can be viewed with the same paradoxical lens and begs the question of how our theories of social understanding can effectively accommodate these discrepancies. Added to this is the finding that although prosociality is robustly related to ToM, as reported in a comprehensive meta-analysis (Imuta et al. 2016), the overall effect accounts for only 3.6% of variance in prosociality. Alternative developmental pathways for the development of prosociality and sharing have been proposed to explain cross-cultural differences (Kärtner and Keller 2012; Paulus 2014). In these alternative accounts, scholars have suggested that children from interdependent or relational cultures are more likely to be driven by situational cues, such as interpersonal responsibility, rather than as an intentional autonomous agent which may be more salient in an independent-oriented culture. Similarly, social-normative models of prosociality emphasise the role of social scaffolding of a normative understanding of the rules surrounding social behaviour, and thus, attending to cultural effects on what is considered normative would seem important (Cheah and Rubin 2003; Paulus 2014).

Thinking about social understanding from an exclusively intentional viewpoint risks not capturing the full explanation for how children understand behaviour. As Naito and Koyama (2006) point out, standard false-belief tasks do not provide situational information, which in turn may disadvantage children from interdependent cultures who have been enculturated to focus more on situational cues. How this might look is still open to interpretation. However, evidence from some recent studies shows that when compared to standard false-belief tasks, younger children make accurate predictions about behaviour when given normative rules within a theory-of-mind paradigm (Bernard et al. 2016; Clement et al. 2011). In these studies, children complete deontic-theory-of-mind-tasks, which attempt to remove the necessity to reflect on mental states to correctly anticipate behaviour, by giving children rules that could be used to predict behaviour. To illustrate, in a standard change of location task, children are given rules that focus on what obligatorily happens to objects (e.g., "in this house, dolls are kept in the box"). Children are then asked to make a prediction about where the protagonist will look for an object (after the object has been moved to a different location). Three-year-old children, who would normally fail at standard false-belief tasks, do much better in these deontic-false-belief tasks. Moreover, when asked to provide reasons for a protagonist's searching patterns, children will also appeal to norms and rules. Our interest in these modifications to standard theory-of-mind tasks is that rules may serve as a useful guide for young children to interpret behaviour, and in particular for children from highly interdependent cultures, where in-group normative rules and obligations are especially salient. As they currently stand, the theory-of-mind suite of tasks are designed in such a way that they require a fundamental attribution error of trait/internal attributes.

Conclusion

This theoretical expansion of the construct of social understanding opens up possibilities for understanding how children from cultures which focus less on mental states effectively navigate their social worlds. For cultures where mental state terms and mentalising are highly infrequent and not part of typical child socialisation, children are likely inducted into a community of minds through different socialisation practices. A new programme of research could examine the frequency with which caregivers discuss rights, obligations and norms as explanations for behaviour, and the relation between these types of interactions, and deontic adaptions of ToM tasks.

References

Adrián, J., Clemente, R., & Villanueva, L. (2007). Mothers' use of cognitive state verbs in picturebook reading and the development of children's understanding of mind: A longitudinal study. *Child Development, 78,* 1052–1067.

Ames, D., Kowles, E., Morris, M., Kalish, C., Rosati, A., & Gopnik, A. (2001). The Social folk theorist: Insights from social and cultural psychology on the contents and contexts of folk theorizing. In B. Malle, L. Moses, & D. Baldwin (Eds.), *Intentions and intentionality: Foundations of social cognition* (pp. 307–330). Cambridge, MA: MIT Press.

Avis, J., & Harris, P. L. (1991). Belief-desire reasoning among Baka children: Evidence for a universal conception of mind. *Child Development, 62*(3), 460–467. https://doi.org/10.1111/j.1467-8624.1991.tb01544.x.

Bernard, S., Clement, F., & Kaufmann, L. (2016). Rules trump desires in preschoolers' predictions of group behavior. *Social Development, 25*(2), 453–467. https://doi.org/10.1111/sode.12150.

Budwig, N. (1999). The contribution of language to the study of mind: A tool for researchers and children. *Human Development, 42,* 362–368.

Budwig, N. (2002). A developmental-functionalist approach to mental state talk. In E. Amsel & J. Byrnes (Eds.), *Language, literacy and cognitive development* (pp. 59–93). New York, NY: Psychology Press.

Callaghan, T., Rochat, P., Lillard, A., Claux, M., Odden, H., Itakura, S. … Singh, S. (2005). Synchrony in the onset of mental-state reasoning: Evidence from five cultures. *Psychological Science, 16,* 378–384.

Carpendale, J., & Lewis, C. (2015). The development of social understanding. In L. Liben & U. Muller (Eds.), *Vol. 2: Cognitive processes* (7th ed., pp. 381–424). Hoboken, NJ: Wiley Blackwell.

Cheah, C. S. L., & Rubin, K. H. (2003). European American and Mainland Chinese mothers' socialization beliefs regarding preschoolers' social skills. *Parenting: Science and Practice, 3,* 1–21.

Clement, F., Bernard, S., & Kaufmann, L. (2011). Social cognition is not reducible to theory of mind: When children use deontic rules to predict the behaviour of others. *British Journal of Developmental Psychology, 29*(4), 910–928. https://doi.org/10.1111/j.2044-835X.2010.02019.x.

De Gracia, M., Peterson, C., & de Rosnay, M. (2016). A cultural conundrum: Delayed false-belief understanding in Filipino children. *Journal of Cross-Cultural Psychology, 47*(7), 929–940. https:// doi.org/10.1177/0022022116655790.

Devine, R., & Hughes, C. (2018). Family correlates of false belief understanding in early childhood: A meta-analysis. *Child Development, 89*(3), 971–987. https://doi.org/10.1111/cdev.12682.

Dixson, H., Komugabe-Dixson, A., Dixson, B., & Low, J. (2017). Scaling theory of mind in a small-scale society: A case study From Vanuatu. *Child Development, 89*, 2157–2175.

Doan, S., Lee, H., & Wang, Q. (2019). Maternal mental state language is associated with trajectories of Chinese immigrant children's emotion situation knowledge. *International Journal of Behavioral Development, 43*, 43–52. https://doi.org/10.1177/0165025418783271.

Doan, S., & Wang, Q. (2010). Maternal discussions of mental states and behaviors: Relations to emotion situation knowledge in European American and immigrant Chinese children. *Child Development, 81*, 1490–1503.

Dunn, J. (1988). *The beginnings of social understanding.* Cambridge: Harvard University Press.

Ensor, R., & Hughes, C. (2008). Content or connectedness? Mother-child talk and early social understanding. *Child Development, 79*, 201–216.

Fivush, R., & Haden, C. (2002). Parent-child reminiscing and the construction of a subjective self. In B. Homer & C. Tamis-LeMonda (Eds.), *The development of social cognition and communication* (pp. 315–336). Mahwah: NJ: Erlbaum.

Fivush, R., Haden, C., & Reese, E. (2006). Elaborating on elaborations: Role of maternal reminiscing style in cognitive and socioemotional sdevelopment. *Child Development, 77*(6), 1568–1588.

Fivush, R., & Nelson, K. (2004). Culture and language in the emergence of autobiographical memory. *Psychological Science, 15*(9), 573–577.

Hughes, C., Devine, R., Ensor, R., Koyasu, M., Mizokawa, A., & Lecce, S. (2014). Lost in translation? Comparing British, Japanese, and Italian children's theory-of-mind performance. *Child Development Research, 2014*, 1–10.

Hughes, C., Devine, R., & Wang, J. (2018). Does parental mind-mindedness account for cross-cultural differences in preschoolers' theory of mind. *Child Development, 89*, 1296–1310.

Imuta, K., Henry, J., Slaughter, V., Selcuk, B., & Ruffman, T. (2016). Theory of mind and prosocial behavior in childhood: A meta-analytic review. *Developmental Psychology, 52*, 1192–1205.

Kalish, C., & Cornelius, R. (2007). What is to be done? Children's ascriptions of conventional obligations. *Child Development, 78*(3), 859–878. https://doi.org/10.1111/j.1467-8624.2007.01037. x.

Kärtner, J., & Keller, H. (2012). Comment: Culture-specific developmental pathways to prosocial behavior: A comment on Bischof-Köhler's universalist perspective. *Emotion Review, 4*(1), 49–50. https://doi.org/10.1177/1754073911421383.

Kuntoro, I., Saraswati, L., Peterson, C., & Slaughter, V. (2013). Micro-cultural influences on theory of mind development: A comparative study of middle-class and pemulung children in Jakarta, Indonesia. *International Journal of Behavioral Development, 37*(3), 266–273. https://doi.org/10. 1177/0165025413478258.

Lecce, S., & Hughes, C. (2010). 'The Italian job?': Comparing theory of mind performance in British and Italian children. *British Journal of Developmental Psychology, 28*(4), 747–766. https://doi. org/10.1348/026151009x479006.

Leslie, A., Friedman, O., & German, T. (2004). Core mechanisms in 'theory of mind'. *Trends in Cognitive Sciences, 8*, 528–533.

Leslie, A., & Thaiss, L. (1992). Domain specificity in conceptual development: Neuropsychological evidence from autism. *Cognition, 43*, 225–251.

Lillard, A. (1998). Ethnopsychologies: Cultural variations in theories of mind. *Psychological Bulletin, 123*, 3–32.

Liu, D., Wellman, H. M., Tardif, T., & Sabbagh, M. A. (2008). Theory of mind development in false-belief understanding Chinese children: A meta-analysis of across cultures and languages. *Developmental Psychology, 44*(2), 523–531. https://doi.org/10.1037/0012-1649.44.2.523.

Lu, H., Su, Y., & Wang, Q. (2008). Talking about others facilitates theory of mind in Chinese preschoolers. *Developmental Psychology, 44*(6), 1726–1736.

Markus, H., & Kitayama, S. (1991). Culture and the self: Implications for cognition, emotion, and motivation. *Psychological Review, 98,* 224–253.

Mayer, A., & Träuble, B. (2013). Synchrony in the onset of mental state understanding across cultures? A study among children in Samoa. *International Journal of Behavioral Development, 37*(1), 21–28. https://doi.org/10.1177/0165025412454030.

Mead, G. H. (1934). *Mind, self and society.* Chicago, IL: University of Chicago Press.

Miller, J. (1986). Early cross-cultural commonalities in social explanation. *Developmental Psychology, 22*(4), 514–520. https://doi.org/10.1037/0012-1649.22.4.514.

Naito, M., & Koyama, K. (2006). The development of false-belief understanding in Japanese children: Delay and difference? *International Journal of Behavioral Development, 30,* 290–304.

Nawaz, S., Hanif, R., & Lewis, C. (2015). 'Theory of mind' development of Pakistani children: Do preschoolers acquire an understanding of desire, pretence and belief in a universal sequence? *European Journal of Developmental Psychology, 12*(2), 177–188. https://doi.org/10.1080/17405629.2014.973843.

Nawaz, S., & Lewis, C. (2018). Mother–child conversation and social understanding in Pakistan. *International Journal of Behavioral Development, 42*(5), 496–505. https://doi.org/10.1177/0165025417741365.

Nelson, K. (1996). *Language in cognitive development.* Cambridge: Cambridge University Press.

Nelson, K. (2003). Entering a community of minds: An experiential approach to 'Theory of Mind'. *Human Development, 46,* 24–46.

Ochs, E., & Schieffelin, B. (1984). Language acquisition and socialization: Three developmental stories and their implications. In R. Shweder & R. Levine (Eds.), *Culture theory: Essays on mind, self and emotion* (pp. 276–320). Cambridge: Cambridge University Press.

Paulus, M. (2014). The emergence of prosocial behavior: Why do infants and toddlers help, comfort, and share? *Child Development Perspectives, 8*(2), 77–81. https://doi.org/10.1111/cdep.12066.

Rakoczy, H., & Schmidt, M. F. H. (2013). The early ontogeny of social norms. *Child Development Perspectives, 7*(1), 17–21. https://doi.org/10.1111/cdep.12010.

Reese, E., & Cleveland, E. (2006). Mother-child reminiscing and children's understanding of mind. *Merrill-Palmer Quarterly, 52,* 17–43.

Ruffman, T., Puri, A., Galloway, O., Su, J., & Taumoepeau, M. (2018). Variety in parental use of "want" relates to subsequent growth in children's theory of mind. *Developmental Psychology, 54,* 677–688.

Ruffman, T., Slade, L., & Crowe, E. (2002). The relation between children's and mothers' mental state language and theory-of-mind understanding. *Child Development, 73,* 734–751.

Shahaeian, A., Peterson, C., Slaughter, V., & Wellman, H. (2011). Culture and the sequence of steps in theory of mind development. *Developmental Psychology, 47,* 1239–1247.

Slaughter, V., Peterson, C., & Mackintosh, E. (2007). Mind what mother says: Narrative input and theory of mind in typical children and those on the autism spectrum. *Child Development, 78*(3), 839–858. https://doi.org/10.1111/j.1467-8624.2007.01036.x.

Taumoepeau, M. (2015). From talk to thought: Strength of ethnic identity and caregiver mental state talk predict social understanding in preschoolers. *Journal of Cross-Cultural Psychology, 46*(9), 1169–1190. https://doi.org/10.1177/0022022115604393.

Taumoepeau, M., & Reese, E. (2013). Maternal reminiscing, elaborative talk, and children's theory of mind: An intervention study. *First Language, 33*(4), 388–410. https://doi.org/10.1177/0142723713493347.

Taumoepeau, M., & Ruffman, T. (2006). Mother and infant talk about mental states relates to desire language and emotion understanding. *Child Development, 77,* 465–481.

Taumoepeau, M., & Ruffman, T. (2008). Stepping stones to others' minds: Maternal talk relates to child mental state language and emotion understanding at 15, 24 and 33 months. *Child Development, 79,* 284–302.

Taumoepeau, M., & Ruffman, T. (2016). Self-awareness moderates the relation between maternal mental state language about desires and children's mental state vocabulary. *Journal of Experimental Child Psychology, 144*(Supplement C), 114–129. https://doi.org/10.1016/j.jecp.2015.11. 012.

Taumoepeau, M., Sadeghi, S., & Nobilo, A. (2019). Cross-cultural differences in children's theory of mind in Iran and New Zealand: The role of caregiver mental state talk. *Cognitive Development, 51*, 32–45.

Tompkins, V., Benigno, J., Lee, B., & Wright, B. (2018). The relation between parents' mental state talk and children's social understanding: A meta-analysis. *Social Development, 27*, 223–246.

Vinden, P. G. (1999). Children's understanding of mind and emotion: A multi-culture study. *Cognition and Emotion, 13*(1), 19–48. https://doi.org/10.1080/026999399379357.

Vygotsky, L. (1978). *Mind in society: The development of higher psychological processes.* Cambridge, MA: Harvard University Press.

Wang, Q. (2013). *The autobiographical self in time and culture.* New York, NY: Oxford University Press.

Welch-Ross, M. (1997). Mother-child participation in conversation about the past: Relationships to preschoolers' theory of mind. *Developmental Psychology, 33*(4), 618–629.

Wellman, H., & Brandone, A. (2009). Early intention understandings that are common to primates predict children's later theory of mind. *Current Opinion in Neurobiology, 19*, 57–62.

Wellman, H., Cross, D., & Watson, J. (2001). Meta-analysis of theory-of-mind development: The truth about false belief. *Child Development, 72*(3), 655–684.

Wellman, H., & Liu, D. (2004). Scaling of theory-of-mind tasks. *Child Development, 75*(2), 523–541. https://doi.org/10.1111/j.1467-8624.2004.00691.x.

Wellman, H., & Miller, J. (2008). Including deontic reasoning as fundamental to heory of mind. *Human Development, 51*(2), 105–135.

Wimmer, H., & Perner, J. (1983). Beliefs about beliefs: Representation and constraining function of wrong beliefs in young children's understanding of deception. *Cognition, 13*(1), 103–128.

Chapter 5
Emotional Development: Cultural Influences on Young Children's Emotional Competence

Nicole B. Capobianco, Caitlin D. Bush and Deborah L. Best

Abstract Children's emotional development follows a complex trajectory, characterized by the interaction of nature and nurture. Although emotional development occurs across the lifespan, basic emotions appear at birth, and secondary or self-conscious emotions appear soon afterward. Children's emotion socialization often begins with parents, but many others, including peers and teachers, serve as agents of socialization. The goal of emotion socialization is to develop emotional competence in children, setting them up for success within their cultural context. Interactions with parents, other family members, and peers teach children to recognize and understand their own and others' emotions. Children also quickly learn culturally acceptable ways to express and regulate their emotions. Parental ethnotheories reflect cultural beliefs about emotions and subsequently influence the ways parents respond to and reminisce about emotional behaviors and events with their children. Though gender and socioeconomic differences also affect the emotion socialization of children, culture has a pervasive influence on emotional competence. Simply put, the study of emotional development cannot be separated from culture.

During a brief break at an academic conference, a Cameroonian Nso mother who had been holding her 1-year-old handed the child over to a Western stranger so she could retrieve a cup of coffee. The child showed no fear which surprised the stranger. When asked about the child's lack of fear, the mother said, "If he had cried, I would not like it. I would blow in his face and say 'No.' He must learn to go to others. A calm baby is a good baby." In the Nso multigenerational households, having multiple caregivers permits mothers to carry out their daily chores, and parenting is regarded as a communal activity. Nso mothers train children to be emotionally inexpressive and to adjust easily to others, reflecting parents' socialization goals (Otto and Keller 2015).

N. B. Capobianco
University of Virginia, Charlottesville, VA, USA

C. D. Bush · D. L. Best (✉)
Wake Forest University, Winston-Salem, NC, USA
e-mail: best@wfu.edu

© Springer Nature Switzerland AG 2019
T. Tulviste et al. (eds.), *Children's Social Worlds in Cultural Context*,
https://doi.org/10.1007/978-3-030-27033-9_5

This example illustrates the ways in which cultural beliefs about appropriate displays of emotion influence the emotional development of children. Cultural norms and emotional scripts shape parental practices, as parents aim to prepare their children for life within a given society. Thus, children's emotional competence develops within a cultural context. It is the aim of this chapter to highlight the ways in which culture influences emotional development, emotion socialization, and the subsequent emotional competencies gained.

Early Emotional Development

Cultural beliefs about emotion influence the ways in which children learn to express emotions (Friedlmeier 2005). Indeed, linguistic distinctions also shape the ways in which people categorize and understand emotions (Matsumoto and Assar 1992; Thompson et al. 2011). Despite cultural variation in emotional development, there are some aspects of this developmental trajectory that transcend culture.

Beginning at birth, infants are able to express emotional arousal. Though they may be unable to self-regulate their emotional responses, infants can express emotions ranging from sadness and fear to delight and contentment (Lewis 2008). Basic emotions, such as interest and fear, emerge in typically developing infants regardless of culture (Lewis 2008). The universal appearance of these emotions may be due in part to the neurobiological underpinnings of emotional development.

Given the complexity of emotional responses and experiences, it is not surprising that many brain regions and systems are involved in the development of emotion. Emotion involves primitive brain regions, such as the limbic system, while also drawing on more sophisticated regions, like the prefrontal cortex (Davidson et al. 2007). Within the limbic system, the amygdala is typically labeled as the "emotion center" of the brain (Johnson 2011). However, the development of the prefrontal cortex and related attentional abilities are needed for more complex emotion understanding and skills, such as emotion regulation (Perry et al. 2016). Furthermore, emotional reactions and development are highly influenced by various hormones and neurotransmitters (Gunnar and Vazquez 2006). Thus, emotional development in infants is dependent on the rapid brain development that occurs during early childhood. For example, the maturation of parasympathetic regulation and the prefrontal cortex allows infants to better regulate emotional arousal (Gunnar and Davis 2003; Perry et al. 2016). Though external forces may influence brain develop in young children, the development of general brain structures and systems can be considered universal for all humans. Thus, neurobiological changes in the brain may explain why certain milestones along the emotional development trajectory are seen across cultures.

Primary, Basic Emotions

Within the first year of life, primary emotions emerge. These are fundamental emotions, such as, interest, joy, distress, and disgust. Primary emotions have been observed in infants worldwide via universal facial expressions (Lewis and Michalson 1983). Regardless of culture, people spontaneously make the same faces to show emotions like disgust, anger, and joy (Matsumoto 2001). Although the precise chronological emergence of primary emotions has not been mapped, babies typically exhibit all primary emotions by the time they reach 12 months of age (Lewis et al. 1989). Shortly after birth, interest, joy, distress, and disgust can be seen (Izard 2013). Anger has been observed in infants as young as 4 months of age, while surprise has been documented at 6 months (Lewis et al. 1989). However, in the appropriate laboratory circumstances, anger, surprise, fear, and sadness can be elicited in infants as young as 10 weeks (Lewis et al. 1990).

Secondary, Self-conscious Emotions

Between the end of the first year and middle of the second year of life, secondary or self-conscious emotions emerge (Lewis et al. 1989). These are emotions such as shame, guilt, pride, or embarrassment. Given the self-reflective nature of secondary emotions, they cannot be experienced until children are able to form cognitive representations of the self (Lewis 2008). During the first two years of life, children learn to differentiate themselves from others, exhibiting self-referential behaviors between 15 and 24 months of age (Lewis et al. 1989). For example, a child will learn to identify him or herself in a mirror. With this newfound skill comes the initial self-conscious emotions, which include embarrassment, empathy, and jealousy (Lewis et al. 1989). As children's cognitive capacities continue to increase, they begin to learn rules about appropriate behavior. With this knowledge, they are able to evaluate themselves, leading to the second class of self-conscious emotions, such as, guilt, shame, and pride (Lewis et al. 1989). Because humans have the unique ability to form cognitive representations of the self and engage in self-reflective processes, self-conscious emotions emerge in children worldwide (Lewis 2014). However, it is important to note that the evocation of specific self-conscious emotions is rooted in the morals, rules, and emotional scripts of a given culture. For example, with an emphasis on modesty and self-criticism, negative self-evaluations are more normative in Japan and Korea, whereas US culture emphasizes individual achievement, favoring positive evaluations of self (Furukawa et al. 2012). When describing their reactions to scenarios characterized by failures or transgressions, Japanese children scored the highest on shame, Korean children were highest on guilt, and US children demonstrated the highest level of pride. The development of self-conscious emotions nicely exemplifies the crossover between emotional and cognitive development. Not only are emotional and cognitive processes closely related in the brain, but it is also clear that certain cognitive abilities are necessary for emotional development (Blankson et al. 2013; Perry et al. 2016). During the preschool years, cognitive and emotional competencies are quickly improving, resulting in skills such as emotion regulation and emotion knowledge. Young children learn strategies for emotion regulation, such as shifting their attention in order to distract themselves from an emotionally arousing stimulus (Perry et al. 2016). Furthermore, preschool-aged children begin to understand the causes and consequences of emotions, as well as the role of emotions in social interactions. Although emotion development continues throughout middle childhood, adolescence, and even adulthood, the current chapter will focus on the early development of emotional competence in young children.

Emotional Competence

Emotional competence is an umbrella term used to encapsulate the ways in which individuals express, understand, identify, and regulate emotions (Min et al. 2018). During the preschool years, children become more adept at understanding and managing their own emotions, as well as those of others (Denham et al. 2003). At this age, children are cognitively able to understand and control their emotions, thus allowing for the development of emotional competence. In many cultures, emotional competence also becomes more socially important upon preschool entry. Denham and colleagues (2003) found that American preschoolers who exhibited more advanced emotional expressiveness, emotion regulation, and emotion knowledge were better liked by peers and were perceived as more socially competent by their teachers.

Although emotional competence is an interesting construct as a whole, it is important to understand each facet of emotional competence individually. Researchers find that the development of specific emotional competence components (e.g., emotional expressiveness, emotion regulation) differs based on cultural values and socially acceptable emotion display rules (Min et al. 2018).

Emotional Expressiveness

Children learn how to express emotions from a variety of influences, including their parents, teachers, and peers. However, a broader perspective reveals that cultural norms influence parenting styles as well as family and social interactions via emotion display rules (McDowell and Parke 2000). It is these rules that guide the intensity and frequency with which children express both positive and negative emotions. In white, middle-class American families, emotions are regarded as intrapersonal experiences and the expression of emotion is viewed as an expression of one's individuality (Lee et al. 2017). Thus, children learn that is acceptable to express both positive and negative emotions (Keller and Otto 2009). In Korea, however, emotions are used to maintain social harmony and the expression of individual needs may be viewed as selfish (Kim et al. 2008). Consequently, children in Korea learn to control negative emotions, resulting in less emotional expression (Lee et al. 2017). Although emotional expressiveness is considered a component of emotional competence regardless of culture, that which is considered an "acceptable" level of emotional expression is clearly culturally specific.

Emotion Knowledge

Another competent of emotional competence is emotion knowledge, which includes the ability to understand, recognize, and label one's own emotions as well as the emotions of others (Voltmer and von Salisch 2017). Children who possess emotion knowledge demonstrate their understanding of emotions through emotion-related conversations and behaviors. For example, they are able to identify emotions based on facial expressions, determine the internal and external causes of emotion, appropriately react to the emotions of others (e.g., display sympathy), and use emotion language (Denham et al. 2003; Voltmer and von Salisch 2017). Preschool is a time in which children rapidly gain emotion knowledge. With exposure to new situations and increased peer interactions, preschoolers learn to identify emotions and the situations that caused those emotions (Yang and Wang 2016). Emotion knowledge is an important part of emotional competence as it contributes to better emotion regulation and coping skills (Eisenberg et al. 2005; Yang and Wang 2016).

From a young age, children gain a great deal of emotion knowledge from their parents. In middle-class European American families, parents engage in emotion conversations with their children (Wang et al. 2006). In these cultures, parents often act as "emotion coaches," helping their children to understand their emotions (Denham et al. 1994). However, parents do not take on the emotion coach role in all cultures. Because Chinese parents view emotions as disruptive and potentially dangerous to social relationships, they teach their children to restrain their emotions (Wang et al. 2006). Wang and colleagues (Wang 2003; Wang et al. 2006) have shown that as early as age 3 years, European American children show greater emotion knowledge when compared to Chinese children living in both Beijing and the USA. This suggests that cultural differences in parenting and emotion socialization may lead to differences in emotion knowledge. Thus, it seems that the amount of emotion knowledge needed in order to be successful in a given society is dependent upon its specific cultural values and norms.

Culture does not only influence the amount of emotion knowledge one may gain, but also the content of that knowledge. This phenomenon is best exemplified by the *in-group advantage* in emotion knowledge. *In-group advantage* is the tendency to better recognize the emotions of others from the same cultural group when compared to the emotions of others from different cultural groups (Elfenbein and Ambady 2002). In a study examining in-group advantage, Chinese children and adults were presented with both Chinese and Caucasian faces (Hu et al. 2014). These Chinese participants looked more at the nose and mouth regions of Chinese faces and more at the eyes of the Caucasian faces. These differential face scanning patterns suggest that Chinese children have already learned to avoid direct eye contact with the more familiar Chinese faces, which is considered appropriate behavior in Chinese culture. However, they do not yet have a well-learned habit of avoiding direct eye contact for less experienced Caucasian faces. When looking at these different types of faces, Chinese children are getting differential emotion-related facial information.

In a study with both African American and European American children (ages 3–7), European American children more accurately recognized emotions in photographs of other European Americans when compared to photographs of African Americans (Tuminello and Davidson 2011). Although the communication of emotion may be universal, cultural groups may differ in their style of emotional expression. Children may learn the emotional styles they see when interacting with members of their cultural group such that familiarity leads to greater accuracy.

Emotion Regulation

Emotion regulation is another important aspect of emotional competence. Emotion regulation processes include behaviors, skills, and strategies that aim to control emotional experiences and expressions (Perry et al. 2016). Because emotion regulation draws on neurophysiological, cognitive, and behavioral processes, emotions can be modified both automatically and with conscious effort (Perry et al. 2016). The goal of emotion regulation is typically to adjust the intensity, duration, or tenor of an emotional experience or expression in order to meet a goal or follow an emotion script (Denham et al. 2003). Although children learn to regulate emotions at a young age (e.g., looking away from an emotionally arousing stimulus), culture greatly shapes the type and amount of emotion regulation children learn to perform.

Culture shapes parents' socialization goals regarding their children's emotion regulation, which, in turn, shapes children's behaviors. Although German Berlin mothers expect to see expressions of emotions at an earlier age than do Cameroonian Nso mothers, they evaluate the expression of these emotions differently (Keller and Otto 2009). Nso mothers believe that infants should learn to control their emotions, particularly negative emotions, during the first three years of life. German mothers disagreed with this goal and value children's autonomy and emotional expression. They try to find reasons for their children's emotional displays (e.g., "Are you hungry?"). As a consequence, Nso infants show an adaptive emotion regulation strategy characterized by calmness and inexpressiveness while German children are more emotionally expressive. Indeed, when Nso children encounter a stranger or are waiting during a delay-of-gratification task, they show little expression of negative affect, decreases in cortisol levels, and little motor activity (Lamm et al. 2018; Otto 2014). The importance of culturally defined emotion socialization goals can be seen with both positive and negative emotions. In European American culture, happiness is an essential goal and is viewed as an indicator of personal success (Ma et al. 2018). Thus, when European Americans experience positive emotions, they typically engage in emotion regulation that allows them to savor rather than dampen those positive feelings (Ma et al. 2018). However, in some East Asian cultures, positive emotions are viewed as fleeting and are thought to lead to negative consequences (e.g., envy, avoidance of reality; Ma et al. 2018). Not surprisingly, Ma and colleagues (2018) found that Japanese participants tried to savor positive emotions significantly less than did U.S. participants. In this case, cultural beliefs about emotions influenced the regulation of the intensity and duration of the positive feelings experienced. It is within the cultural context of these emotion beliefs and display rules that children learn to regulate their emotional experiences and expressions.

Emotion Socialization

Emotional competence is primarily gained through emotion socialization. Parents aim to provide their children with skills that will allow them to be successful in society. Thus, the goal of emotion socialization is to equip children with the level of emotional competence needed to thrive within a specific culture. Of course, there are a variety of emotion socialization forces, including siblings, relatives, peers, and teachers. However, parents begin the emotion socialization process from an early age. The goals of emotion socialization are quickly transformed into one's beliefs about parenting, or ethnotheories (Keller and Otto 2009; Super and Harkness 1986). These ethnotheories are reflected in parenting style, influencing the ways in which parents choose to communicate and interact with their children (Keller and Otto 2009). Ethnotheories and their subsequent parenting styles take shape even before a child is born, meaning that the emotion socialization process begins during early infancy and continues throughout childhood. Because beliefs about parenting and emotions vary widely from culture to culture, the factors that influence emotion socialization must be examined within a cultural context.

Agents of Emotion Socialization

Parents

For infants, the primary function of emotions is to regulate the actions of their care-givers (Holodynski and Friedlmeier 2012). Crying leads to the caregiver acting to sat-isfy the baby's needs, an interpersonal interaction that shapes the caregiver's behavior. But, caregivers also shape the baby's emotional behavior in ways that are consistent with parental ethnotheories regarding emotions. For example, Cameroonian Nso mothers do not consider an infant smile to be a means of social contact so they rarely engage in face-to-face interactions and mutual gaze with their infants. Thus, when Nso infants smile at their mothers, the mothers do not smile back contingently. By comparison, German mothers and infants often engage in face-to-face interactions, and mothers reinforce infants' smiles by smiling back. As a result, compared with Nso infants, German babies show increased smiling even in the first three months of life (Wörmann et al. 2014).

Social Referencing

During the second half of their first year, when in ambiguous situations, infants monitor the emotional cues and reactions of parents and others to decide how they should respond, a phenomenon called *social referencing* (Feinman 1992). If a stranger approaches, infants watch their mother's reaction as a cue for how they should react. They are especially attuned to the caregiver's negative reactions, as if these are warning signals (Carver and Vaccaro 2007). Thus, young children primarily learn about their emotions by observing and imitating the emotional expressiveness of their caregivers (Eisenberg et al. 1998).

As mothers and infants engage in face-to-face interaction, infants gaze at their mothers' emotional expressions and imitate the affective state their mothers demonstrate. Maternal displays of joy elicit infants' positive emotional displays while maternal displays of sadness elicit infants' negative emotional displays (Termine and Izard 1988). Accordingly, mothers who show more frequent happy displays have children who also display more frequent happy emotional expressions and less sad and angry emotional expressions (Denham 1989). When mothers show more frequent displays of anger, their children are more likely to express other negative emotions, such as sadness and fear, and are less likely to express happiness (Denham 1989).

It is evident that parents' emotional expressivity has a significant influence on children's early display of emotions, and consequently there is a long-term impact of parent expressivity on children's emotional competence. Children whose parents model expressive styles and emotional responsiveness have greater emotional competence and overall social competence (Denham et al. 1997). Parents who display a wide range of emotional expressions in front of their children, including tension and intense sadness, have children with greater emotional understanding (Denham and Grout 1992).

As children approach preschool age, parents may begin talking to their children about emotions. Parents may guide their children's emotional development by discussing feelings and actively coaching children on how to express their emotions. Parents who are more reflective about their own and their child's emotions are able to engage in sensitive interactions, contributing to young children's growing awareness and understanding of emotions (Brophy-Herb et al. 2009). Caregivers who express higher negativity are more likely to have children who develop internalized behavior problems (McCoy and Raver 2011). On the other hand, mothers who discuss desires and feelings with their children as early as 15 months of age have children who exhibit greater emotion understanding later in life (Taumoepeau and Ruffman 2006). Research such as this highlights the influence of the family emotional climate on the emotional development of preschool-aged children.

Joint Emotional Reminiscing

When parents discuss emotions with children they may reflect on and remember past emotional events, thus engaging in *joint emotional reminiscing* (Van Bergen and Salmon 2010). This form of reflective conversation provides parents with an opportunity to discuss feelings with their children and to guide their children's understanding and appropriate expression of emotions in different settings. While engaging in discussion about a past shared event, the focus is on the emotional aspect of that event, the affect experienced during the event, and how the event was personally meaningful. Emotional reminiscing reflects the parents' socialization goal of helping children better understand their own emotions and the emotions of others. Parents may reminisce with their children about a variety of emotional experiences, including both positive and negative emotions (Bush 2016).

Different cultural contexts place different value on the role of reminiscing and child development. Thus, parents may utilize unique styles of emotional reminiscing that are rooted in their culturally influenced parenting models. Wang and Fivush (2005) found that compared with Chinese mothers, European American mothers engaged in more interactive and elaborative emotional reminiscing (e.g., talking about the causes of emotional experiences) with their 3-year-old children. Chinese mothers focused on social interaction and being in harmony with others when reminiscing with their children about emotionally salient events. Children's reflections were consistent with parenting style differences. For example, European American children talked more about the causes of emotional experiences, while Chinese children talked about the social aspect of emotional experiences.

In another study, Fivush and Wang (2005) found cultural differences in the way parents and children discuss positive versus negative events of the past. Compared with European American mother-child dyads, Chinese mothers and children tend to use more negative emotion words when discussing the past. However, European American mothers and children were more likely to express disagreement about the emotional reaction experienced when discussing a past event. Both European American and Chinese mothers typically agreed with their children's emotional perspective when discussing a positive event but tended to negotiate the emotional perspective when discussing a negative event. Sadness was the most frequent negative emotion discussed by the European American dyads, but Chinese dyads discussed more anger than sadness. Sadness may be difficult to resolve other than to share it with others for emotional support, which is considered appropriate in U.S. culture but not in Chinese culture. Anger needs to be resolved to maintain social harmony which is central in Chinese culture.

Similarly, Chilean parents' emotional reminiscing also differs based on the valence of the emotional experience. When discussing negative experiences with their children, Chilean parents used richer emotional content (e.g., facial expressions, evaluation of causes) than when discussing positive experiences (Nolivos and Leyva 2013). In contrast, Italian dyads show a consistent decrease in elaborations and evaluations when discussing negative events in comparison with positive events (Coppola et al. 2014). Mothers may have been motivated to dampen their child's emotional reactivity during conversations about negatively valenced events which would be consistent with the collectivistic tendencies of the Italian culture that exist alongside their general individualistic orientation (Oyserman et al. 2002).

Display Rules

Along with cultural differences in reminiscing styles, there are cultural variations in parents' emotion socialization goals and children's internalization of culturally appropriate display rules. In Indian culture, interdependence and avoidance of social disruption are emphasized in emotion socialization. Indian mothers in India and immigrant Indian American mothers believe it is less acceptable for children to display anger and sadness than do European American mothers (McCord and Raval 2016; Raval and Martini 2009). Indeed, Indian and Indian American mothers who more strongly endorsed these beliefs had children who reported that they would conceal their anger and sadness from others.

Looking more closely at the role of socialization, an instructive study compared the emotional expressiveness of four groups of 3-year-olds: Chinese girls in Mainland China, Chinese girls reared in the USA by Chinese parents, Chinese adopted girls reared in the USA by European American parents, and European American girls (Camras et al. 2006). Compared with the European American girls, children of Chinese heritage had less intense displays of positive and negative emotion which were probably due to socialization factors.

Peers

When children have the opportunity to interact with same-age peers, peer groups can serve as another influential agent of emotion socialization. Of course, a child growing up on an isolated farm will have limited interactions with peers. Conversely, children in hunter-gatherer, pastoral, or agricultural subsistence societies may be surrounded by many peers from a young age, but these tend to be multiple-age peers rather than same-age groups (Rogoff 2003; Whiting and Edwards 1988). In many industrialized societies which tend to emphasize age-graded institutions (e.g., schools, organized sports or activities), children spend a great deal of time with same-age peers. Peer groups form spontaneously among children, usually sprouting from a common interest or shared activity (Chen et al. 2005). Although the impact of peer groups on emotion socialization may be strongest during middle childhood and adolescence, children begin influencing and reinforcing behaviors in one another at a young age.

For children in industrialized societies, preschool may be the first environment in which they are constantly surrounded by same-age peers. When children interact with peers, they learn new social and emotional skills as they constantly evaluate and react to each other's behavior (Chen et al. 2005). Children base these evaluations and reactions on the norms and emotional scripts they have come to learn (Chen et al. 2005). In this way, children reinforce the emotion socialization that has been taught to them by their parents. Denham and colleagues (2003) found that U.S. preschoolers who exhibited emotional competence by frequently expressing happy feelings, regulating their emotions, and excelling in tasks of emotion knowledge (e.g., identifying emotions), were liked more by their peers. This liking and acceptance by peers undoubtedly reinforces culturally valued emotional competence behaviors, thus contributing to emotion socialization.

In a longitudinal study of elementary school children in Indonesia, Eisenberg and colleagues (Eisenberg et al. 2001a, b; 2004) found that children who had well-regulated emotions, low negative emotionality, and exhibited prosocial behaviors, were positively evaluated by their peers. Conversely, children who were seen by their peers as prone to anger were evaluated negatively. Like the U.S. preschoolers, children in Indonesia seem to approve of children who follow the culturally acceptable emotional scripts and display rules that they have come to learn. Thus, peer approval serves to reinforce the emotion socialization processes that have already begun prior to school entry.

Teachers

Upon school entry, teachers become another source of emotion socialization, further contributing to the development of children's emotional competence. When teachers create an emotionally supportive classroom environment and have positive relationships with their students, children are able to improve their social skills and emotional competencies (Bassett et al. 2017; Curby et al. 2013). However, teachers also engage in discrete emotion socialization behaviors, similar to those of parents (Ahn and Stifter 2006). In other words, teachers may respond in supportive ways (e.g., accepting, comforting) when children's emotional expressions are deemed appropriate, while they may be unsupportive (e.g., ignoring, minimizing, punishing) when displays of emotion are considered inappropriate (Bassett et al. 2017). In this way, teachers reinforce culturally accepted emotional scripts and display rules. For example, qualitative observations in U.S. child care centers and preschools have shown that teachers reinforce behaviors related to positive emotions (e.g., smiling, laughing, affection-seeking), which are valued in U.S. culture (Ahn 2005; Denham et al. 2017).

Just as parents and peers socialize children in accordance with cultural beliefs about emotions, teachers' emotion socialization goals are also reflective of cultural norms. In an ambitious project, researchers observed preschool classrooms in China, Japan, and the USA (Tobin et al. 1991; Unnithan 1993). In China, teachers aimed to promote collectivism and selflessness in their students, while diminishing spoiled behaviors. The Chinese preschool classrooms were highly regimented, even requiring children to use the bathroom at a designated time. Children in the US preschools were often given choices about what they wanted to do next, perhaps laying the foundation for independent decision making and democracy. In Japan, teachers valued obedience and dependence in children, yet when a difficult child was seen to act out, the Japanese teachers explained that the child was cognitively unable to be obedient and sensitive to others. As a result, these teachers did not punish the child in the same way that an U.S. teacher might have done. Clearly, teachers respond to children's emotional behaviors in ways that promote cultural values and rules about emotion. Therefore, teachers act as agents of socialization in order to develop the emotional competencies children need within their cultural context.

Differences in Emotion Socialization

Gender Differences

Though culture has a pervasive influence on emotion socialization practices and goals, there are many other factors that produce differences in emotion socialization and the subsequent emotional competencies. For example, there are differing cultural expectations for male and female emotional expression. Gender-appropriate emotional expressiveness begins early; crying is viewed as acceptable for female toddlers but not for male toddlers by parents (Brophy-Herb et al. 2009). A recent meta-analysis of 166 studies across infancy through adolescence revealed that overall, girls expressed more positive emotions and more internalizing negative emotions (e.g., sadness, anxiety) than did boys. However, boys expressed more externalizing emotions (e.g., anger) when compared with girls (Chaplin and Aldao 2013). It is important to note that most of the studies in the meta-analysis utilized primarily of Caucasian samples. Interestingly, few gender differences in emotional expression were found in infancy, but those differences soon emerged during toddlerhood and the preschool years, suggesting the role of socialization.

Not only do emotion socialization expectations differ based on gender, but there is also a difference in emotion understanding between young girls and boys. At age 3, girls outperformed boys on an emotion understanding task (e.g., explaining how a story protagonist felt) and at age 6, girls outperformed boys on a conflicting emotions task (e.g., explaining why someone feels happy and also sad on the last day of school; Brown and Dunn 1996).

Just as parents talk to girls and boys about emotions differently, parents also engage in differential emotional reminiscing with their children based on the child's gender. Mothers and fathers both use more emotion words when reminiscing with their daughters than when reminiscing with their sons, and they also use a greater variety of emotion words with their daughters (Kuebli and Fivush 1992). Parents seem to reminisce differently about negative emotions with girls than with boys. For example, parents reminisce about sadness and disliking more with their daughters than with their sons (Adams et al. 1995; Kuebli and Fivush 1992). When reminiscing about sadness, mothers emphasize the causes of sadness in their conversations with daughters more than in those with sons (Fivush 1991). However, mothers have longer reminiscing conversations about anger with their sons than with their daughters because they view it as more acceptable for boys to express anger and retaliation (Fivush 1991).

Not only do parents reminisce about different emotions with their children based on the child's gender, but there is also evidence suggesting that parents' responses to these emotional discussions are significantly influenced by child gender. When reminiscing about sad events, mothers seemed more concerned with comforting their daughters during the discussion than they did comforting sons (Fivush 1991). In response to discussions of anger, mothers are more accepting of their sons' retaliation to anger-inducing events, while they encouraged their daughters to reestablish the damaged relationship.

Gender also interacts with culture when mothers and children are talking about past emotional events. Contrary to findings in the USA, when Peruvian mothers talk with their sons, they use more emotion references than when talking with their daughters (Melzi and Fernandez 2004). There were no gender differences in Peruvian mothers' use of negative emotion words, but mothers of boys used more positive emotion words than did mothers of girls. With more questions about positive events, mothers may be encouraging boys to be more assertive about their preferences. By not discussing negative events, mothers encourage boys not to display vulnerability, a culturally undesirable trait for boys.

Clearly, a child's gender influences the ways in which parents approach emotional discussions and respond to emotional expressiveness. However, it is important to note that gender differences in emotion socialization are couched within cultural beliefs about gender norms. Thus, parental emotion socialization practices are reflective of the gender-specific emotion display rules within a given culture.

Socioeconomic Status Differences

Socioeconomic status (SES) is an indicator of a family's wealth and well-being based on factors such as income and parental educational attainment (Diemer et al. 2013). A large body of research examining SES differences in the USA has highlighted differences in both parenting styles and emotion beliefs (Conger and Dogan 2007). Not surprisingly, these SES differences produce differences in the emotion social-ization of children. For example, low-income parents of preschoolers in the USA tend to misinterpret their children's emotional displays, perceiving them as attempts at manipulation rather than as legitimate expressions of feelings (Brophy-Herb et al. 2009). Thus, lower SES parents may not frequently encourage emotion expression in their children. Because lower SES families often live in high-risk environments, learning to be less emotionally expressive may be adaptive as it prevents one from attracting potentially harmful attention. Similarly, some authors have suggested that low-income children may avoid displays of sadness so as not to appear vulnerable to others, while expressions of anger may be perceived as "toughness" in some low-income neighborhoods (Garner and Spears 2000).

Of course, the USA is not the only country that sees SES differences in emotion socialization. A study conducted by Okur and Corapci (2016) examined the differences in parental emotion socialization and child emotion expression among middle-high and lower SES families in Turkey. The results revealed that Turkish children from middle-high SES families were more likely to express anger than were their lower SES peers. The researchers suggested that this difference in emotion expression was largely due to SES differences in ethnotheories. When compared to lower SES mothers, mothers from middle-high SES families are more likely to encourage autonomy, are more tolerant of both positive and negative emotional expression, and are less likely to minimize children's emotions. These emotion beliefs undoubtedly influence emotion socialization and may make children from middle-high SES families feel more comfortable expressing anger.

Conclusion

The emotional development trajectory is an excellent example of the complex interaction of nature and nurture. Of course, there are neurobiological underpinnings to emotional development which exist in nearly all humans worldwide. This neurobiological foundation coupled with the inherently social nature of human beings may explain why certain aspect of emotional development are universal. However, the development of emotional competence does not occur in a vacuum. Culture permeates every aspect of emotional development. Cultural beliefs about emotions shape parental ethnotheories which are translated into emotion socialization goals. Emotion socialization goals are then reflected in parenting styles. Some parents may choose to act as emotion coaches for their children or may reminisce about past emotional events, while others may teach their children to restrain their emotions. Though the emotion socialization goals may differ, the end result is the same: children gain a level of emotional competence that is suited for the cultural context in which they live.

As should be evident, research reviewed in this chapter has demonstrated that emotions are inextricably tied to culture. In fact, it has been suggested that emotions are at the heart of culture (Lutz 1983). Emotions are a medium by which cultural norms and ideals may be communicated. When parents teach children about emotions, they are also teaching them about culture. Indeed, emotions are a central component of socialization. Parents, and other individuals in a child's life, may not consciously think about the development of emotional competence. However, the growth of emotional competence skills is a central goal of socialization in all cultures. The pervasive influence of emotions is not surprising; human beings are social beings and emotions play a significant role in social interactions. Still, the importance of emotions is often underestimated. Emotions are not only a way in which culture is communicated to children, but also a ubiquitous goal of child development.

References

Adams, S., Kuebli, J., Boyle, P. A., & Fivush, R. (1995). Gender differences in parent-child conversations about past emotions: A longitudinal investigation. *Sex Roles, 33*(5–6), 309–323.

Ahn, H. J. (2005). Child care teachers' strategies in children's socialization of emotion. *Early Child Development and Care, 175*(1), 49–61. https://doi.org/10.1080/0300443042000230320.

Ahn, H. J., & Stifter, C. (2006). Child care teachers' response to children's emotional expression. *Early Education and Development, 17*(2), 253–270. https://doi.org/10.1207/s15566935eed1702_3.

Bassett, H. H., Denham, S. A., Fettig, N. B., Curby, T. W., Mohtasham, M., & Austin, N. (2017). Temperament in the classroom: Children low in surgency are more sensitive to teachers' reactions to emotions. *International Journal of Behavioral Development, 41*(1), 4–14. https://doi.org/10.1177/0165025416644077.

Blankson, A. N., O'Brien, M., Leerkes, E. M., Marcovitch, S., Calkins, S. D., & Weaver, J. M. (2013). Developmental dynamics of emotion and cognition processes in preschoolers. *Child Development, 84*(1), 346–360. https://doi.org/10.1111/j.1467-8624.2012.01841.x.

Brophy-Herb, H. E., Horodynski, M., Dupuis, S. B., Bockneck, E., Schiffman, R., Onaga, E., et al. (2009). Early emotional development in infants and toddlers: Perspectives of early Head Start staff and parents. *Infant Mental Health Journal, 30*, 203–222. https://doi.org/10.1002/imhj.20211.

Brown, J. R., & Dunn, J. (1996). Continuities in emotion understanding from 3 to 6 years. *Child Development, 67*(3), 789–802. https://doi.org/10.2307/1131861.

Bush, C. D. (2016). *The socialization of emotion through negative emotional reminiscing with children* (unpublished master's thesis). Wake Forest University, Winston-Salem, NC, USA.

Camras, L. A., Chen, Y., Bakeman, R., Norris, K., & Cain, T. R. (2006). Culture, ethnicity, and children's facial expressions: A study of European American, Mainland Chinese, Chinese American, and adopted Chinese girls. *Emotion, 6*, 103–114.

Carver, L. J., & Vaccaro, B. G. (2007). 12-month old infants allocate increased neural resources to stimuli associated with negative adult emotion. *Developmental Psychology, 43*, 54–69.

Chaplin, T. M., & Aldao, A. (2013). Gender differences in emotion epression in children: A meta-analytic review. *Psychological Review, 139*, 735–765.

Chen, X., Chang, L., He, Y., & Liu, H. (2005). The peer group as a context: Moderating effects on relations between maternal parenting and social and school adjustment in Chinese children. *Child Development, 76*(2), 417–434. https://doi.org/10.1111/j.1467-8624.2005.00854.x.

Conger, R. D., & Dogan, S. J. (2007). Social class and socialization in families. In J. E. Grusec & P. D. Hastings (Eds.), *Handbook of socialization: Theory and research* (pp. 433–460). New York: Guilford.

Coppola, G., Ponzetti, S., & Vaughn, B. E. (2014). Reminiscing style during conversations about emotion-laden events and effects of attachment security among Italian mother–child dyads. *Social Development, 23*(4), 702–718.

Curby, T. W., Brock, L. L., & Hamre, B. K. (2013). Teachers' emotional support consistency predicts children's achievement gains and social skills. *Early Education and Development, 24*(3), 292–309. https://doi.org/10.1080/10409289.2012.665760.

Davidson, R. J., Fox, A., & Kalin, N. H. (2007). Neural bases of emotion regulation in non-human primates and humans. In J. J. Gross (Ed.), *Handbook of emotion regulation* (pp. 47–68). New York, NY: Guilford.

Denham, S. A. (1989). Maternal affect and toddlers' social-emotional competence. *American Journal of Orthopsychiatry, 59*(3), 368–376.

Denham, S. A., & Grout, L. (1992). Mothers' emotional expressiveness and coping: Relations with preschoolers' social-emotional competence. *Genetic, Social, and General Psychology Monographs, 118*(1), 73–101.

Denham, S. A., Zoller, D., & Couchoud, E. A. (1994). Socialization of preschoolers' emotion understanding. *Developmental Psychology, 30*(6), 928–936. https://doi.org/10.1037/0012-1649.30.6.928.

Denham, S. A., Mitchell-Copeland, J., Strandberg, K., Auerbach, S., & Blair, K. (1997). Parental contributions to preschoolers' emotional competence: Direct and indirect effects. *Motivation and Emotion, 21*(1), 65–86.

Denham, S. A., Blair, K. A., DeMulder, E., Levitas, J., Sawyer, K., Auerbach-Major, S., et al. (2003). Preschool emotional competence: Pathway to social competence. *Child Development, 74*(1), 238–256. https://doi.org/10.1111/1467-8624.00533.

Denham, S. A., Bassett, H. H., & Miller, S. L. (2017). Early childhood teachers' socialization of emotion: Contextual and individual contributors. *Child & Youth Care Forum, 46*(6), 805–824. https://doi.org/10.1007/s10566-017-9409-y.

Diemer, M. A., Mistry, R. S., Wadsworth, M. E., López, I., & Reimers, F. (2013). Best practices in conceptualizing and measuring social class in psychological research. *Analyses of Social Issues and Public Policy, 13*, 77–113.

Eisenberg, N., Cumberland, A., & Spinrad, T. L. (1998). Parental socialization of emotion. *Psychological Inquiry, 9*, 241–273.

Eisenberg, N., Liew, J., & Pidada, S. U. (2001a). The relations of parental emotional expressivity with quality of Indonesian children's social functioning. *Emotion, 1*, 116–136.

Eisenberg, N., Pidada, S., & Liew, J. (2001b). The relations of regulation and negative emotionality to Indonesian children's social functioning. *Child Development, 72*, 1747–1763.

Eisenberg, N., Liew, J., & Pidada, S. U. (2004). The longitudinal relations of regulation and emotionality to quality of Indonesian children's socioemotional functioning. *Developmental Psychology, 40*, 805–812.

Eisenberg, N., Sadovsky, A., & Spinrad, T. L. (2005). Associations of emotion-related regulation with language skills, emotion knowledge, and academic outcomes. *New Directions for Child and Adolescent Development, 2005*(109), 109–118. https://doi.org/10.1002/cd.143.

Elfenbein, H. A., & Ambady, N. (2002). On the universality and cultural specificity of emotion regulation: A meta-analysis. *Psychological Bulletin, 128*, 203–235.

Feinman, S. (1992). Social referencing and conformity. In S. Feinman (Ed.), *Social referencing and the social construction of reality in infancy* (pp. 229–267). New York, NY: Plenum Press.

Fivush, R. (1991). Gender and emotion in mother-child conversations about the past. *Journal of Narrative & Life History, 1*(4), 325–341.

Fivush, R., & Wang, Q. (2005). Emotion talk in mother-child conversations of the shared past: The effects of culture, gender, and event valence. *Journal of Cognition and Development, 6*(4), 489–506.

Friedlmeier, W. (2005). Emotional development and culture: Reciprocal contributions of cross-cultural research and developmental psychology. In Friedlmeier, W., Chakkarath, P., & Schwarz, B. (Eds), *The importance of cross-cultural research for the social sciences* (pp. 125–152). Hove, England: Psychology Press/Erlbaum (UK) Taylor & Francis.

Furukawa, E., Tangney, J., & Higashibara, F. (2012). Cross-cultural continuities and discontinuities in shame, guilt, and pride: A study of children residing in Japan, Korea, and the USA. *Self and Identity, 11*, 90–113.

Garner, P. W., & Spears, F. M. (2000). Emotion regulation in low-income preschoolers. *Social Development, 9*(2), 246–264. https://doi.org/10.1111/1467-9507.00122.

Gunnar, M. R., & Davis, E. P. (2003). Stress and emotion in early childhood. In *Handbook of psychology* (pp. 113–134). American Cancer Society. https://doi.org/10.1002/0471264385.wei0605.

Gunnar, M. R., & Vazquez, D. (2006). Stress neurobiology and developmental psychopathology. In D. Cicchetti & D. Cohen (Eds.), *Developmental psychopathology, vol. 1: Developmental neuroscience* (2nd ed., pp. 522–577), New York, NY: Wiley.

Holodynski, M., & Friedlmeier, W. (2012). Affect and culture. In J. Valsiner (Ed.), *The Oxford handbook of culture and psychology* (pp. 957–986). Oxford: Oxford University Press.

Hu, C., Wang, Q., Fu, G., Quinn, P. C., & Lee, K. (2014). Both children and adults scan faces of own and other races differently. *Vision Research, 102*, 1–10.

Izard, C. E. (2013). *Human emotions*. Springer Science & Business Media.

Johnson, M. H. (2011). Developmental neuroscience, psychophysiology, and genetics. In M. H. Bornstein & M. E. Lamb (Eds.), *Developmental science: An advanced textbook* (pp. 201–239). New York, NY. Psychology Press.

Keller, H., & Otto, H. (2009). The cultural socialization of emotion regulation during infancy. *Journal of Cross-Cultural Psychology, 40*(6), 996–1011. https://doi.org/10.1177/0022022109348576.

Kim, H. S., Sherman, D. K., & Taylor, S. E. (2008). Culture and social support. *American Psychologist, 63*(6), 518–526. https://doi.org/10.1037/0003-066X.

Kuebli, J., & Fivush, R. (1992). Gender differences in parent-child conversations about past emotions. *Sex Roles, 27*(11–12), 683–698.

Lamm, B., Keller, H., Telser, J., Gudi, H., Yovsi, R. D., Freitag, C., et al. (2018). Waiting for the second treat: Developing culture-specific modes of self-regulation. *Child Development, 89,* e261–e277.

Lee, J. H., Eoh, Y., Jeong, A., & Park, S. H. (2017). Preschoolers' emotional understanding and psychosocial adjustment in Korea: The moderating effect of maternal attitude towards emotional expressiveness. *Journal of Child and Family Studies, 26*(7), 1854–1864. https://doi.org/10.1007/s10826-017-0703-y.

Lewis, M. (2008). The emergence of human emotions. In M. Lewis, J. M. Haviland-Jones, & L. Barrett (Eds.), *Handbook of emotions* (3rd ed.). New York, NY: Guilford Press.

Lewis, M. (2014). *The rise of consciousness and the development of emotional life.* New York, NY: Guilford.

Lewis, M., & Michalson, L. (1983). The socialization of emotion. In *Children's emotions and moods* (pp. 193–230). Boston, MA: Springer. https://doi.org/10.1007/978-1-4613-3620-4_7.

Lewis, M., Sullivan, M. W., Stanger, C., & Weiss, M. (1989). Self-development and self-conscious emotions. *Child Development, 60*(1), 146–156. https://doi.org/10.2307/1131080.

Lewis, M., Alessandri, S. M., & Sullivan, M. W. (1990). Violation of expectancy, loss of control, and anger expressions in young infants. *Developmental Psychology, 26*(5), 745–751. https://doi.org/10.1037/0012-1649.26.5.745.

Lutz, C. (1983). Parental goals, ethnopsychology, and the development of emotional meaning. *Ethos, 11,* 246–262.

Ma, X., Tamir, M., & Miyamoto, Y. (2018). A socio-cultural instrumental approach to emotion regulation: Culture and the regulation of positive emotions. *Emotion, 18*(1), 138–152. https://doi.org/10.1037/emo0000315.

Matsumoto, D. (2001). Culture and emotion. In D. Matsumoto (Ed.), *The handbook of culture and psychology* (pp. 171–194). New York, NY: Oxford University Press.

Matsumoto, D., & Assar, M. (1992). The effects of language on judgments of universal facial expressions of emotion. *Journal of Nonverbal Behavior, 16,* 85–99.

McCord, B. L., & Raval, V. V. (2016). Asian Indian immigrant and White American maternal emotion socialization and child socio-emotional functioning. *Journal of Child and Family Studies, 25,* 464–474.

McCoy, D., & Raver, C. (2011). Caregiver emotional expressiveness, child emotion regulation, and child behavior problems among head start families. *Social Development, 20,* 741–761. https://doi.org/10.1111/j.1467-9507.2011.00608.x.

McDowell, D. J., & Parke, R. D. (2000). Differential knowledge of display rules for positive and negative emotions: Influences from parents, influences on peers. *Social Development, 9,* 415–432.

Melzi, G., & Fernandez, D. (2004). Talking about past emotions: Conversations between Peruvian mothers and their preschool children. *Sex Roles, 50,* 641–657.

Min, M. C., Islam, M. N., Wang, L., & Takai, J. (2018). Cross-cultural comparison of university students' emotional competence in Asia. *Current Psychology: A Journal for Diverse Perspectives on Diverse Psychological Issues.* https://doi.org/10.1007/s12144-018-9918-3.

Nolivos, V., & Leyva, D. (2013). Fun and frustrations: Low-income Chilean parents reminiscing with their children about past emotional experiences. *Actualidades En Psicología, 27*(115), 31–48.

Okur, Z. E., & Corapci, F. (2016). Turkish children's expression of negative emotions: Intracultural variations related to socioeconomic status. *Infant and Child Development, 25*(5), 440–458. https://doi.org/10.1002/icd.1945.

Otto, H. (2014). Don't show your emotions! Emotion regulation and attachment in the Cameroonian Nso. In H. Otto & H. Keller (Eds.), *Different faces of attachment* (pp. 215–229). Cambridge, UK: Cambridge University Press.

Otto, H., & Keller, H. (2015). A good child is a calm child: Mothers' social status, maternal conceptions of proper demeanor, and stranger anxiety in one-year old Cameroonian Nso children. *Psihologijske Teme, 24,* 1–25.

Oyserman, D., Coon, H. M., & Kemmelmeier, M. (2002). Rethinking individualism and collectivism: Evaluation of theoretical assumptions and meta-analyses. *Psychological Bulletin, 128,* 3–72.

Perry, N. B., Swingler, M. M., Calkins, S. D., & Bell, M. A. (2016). Neurophysiological correlates of attention behavior in early infancy: Implications for emotion regulation during early childhood. *Journal of Experimental Child Psychology, 142,* 245–261. https://doi.org/10.1016/j.jecp.2015.08.007.

Raval, V. V., & Martini, T. S. (2009). Maternal socialization of children's anger, sadness, and physical pain in two communities in Gujarat, India. *International Journal of Behavioral Development, 33,* 215–229.

Rogoff, B. (2003). *The cultural nature of human development.* New York, NY: Oxford University Press.

Super, C. M., & Harkness, S. (1986). The Developmental Niche: A conceptualization at the interface of child and culture. *International Journal of Behavioral Development, 9*(4), 545–569. https://doi.org/10.1177/016502548600900409.

Taumoepeau, M., & Ruffman, T. (2006). Mother and infant talk about mental states relates to desire language and emotion understanding. *Child Development, 77,* 465–481. https://doi.org/10.1111/j.1467-8624.2006.00882.x.

Termine, N. T., & Izard, C. E. (1988). Infants' responses to their mothers' expressions of joy and sadness. *Developmental Psychology, 24*(2), 223–229.

Thompson, R. A., Winer, A. C., & Goodwin, R. (2011). The individual child: Temperament, emotion, self, and personality. In M. H. Bornstein & M. E. Lamb (Eds.), *Developmental science: An advanced textbook* (6th ed., pp. 427–468). New York, NY: Psychology Press.

Tobin, J. J., Wu, D. Y. H., & Davidson, D. H. (1991). *Preschool in three cultures: Japan, China, and the United States.* New Haven, CT: Yale University Press.

Tuminello, E. R., & Davidson, D. (2011). What the face and body reveal: In-group emotion effects and stereotyping of emotion in African American and European American children. *Journal of Experimental Child Psychology, 110,* 258–274.

Unnithan, N. P. (1993). Review of preschool in three cultures: Japan, China and the United States, by J. J. Tobin, D. Y. H. Wu, & D. H. Davidson, *Journal of Comparative Family Studies, 24*(1), 153–155.

Van Bergen, P., & Salmon, K. (2010). The association between parent-child reminiscing and children's emotion knowledge. *New Zealand Journal of Psychology, 39,* 51–56.

Voltmer, K., & von Salisch, M. (2017). Three meta-analyses of children's emotion knowledge and their school success. *Learning and Individual Differences, 59,* 107–118. https://doi.org/10.1016/j.lindif.2017.08.006.

Wang, Q. (2003). Emotion situation knowledge in American and Chinese preschool children and adults. *Cognition and Emotion, 17*(5), 725–746. https://doi.org/10.1080/02699930302285.

Wang, Q., & Fivush, R. (2005). Mother-Child conversations of emotionally salient events: Exploring the functions of emotional reminiscing in European-American and Chinese families. *Social Development, 14*(3), 473–495.

Wang, Q., Hutt, R., Kulkofsky, S., McDermott, M., & Wei, R. (2006). Emotion situation knowledge and autobiographical memory in Chinese, immigrant Chinese, and European American 3-year-olds. *Journal of Cognition and Development, 7*(1), 95–118. https://doi.org/10.1207/s15327647jcd0701_5.

Whiting, B. B., & Edwards, C. P. (1988). *Children of different worlds: The formation of social behavior*. Cambridge, MA, USA: Harvard University Press.

Wörmann, V., Holodynski, M., Kärtner, J., & Keller, H. (2014). The emergence of social smiling: The interplay of maternal and Infant imitation during the first three months in cross-cultural comparison. *Journal of Cross-Cultural Psychology, 45,* 339–361.

Yang, Y., & Wang, Q. (2016). The relation of emotion knowledge to coping in European American and Chinese immigrant children. *Journal of Child and Family Studies, 25*(2), 452–463. https://doi.org/10.1007/s10826-015-0224-5.

Chapter 6
Young Children's Gender Development

Deborah L. Best and Judith L. Gibbons

Abstract Gender is one of the most salient influences on children's social development. As infants, girls and boys are often difficult to distinguish, yet from birth onward gender matters and is defined within the child's cultural context. Differential gender socialization determines children's names, how they are dressed, the toys they are given, the playmates they interact with, as well as their chores, responsibilities, and education. Nevertheless, in many modern industrialized societies, gender differences have begun to blur with similarities in educational opportunities, occupations, and domestic activities. Cultural expectations about gender shape children's gender identities, roles, stereotypes, social interactions, and other aspects of gender. These facets of gender development are the focus of the present chapter.

A recent article in the U.S. monthly *Parents* magazine gave suggestions to expectant parents about how to host a "Gender-Reveal Party" (DeLoach 2018). The reader is told that because learning the sex of your baby is magical, you should share that moment with friends and family in a gender-reveal party. After the ultrasound at 18–20-week gestation when the sex of the baby can be determined, expectant parents are told to have the technician write the sex of the fetus on a piece of paper and place it in a sealed envelope. Then, they are to take the envelope to a bakery and order a cake or cupcakes with either pink or blue icing inside and neutral colors on the outside, and they are not to open the envelope. At the gender-reveal party, the parents and guests bite into the prognosticating dessert to discover the sex of the anticipated addition to the family. Rather than revealing the secret with a dessert, some parties have used pink or blue balloons released from a large box in the front yard or pink or blue baby clothes wrapped for the expectant parents to open. One party even had the family pet alligator chomping into a watermelon filled with blue Jell-O to reveal the baby's gender. Gender-reveal parties have begun showing up in Australia with

D. L. Best (✉)
Wake Forest University, Winston-Salem, NC, USA
e-mail: best@wfu.edu

J. L. Gibbons
Saint Louis University, St. Louis, MO, USA
e-mail: judith.gibbons@slu.edu

© Springer Nature Switzerland AG 2019
T. Tulviste et al. (eds.), *Children's Social Worlds in Cultural Context*,
https://doi.org/10.1007/978-3-030-27033-9_6

plumes of blue or pink smoke from car exhausts and appropriately colored cupcakes in the UK (Williams 2018).

It is understandable that some expectant parents would like to know the sex of the coming arrival in order to plan. However, before technology permitted anyone to know the sex of the baby prenatally, when expectant parents were asked whether they hoped for a girl or boy, the usual response was, "We don't care, as long as it's healthy." Throwing a party just to celebrate the baby's sex indicates that expectant parents do care, suggesting that biology is all one needs to know about the coming arrival (Gieseler 2017). When parents-to-be discover the biological sex, do they expect their daughter to wear hair bows and lacy dresses or their son to like trucks and toy guns? What if the new baby grows up not conforming to these traditional gender expectations? Gender is more than just the biological sex and is defined within the child's cultural social context. Before looking more closely at gender socialization and behaviors, the role of biology will be explored.

Biology and Gender

Although sex chromosomes and sex hormones play an important role in determining whether a newborn will be labeled a girl or boy, neither are necessary or sufficient to cause gendered behaviors. Genetic and environmental factors interact in a dynamic system leading to sexual dimorphism in which males and females have different anatomical, physiological, and behavioral characteristics in addition to differences in sexual organs. Sexual differentiation functions on a continuum rather than a dichotomy with sex differences waxing and waning across the course of development (Fausto-Sterling et al. 2011). Indeed, at birth males are heavier with more muscle development and have a higher activity level, basal metabolism, and pain threshold (Campbell and Eaton 1999; Eaton and Enns 1986). Sex differences in cortical brain structures vary with levels of circulating gonadal steroids that occur during the neonatal and adult periods, but not during childhood. These reflect the interplay of biology (e.g., sex-chromosomes, hormones) and experience (e.g., parental expectations, social interactions, cultural context; Rutter et al. 2003). Prenatal hormones contribute to sexually dimorphic behavior, as girls exposed to testosterone prenatally show increased preferences for boys as playmates, weapons and vehicles as toys, and engage in more rough-and-tumble play (Hines 2006, 2013). Studies of normal variations in prenatal testosterone are less consistent, with some studies relating testosterone levels to children's behavior and others not (Hines 2006). Sex differences in hormones, brain anatomy, weight, strength and activity levels influence the ways in which parents and others socialize children into their culturally defined gender world.

Socialization of Gender

Importance of Child Gender for Parents

Although the baby's sex may be important to parents in the United States, in some parts of the world, the baby's sex determines her future. During enforcement of the one-child policy in China, virtually all of the illegally abandoned babies were girls (see Julian et al., Chap. 16 in this volume). Girls were taken in by orphanages and/or relinquished for intercountry adoption, while their brothers were cherished and spoiled.

On the other hand, in some instances the baby's biological sex has been considered irrelevant or even secret. There is a movement in Sweden and the United States to raise children as "theybies," not revealing the child's sex in order to encourage gender-neutral treatment. Parents of "theybies" share hints on websites, such as raisingzoomer.com, on topics such as gender-creative hairstyles and dealing with formal documents. Currently there are at least 10 countries (Australia, Bangladesh, Canada, Denmark, Germany, India, Malta, Nepal, New Zealand, and Pakistan) that permit gender-neutral options on passports or national identity cards. Beginning in 2005, members of the Indian hijra community were permitted to put an "E" on their passport, for eunuch (Newman 2018).

Although we could not find any formal studies of the developmental course of children raised as gender neutrals, this area provides fertile ground for understanding gender development in young children. While parents sometimes choose to raise their children as gender neutrals, some children also choose to be gender non-conforming or transgender (Rahilly 2015). Parents of non-conforming children report that their children had expressed interests and preferences of the other gender at about the age of 2 years. At first, parents often restricted cross-gender dressing and toys (e.g., you can wear a dress at home, but not out in public), but some eventually adopted a non-binary approach (Rahilly 2015).

Parental Expectations and Behavior

Parent Expectation. The transition to parenthood shifts attitudes about gender toward more traditional thinking (Perales et al. 2018). Newborn babies are perceived in gender-stereotyped ways. In an early study, a baby labeled as a girl ("Baby X") was more often offered a doll than when the same baby was labeled as a boy (Seavey et al. 1975; Sidorowicz and Lunney 1980). Children (ages 5 through 15) characterized infants labeled as girls (independent of actual gender) as smaller, nicer, softer, and more beautiful than infants labeled as boys (Vogel et al. 1991). Both college students and mothers attributed masculinity and strength to babies labeled as males compared to those labeled as females (Burnham and Harris 1992). In yet another study, women referred to the baby's motor activity when labeled as a boy (Pomerleau et al. 1997).

Even before babies are born, when parents find out the baby's sex via ultrasound, they describe boys as "more coordinated" and girls as "finer and quieter" (Sweeney and Bradbard 1989). In sum, the "Baby X" studies show that babies may be ascribed different traits and treated differently depending on perceived gender.

Parental expectations can also be seen in other countries. Zincanteco newborns in Mexico traditionally were given gender appropriate objects: cooking utensils, weaving tools, and flowers for girls and a billhook, digging stick, palm leaf (to be woven as an adult) and chilies (to buy in adulthood) for boys (Greenfield et al. 1989). Culture certainly plays a role in these parental expectations and behaviors, and they demonstrate that parents assume their children's futures will reflect cultural experiences similar to their own.

Parent Behaviors. Despite these pervasive findings regarding gender differential expectations, the evidence that parents treat infant and toddler daughters and sons differently is more limited. A meta-analysis by Lytton and Romney (1991) revealed only small effects for encouragement of sex-typed activities. In Western countries other than the U.S., parents used more physical punishment with boys. Another meta-analysis revealed that parents used more controlling strategies with young sons (less than 2 years old) than with their female counterparts (Endendijk et al. 2016).

In a review of the literature, Leaper (2002) examined differential parental behaviors that had not been examined in previous research. Perhaps because infant boys were more irritable than girls, mothers responded more contingently to them, which supported the development of emotional self-regulation. Mothers talked more than fathers, especially to daughters, and they talked more about emotional experiences with daughters than with sons. Mothers discussed sadness more with daughters and anger with sons. Fathers' behaviors, especially with boys, indicate which behaviors are considered appropriate and which undesirable, and boys have less latitude in their behaviors (Langois and Downs 1980). Although there may be subtle differences in the way parents treat girls and boys, the same parental behaviors may affect boys and girls differently.

In contrast to the differences in how parents overtly treat boys and girls, parents also promote gender-stereotyped behavior in indirect ways, for example, by provision of gender-typed experiences and toys (Boe and Woods 2018). When looking at the contents of young children's rooms (1–6 years of age), Rheingold and Cook (1975) found that boys' rooms had animal motifs, more vehicles, and sports equipment. Girls' rooms had ruffles, dolls, and domestic toys. Children's home environments are highly gender-stereotyped (MacPhee and Prendergast 2019) and children's preferences for toys are strongly correlated with familiarity. In other words, children like the toys they are given; while boys' toys promote action and aggression, girls' toys promote nurturance and cooperation.

Parents also engage in more implicit gender socialization (Mesman and Groeneveld 2018). For example, in book reading, parents make more positive comments about drawings of people in gender-stereotypical behaviors than people in counter-stereotypical activities (Endendijk et al. 2014). Another indirect way to convey gender messages is through modeling; parents' division of household tasks sends messages to children about what men and women do (Bussey and Bandura

1999). In the classic Four Culture Study, Munroe and Munroe (1982) found that children develop an understanding of gender roles and concepts more slowly in more traditional cultures in which childcare is a maternal responsibility and they have little contact with male figures (Kenya, Nepal) compared with cultures with more contact and less distinctive gender roles (Belize, Samoa). Not surprisingly, overall, it seems that parents have little insight into how they contribute to the gender socialization of their children.

Task Assignment. In non-industrial societies, even very young children contribute to their households by performing chores delegated by adults or performed voluntarily. For example, among forager-horticulturalists of lowland Bolivia, children are assigned or voluntarily perform many tasks by the age of 4, including fetching water, washing plates, tending the fire, washing rice, as well as feeding, dressing, and bathing younger siblings, and tending the garden (Stieglitz et al. 2013). Although there is a great deal of overlap in household tasks, girls are more likely to be assigned domestic tasks such as cooking, tending fires, washing plates, and childcare, whereas boys are more likely to be delegated harvesting tasks. In an early survey of the anthropological record, Barry et al. (1957) concluded that boys, more than girls, were socialized for self-reliance and achievement, whereas socialization pressure for girls was for nurturance, responsibility, and obedience. A recent review of hunter-gatherer societies by Lew-Levy et al. (2017) revealed no gender differentiated pressure or training for young children. In sum, pre-industrial cultures may vary widely in terms of the salience of gender socialization.

Peer Influences

Throughout childhood, and certainly in adolescence, peers play an increasingly important role in the socialization of gender. Maccoby (1998) speculates that peers are perhaps more important than parents in the socialization of gender roles. She noted the almost universal tendency for children to prefer same-sex peers, which was found as early as 2 years of age in the classic Six Culture Study (India, Kenya, Mexico, Okinawa, Philippines, United States; Edwards 1992; Edwards and Whiting 1993). In some cultures, girls and boys are mostly separated by the beginning of toddlerhood, and separation becomes more pronounced in free-play situations as children grow older (Fouts et al. 2013; Whiting and Edwards 1988).

Most studies of gender segregation have focused on children's play groups in Western countries (Pelligrini 2009). In free play situations, children seek out same-sex playmates and avoid children of the other sex; these tendencies increase across the preschool years. In these segregated play groups, boys play rough, strive for dominance, take risks, and grandstand, and girls self-disclose, try to maintain positive relationships, and avoid conflict (Maccoby 1998). Boys' groups are more cohesive, exclusionary, and separate from adult supervision. Gender segregation goes beyond behavioral compatibility with children selecting playmates because they share similar interests in gender-typed activities (Martin et al. 2013). Once these interactional ties form, children reinforce each other for engaging in these gendered activities, which amplifies the children's tendency to segregate by gender.

Gender segregation is also seen among non-Western children. (See also Tõugu, Chap. 2 in this volume.) In a study with 1- to 4-year-old Bofi farmer and Bofi forager children in Central Africa, similar sex segregation by age 3 was found (Fouts et al. 2013). However, *how* gender segregation occurred differed from that seen in Western countries. Gender segregation was more prominent among Bofi farmer children than among Bofi forager children, but for both groups 3- and 4-year-old boys showed significant gender segregation and girls did not. In the Bofi farmer community, there is a clear division of labor with women responsible for farming and household tasks, and men for hunting and political activities. Girls help their mothers with daily tasks, and boys roam freely. Those who do not adhere to prescribed gender roles are ridiculed. Even though Bofi foragers have distinct gender roles, they are more fluid than seen in the farmer community. Perhaps the flexibility of forager gender roles shapes these children to be less attuned than the farmer children to gender role differences at an early age.

Children's Self-socialization

Cognitive developmental theories emphasize children's active participation in their own gender socialization (e.g., Martin et al. 2002; Tobin et al. 2010). In one study of ethnically diverse 2-year-olds in the United States, a toddler's gender-typed style of dressing was unrelated to his/her mother's gender role attitudes, but was related to the toddler's own gender labeling (Halim et al. 2018). In another study, accounts by parents confirmed that the majority of 3- and 4-year olds pass through a period of gender appearance rigidity (Halim et al. 2014). Although there is widespread cross-cultural evidence for the sequence of gender developmental milestones: gender identity, gender stability, and gender constancy (e.g., De Lisi and Gallagher 1991; Gibbons 2000; Munroe et al. 1984), the consequences of achieving gender constancy may or may not include increased sex-typing (e.g., Arthur et al. 2009). The concept of gender constancy, that gender is permanent and irreversible, is related to a similar concept of gender essentialism. Meyer and Gelman (2016) found that belief in gender essentialism was associated with increased sex-typed preferences among children. At an early age, as young as two, some children may express the belief that they are the opposite gender from their biological sex (Fast and Olson 2018). Their sex-typed beliefs and behaviors did not differ from siblings or controls, matched for expressed gender. They were, however, less likely than others to believe that gender is stable (Fast and Olson 2018). Although not common, transgender in young children supports the notion that children are actively involved in their own gender socialization. The children express their gender identity early (about age 2) and they proceed to become sex-typed according to their own expressed gender.

Children's Gendered Behaviors and Beliefs

Gender Schemes and Preferences

Within children's cultural contexts, they are exposed to adults and peers of both sexes and they build gender categories, incorporating sex-differentiated attributes into these gender schemes (Leinbach and Fagot 1993). Gender schemes serve as organizing principles, helping them learn what behaviors are appropriate for each sex, guiding their behaviors, and helping them predict the behavior of others.

During the first year of life, Japanese children reliably discriminate between male and female faces (8 months of age; Yamaguchi 2000) as do children in the USA (9–12 months; Leinbach and Fagot 1993). By 19 months of age, children stereotype objects as feminine or masculine (Zosuls et al. 2009), and by 3–4 years of age, they readily label toys, activities, and occupations (Guttentag and Longfellow 1977). Across the toddler and preschool years, children show a growing preference for gender stereotypic toys (e.g., dolls for girls, construction vehicles and weapons for boys) in Italy (DeCaroli and Sagone 2007), Senegal (Bloch and Adler 1994), the USA (Weisgram et al. 2014), and the UK (Todd et al. 2017). Playing with different kinds of toys helps children learn various skills and how they should or should not behave, helping to solidify gender stereotypes and later social roles.

Along with gender-differentiated toys, children in Western industrialized cultures (USA, Picariello et al. 1990; UK, Wong and Hines 2015) show a gender-typed color preference: pink for girls and blue for boys. A recent study in Hong Kong, a culture that has had a great deal of Western contact, found the same strong gender-color preference among Chinese children (Yeung and Wong, 2018). Indeed, when yellow and green, gender-neutral colors, were arbitrarily labeled as "for girls" or "for boys," the Chinese children showed a preference for their own gender colors. Although non-Western children's color preferences have not been explored, a study with Namibian Himba adults found their color preferences to be quite different from those of British adults (Taylor et al. 2013), suggesting Himba children also may show similar non-Western preferences if they were questioned. It appears that cultural gender messages regarding toys, activities, and colors are very clear for young children.

Gendered Activities and Tasks

Tasks that children are assigned also help shape their later gender role behaviors. Although preschool children, particularly in Western countries, do few if any household tasks, their play often emulates what adults do (e.g., playing house, school). Rogoff (1981) found that two-thirds of Guatemalan Mayan children's non-game play was imitation of adult roles, and as early as age 5 they were eager to contribute to household economic activities. In the Six Culture Study, when both girls and boys cared for younger siblings and did household chores, few gender differences in their behaviors were found (Kenya, Philippines, USA). Larger gender differences were found where girls were more engaged in these activities than boys (India, Mexico, Okinawa; Whiting and Edwards, 1973). In the USA, girls do more chores than boys, often kitchen-related tasks and babysitting, and boys take out the trash or have no chores, and none babysat (Etaugh and Liss 1992; Giles et al. 2014). Such variations in activities certainly influence gender differences in children's behaviors. Indeed, boys were pressured to conform to their roles more than girls who have greater role variability (Welch et al. 1981).

Gender Behavior Differences

Nurturance, aggression, and proximity to adults are three behaviors that have clearly shown gender differences in studies across the years. The Six Culture Study (Edwards and Whiting 1980) found that girls who spent more time with infants demonstrated more nurturant behavior than did boys who did not interact much with infants or younger children. This finding is consistent with an older study (Barry et al. 1957) that found that across 110 cultures, girls were socialized to be more nurturant, obedient, and responsible than boys. Indeed, nurturance is consistent with the expectation that as girls grow up they will be more involved with childcare.

In a similar fashion, the Four Culture Study found consistent gender differences in aggression (Munroe et al. 2000). Boys were more competitive, dominance seeking, and were involved in more rough-and-tumble play than girls. In a recent meta-analysis of 3- to 14-year-olds across 12 countries, boys displayed more direct aggression (i.e., physical aggression) than girls but there were no gender differences in indirect or social aggression (i.e., rejection, exclusion; Card et al. 2008). It is clear that situational factors such as family violence, early parenting that reinforces aggression in very young boys, and cultural factors such as gender stereotypes, interact to place some boys at risk for greater physical aggression (Dayton and Malone 2017).

Another interesting observation from the Four Culture Study was that boys were found further from home than girls which provided them with an important source of environmental experience for learning spatial skills (Munroe et al. 1985). A study with a large, nationally representative sample of 2- to 7-year-olds in the USA confirms the importance of boys' spatial experience. The study found that boys played more with spatial toys (e.g., puzzles, blocks, board games) than girls and when controlling for general cognitive abilities, boys outperformed girls on spatial tasks (Jirout and Newcombe 2015). It appears that boys' spatial advantage is related to their greater experience in spatial activities.

Additional widespread gender differences among preschool age children have been described in other chapters of this book. Across cultures there is evidence for girls' greater participation in helping and sharing. (See Poelker and Gibbons, Chap. 7 in this volume.) Moreover, Chap. 5 (Capobianco et al. in this volume) provides evidence of girls' greater expressiveness of positive emotions, sadness, and anxiety, and boys' greater expression of anger. In addition, girls out-performed boys in emotional understanding.

Gender Stereotypes

Girls' and boys' different experiences and role models support their learning of culturally defined gender stereotypes about men and women, boys and girls. Williams and Best (1990) administered the Sex Stereotype Measure II (SSM II) to children in 25 countries to assess their knowledge of adult-defined gender trait stereotypes. They found that stereotypic responses rose from around 60% at age 5 to 70% at age 8. Men were described as strong, aggressive, cruel, coarse, and adventurous at both ages, and women were consistently associated with weak, appreciative, softhearted, gentle, and meek. Boys and girls learned these stereotypes at the same rate, but there was a tendency for the male stereotype traits to be learned earlier than the female traits. Scores were particularly high in Pakistan and relatively high in New Zealand and England. Scores were low in Brazil, Taiwan, Germany, and France. Gender stereotypes have been found to be more differentiated in the early years, but they become more flexible as children recognize that gender roles are not always rigid (e.g., girls can play with trucks too; Banse et al. 2010).

Gender Non-conforming Children

In recent years, there has been a substantial shift in how children who do not conform to traditional gender norms are regarded by their families, peers, and professionals. These children, sometimes described as gender independent, may push the boundaries of usual gendered behaviors, reject the usual gender labels, or identify with a different gender than expected (Pyne 2014). Like their older counterparts, even very young gender non-conforming children may face backlash for violating gender stereotypes (Sullivan et al. 2018).

Conclusions

Although the specific demands vary, all cultures use gender as a salient category for structuring children's environments, prescribing and proscribing behaviors, and preparing young children for their future roles as adults. The cultural demands interact with children's biological predispositions, the specific ideologies of the parents and community, and the environmental niche of the child. Depending on the cultural setting and the intersection of identities, gender norms often differ and lead to different behaviors and expectations for girls and boys. For example, a girl from a hunter-gatherer society has expectations about her gender roles that differ not only from her male counterparts, but also from a girl living in a contemporary industrialized Western society. Moreover, many scholars (e.g., Hyde et al. 2019) have pointed out that the gender binary, the idea that all human beings can be clearly classified as male or female, does not fit evidence from neurobiology, psychological research with transgender persons, or cross-cultural psychology. Future research needs to admit the complexity of sex and gender in order to tease out the meaning of gender in different cultural contexts. Imagine for a moment a gender reveal party in which the icing inside the cupcake is neither pink, nor blue, but purple, or even green.

References

Arthur, A. E., Bigler, R. S., & Ruble, D. N. (2009). An experimental test of the effects of gender constancy on sex typing. *Journal of Experimental Child Psychology, 104*(4), 427–446.

Banse, R., Gawronski, B., Rebetez, C., Gutt, H., & Morton, J. B. (2010). The development of spontaneous gender stereotyping in childhood: Relations to stereotype knowledge and stereotype flexibility. *Psychological Science, 13,* 298–306.

Barry, H., III, Bacon, M. K., & Child, I. L. (1957). A cross-cultural survey of some sex differences in socialization. *Journal of Abnormal and Social Psychology, 55,* 327–332.

Bloch, M. N., & Adler, S. M. (1994). African children's play and the emergence of the sexual division of labor. In J. L. Roopnarine, J. E. Johnson, & F. H. Hooper (Eds.), *Children's play in diverse cultures* (pp. 148–178). Albany, NY: State University of New York Press.

Boe, J. L., & Woods, R. J. (2018). Parents' influence on infants' gender-typed toy preferences. *Sex Roles, 79,* 358–373. https://doi.org/10.1007/s11199-017-0858-4.

Burnham, D. K., & Harris, M. B. (1992). Effects of real gender and labeled gender on adults' perceptions of infants. *The Journal of Genetic Psychology, 153*(2), 165–183. https://doi.org/10.1080/00221325.1992.10753711.

Bussey, K., & Bandura, A. (1999). Social–cognitive theory of gender development and differentiation. *Psychological Review, 106,* 676–713. https://doi.org/10.1037/0033-295X.106.4.676.

Campbell, D. T., & Eaton, W. O. (1999). Sex differences in the activity level of infants. *Infant and Child Development, 8,* 1–17. https://doi.org/10.1002/(SICI)1522-7219(199903)8:1%3c1:AID-ICD186%3e3.0.CO;2-O.

Card, N. A., Stucky, B. D., Sawalani, G. M., & Little, T. D. (2008). Direct and indirect aggression during childhood and adolescence: A meta-analytic review of gender differences, intercorrelations, and relations to maladjustment. *Child Development, 79,* 1185–1229. https://doi.org/10.1111/j.1467-8624.2008.01184.x.

Dayton, C. J., & Malone, J. C. (2017). Development and socialization of physical aggression in very young boys. *Infant Mental Health Journal, 38*(1), 150–165. https://doi.org/10.1002/imhj.2162.

De Caroli, M. E., & Sagone, E. (2007). Toys, sociocognitive traits, and occupations: Italian children's endorsement of gender stereotypes. *Psychological Reports, 100,* 1298–1311.

De Lisi, R., & Gallagher, A. M. (1991). Understanding of gender stability and constancy in Argentinean children. *Merrill-Palmer Quarterly, 37*(3), 483–502.

DeLoach. C. (2018). How to host a gender reveal party. *Parents.* Retrieved from https://www.parents.com/pregnancy/my-baby/gender-prediction/how-to-host-a-gender-reveal-party/.

Eaton, W. O., & Enns, L. R. (1986). Sex differences in human motor activity level. *Psychological Bulletin, 100,* 19–28. https://doi.org/10.1037/0033-2909.100.1.19.

Edwards, C. P. (1992). Cross-cultural perspectives on family-peer relations. In R. D. Parke & G. W. Ladd (Eds.), *Family-peer relationships: Modes of linkages* (pp. 285–315). Mahwah, NJ: Erlbaum.

Edwards, C. P., & Whiting, B. B. (1980). Differential socialization of girls and boys in light of cross-cultural research. *New Directions for Child Development, 8,* 45–57.

Edwards, C. P., & Whiting, B. B. (1993). "Mother, older sibling, and me": The overlapping roles of caretakers and companions in the social world of 2–3 year olds in Ngeca, Kenya. In K. MacDonald (Ed.), *Parent-child play: Descriptions and implications* (pp. 305–329). Albany, NY: State University of New York Press.

Endendijk, J. J., Groeneveld, M. G., Bakermans-Kranenburg, M. J., & Mesman, J. (2016). Gender-differentiated parenting revisited: Meta-analysis reveals very few differences in parental control of boys and girls. *PLoS ONE, 11*(7), e0159193. https://doi.org/10.1371/journal.pone.0159193.

Endendijk, J. J., Groeneveld, M. G., Mesman, J., Van der Pol, L. D., Van Berkel, S. R., Hallers-Haalboom, E. T., et al. (2014). Boys don't play with dolls: Mothers' and fathers' gender talk during picture book reading. *Parenting: Science and Practice, 14,* 141–161.

Etaugh, C., & Liss, M. B. (1992). Home, school, and playroom: Training grounds for adult gender roles. *Sex Roles, 26,* 129–147. https://doi.org/10.1080/15295192.2014.972753.

Fast, A. A., & Olson, K. R. (2018). Gender development in transgender preschool children. *Child Development, 89*(2), 620–637. https://doi.org/10.1111/cdev.12758.

Fausto-Sterling, A., García Coll, D., & Lamarre, M. (2011). Sexing the baby: Part 1—what do we really know about sex differentiation in the first three years of life? *Social Science and Medicine, 74,* 1684–1692. https://doi.org/10.1016/j.socscimed.2011.05.051.

Fouts, H. N., Hallam, R. A., & Purandare, S. (2013). Gender segregation in early-childhood social play among the Bofi foragers and Bofi farmers in Central Africa. *American Journal of Play, 5*(3), 333–356.

Gibbons, J.L. (2000). Gender development in cross-cultural perspective. In T. Eckes, & H. M. Trautner (Eds.), *The developmental social psychology of gender,* (pp. 389–415). Mahwah, NJ: Erlbaum.

Gieseler, C. (2017). Gender-reveal parties: Performing community identity in pink and blue. *Journal of Gender Studies, 27,* 661–671. https://doi.org/10.1080/09589236.2017.1287066.

Giles, A. C., Cantin, K. D., Best, D. L., Tyrrell, H. P., & Gigler, M. E. (2014, February). Filial responsibilities of Hispanic and Anglo children in the United States. Paper presented in Symposium, Developmental Issues. In Paper presented in Symposium, *Developmental Issues in Different Cultural Settings,* D. L. Best & J. L. Gibbons (Conveners). Symposium at the meeting of the Society for Cross-Cultural Research, Charleston, SC.

Greenfield, P. M., Brazelton, T. B., & Childs, C. P. (1989). From birth to maturity in Zinacantan: Ontogenesis in cultural context. In V. Bricker & G. Gossen (Eds.), *Ethnographic encounters in southern Mesoamerica: Celebratory essays in honor of Evon Z. Vogt* (pp. 177–346). Albany, NY: Institute of Mesoamerican Studies, State University of New York.

Guttentag, M., & Longfellow, C. (1977). Children's social attributions: Development and change. In C. B. Keasey (Ed.), *Nebraska symposium on motivation* (pp. 305–341). Lincoln, NB: University of Nebraska Press.

Halim, M. L., Ruble, D. N., Tamis-LeMonda, C. S., Zosuls, K. M., Lurye, L. E., & Greulich, F. K. (2014). Pink frilly dresses and the avoidance of all things "girly": Children's appearance rigidity and cognitive theories of gender development. *Developmental Psychology, 50*(4), 1091–1101. https://doi.org/10.1037/a0034906.

Halim, M. L. D., Walsh, A. S., Tamis-LeMonda, C. S., Zosuls, K. M., & Ruble, D. N. (2018). The roles of self-Socialization and parent socialization in toddlers' gender-typed appearance. *Archives of Sexual Behavior, 47*(8), 2277–2285. https://doi.org/10.1007/s10508-018-1263-y.

Hines, M. (2006). Prenatal testosterone and gender-related behaviour. *European Journal of Endocrinology, 155,* S115–S121. https://doi.org/10.1530/eje.1.02236.

Hines, M. (2013). Sex and sex differences. In P. D. Zelazo (Ed.), *The Oxford handbook of developmental psychology* (Vol. 1, pp. 164–201)., Body and mind Oxford, UK: Oxford University Press.

Hyde, J. S., Bigler, R. S., Joel, D., Tate, C. C., & van Anders, S. M. (2019). The future of sex and gender in psychology: Five challenges to the gender binary. *American Psychologist, 74*(2), 171. https://doi.org/10.1037/amp0000307.

Jirout, J. J., & Newcombe, N. S. (2015). Building blocks for building spatial skills: Evidence from a large, representative U.S. sample. *Psychological Science, 26,* 302–310. https://doi.org/10.1177/0956797614563338.

Langlois, J. H., & Downs, C. (1980). Mothers, fathers and peers as socialization agents of sex-typed play behavior in young children. *Child Development, 51,* 1217–1247.

Leaper, C. (2002). Parenting girls and boys. In M. H. Bornstein (Ed.), *Handbook of parenting: Children and parenting* (Vol. 1, 2nd ed., pp. 189–225). Mahwah, NJ: Lawrence Erlbaum.

Leinbach, M. D., & Fagot, B. I. (1993). Categorical habituation to male and female faces: Gender schematic processing in infancy. *Infant Behavior and Development, 16,* 317–332.

Lewy-Levy, S., Reckin, R., Lavi, N., Cristóbal-Azkarate, J., & Ellis-Davies, K. (2017). How do hunter-gatherer children learn subsistence skills? A meta-ethnographic review. *Human Nature, 28,* 367–394.

Lytton, H., & Romney, D. M. (1991). Parents' differential socialization of boys and girls: A meta-analysis. *Psychological Bulletin, 109*(2), 267–296. https://doi.org/10.1037/0033-2909.109.2.267.

Maccoby, E. E. (1998). *The two sexes: Growing up apart, coming together.* Cambridge, MA: Belnap Press.

MacPhee, D., & Prendergast, S. (2019). Room for improvement: Girls' and boys' home environments are still gendered. *Sex Roles, 80*(5–6), 332–346. https://doi.org/10.1007/s11199-018-0936-2.

Martin, C., Kornienko, O., Schaefer, D. R., Hanish, L. D., Fabes, R. A., & Goble, P. (2013). The role of sex of peers and gender-typed activities in young children's peer affiliative networks: A longitudinal analysis of selection and influence. *Child Development, 84*(3), 921–937. https://doi.org/10.1111/cdev.12032.

Martin, C. L., Ruble, D. N., & Szkrybalo, J. (2002). Cognitive theories of early gender development. *Psychological Bulletin, 128*(6), 903–933. https://doi.org/10.1037/0033-2909.128.6.903.

Mesman, J., & Groeneveld, M. G. (2018). Gendered parenting in early childhood: Subtle but unmistakable if you know where to look. *Child Development Perspectives, 12*(1), 22–27. https://doi.org/10.1111/cdep12250.

Meyer, M., & Gelman, S. A. (2016). Gender essentialism in children and parents: Implications for the development of gender stereotyping and gender-typed preferences. *Sex Roles, 75*(9–10), 409–421. https://doi.org/10.1007/s11199-016-0646-6.

Munroe, R. L., Hulefeld, R., Rodgers, J. M., Tomeo, D. L., & Yamazaki, S. K. (2000). Aggression among children in four cultures. *Cross-Cultural Research: The Journal of Comparative Social Science, 34,* 3–25. https://doi.org/10.1177/106939710003400101.

Munroe, R. H., & Munroe, R. L. (1982). The development of sex-gender constancy among children in four cultures. In R. Rath, H. S. Asthana, D. Sinha, & J. B. P. Sinha (Eds.), *Diversity and unity in cross-cultural psychology.* Lisse, The Netherlands: Swets & Zeitlinger B. V.

Munroe, R. H., Munroe, R. L., & Brasher, A. (1985). Precursors of spatial ability: A longitudinal study among the Logoli of Kenya. *The Journal of Social Psychology, 125,* 23–33. https://doi.org/10.1080/00224545.1985.9713505.

Munroe, R. H., Shimmin, H. S., & Munroe, R. L. (1984). Gender understanding and sex role preference in four cultures. *Developmental Psychology, 20,* 673–682.

Newman, A. (2018, September 27). Male, female or 'X': The push for a third choice on official Forms. *New York Times.* Retrieved from https://www.nytimes.com/2018/09/27/nyregion/gender-neutral-birth-certificate.html.

Pellegrini, A. D. (2009). *The role of play in human development.* Oxford, UK and New York: Oxford University Press.

Perales, F., Jarallah, Y., & Baxter, J. (2018). Men's and women's gender-role attitudes across the transition to parenthood: Accounting for child's gender. *Social Forces, 97*(1), 251–276. https://doi.org/10.1093/sf/soy015.

Picariello, M. L., Greenberg, D. N., & Pillemer, D. B. (1990). Children's sex-related stereotyping of colors. *Child Development, 61*, 1453–1460. https://doi.org/10.2307/1130755.

Pomerleau, A., Malcuit, G., Turgeon, L., & Cossette, A. L. (1997). Effects of labelled gender on vocal communication of young women with 4-month-old infants. *International Journal of Psychology, 32*(2), 65–72. https://doi.org/10.1080/002075997400872.

Pyne, J. (2014). Gender independent kids: A paradigm shift in approaches to gender non-conforming children. *Canadian Journal of Human Sexuality, 23*, 1–8. https://doi.org/10.3138/cjhs.23.1.co1.

Rahilly, E. P. (2015). The gender binary meets the gender-variant child: Parents' negotiations with childhood gender variance. *Gender & Society, 29*(3), 338–361. https://doi.org/10.1177/0891243214563069.

Rheingold, H. L., & Cook, K. V. (1975). The contents of boys' and girls' rooms as an index of parents' behavior. *Child Development, 46*, 459–463. https://doi.org/10.2307/1128142.

Rogoff, B. (1981). Adults and peers as agents of socialization: A highland Guatemalan profile. *Ethos, 9*, 18–36. https://doi.org/10.1525/eth.1981.9.1.02a00030.

Rutter, M., Caspi, A., & Moffitt, T. E. (2003). Using sex differences in psycho-pathology to study causal mechanisms: Unifying issues and research strategies. *Journal of Child Psychology and Psychiatry, 44*, 1092–1115.

Seavey, C. A., Katz, P. A., & Zalk, S. R. (1975). Baby X. *Sex Roles, 1*(2), 103–109. https://doi.org/10.1007/bf0028804.

Sidorowicz, L. S., & Lunney, G. S. (1980). Baby X revisited. *Sex Roles, 6*(1), 67–73. https://doi.org/10.1007/bf00288362.

Sullivan, J., Moss-Racusin, C., Lopez, M., & Williams, K. (2018). Backlash against gender stereotype-violating preschool children. *PLoS ONE, 13*(4), e0195503. https://doi.org/10.1371/journal.pone.0195503.

Sweeney, J., & Bradbard, M. R. (1989). Mothers' and fathers' changing perceptions of their male and female infants over the course of pregnancy. *Journal of Genetic Psychology, 149*, 393–404. https://doi.org/10.1080/00221325.1988.10532167.

Stieglitz, J., Gurven, M., Kaplan, H., & Hooper, P. L. (2013). Household task delegation among high-fertility forager-horticulturalists of lowland Bolivia. *Current Anthropology, 54*(2), 232–241. https://doi.org/10.1086/669708.

Taylor, C., Clifford, A., & Franklin, A. (2013). Color preferences are not universal. *Journal of Experimental Psychology: General, 142*, 1015–1027. https://doi.org/10.1037/a0030273.

Tobin, D. D., Menon, M., Menon, M., Spatta, B. C., Hodges, E. V., & Perry, D. G. (2010). The intrapsychics of gender: A model of self-socialization. *Psychological Review, 117*(2), 601–622. https://doi.org/10.1037/a0018936.

Todd, B. K., Barry, J. A., & Thommessen, S. A. O. (2017). Preferences for "gender-typed" toys in boys and girls aged 9 to 32 months. *Infant and Child Development, 26*, 198e. https://doi.org/10.1002/icd.1986.

Vogel, D. A., Lake, M. A., Evans, S., & Karraker, K. H. (1991). Children's and adults' sex-stereotyped perceptions of infants. *Sex Roles, 24*(9–10), 605–616. https://doi.org/10.1007/bf00288417.

Weisgram, E. S., Fulcher, M., & Dinella, L. M. (2014). Pink gives girls permission: Exploring the role of explicit gender labels and gender-typed colors on preschool children's toy preferences. *Journal of Applied Developmental Psychology, 35*, 401–409. https://doi.org/10.1016/j.appdev.2014.06.004.

Welch, M. R., Page, B. M., & Martin, L. L. (1981). Sex differences in the ease of socialization: An analysis of the efficiency of child training processes in preindustrial societies. *Journal of Social Psychology, 113*, 3–12.

Whiting, B., & Edwards, C. P. (1973). A cross-cultural analysis of sex differences in the behavior of children aged 3 to 11. *Journal of Social Psychology, 91*, 171–188.

Whiting, B. B., & Edwards, C. P. (1988). *Children of different worlds: The formation of social behavior.* Cambridge, MA: Harvard University Press.

Williams, J. E., & Best, D. L. (1990). *Measuring sex stereotypes: A multination study.* Newbury Park, CA: Sage.

Williams, Z. (2018, November 30). The rise of the gender-reveal party—reckless, pointless and bizarrely old-fashioned. *The Guardian.* Retrieved from https://www.theguardian.com/world/shortcuts/2018/nov/30/the-rise-of-the-gender-reveal-party-reckless-pointless-and-bizarrely-old-fashioned.

Wong, W. I., & Hines, M. (2015). Preferences for pink and blue: The development of color preferences as a distinct gender-typed behavior in toddlers. *Archives of Sexual Behavior, 44,* 1243–1254. https://doi.org/10.1007/s10508-015-0489-1.

Yamaguchi, M. K. (2000). Discriminating the sex of faces by 6- and 8-mo-old infants. *Perceptual and Motor Skills, 91,* 653–664.

Yeung, S. P., & Wong, W. I. (2018). Gender labels on gender-neutral colors: Do they affect children's color preferences and play performance? *Sex Roles, 79,* 260–272. https://doi.org/10.1016/j.appdev.2014.06.004.

Zosuls, K. M., Ruble, D. N., Tamis-LeMonda, C. S., Shrout, P. E., Bornstein, M. H., & Greulich, F. K. (2009). The acquisition of gender labels in infancy: Implications for gender-typed play. *Developmental Psychology, 45,* 688–701.

Chapter 7
Sharing and Caring: Prosocial Behavior in Young Children Around the World

Katelyn E. Poelker and Judith L. Gibbons

Abstract Young children around the world help others. Yet, the ways in which they help and the conditions under which they provide assistance differ by age and cultural context. Prosocial behavior can be defined as instrumental, empathic, or altruistic, or conceptualized as helping, sharing, or comforting. In this chapter, we explore the developmental trends and diversity behind young children's helpfulness. For example, instrumental helping is most common among younger children and empathic helping becomes more frequent with age; altruism is rare, likely due to its costliness. In addition to developmental patterns, a major focus of our chapter is the role of cultural context in shaping children's helping behavior. Although most of the laboratory research on children's prosocial behavior has been conducted in the minority world, the literature outside of those contexts reveals noteworthy cross-cultural differences in a variety of domains including: what constitutes helping, the available opportunities to help, and the necessity of developmental milestones like self-recognition as precursors to prosocial behavior. Given that helping behavior is such a positive component of social relationships, we suggest circumstances that may promote helping across cultures like insuring there are sufficient developmentally appropriate opportunities to help and the role of cultural values (e.g., autonomy, relatedness). Lastly, we argue for the need to understand the mechanism(s) driving cultural differences, using the developmental niche to frame future research in this area.

Young children help others in myriad ways. At home they may help a parent by carrying a cup to the table, gathering firewood, or providing care for younger siblings; at school, they may help a classmate pick up spilled crayons, offer to share a popular toy, or give comfort during upsetting times. Prosocial behavior, social scientists' term for helping and sharing, evolves across the lifespan and varies across

K. E. Poelker (✉)
Hope College, 35 E. 12th Street, Holland, MI, USA
e-mail: katepoelker@gmail.com

J. L. Gibbons
Saint Louis University, St. Louis, MO, USA
e-mail: judith.gibbons@slu.edu

© Springer Nature Switzerland AG 2019　　　　　　　　　　　　89
T. Tulviste et al. (eds.), *Children's Social Worlds in Cultural Context*,
https://doi.org/10.1007/978-3-030-27033-9_7

cultural contexts in the type of help, the recipient, and the motivation for helping (de Guzman et al. 2014). In this chapter, we focus on how young children help those in their social worlds—parents, siblings, friends, and strangers—emphasizing both the cultural similarities and differences in those behaviors.

Defining Prosocial Behavior

Prosocial behavior has a rich history in psychology and has often been of particular interest to developmental psychologists to further understanding of how social behavior varies throughout the lifespan (Mussen and Eisenberg-Berg 1977; Radke Yarrow et al. 1976; Zahn-Waxler and Smith 1992). As is often the case with frequently researched constructs, a multitude of definitions exists in the literature. At the most basic level, prosocial behavior is akin to helping, caring, and sharing and can be formally defined as "a voluntary behavior meant to help another" (Padilla-Walker and Carlo 2014, p. 6). It is also commonly associated with empathy, or the ability to identify and feel others' emotions (Eisenberg and Miller 1987). Recently, scholars have begun to emphasize the multiple influences on prosocial behavior—that is, its connections to other facets of development including biology, socialization practices, and culture (Dunfield 2014; Padilla-Walker and Carlo 2014). The role of culture in shaping prosocial norms and behavior in children has been of interest for decades (e.g., Eisenberg et al. 1985; Eisenberg and Mussen 1989), but in the current chapter we examine the connection between the two constructs more deeply.

Some scholars have proposed that the umbrella term of helping is best understood when broken down into three subtypes: instrumental helping, empathic helping, and altruism (Svetlova et al. 2010). Instrumental helping is rooted in actions like helping a friend to clean up her spilled milk or assisting a parent by clearing the dinner table. Giner Torréns and Kärtner (2017) defined instrumental helping as "any behavior that is intended to fulfill others' goal-directed needs" (p. 353). Empathic helping, or helping rooted in emotion-laden situations, is more complex and more relational than instrumental helping. It involves, for example, comforting someone who is sad or upset. Altruism emerged as the most sophisticated and by most definitions, the costliest type of prosocial behavior to the helper or benefactor, such as positioning oneself in front of a moving train to save another person's life (Svetlova et al. 2010). Scholars have proposed many different definitions of altruism. One such definition is that altruism is "a motivational state with the ultimate goal of increasing another's welfare" (Batson and Shaw 1991, p. 6). Others have emphasized that altruistic actions must come at a cost to the benefactor and that the benefactor must have no expectation that the kindness will be returned (Hoffman 1981).

Others have suggested three alternative subtypes of prosocial behavior that include helping, sharing, and comforting (Dunfield 2014; Mussen and Eisenberg-Berg 1977). Dunfield argues that helping, sharing, and comforting arise in response to others' negative feelings or situations—respectively, "an instrumental need, [an] unmet material desire, and emotional distress" (Dunfield 2014, p. 1).

Developmental Patterns of Prosocial Behavior

Developmentally speaking, instrumental helping emerges as early as 12–14 months of age and is more common among younger children than empathic helping or altruism (Svetlova et al. 2010; Warneken and Tomasello 2007). Instead of the more sophisticated cognitive skills required to engage in other types of prosocial behavior, instrumental helping demands that a child understands that behaviors are often dictated by goals (Svetlova et al. 2010). Not only is instrumental helping common in toddlers, it often appears without prompting and without the expectation of a reward (Rheingold 1982; Warneken and Tomasello 2008). In fact, Warneken and Tomasello (2008) argued that the 20-month-olds in their sample were less likely to help when rewarded for their helping behavior because their initial inclination to help was intrinsic (as opposed to extrinsic).

Empathic helping is more likely to appear as children get older (Svetlova et al. 2010). The ability to engage in empathic helping seems to depend on the ability to recognize oneself, which emerges around 18 months (Svetlova et al. 2010). In Hoffman's (2000) well-known theory of empathy development, he argues that empathy has its roots in infancy (with empathic, contagious crying), but that children's ability to empathize becomes progressively more complex as they move through the remaining four stages of his model. According to Hoffman's (2000) model, empathy before age 2 is limited to "egocentric empathic distress" (Laible and Karahuta 2014, p. 353); after age 2 when the child has achieved self-recognition (and is able to make the distinction between the self and others), the empathy becomes more other-focused. These advances are due, at least in part, to the cognitive processes of declining egocentrism and increasing perspective-taking.

With respect to altruism, although advances in social cognition may facilitate a more complete understanding of situations that require an altruistic response, having such social cognitive skills does not automatically translate to rates of increased altruism as children age. In fact, some scholars argue that altruism rates decrease as children get older and are better able to assess what is required of them to behave altruistically. Thus, children engage in altruistic helping less frequently than the other types of prosocial behavior (Laible and Karahuta 2014; Svetlova et al. 2010).

Sharing is another important type of prosocial behavior; spontaneous sharing is among the first social acts to emerge in childhood (Brownell et al. 2013; Dunfield 2014; Laible and Karahuta 2014). Even before age 1, children will voluntarily and without provocation offer a toy or other resource to an adult (Laible and Karahuta 2014). Shortly thereafter, children offer to give objects in response to others' verbal and nonverbal requests (Hay and Murray 1982). However, it is important to note that not all sharing is other-oriented or prosocial in nature. For example, younger children might offer a toy to another child or adult as a way to attract attention or incite a positive emotional response (Brownell et al. 2013).

In a study specifically focused on other-oriented sharing with 18–24-month-olds in the USA, the 24-month-olds shared resources more quickly and more frequently than their younger peers (Brownell et al. 2013). The older children also required less verbal prompting before engaging in the sharing behavior. For 18-month-olds, the request for sharing had to be explicit. A similar pattern emerged in a study by Hay and colleagues; other-oriented sharing (in this case sharing when only a few toys were available) increased in toddlers between the ages of 12 and 30 months (Hay et al. 1999). Like altruism, sharing can also be costly, as it requires the sharer to cede something desired or valued to another person. Rates of sharing are oftentimes lower among toddlers than other types of prosocial behavior likely because of the costliness to the sharer (Brownell et al. 2013; Laible and Karahuta 2014).

Emotion Socialization, Social Cognitive Processes, and Prosocial Behavior

In addition to their developmental stage, children's socialization may also influence their prosocial behavior—in particular, socialization about emotion. Parents who asked their 18–30-month-old children to name and describe emotions had children who shared faster and with greater frequency than parents who did not engage their children in those conversations, even when controlling for age (Brownell et al. 2013). Furthermore, results revealed that the direction of the emotion talk was essential. In other words, it was critical that the parents solicited this emotion information from their young children, not just that the parents themselves frequently discussed emotions (Brownell et al. 2013).

Along with sharing, empathic helping may also be encouraged by parental socialization of emotions (Drummond et al. 2014). When parents read books with their children they use more affect words (e.g., happy or sad) and when playing with their children they use more mental state words (e.g., think or know). The children whose parents urged them to discuss emotions during book reading and used mental state and emotion words during joint play were more likely to engage in empathic helping.

Children's theory of mind (ToM), or their ability to assume another's mental state (Wellman et al. 2001), may also be related to the interpersonal act of sharing (Wu and Su 2014). In a laboratory study with Chinese 2-, 3-, and 4-year-olds, patterns emerged with respect to age and ToM status. In a laboratory task, both 2- and 3-year-olds required more prompting before sharing toys with a puppet; the 4-year-olds shared more spontaneously. However, regardless of age, children who had achieved more advanced ToM understanding shared more readily, suggesting that perspective-taking does enhance one's ability to behave prosocially. This finding has been further supported by the results of a meta-analytic review of the relation between theory of mind and prosocial behavior in childhood (Imuta et al. 2016). Although the authors acknowledged previously mixed evidence that ToM promotes prosocial behavior, the meta-analysis confirmed that the ability to take others' thoughts and feelings into account promotes prosocial actions (Imuta et al. 2016). With that said, the authors cautioned that the magnitude of the association between prosocial behavior and ToM may be weak.

Young children's understanding of reciprocity might also affect their propensity to help and to share (Laible and Karahuta 2014; Warneken and Tomasello 2013). In a study with 6- and 10-month olds, Hamlin et al. (2007) reported that infants as young as 6 months of age prefer instances in which characters help, as opposed to hinder, others' actions, suggesting that even preverbal human infants may evaluate other's behavior to ascertain the likelihood of helpfulness and reciprocity. In a separate study with toddlers, 3-year-olds were more likely to share with partners who had previously shared with them than 2-year-olds (Warneken and Tomasello 2013). Prior helping behavior did not seem to increase 3-year-olds' tendency to share. No preference for sharing with those who had previously helped or shared with them emerged for 2-year-olds, indicating reciprocity was not incorporated into 2-year-olds' decisions to behave prosocially. Warneken and Tomasello (2013) concluded that although some scholars argue that reciprocity is essential for prosocial behavior, helping behavior likely emerges independently of reciprocity but that later in development, reciprocity mediates prosocial behavior.

Gender Differences in Prosocial Behavior

With respect to gender differences in prosocial and sharing behavior, many studies have suggested that girls share and are more prosocial than boys (e.g., Burford et al. 1996), but some have reported no gender differences (Grusec et al. 2002; Radke-Yarrow et al. 1983). Some have explained the gender differences using gender role expectations, such that it is more acceptable for a girl to share and help and for a boy to behave aggressively (Sebanc et al. 2003). Others have argued that gender differences in prosocial behavior may become more exaggerated as children get older (Tisak et al. 2007). See Chap. 6 in this volume by Best and Gibbons for more information.

Motivations for Prosocial Behavior

In addition to considering the different types of prosocial behavior and the roles of social cognitive processes like reciprocity and theory of mind, it is also important to recognize the diversity in motivations for helping, which may vary by culture and developmental stage. Eisenberg (1986) argues that children's prosocial moral reasoning underlies their motivations for helping. For example, children motivated by receiving praise or recognition for their helpfulness will be less likely to help in anonymous helping situations (Eisenberg and Spinrad 2014). If they are motivated by feelings of empathy or sympathy, children will be quick to help in situations that allow them to relieve another's distress and less likely to assist when another's needs or distress are less explicit or apparent.

Moreover, researchers have proposed many frameworks for why young children help others (Paulus 2014). Paulus (2014) argues that prosocial behavior likely stems from one of four motives: emotion-sharing, goal-alignment, social interaction, or social normative. When motivated by emotion-sharing, young children help because they recognize others' emotional distress (Paulus 2014). According to the theory, then, this motive requires that children have acquired self-recognition. Children must transform their own negative feelings and concern about another person into a solution to help that individual. Studies that have suggested that children are able to experience empathy before gaining self-recognition threaten the validity of this motive (e.g., Brownell et al. 2013).

The goal-alignment motive most closely fits with acts of instrumental helping (Paulus 2014). Although goal-alignment models of helping do not impose self-recognition as a prerequisite for helping, they are limited in that other types of prosocial behavior, such as empathic helping or altruism, are difficult to explain. The social interaction approach is based on the basic tenet that humans are social creatures who find interacting with others to be enjoyable and rewarding (Paulus 2014). Thus, prosocial behavior is one avenue to engage socially with others. Lastly, according to Paulus (2014), children's social environments may promote helping behavior yielding the social normative model. Using this approach, children learn from social cues and rules to engage in prosocial acts by scaffolding (e.g., providing greater support initially and then gradually reducing that support once the child has acquired more skills and experience) or other means.

Others argue more succinctly that children's motivations for helping are intrinsic (Hepach et al. 2017). When toddlers accomplished a goal or helped others, their body posture was elevated (Hepach et al. 2017). When they helped someone in need or saw someone else assist that person, their pupils dilated—a sign of sympathetic arousal (Hepach et al. 2012). These findings suggest that even young children hold a concern for others and want that person to receive the assistance he or she needs.

Cross-Cultural Prosocial Behavior in Early Childhood

Prosocial behavior in young children has been studied experimentally more often in WEIRD (Western, Educated, Industrialized, Rich, and Democratic; Henrich et al. 2010) cultures than in the majority world, although anthropological ethnographies have also been probed extensively (de Guzman et al. 2014; Lancy 2018). Research by psychologists has focused on the motivation for helping, as well as age and gender differences in prosocial behavior among children living in the minority world (Burford et al. 1996; Warneken and Tomasello 2013). A recent explosion of research of the helping behavior of toddlers shows that young children routinely assist others (e.g., Lancy 2018; Rogoff et al. 2014; Warneken 2016; Warneken and Tomasello 2008).

Around the world, children as young as 12 months of age help others in daily tasks (e.g., Lancy 2018). Lancy and others argue that children are intrinsically helpful and that their participation in daily tasks allows them to be a part of their social group. The behaviors they show are instrumental helping as described above, and directly or potentially benefit the family or community. Examples include 3-year-old Huaroani children joining a search for forest food, a 15-month-old Mapuche boy feeding the household's chickens, 3-year-old Gusii children hoeing garden plots, and Taira toddlers carrying rice stalks (Lancy 2018). A short film depicts Tiny Katerina of Siberia (Golovnev 2004). At the age of 25 months, the wobbly toddler Katerina helps gather firewood, ladles soup from a large pot, and plucks the feathers from hunted birds to assist those around her. Through these vivid examples, as well as a survey of the anthropological literature, Lancy (2018) argues that contributing to the family and community emerges universally at early ages and serves as a precursor to adolescent and adult work.

Among Mayan children, helping is a primary way of learning, "learning by observing and pitching in" (LOPI, Rogoff et al. 2015). See also Chap. 3 this volume. At young ages, children assist their family members in ongoing daily tasks, learning not only the skills required, but also processes of seamless coordination and collaboration. Because keen observation and participation are so much a part of everyday cultural practices, indigenous children may be less likely than others to encode their behavior as helping (e.g., Gibbons 2013), and instead consider that "it is just what we do."

Although few would dispute the pervasiveness of toddlers' helpfulness, questions as to its motivation, cross-cultural similarities and differences, and social influences remain. An intrinsic need and desire to be helpful is posited by some (Lancy 2018; Warneken 2016; Warneken and Tomasello 2009). Lancy argues that children have a compulsion to help and that helping makes them happy. Warneken (2016) argues for a biological disposition for altruism and helpfulness; helping emerges at a very early age, even when not explicitly encouraged by parents. As described above, concrete rewards for helping do not drive helping, but may even diminish it (Warneken and Tomasello 2008).

Others take issue with the natural emergence of helping based on a biological disposition (Dahl 2015; Dahl et al. 2017). Scaffolding, rewards, and punishment may influence the expression of helping behavior. In a laboratory study by Dahl et al. (2017), scaffolding increased the helping behavior of children who were younger than 15 months of age, but not of older children, 15–18 months old. Another laboratory study revealed that a mother's scaffolding of her child's assistance in a clean-up task predicted her child's helpfulness with an experimenter (Hammond and Carpendale 2015). Thus, individual differences were a consequence of mother's scaffolding. In naturalistic observations of U.S. middle class toddlers at home, instances of helping were often accompanied by encouragement, thanking, or praising (Dahl 2015). Toddlers in India were often chastised for not helping, but rarely praised for assisting others (Giner Torréns and Kärtner 2017). These findings suggest that helping behavior is often promoted or discouraged through others' responses. Furthermore, in some cases the helping is viewed as expected (as in India) or somewhat surprising (as in the USA).

Cross-cultural comparisons in young children's helping behavior are scarce (Giner Torréns and Kärtner 2017; Köster et al. 2015). In a study of rural toddlers from India, Canada, and Peru, the authors found few cultural differences in children's assistance in five tasks (Callaghan et al. 2011). However, the lack of differences might have been due to the high difficulty of the tasks, which required sophisticated perspective-taking (Giner Torréns and Kärtner 2017). In a comparison of helping among 18-month-old children from Germany and India, the Indian children helped more than the German children (Giner Torréns and Kärtner 2017). Indian children were provided more opportunities to help, and more often reprimanded for not helping. Punitive responses to failure to help were positively correlated with helping behavior among Indian children and negatively correlated for German children (Giner Torréns and Kärtner 2017). The authors hypothesize that children from relational cultures are provided more opportunities to help and that helping is expected as a part of interpersonal responsibilities (see also Köster et al. 2015); in Germany providing opportunities to help was a strategy used by mothers whose children were not being helpful. In another cross-national study conducted in urban Germany, urban Brazil, and rural Brazil, mothers were instructed to ask their child (in the way they usually would) to carry objects to a table (Köster et al. 2016). Assertive scaffolding (in which mothers assigned tasks in a serious and insistent tone accompanied by corresponding nonverbal behaviors and facial expressions) was associated with toddlers' helping in rural Brazil, whereas deliberate scaffolding (asking, pleading, providing reasons) was associated with toddlers' helping in Germany. The contribution of this research is that not only the outcomes, but also the processes involved in children's helping may differ cross-culturally. In another cross-national study looking at the variables associated with prosocial behavior, researchers found that self-concept (as indexed by mirror recognition) predicted prosocial behavior in German toddlers, but not in Indian toddlers (Kärtner et al. 2010).

Other investigators have examined prosocial behavior among young children outside the minority world context. Aime et al. (2017) found that in the Pacific island nation of Vanuatu, a small-scale rural environment, most children helped the experimenter, even without a specific request to do so. De Guzman et al. (2005) performed naturalistic observations of prosocial behavior among Gikuyu children of Ngecha, Kenya. They found that prosocial behavior was most often expressed during labor or chores and least likely expressed during self-care. Other than participation in routine household tasks, many children cared for siblings; although childcare was rare for the youngest age group, 4–6-year-olds were caring for younger children in about one third of the spot observations.

Along with other forms of helping, sibling caretaking is widespread throughout the world, and is a part of assisting the family by participating in ongoing household tasks (Edwards 1986; Weisner et al. 1977; Whiting 1983). Children as young as 4 or 5 years old are frequently observed caring for younger siblings (Gosso 2010; Lancy 2018; Nag et al. 1978). The child caretaker learns responsibility and nurturance, while the younger child benefits from shared caregiving (Edwards 1986). For a review of the role of siblings in young children's social development, see Maynard, Chap. 11 this volume.

A related area of research is children's imitation of prosocial behaviors of others, including parents, siblings, and unrelated adults (Legare and Nielsen 2015). To some extent, children's helping may result simply from imitation of others' behavior. Children are more likely to imitate those who are responsive and available. In a Canadian laboratory study, children imitated parents who showed higher responsiveness and availability; those parental qualities were also associated with higher levels of help-ing "in girls" (Brooker and Poulin-Dubois 2013). Moreover, there may be cultural differences in children's imitation of adults' helping behavior, and imitation may be one way that children learn about the values and customs of their culture. In a cross-national study, children from India imitated both generous and stingy adults, but children in the United States imitated only the stingy model (Blake et al. 2016).

Circumstances that Promote Helping

Given that prosocial behavior promotes positive interpersonal interactions, it is important to consider the situations or circumstances that may promote helping. In light of the literature reviewed above, both from the minority and majority worlds, it is clear that children first readily help close others—those in their in-groups and familiar social worlds using the methods that are modeled for them. For example, tiny Katerina helped in ways that were in concert with the actions of those around her (Golovnev 2004). In other words, Katerina's helpful acts were closely tied to what her mother or more expert others were doing. Based on available anthropological evidence, young children's helping is most compatible with situations that invite small contributions and that children can easily discern how they may assist without being explicitly told to do so (although a child's response to an explicit call for help would also certainly "count" as helping; Lancy 2018).

Thus, we must consider the availability of helping tasks, as it seems likely that some cultures vary in the number of suitable helping tasks available for young chil-dren (Giner Torréns and Kärtner 2017; Köster et al. 2015). For example, there are some tasks that young children simply are not developmentally equipped to help with, like driving a car or writing this chapter, while others are more developmentally fea-sible and appropriate (e.g., gathering small pieces of wood). As described above in the Giner Torréns and Kärtner (2017) study with Indian and German children and their mothers, the Indian mothers provided more opportunities for their children to help. This finding is consistent with prior literature that has revealed cultures high on relatedness (like much of the majority world) provide more opportunities for helping than those from more autonomous backgrounds (like many minority world coun-tries; Keller et al. 2004; Köster et al. 2015). In particular, children living in cultures in which their participation in household chores, including childcare, is readily inte-grated into daily life may be particular poised to help at home (Giner Torréns and Kärtner 2017).

In addition to providing children with opportunities to help, cultures that use LOPI (Rogoff et al. 2015) and encourage imitation (Legare and Nielsen 2015) to teach cul-turally specific expectations, values, and behaviors would likely encourage prosocial behavior as well. Both strategies are participatory and encourage the child's cooper-ation and presence in daily routines. Their contributions are likely to be recognized and valued and those actions that are consistent with the cultural system are likely reinforced. Behaviors that are inconsistent with cultural practices may be corrected, so the child can learn for the next time.

Conclusions

When comparing the psychological and anthropological literatures on helping, anthropologists readily privilege children's everyday social and cultural systems, oftentimes using ethnographic methods to characterize children's helping behavior (e.g., Lancy 2018). This approach generates a rich narrative of children's daily helping behaviors and provides many examples of how children respond to calls for help in familiar circumstances and situations. Psychologists, in contrast, more often depend on laboratory studies that yield greater experimental control, but likely sacrifice ecological validity. Furthermore, generally speaking, the child's cultural context and values have not been traditionally emphasized in those investigations.

The two approaches also differ in their discussions of the motivations and developmental trajectories of helping. As explained earlier, many anthropologists (e.g. Lancy 2018) imply that all children have an identical intrinsic desire or motivation to help. In other words, a young child's motivation to help is universal—to contribute to the well-being of their family and community. Although some psychologists have made similar claims—that a child's desire to help is intrinsic (Hepach et al. 2017)—the motivation driving children's prosocial behavior is certainly an important and unresolved issue in the literature. Systematic investigations designed to reveal cultural differences and similarities behind children's motivations to help (or not) would make an important contribution to the literature (see Tisak et al. 2007 for one example).

A crucial direction for future research is to focus on the mechanisms and processes that facilitate or promote prosocial behavior in children in different contexts. A useful framework for describing the cultural ecology is that of the developmental niche, which is comprised of (A) the physical and social settings, (B) the customs of child care and child rearing, and (C) the psychology of the caretakers (Harkness and Super 1996). Parental goals and ethnotheories (i.e., parental beliefs about childrearing) vary and parents may differ in their conceptions of responsible behavior (Köster et al. 2016). In the minority world, only psychologically autonomous behavior is considered prosocial, whereas in the majority world, interpersonal responsibility can be considered prosocial (see also Miller and Bersoff 1994). This may be a distinct cultural variable in prosocial behavior, as evidenced by the finding that self-recognition was a prerequisite for prosocial behavior in German toddlers, but not in Indian toddlers (Kärtner et al. 2010). Customs of childcare may also provide differential opportunities for helping. For example, in many cultural settings, it is customary for older siblings, themselves as young as 4 years old, to care for younger siblings (Edwards 1986). Physical and social settings also dictate much of children's opportunity to help. Children confined in playpens have fewer opportunities to collaborate on and participate in tasks with others, simply because their mobility and autonomy are more limited (Harkness and Super 1996). When parents or other adults have a higher workload, children's helping is more likely (Whiting 1963).

So as not to focus entirely on differences, another issue is whether there are cultural universals with respect to children's prosocial behavior. The study of trajectories of prosocial development among young children in different cultures is a fruitful avenue to deepen our understanding of human interaction.

References

Aime, H., Broesch, T., Aknin, L. B., & Warneken, F. (2017). Evidence for proactive and reactive helping in two- to five-year-olds from a small-scale society. *PloSOne, 12*(11), 1–16. https://dx.doi.org/10.1371/journal.pone.0187787.

Batson, C. D., & Shaw, L. L. (1991). Evidence for altruism: Toward a pluralism of prosocial motives. *Psychology Inquiry, 2,* 107–122. https://doi.org/10.1207/s15327965pli0202_1.

Blake, P. R., Corbit, J., Callaghan, T. C., & Warneken, F. (2016). Give as I give: Adult influence of children's giving in two cultures. *Journal of Experimental Child Psychology, 152,* 149–160. https://doi.org/10.1016/j.jcep.2016.07.010.

Brooker, I., & Poulin-Dubois, D. (2013). Is parental emotional reliability predictive of toddlers' learning and helping? *Infant Behavior and Development, 36,* 403–418.

Brownell, C. A., Svetlova, M., Anderson, R., Nichols, S. R., & Drummond, J. (2013). Socialization of early prosocial behavior: Parents' talk about emotions is associated with sharing and helping in toddlers. *Infancy, 18,* 91–119. https://doi.org/10.1111/j.1532-7078.2012.00125.x.

Burford, H. C., Foley, L. A., Rollins, P. G., & Rosario, K. S. (1996). Gender differences in preschoolers' sharing behavior. *Journal of Social Behavior and Personality, 11,* 17–25.

Callaghan, T., Moll, H., Rakoczy, H., Warneken, F., Liszkowski, U., Behne, T., et al. (2011). Early social cognition in three cultural contexts. *Monographs of the Society for Research in Child Development, 76,* 1–142.

Dahl, A. (2015). The developing social context of infant helping in two U.S. samples. *Child Development, 86,* 1080–1093. https://doi.org/10.1111/cdev.12361.

Dahl, A., Satlof-Bedrick, E. S., Hammond, S. I., Drummond, J. K., Waugh, W. E., & Brownell, C. A. (2017). Explicit scaffolding increases simple helping in younger infants. *Developmental Psychology, 53,* 407–416. https://doi.org/10.1037/dev0000244.

de Guzman, M. R. T., Do, K. A., & Kok, C. M. (2014). The cultural contexts of children's prosocial behaviors. In L. M. Padilla-Walker & G. Carlo (Eds.), *Prosocial development: A multidimensional approach* (pp. 221–241). New York: Oxford University Press.

de Guzman, M. R. T., Edwards, C. P., & Carlo, G. (2005). Prosocial behaviors in context: A study of Gikuyu children of Ngecha, Kenya. *Applied Developmental Psychology, 26,* 542–558. https://doi.org/10.1016/j.appdev.2005.06.006.

Drummond, J., Paul, E. F., Waugh, W. E., Hammond, S. I., & Brownell, C. A. (2014). Here, there and everywhere: emotion and mental state talk in differnet social contexts predicts empathic helping in toddlers. *Frontiers in Psychology, 5*(365), 1–11. https://doi.org/10.3389/fpsyg.2014.00361.

Dunfield, K. A. (2014). A construct divided: Prosocial behavior as helping, sharing, and comforting subtypes. *Frontiers in Psychology, 5*(958), 1–13. https://doi.org/10.3389/fpsyg.2014.00958drumm.

Edwards, C. P. (1986). Another style of competence: The caregiving child. In A. Fogel & G. F. Melson (Eds.), *Origins of nurturance: Developmental, biological and cultural perspectives on caregiving* (pp. 95–111). Hillsdale, NJ: Lawrence Erlbaum.

Eisenberg, N. (1986). *Altruistic emotion, cognition, and behavior.* Hillsdale, NJ: Erlbaum.

Eisenberg, N., Boehnke, K., Schuhler, P., & Silbereisen, R. K. (1985). The development of prosocial behavior and cognitions in German children. *Journal of Cross-Cultural Psychology, 16,* 69–82. https://doi.org/10.1177/0022002185016001006.

Eisenberg, N., & Miller, P. A. (1987). The relation of empathy to prosocial and related behaviors. *Psychological Bulletin, 101,* 91–119. https://doi.org/10.1037/0033-2909.101.1.91.

Eisenberg, N., & Mussen, P. H. (1989). *The roots of prosocial behavior in children.* New York: Cambridge University Press.

Eisenberg, N., & Spinrad, T. L. (2014). Multidimensionality of prosocial behavior: Rethinking the conceptualization and development of prosocial behavior. In L. M. Padilla-Walker & G. Carlo (Eds.), *Prosocial development: A multidimensional approach* (pp. 17–39). New York: Oxford University Press.

Gibbons, J. L. (2013). Guatemalan adolescents' reports of helping in urban and rural Mayan communities. In D. A. Vakoch (Ed.), *Altruism in cross-cultural perspective* (pp. 45–56). New York, NY: Springer. https://dx.doi.org/10.1007/978-1-4614-6052-0_4.

Giner Torréns, M., & Kärtner, J. (2017). The influence of socialization on early helping. *Journal of Cross-Cultural Psychology, 48,* 353–368. https://doi.org/10.1177/0022022117690451.

Golovnev, I. (Producer & Director). (2004). *Tiny Katarina* (Motion picture). Ekaterinburg, Russia: Bureau Studio.

Gosso, Y. (2010). Play in different cultures. In P. K. Smith (Ed.), *Children and play* (pp. 80–98). Chichester, UK: Wiley-Blackwell.

Grusec, J. E., Davidov, M., & Lundell, L. (2002). Prosocial and helping behavior. In P. K. Smith & G. H. Hart (Eds.), *Blackwell handbook of childhood social development* (pp. 457–474). Malden, MA: Blackwell.

Hamlin, J. K., Wynn, K., & Bloom, P. (2007). Social evaluation by preverbal infants. *Nature, 450,* 557–560. https://doi.org/10.1038/nature06288.

Hammond & Carpendale. (2015). Helping children help: The relation between maternal scaffolding and children's early help. *Social Development, 24,* 367–383. https://doi.org/10.1111/sode.12104.

Harkness, S., & Super, C. M. (1996). *Parents' cultural belief systems: Their origins, expressions, and consequences.* New York: Guilford Press.

Hay, D. F., Castle, J., Davies, L., Demetriou, H., & Stimson, C. A. (1999). Prosocial action in very early childhood. *Journal of Child Psychology and Psychiatry, 40,* 905–916. https://doi.org/10.1111/1469-7610.00508.

Hay, D. F., & Murray, P. (1982). Giving and requesting: Social facilitation of infants' offers to adults. *Infants Behavior and Development, 5,* 301–310. https://doi.org/10.1016/S0163-6383(82)80039-8.

Henrich, J., Heine, S. J., & Norenzayan, A. (2010). The weirdest people in the world? *Behavioral and Brain Science, 33,* 61–83. https://doi.org/10.1017/s0140525x0999152x.

Hepach, R., Vaish, A., & Tomasello, M. (2012). Young children are intrinsically motivated to see others helped. *Psychological Science, 23,* 967–972. https://dx.doi.org/10.1177/09568797612440571.

Hepach, R., Vaish, A., & Tomasello, M. (2013). Young children sympathize less in response to unjustified emotional distress. *Developmental Psychology, 49,* 1132–1138. https://dx.doi.org/10.1037/a0029501.

Hoffman, M. L. (1981). Is altruism part of human nature? *Journal of Personality and Social Psychology, 40,* 121–137. https://doi.org/10.1037/0022-3514.40.1.121.

Hoffman, M. (2000). *Empathy and moral development: Implications for justice and caring.* New York: Cambridge University Press.

Imuta, K., Henry, J. D., Slaughter, V., Selcuk, B., & Ruffman, T. (2016). Theory of mind and prosocial behavior in childhood: A meta-analytic review. *Developmental Psychology, 52,* 1192–1205. https://doi.org/10.1037/dev0000140.

Kärtner, J., Keller, H., & Chaudhary, N. (2010). Cognitive and social influences on early prosocial behavior in two sociocultural contexts. *Developmental Psychology, 46,* 905–914. https://doi.org/10.1037/a0019718.

Keller, H., Yovsi, R., Borke, J., Kärter, J., Jensen, H., & Papalogoura, Z. (2004). Developmental consequences of early parenting experiences: Self-recognition and self-regulation in three cultural communities. *Child Development, 75,* 1745–1760. https://doi.org/10.1111/j.1467-8624.2004.00814.x.

Köster, M., Cavalcante, L., Cruz de Carvalho, R., Dôgo Resende, B., & Kärtner, J. (2016). Cultural influences on toddlers' prosocial behavior: How maternal task assignment relates to helping others. *Child Development, 87,* 1727–1738. https://doi.org/10.1111/cdev.12636PMID:28262931.

Köster, M., Schuhmacher, N., & Kärtner, J. (2015). A cultural perspective on prosocial development. *Human Ethology Bulletin, 30,* 71–82.

Laible, D., & Karahuta, E. (2014). Prosocial behaviors in early childhood: Helping others, responding to the distress of others, and working with others. In L. M. Padilla-Walker & G. Carlo (Eds.), *Prosocial development: A multidimensional approach* (pp. 350–373). New York: Oxford University Press.

Lancy, D. F. (2018). *Anthropological perspectives on children as helpers, workers, artisans, and laborers.* New York: Palgrave Macmillan.

Legare, C. H., & Nielsen, M. (2015). Imitation and innovation: The dual engines of cultural learning. *Threads in Cognitive Sciences, 19,* 688–699. https://doi.org/10.1016/j.tics.2015.08.005.

Miller, J. G., & Bersoff, D. M. (1994). Cultural influences on the moral status of reciprocity and the discounting of endogenous motivation. *Personality and Social Psychology Bulletin, 20,* 592–602. https://doi.org/10.1177/0146167294205015.

Mussen, P., & Eisenberg-Berg, N. (1977). *Roots of caring, sharing, and helping: The development of pro-social behavior in children.* Oxford, England: W. H. Freeman.

Nag, M., White, B. N. F., Peet, R. C., Bardhan, A., Hull, T. H., Johnson, A., et al. (1978). An anthropological approach to the study of the economic value of children in Java and Nepal [and comments and reply]. *Current Anthropology, 19,* 293–306. https://dx.doi.org/10.1086/202076.

Padilla-Walker, L. M., & Carlo, G. (2014). The study of prosocial behavior: Past, present, and future. In L. M. Padilla-Walker & G. Carlo (Eds.), *Prosocial development: A multidimensional approach* (pp. 350–373). New York: Oxford University Press.

Paulus, M. (2014). The emergence of prosocial behavior: Why do infants and toddlers help, comfort, and share? *Child Development Perspectives, 8,* 77–81. https://dx.doi.org/10.1111cdep.12066.

Radke Yarrow, M., Zahn Wexler, C., Barrett, D., Darby, J., King, R., Pickett, M., et al. (1976). Dimensions and correlates of prosocial behavior in young children. *Child Development, 47,* 118–125. https://doi.org/10.2307/1128290.

Radke-Yarrow, M., Zahn-Wexler, C., & Chapman, M. (1983). Children's prosocial disposition and behavior. In P. H. Mussen (Ed.), *Carmichael's manual of child psychology* (Vol. 4, pp. 469–546). New York: Wiley.

Rheingold, H. L. (1982). Little children's participation in the work of adults, a nascent prosocial behavior. *Child Development, 53*(1), 114–125. https://doi.org/10.2307/1129643.

Rogoff, B., Najafi, B., & Mejía-Arauz, R. (2014). Constellations of cultural practices across generations: Indigenous American heritage and learning by observing and pitching in. *Human Development, 57,* 82–95. https://dx.doi.org/10.1159/000356761.

Sebanc, A. M., Pierce, S. L., Cheatham, C. L., & Gunnar, M. R. (2003). Gendered social worlds in preschool: Dominance, peer acceptance, and assertive social skills in boys' and girls' peer groups. *Social Development, 12,* 91–106. https://doi.org/10.1111/1467-9507.00223.

Svetlova, M., Nichols, S. R., & Brownell, C. A. (2010). Toddlers' prosocial behavior: From instrumental to empathic to altruistic helping. *Child Development, 81,* 1814–1827. https://doi.org/10.1111/j.1467-8624.2010.01512.x.

Tisak, M. S., Holub, S. C., & Tisak, J. (2007). What nice things do boys and girls do? Preschoolers' perspectives of peers' behaviors at school and at home. *Early Education and Development, 18,* 183–199. https://doi.org/10.1080/10409280701282686.

Warneken, F. (2016). Insights into biological foundation of human altruistic sentiments. *Current Opinion in Psychology, 7,* 51–56. https://doi.org/10.1016/j.copsyc.2015.07.013.

Warneken, F., & Tomasello, M. (2007). Helping and cooperation at 14 months of age. *Infancy, 11*, 271–294. https://doi.org/10.1111/j.1532-7078.2007.tb00227.x.

Warneken, F., & Tomasello, M. (2008). Extrinsic rewards undermine altruistic tendencies in 20-month-olds. *Developmental Psychology, 44*, 1785–1788. https://doi.org/10.1037/a0013860.

Warneken, F., & Tomasello, M. (2009). Varieties of altruism in children and chimpanzees. *Trends in Cognitive Science, 13*, 307–402. https://doi.org/10.1016/j.tics.2009.06.008.

Warneken, F., & Tomasello, M. (2013). The emergence of contingent reciprocity in young children. *Journal of Experimental Child Psychology, 116*, 338–350. https://doi.org/10.1016/j.jcep.2013.06.002.

Weisner, T. S., Gallimore, R., Bacon, M. K., Barry, H., Bell, C., Caiuby Novaes, S., et al. (1977). My brother's keeper: Child and sibling caretaking [and comments and reply]. *Current Anthropology, 18*, 169–190. https://doi.org/10.1086/201883.

Wellman, H. M., Cross, D., & Watson, J. (2001). Meta-analysis of theory-of-mind development: The truth about false belief. *Child Development, 72*, 655–684. https://doi.org/10.1111/1467-8624.00304.

Whiting, B. B. (1963). *Six cultures: Studies of child rearing*. Oxford, England: Wiley.

Whiting, B. B. (1983). The genesis of prosocial behavior. In D. L. Bridgeman (Ed.), *The nature of prosocial development: Interdisciplinary theories and strategies* (pp. 221–242). New York: Academic Press.

Wu, W., & Su, Y. (2014). How do preschoolers' sharing behaviors relate to their theory of mind understanding? *Journal of Experimental Child Psychology, 120*, 73–86. https://doi.org/10.1016/j.jecp.2013.11.007.

Zahn-Waxler, C., & Smith, K. D. (1992). The development of prosocial behavior. In V. B. Van Hasselt & M. Hersen (Eds.), *Perspectives in developmental psychology: Handbook of social development: A lifespan perspective* (pp. 229–256). New York: Plenum Press.

Chapter 8
Peer Interactions: Culture and Peer Conflict During Preschool Years

Anni Tamm

Abstract Early peer conflict has received much research attention in developmental psychology, but cross-cultural research is still scarce. This chapter reviews some of the existing studies to explore to what degree early peer interactions during conflicts reflect cultural values. The chapter is divided into four subsections: (1) overview of the theoretical perspectives suggesting cultural differences in early peer conflict, (2) methodological issues that somewhat limit the comparability of cross-cultural studies, (3) cultural similarities and differences in preschool children's conflicts and their managements, and (4) main conclusions and future directions. The reviewed studies show that early peer interactions during conflicts do reflect dominant cultural values. Cultural differences in the way children resolve conflicts with peers tend to be most emphasized. More specifically, cultural values shape the way children balance autonomy and relatedness during peer conflicts. These differences are observable as early as among 3-year-old children. There is less evidence about cultural differences in other aspects of preschool children's peer conflicts. More research is needed to examine cultural differences in outcomes of conflicts, their intensity, reconciliation, third-party interventions, and in preschool children's perceptions of conflicts.

The chapter discusses the role of culture in the nature of peer conflict during preschool. Conflict is generally defined in terms of incompatible behaviors or goals: one person overtly expresses his/her opposition to another person's statements or goals (Laursen and Hafen 2010; Shantz 1987). Sometimes the term conflict has been used as a synonym to aggression. Aggression, however, involves acts that harm another person. As Shantz (1987) points out, aggressive behavior does usually involve conflict, but the converse is not true: conflicts often do not involve aggression. Making this distinction between conflict and aggression enables us to also acknowledge the positive aspects of conflicts. According to Piaget (1932), peer conflict has a unique role in children's socio-cognitive development. Compared with parent-child relations, peers are more equal in terms of power—they share similar level of knowledge and experience. Children thus have many opportunities to negotiate and practice com-

A. Tamm (✉)
Department of Psychology, University of Tartu, Näituse 2, Tartu 50409, Estonia
e-mail: anni.tamm@ut.ee

© Springer Nature Switzerland AG 2019
T. Tulviste et al. (eds.), *Children's Social Worlds in Cultural Context*,
https://doi.org/10.1007/978-3-030-27033-9_8

promise in the peer context, and this facilitates the development of cognitive skills (Ames and Murray 1982; Piaget 1932), emotional understanding (Kramer 2014), and morality and autonomy (Killen and Nucci 1999; Ross et al. 1990). More generally, conflict management affects, but also reflects children's social competence, social and psychological adjustment, and the quality of interpersonal relationships. Much research has been conducted to understand early peer conflict from a developmental perspective. Yet, cross-cultural research is still scarce. This chapter reviews some of the existing studies to explore to what degree early peer interactions during conflicts reflect cultural values. Do children from different cultures deal with the tension stemming from balancing autonomy and relatedness during conflicts differently? At what age are cultural differences observable?

The chapter is divided into four subsections: (1) overview of the theoretical perspectives suggesting cultural differences in early peer conflict, (2) methodological issues that somewhat limit the comparability of cross-cultural studies, (3) cultural similarities and differences in preschool children's conflicts and their managements, and (4) main conclusions and future directions.

Autonomy and Relatedness Values Shape Peer Interactions

Culture can be defined as "a socially interactive process of construction comprising two main components: shared activity (cultural practices) and shared meaning (cultural interpretation)" (Greenfield et al. 2003, p. 462). Culture organizes children's developmental environments and shapes their values, expectations, behaviors, and interactions and relationships with other people (Super and Harkness 2002). In diverse sociocultural contexts, autonomy (i.e., volitional agency) and relatedness (i.e., connectedness to others) are considered universal developmental needs, but the relative emphasis put on these dimensions in children's socialization varies according to what values and beliefs are more adaptive in the particular sociocultural environment (Chirkov and Ryan 2001; Greenfield et al. 2003; Kagitçibaşi 2013; Rothbaum and Trommsdorff 2007). Parents need to find a balance between promoting autonomy and relatedness in their children (Greenfield et al. 2003; Kagitçibaşi 2013). Drawing upon Kagitçibaşi's family change theory (1996, 2013), we can distinguish among three models: (1) The model of interdependence, in which relatedness, conformity, and obedience are socialized in children, that is prevalent in many nonwestern, rural agrarian and urban low-income societies oriented to collectivistic values; (2) the model of independence, in which autonomy, self-enhancement, and self-maximization are of high importance in children's socialization, that is prevalent in many western, urban industrial societies oriented to individualistic values; and (3) the synthesis of the two previous models—an autonomy-relatedness model—in which both autonomy and relatedness are valued, that is common in urban, relatively wealthy societies oriented to both individualistic and collectivistic values.

Also relevant here is the theory of independent and interdependent self-construals (Markus and Kitayama 1991) that helps to explain cultural differences in the way children relate to each other and form relationships. In many western cultures, independent self-construal is promoted in children—children learn to define themselves mainly through their inner attributes and characteristics. In many nonwestern cultures, interdependent self-construal is prevalent—children learn to define themselves mainly through their relationships, and their behavior is more strongly influenced by others.

Conflict resolution skills are an important part of children's social competence and acquiring this competence is crucial in various cultures for developing and maintaining relationships with peers and others (Chen and French 2008). There are, however, cultural differences in the meaning of social competence (Chen and French 2008). In many western autonomy-oriented cultures, characteristics like self-assertiveness and social initiative are viewed as indicators of social competence. In many nonwestern relatedness-oriented cultures, self-regulation and attending to others' needs are valued more highly.

Balancing autonomy and relatedness, more specifically self and other interests, is a critical aspect of conflict resolution. It is especially challenging for preschoolers whose perspective taking skills and abilities to coordinate different perspectives and goals are still developing. Children in diverse cultural contexts experience conflicts with peers (French et al. 2005; Martínez-Lozano et al. 2011; Rourou et al. 2006), but these experiences are likely to differ largely as a function of the degree to which orientation-to-personal and orientation-to-group interests are promoted by socialization agents, such as parents and teachers. Emphasis put on autonomy and relatedness is likely to affect the way children address conflicts—their tolerance of overt conflict, their strategies of resolution and reconciliation of conflicts (Chen and French 2008).

Although researchers have not always made it explicit, autonomy and relatedness orientations can be seen as the basis of most categorizations of conflict resolution strategies. For example, Singer et al. (2012) distinguished between unilateral (oriented to individual interests) and bilateral strategies (oriented to individual and others' interests simultaneously). In another study, children's conflict resolution strategies were classified into five categories (dominating, integrating, compromising, obliging, and avoiding) based on two dimensions: concern for the self and concern for the other (Maruyama et al. 2015). Laursen et al. (2001) reviewed the relevant literature and concluded that there are three main strategies: negotiation (mutual interests are taken into account), coercion (focus only on individual interest), and disengagement (leave conflict unresolved). Research in this field thus largely deals with the question of to what degree children are oriented to only their individual interests and to what degree they also attend to others' interests.

Methodological Issues in Studies on Early Peer Conflict

Conflict is a complex phenomenon. While the main focus in this chapter is on the role of culture in preschool children's conflicts, we cannot overlook other factors that are known to significantly influence conflicts and their management. As there are still rather few cross-cultural studies on preschool children's conflicts, the variation in other factors and different methodological decisions made by different researchers makes it somewhat difficult to compare the findings of cross-cultural studies. Some of these issues are outlined below and discussed further in the next section.

Definition of Conflict

There are a couple of issues related to the definition of conflict. One that was already mentioned in the beginning of this chapter is whether conflict is differentiated from aggression or not. It is problematic that there are cross-cultural studies that have not provided a definition of conflict. In many studies, where the definition is given, conflict is explicitly defined in terms of opposition and thus not equated with aggression. For example, conflict has been defined as *"an interactional event, which follows after an opposition to a request, a remark, or an action, and ends with a resolution."* (Martínez-Lozano et al. 2011, p. 897). In some studies, however, conflict has not been clearly distinguished from aggression and defined, for example, as *"any act directed toward another child which involved treating the other child in an inconsiderate, aggressive, or destructive manner."* (Orlick et al. 1990, p. 22). When interpreting and comparing research findings, the definition of conflict must be taken into account. Moreover, especially in observational studies, the results can be somewhat different depending on whether a two-turn (opposition from one child is needed) or three-turn criterion (opposition from both parties is needed) is used to identify conflicts (Hartup et al. 1988).

Real or Hypothetical Conflicts

In general, data collection methods vary less in studies done among preschool children than in studies conducted with older samples. Observation has been frequently used for assessing preschool children's conflicts in diverse cultures. Some researchers have also used hypothetical conflict scenarios and asked children to finish vignette stories. It has been claimed that with hypothetical conflicts one can examine how children think about conflicts, while by observing real conflicts one can examine how children actually resolve conflicts (Rubin and Krasnor 1992). Research evidence suggests that differences between responses to real and hypothetical conflicts are larger in preschool than in older samples (Laursen et al. 2001). However, how children think and how they act are both important to examine and by combining different methods we get richer data about how children address conflicts.

Situational Factors

The nature of children's conflicts and their resolution is dependent on many situational factors (Laursen et al. 2001; Tamm et al. 2014; Thornberg 2006; Walker et al. 2002) and this makes cross-cultural comparison more challenging. The following often varies in different studies:

- Which conflicts are assessed—object-related or social conflicts?
- In which setting are children observed—open-field or closed-field, during structured activities or free play?
- Between whom are conflicts observed or described to children (in case of hypothetical conflicts)—same sex and age peers or in mixed age and sex groups? Between friends or non-friends?

Children's Age

It is well established that with age conflict management strategies improve along with social cognitive abilities (Dunn and Herrera 1997; Hu et al. 2010; Piaget 1932). Some cross-cultural studies have included 2–7-year-olds in their sample and some have focused on a narrower age range. Significant differences occur between younger and older preschool children in conflict resolution (Chen et al. 2001).

The Role of Culture in Early Peer Conflict

Children's conflicts can mainly be described by their incidence and duration, the conflict issue, strategies that parties use, and outcomes (Shantz 1987). Although theoretical perspectives suggest cultural differences in all of these aspects, most cross-cultural studies tend to focus only on children's conflict resolution strategies. Comparisons are typically made between cultures that are oriented toward values related to independence and autonomy and cultures that consider collective goals and relatedness highly important. Researchers have, however, also started to pay more attention to similarities and differences between cultures that in some other studies are grouped under the same category (e.g., Western Europe or Asian countries). In this chapter, cultural similarities and differences in preschool children's conflicts and their resolution are illustrated through examining (1) a comparison of North American countries and East Asian countries, (2) East Asian countries, (3) Middle East countries, and (4) Western and Southwestern Europe countries.

North America and East Asia

Comparisons between North American and East Asian countries are most popular in psychological literature as they are thought to represent very different types of cultures. North America is characterized by lower interdependence between individuals than East Asia (Hofstede 2001). In the U.S. and Canada, independent self-construal is prevalent and autonomy and independence are promoted in children (Markus and Kitayama 1991; Suizzo et al. 2008; Trommsdorff 2012). In China and Japan, interdependent self-construal is prevalent and collective goals and relatedness are given priority (Georgas et al. 2001; Markus and Kitayama 1991; Trommsdorff 2012). Are those differences reflected in preschool children's conflict resolution strategies? The four cross-cultural studies reviewed (Chen and Rubin 1992; Kyratzis and Guo 2001; Orlick et al. 1990; Zahn-Waxler et al. 1996) do not provide a simple answer.

Orlick et al. (1990) observed that Chinese 5-year-olds engaged in cooperation (i.e., helping and sharing) more frequently and in conflict behavior (defined as inconsiderate, aggressive, or destructive behavior) less frequently than their Canadian peers. Another study indicated that compared with 4–6-year-old Japanese children, U.S. children showed more anger and suggested more coercive strategies as a resolution to various hypothetical conflicts (Zahn-Waxler et al. 1996). These findings are in accordance with the above-mentioned differences in cultural values. The authors of both studies point out the cultural differences in children's socialization. In Chinese and Japanese cultures, children are socialized to be considerate, interdependent, and maintain harmony with others. Parents promote children's self-regulation skills that, in turn, support children in behaving in accordance with the society's rules, norms, and expectations (Trommsdorff 2012). Japanese mothers have found to be disappointed when their children's behavior does not meet the society's standards and they draw children's attention to the consequences of hurting others more frequently than do U.S. mothers (Zahn-Waxler et al. 1996). In U.S., coercive behavior is also discouraged but at the same time, it is more often tolerated due to high emphasis being placed on self-oriented values. Many observational studies conducted among U.S. preschool children show that although negotiation is used, coercive strategies are also fairly frequent and many conflicts end in one child's withdrawal or yielding (Chen et al. 2001; O'Brien et al. 1999; Rourke et al. 1999; Spivak 2016).

There are somewhat contradictory findings as well. Namely, while 6-year-old children in Canada and China most frequently suggested prosocial strategies to hypothetical conflicts over resources, Chinese children suggested these strategies less frequently and coercive strategies more frequently than Canadian children (Chen and Rubin 1992). Furthermore, in same-sex groups, 3–4-year-old U.S. boys and Chinese girls used coercive strategies more frequently than U.S. girls and Chinese boys (Kyratzis and Guo 2001). These findings show the complex interplay of various factors that affect children's conflicts. For example, it might be questioned whether Canadian and Chinese children in Chen and Rubin's (1992) study interpreted the hypothetical scenarios similarly and whether object-related conflicts are equally common in both cultural contexts. Many studies show that among U.S.

preschool children, conflicts over resources are more frequent than other types of conflicts (Chen et al. 2001; O'Brien et al. 1999; Rourke et al. 1999). There is some indication though, with other cultures, that conflicts over objects are less frequent in cultures that consider other-oriented values highly important (Martínez-Lozano et al. 2011). Additionally, children's behavior might differ in same-sex and mixed-sex groups. Kyratzis and Guo (2001) point out the different gender roles in the U.S. and China stemming from cultural values and independent versus interdependent self-construal. They also suggest that these gender roles are especially evident in same-sex peer groups and help to clarify the differences between U.S. and Chinese children's conflict resolution strategies.

One can conclude that differences in conflict resolution strategies between children from North American and East Asian countries are already observable in early preschool years. These differences are, however, to some degree situation-specific. Conclusions derived from hypothetical conflicts should not be generalized to real conflicts, from one type of conflict to another, or from same-sex conflict interactions to mixed-sex interactions.

East Asia

Maruyama et al. (2015) compared conflict resolution strategies of children from China, Japan, and South Korea. As the authors point out, the three countries tend to be seen as rather similar and little attention has been paid to examining differences between them. When using the Hofstede's (2001) measure of cultural dimensions, Japan, China, and South Korea are indeed similarly low in individualism. Maintaining harmony in the group and accommodating to social rules and others' expectations are of high importance in all three cultural contexts (Trommsdorff 2012).

The researchers presented hypothetical conflicts about differing opinions and distribution of resources to 3–6-year-olds whose task was to continue the stories (Maruyama et al. 2015). The findings show that cultural similarities and differences are tied to situational factors. In conflicts over different opinions, 3–year-olds from the three countries were similar in preferring coercive, rather self-oriented, strategies. In conflicts over resources—type of conflicts that seem to trigger the use of more coercive strategies from U.S. children—3–5-year-old Chinese and Japanese children tended to suggest strategies that indicate concern for both parties' interests. South Korean children suggested a wider array of strategies and none of them could be said to be prevalent.

This study points out another methodological factor that can affect the results. Namely, researchers use very different categorizations of children's conflict resolution strategies. Obviously, the results can differ depending on whether there are three broad categories (e.g., negotiation, coercion, and withdrawal) or ten narrower categories (e.g., distinguish between compromise and negotiation or between verbal and physical aggression). Maruyama et al. (2015) distinguished between compromise and integration—intermediate concern for self and other versus high concern for self and other—that more often are seen as belonging to the same category. As a result, however, the researchers were able to detect differences between Chinese, Japanese, and South Korean children's strategies that would probably not have been noticed with broader categories.

Middle East

Feldman et al. (2010) compared Israeli and Palestinian children's conflict resolution strategies in parent-child and peer conflicts. Previous studies had pointed out many similarities as well as differences between the two cultures (Feldman and Masalla 2007; Kagitçibaşi et al. 2010; Seginer et al. 2007). Israeli and Palestinian families are similar in considering values related to interdependence important. Palestinian parents are, however, more traditional in their socialization goals and family relationships than Israeli parents. It has been suggested that Israeli parents follow the model of autonomy-relatedness: they rate socialization goals like self-expression, creativity, and assertiveness highly (Ben-Arieh et al. 2006; Feldman and Masalla 2007; Kagitçibaşi et al. 2010). Palestinian parents follow the model of interdependence: they use more behavioral control and consider family cohesion, compliance, and collective goals as more important (Ben-Arieh et al. 2006; Feldman and Masalla 2007; Kagitçibaşi et al. 2010).

In conflicts with peers, 3-year-old Israeli children used compromise more frequently and turned to adults less frequently than their Palestinian peers (Feldman et al. 2010). The authors see these findings being consistent with the cultural values and socialization practices in the respective cultures. Namely, Israeli children are taught to be self-sufficient and to manage interpersonal conflicts (Feldman et al. 2010). In Palestinian children's socialization, higher emphasis is put on dependence on others and compliance with authority figures (Feldman et al. 2010).

Western and Southwestern Europe

Studies have compared conflict issues and resolution strategies among Dutch and Andalusian children (Martínez-Lozano et al. 2011; Sánchez-Medina et al. 2001). Dutch families have been found to follow the model of independence where self-oriented values are emphasized (Georgas et al. 2001; Mayer 2013). In Andalusia, interdependence in the family is high and in addition to emotional support, family members are expected to provide economic support that is characteristic of the model of interdependence (Kagitçibaşi 2013; Tobio and Cordón 2013).

Dutch children, ages 4–6 years, have been found to experience many conflicts over objects and to resolve conflicts by using directives more frequently than their Andalusian peers (Martínez-Lozano et al. 2011; Sánchez-Medina et al. 2001). Andalusian children were more likely than Dutch children to be involved in conflicts over social behavior (Martínez-Lozano et al. 2011; Sánchez-Medina et al. 2001). They also more often used negotiation to reach an agreement and tended to maintain the social interaction after the conflict. As explained earlier in this chapter, conflict situations require children to find a balance between autonomy and relatedness. Dutch and Andalusian children seem to resolve this tension differently (Sánchez-Medina et al. 2001). Andalusian children try to coordinate different interests for the benefit of the group. Dutch children are more oriented to their individual interests in peer interactions and see more value in achieving their goals than continuing social interactions.

Studies comparing children's conflict resolution and adult intervention among native Dutch and those with Moroccan and Antillean backgrounds in the Netherlands provide further insight into the role of culture in shaping children's peer interactions. Observations conducted in Dutch preschools showed that 2–3-year-old native Dutch, Moroccan, and Antillean children experienced conflicts with similar frequency and resolved these conflicts by using similar strategies (Rourou et al. 2006). Moreover, native Dutch, Moroccan, and Antillean kindergarten teachers had similar daycare-specific child-rearing beliefs, including how to intervene in children's conflicts despite having somewhat different general child-care beliefs (Huijbregts et al. 2008). It thus seems that along with one's family cultural background, the larger sociocultural context has a strong influence on socialization of children. Parents and teachers are likely to socialize children toward these broader cultural values and characteristics that will be desirable in their particular cultural setting (Tam and Lee 2010).

Conclusions

The reviewed studies show that early peer interactions during conflicts do reflect dominant cultural values. Cultural differences in the way children resolve conflicts with peers are apparent in how they think about conflicts as well as how they resolve them. Children in diverse cultural contexts use a wide array of conflict resolution strategies—they can be seen asserting their autonomy as well as being oriented to relationship maintenance and conflict avoidance. However, cultural values do shape the way children balance autonomy and relatedness during peer conflicts. In cultures in which autonomy, self-enhancement, and self-maximization are promoted in children, preschool-aged children can often be seen being mainly oriented to maintaining their autonomy and achieving personal goals during peer conflicts. In cultures in which conformity, obedience, and relatedness and harmony in relationships are stressed in children's socialization, children are more likely to be oriented to maintaining relatedness with their peers in conflict situations and to subordinate their personal goals to group goals. Based on the reviewed studies, these differences are observable among 3-year-old and older children. It is yet to be determined whether we can see such cultural differences in even younger children.

There is less evidence about cultural differences in other aspects of preschool children's peer conflicts. When generalizing the findings of some previous studies (Martínez-Lozano et al. 2011; Maruyama et al. 2015; Sánchez-Medina et al. 2001), it might be suggested that object-related conflicts occur more frequently between preschool children in autonomy-oriented cultures and trigger more coercive responses by its participants. In relatedness-oriented cultures, social conflicts (i.e., about social behavior and decision-making) may be more common and may be the type of conflict in which preschool children use more coercion. A question has also been posed about whether conflicts in autonomy-oriented cultures are more frequently experienced in dyads rather than in larger groups (Tamm et al. 2014). More research is needed to test these hypotheses as well as to examine cultural differences in the outcomes of conflicts, their intensity, reconciliation, third-party interventions, and in preschool children's perception of conflicts. Drawing upon the autonomy-relatedness framework, it would be logical to assume that children are socialized to think about conflicts in different ways. They might be socialized to consider conflict primarily as a threat to their autonomy or as a threat to relationship. From a slightly different point of view, there could be cultural differences in whether conflicts are seen as moral issues or as social-conventional issues (e.g., Tulviste and Koor 2005).

More research that includes a larger number of different cultures is needed to better understand cultural influences on preschool children's experiences with peer conflict and how culture interacts with various situational factors in affecting children's responses to conflict. Studies comparing cultures typically seen as highly similar in terms of cultural values could potentially provide an even more nuanced understanding of these issues.

Acknowledgements The writing of this chapter was supported by the Estonian Research Council (grant no. PUT1359).

References

Ames, G. J., & Murray, F. B. (1982). When two wrongs make a right: Promoting cognitive change by social conflict. *Developmental Psychology, 18*(6), 894–897.

Ben-Arieh, A., Khooury-Kassabri, M., & Haj-Yahia, M. M. (2006). Generational, ethnic, and national differences in attitudes toward the rights of children in Israel and Palestine. *American Journal of Orthopsychiatry, 76,* 381–388.

Chen, D. W., Fein, G. G., Killen, M., & Tam, H. P. (2001). Peer conflicts of preschool children: Issues, resolution, incidence, and age-related patterns. *Early Education and Development, 12*(4), 523–544.

Chen, X., & French, D. C. (2008). Children's social competence in cultural context. *Annual Review of Psychology, 59,* 591–616.

Chen, X., & Rubin, K. H. (1992). Correlates of peer acceptance in a Chinese sample of six-year-olds. *International Journal of Behavioral Development, 15*(2), 259–273.

Chirkov, V. I., & Ryan, R. M. (2001). Parent and teacher autonomy-support in Russian and U.S. adolescents: Common effects on well-being and academic motivation. *Journal of Cross-Cultural Psychology, 32,* 618–635.

Dunn, J., & Herrera, C. (1997). Conflict resolution with friends, siblings, and mothers: A developmental perspective. *Aggressive Behavior, 23*, 343–357.

Feldman, R., & Masalha, S. (2007). The role of culture in moderating the links between early ecological risk and young children's adaptation. *Development and Psychopathology, 19*, 1–21.

Feldman, R., Masalha, S., & Derdikman-Eiron, R. (2010). Conflict resolution in the parent–child, marital, and peer contexts and children's aggression in the peer group: A process-oriented cultural perspective. *Developmental Psychology, 46*(2), 310–325.

French, D. C., Pidada, S., Denoma, J., McDonald, K., & Lawton, A. (2005). Reported peer conflicts of children in the United States and Indonesia. *Social Development, 14*(3), 458–472.

Georgas, J., Mylonas, K., Bafiti, T., Poortinga, Y. H., Christakopoulou, S., Kagitcibasi, C., et al. (2001). Functional relationships in the nuclear and extended family: A 16-culture study. *International Journal of Psychology, 36*(5), 289–300.

Greenfield, P. M., Keller, H., Fuligni, A., & Maynard, A. E. (2003). Cultural pathways through universal development. *Annual Review of Psychology, 54*, 461–490.

Hartup, W. W., Laursen, B., Stewart, M. I., & Eastenson, A. (1988). Conflict and the friendship relations of young children. *Child Development, 59*, 1590–1600.

Hofstede, G. (2001). *Culture's consequences: Comparing values, behaviors, institutions, and organizations across nations.* Thousand Oaks, CA: Sage.

Hu, Z., Chan, R. C., & McAlonan, G. M. (2010). Maturation of social attribution skills in typically developing children: An investigation using the social attribution task. *Behavioral and Brain Functions, 6*, 1–8.

Huijbregts, S. K., Leseman, P. P., & Tavecchio, L. W. (2008). Cultural diversity in center-based childcare: Childrearing beliefs of professional caregivers from different cultural communities in the Netherlands. *Early Childhood Research Quarterly, 23*(2), 233–244.

Kagitçibaşi, Ç. (1996). *Family and human development across cultures.* Mahwah, NJ: Lawrence Erlbaum.

Kagitçibaşi, Ç. (2013). Adolescent autonomy-relatedness and the family in cultural context: What is optimal? *Journal of Research on Adolescence, 23*, 223–235.

Kagitcibasi, C., Ataca, B., & Diri, A. (2010). Intergenerational relationships in the family: Ethnic, socioeconomic, and country variations in Germany, Israel, Palestine, and Turkey. *Journal of Cross-Cultural Psychology, 41*(5–6), 652–670.

Killen, M., & Nucci, L. P. (1999). Morality, autonomy, and social conflict. In M. Killen & D. Hart (Eds.), *Morality in everyday life: Developmental perspectives* (pp. 52–86). Cambridge: Cambridge University Press.

Kramer, L. (2014). Learning emotional understanding and emotion regulation through sibling interaction. *Early Education and Development, 25*(2), 160–184.

Kyratzis, A., & Guo, J. (2001). Preschool girls' and boys' verbal conflict strategies in the United States and China. *Research on Language and Social Interaction, 34*(1), 45–74.

Laursen, B., Finkelstein, B. D., & Betts, N. T. (2001). A developmental meta-analysis of peer conflict resolution. *Developmental Review, 21*(4), 423–449.

Laursen, B., & Hafen, C. A. (2010). Future directions in the study of close relationships: Conflict is bad (except when it's not). *Social Development, 19*, 858–872.

Markus, H. R., & Kitayama, S. (1991). Culture and the self: Implications for cognition, emotion, and motivation. *Psychological Review, 98*, 224–253.

Martínez-Lozano, V., Sánchez-Medina, J. A., & Goudena, P. P. (2011). A cross-cultural study of observed conflicts between young children. *Journal of Cross-Cultural Psychology, 42*(6), 895–907.

Maruyama, H., Ujiie, T., Takai, J., Takahama, Y., Sakagami, H., Shibayama, M., et al. (2015). Cultural difference in conflict management strategies of children and its development: Comparing 3-and 5-year-olds across China, Japan, and Korea. *Early Education and Development, 26*(8), 1210–1233.

Mayer, B. (2013). Family change theory: A preliminary evaluation on the basis of recent cross-cultural studies. In I. Albert & D. Ferring (Eds.), *Intergenerational relations: European perspectives on family and society* (pp. 167–187). Cambridge: Policy Press.

O'Brien, M., Roy, C., Jacobs, A., Macaluso, M., & Peyton, V. (1999). Conflict in the dyadic play of 3-year-old children. *Early Education and Development, 10*(3), 289–313.

Orlick, T., Zhou, Q. Y., & Partington, J. (1990). Co-operation and conflict within Chinese and Canadian kindergarten settings. *Canadian Journal of Behavioural Science, 22*(1), 20–25.

Piaget, J. (1932). *The moral judgement of the child.* London: Routledge & Kegan Paul.

Ross, H., Tesla, C., Kenyon, B., & Lollis, S. (1990). Maternal intervention in toddler peer conflict: The socialization of principles of justice. *Developmental Psychology, 26*(6), 994–1003.

Rothbaum, F., & Trommsdorff, G. (2007). Do roots and wings complement or oppose one another? The socialization of relatedness and autonomy in cultural context. In J. E. Grusec & P. D. Hastings (Eds.), *Handbook of socialization: Theory and research* (pp. 461–489). New York, NY, US: Guilford Press.

Rourke, M. T., Wozniak, R. H., & Wright Cassidy, K. (1999). The social sensitivity of preschoolers in peer conflicts: Do children act differently with different peers? *Early Education and Development, 10*(2), 209–227.

Rourou, A., Singer, E., Bekkema, N., & De Haan, D. (2006). Cultural perspectives on peer conflicts in multicultural Dutch child care centres. *European Early Childhood Education Research Journal, 14*(2), 35–53.

Rubin, K. H., & Krasnor, L. R. (1992). Interpersonal problem-solving and social competence in children. In V. B. Hasselt & M. Hersen (Eds.), *Handbook of social development: A lifespan perspective* (pp. 283–323). New York: Plenum.

Sánchez-Medina, J. A., Martínez-Lozano, V., & Goudena, P. P. (2001). Conflict management in pre-schoolers: A cross-cultural perspective La Gestion des Conflits chez les Enfants d'Aˆge Preˊ scolaire: Une perspective interculturelle Gestioˊ n de Conflictos en los Preescolares: Una perspectiva inter-cultural. *International Journal of Early Years Education, 9*(2), 153–160.

Seginer, R., Shoyer, S., Hossessi, R., & Tannous, H. (2007). Adolescent family and peer relationships: Does culture matter? *New Directions for Child and Adolescent Development, 116,* 83–99.

Shantz, C. U. (1987). Conflicts between children. *Child Development, 58,* 283–305.

Singer, E., Van Hoogdalem, A. G., De Haan, D., & Bekkema, N. (2012). Day care experiences and the development of conflict strategies in young children. *Early Child Development and Care, 182,* 1661–1672.

Spivak, A. L. (2016). Dynamics of young children's socially adaptive resolutions of peer conflict. *Social Development, 25*(1), 212–231.

Suizzo, M. A., Chen, W. C., Cheng, C. C., Liang, A. S., Contreras, H., Zanger, D., et al. (2008). Parental beliefs about young children's socialization across US ethnic groups: Coexistence of independence and interdependence. *Early Child Development and Care, 178*(5), 467–486.

Super, C. M., & Harkness, S. (2002). Culture structures the environment for development. *Human Development, 45*(4), 270–274.

Tam, K. P., & Lee, S. L. (2010). What values do parents want to socialize in their children? The role of perceived normative values. *Journal of Cross-Cultural Psychology, 41,* 175–181.

Tamm, A., Tõugu, P., & Tulviste, T. (2014). The influence of individual and situational factors on children's choice of a conflict management strategy. *Early Education & Development, 25*(1), 93–109.

Thornberg, R. (2006). The situated nature of preschool children's conflict strategies. *Educational Psychology, 26,* 109–126.

Tobío, C., & Cordón, J. A. F. (2013). Family networks in Andalusia, Spain. *International Review of Sociology, 23*(1), 68–84.

Trommsdorff, G. (2012). Development of "agentic" regulation in cultural context: The role of self and world views. *Child Development Perspectives, 6*(1), 19–26.

Tulviste, T., & Koor, M. (2005). "Hands off the car, it's mine!" and "The teacher will be angry if we don't play nicely": Gender-related preferences in the use of moral rules and social conventions in preschoolers' dyadic play. *Sex Roles, 53*(1–2), 57–66.

Walker, S., Irving, K. A., & Berthelsen, D. C. (2002). Gender influences on preschool children's social problem-solving strategies. *Journal of Genetic Psychology, 163,* 197–210.

Zahn-Waxler, C., Friedman, R. J., Cole, P. M., Mizuta, I., & Hiruma, N. (1996). Japanese and United States preschool children's responses to conflict and distress. *Child Development, 67*(5), 2462–2477.

Chapter 9
Together or Better Singular? German Middle Class Children's Problem Solving in Dyads and Triads

Heidi Keller, Swantje Decker and Paula Döge

Abstract Socialization strategies in German middle class families focus on psychological autonomy with a special emphasis on individuality and the inner world. Small children experience mainly dyadic communication structures. It can be assumed that these experiences affect their cooperative behavior with other children. In a structured observational situation, we observed that triads of 4–5 years old German children do solve a cooperation task less than 10% of the time, despite the explicit instruction to do so. Only one of 20 triads worked predominantly triadically. Most of the children worked in an isolated mode. Children in a comparison group of dyads acted at least half of the time dyadically. Cooperation seems to be easier for children in dyads compared to triads. The results highlight consequences of cultural practices that may not be intended.

Cooperation is a basic human capacity. It is generally assumed that cooperation is part of human sociality that evolved during the history of human kind. The reference to evolution dates back to Charles Darwin who had observed that most animals form social groups in which individuals cooperate. He tried to explain the seeming contradiction between cooperation and the aim for individual fitness with several proposals (Darwin 1871): one proposal was that natural selection could have supported altruistic behavior among kin, the later principle of inclusive fitness (Hamilton 1964), another proposal was the principle of reciprocity, indicating that supporting unrelated persons would eventually be returned through the principle of altruism.

Although the dimensions of cooperation, sharing, and fairness are visible very early in human ontogeny, social behavior is nevertheless largely shaped by explicit moral teaching and by everyday social experiences (Olson and Spelke 2008). However, cultures provide very different learning environments for children.

H. Keller (✉)
Osnabrück University, Osnabrück, Germany
e-mail: heidi.keller@me.com

S. Decker
AWO Münsterland-Recklinghausen, Recklinghausen, Germany

P. Döge
Diakonie Deutschland, Berlin, Germany

© Springer Nature Switzerland AG 2019
T. Tulviste et al. (eds.), *Children's Social Worlds in Cultural Context*,
https://doi.org/10.1007/978-3-030-27033-9_9

117

Most research about children's development, including the development of coop-eration, generated from Western industrialized societies (Arnett 2008; Henrich et al. 2010; Nielsen et al. 2017). In this context, children's development is conceived from a subjective, individual perspective. Therefore, the development of the self as inde-pendent from others is the primary developmental task (Keller 2018). From this per-spective, children develop cooperative behaviors during the first years of life within meaningful social everyday encounters. Children's social encounters, i.e., interac-tional exchanges, in the Western middle class world are mainly verbally framed between one child and one adult partner. These children start social exchange with other children only later, between 16 and 28 months of age with an especially steep increase between 24 and 28 months. Only from then on are children considered to be capable to coordinate their actions jointly toward a goal or a particular topic (see Brownell 2011 for an overview).

Children's Dyadic Interactions

Interactions in the Family

Although the importance of children's social experiences with other children in peer groups is often stressed (see e.g., Corsaro 1992; Corsaro and Eder 1990; Hartup 1992; Hammes-Di Bernardo and Speck-Hamdan 2010), the bulk of empirical stud-ies regarding children's cooperative behavior is devoted to dyadic situations, mainly between one child and one adult or two children (see e.g., Warneken and Tomasello 2009). This research strategy mirrors the social reality of Western middle class life where social exchange is mainly dyadically organized. Even in larger groups, indi-viduals' interactions are a series of dyadic encounters.

When looking at the social interactions of animals or humans, researchers have used Markov models to illustrate and study their interrelationships (Haccou, et al. 1988; Ntwiga and Ogutu 2018). Markov models are stochastic probability models that have been applied to a wide variety of behaviors from a baby's activities to consumer behavior. In the yellow portion (a) of Fig. 9.1 is a hypothetical model portraying the dyadic social interactions found in Western cultures. Such dyadic organization is often observed even when larger social units exit. In the green portion (b) of the figure, there is a more complex pattern depicting the dense social networks found more frequently in other societies, such as Eastern cultures.

Concurrent multiparty interactions with overlapping conversational contributions are evaluated as grossly impolite in a Western middle class environment. Individuals are expected to devote their exclusive attention to the person who speaks and not to start one's own contributions before the other person has finished (turn taking). This pattern can already be observed between mothers/fathers and their few weeks old children (Keller 2018; Morelli et al. 2017).

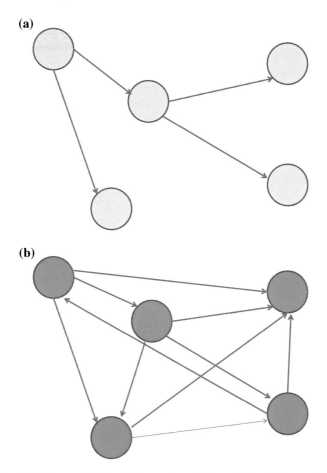

Fig. 9.1 a Simple Markov model of social interactions similar to the dyadic interactions frequently found in Western Societies. **b** Higher-order Markov model of social interactions similar to the dyadic interactions frequently found in Eastern and other Non-Western societies

This behavioral pattern is representative of families with a particular sociodemographic profile, organized by a high degree of formal education. The higher the level of formal education, the later the occurrence of first parenthood and the fewer children are born compared with families with less formal education. Higher formally-educated families live predominantly in nuclear, two generation households, i.e., parents and children. From the first day of life, babies experience exclusive dyadic attention and sensitive responsiveness to their signals, mainly in the face-to-face mode with extensive verbal accompaniment and monitoring (Keller 2016, 2018). From birth onward, toys are introduced into the dyadic interaction as well, and these facilitate and support processes of joint and coordinated attention. In Western middle class families, joint attention in this context means reference to an object within a dyadic setting (Bakeman and Adamson 1984, but also see Bard and Leavens 2009).

Familiarity with objects allows children to entertain themselves and spend time without social partners. Toys distract children from social others and can act as (emotional) security objects. Western middle class families emphasize in their socialization agendas the importance of children's learning to spend time on their own from early on and to develop relationships with themselves. Too much social interaction is regarded as disturbing and irritating for small children (Keller 2016).

Children's Interactions Outside the Family: Teachers and Caregivers

Also, in extra-familial care, children from Western middle class families experience a similar emphasis on dyadic social interactions between one teacher or day care provider and one child. The pedagogical credo of daycare centers that is considered to indicate high quality stresses the importance of dyadic adult-child encounters, since adults are understood as being the best (and only) educational partners for children.

On the other hand, Western middle class parents refer their children to daycare institutions earlier than families belonging to lower social classes (Schlack et al. 2007; Tietze et al. 2013) in order for their children to meet other children. With German families being small (fertility rate of 1.46 children per German woman [Statistisches Bundesamt (Federal office for statistics) 2018], having more than one other sibling for a child to interact with in the family is the exception rather than the rule.

Free Play and Autonomy

Another Western cornerstone of quality pedagogy is free play, which covers about half of the typical daycare and kindergarten day (Gernhardt 2017). Free play means that every child can decide, where, what, and with whom he or she wants to play. The emphasis on free play is based in constructivist approaches to early education stressing the self-educational potential of children's play. Children, not adults, are the initiators of their activities, so that children can structure their learning experiences on their own. It is particularly stressed that these processes are most successful when children play alone or with only a few other children (Andres and Laewen 2016). Children from middle class families thus experience continuity between home and institution, which reinforces educational processes, whereas children from other sociodemographic backgrounds may have disruptive experiences (Bossong and Keller 2018).

Thus, sociodemographic contexts are represented in cultural norms, values and behavioral conventions, i.e., cultural models. The Western middle class educational strategy supports the cultural model of psychological autonomy. Psychological autonomy rests on the assumption that human behavior and mental representations are based in personal preferences and decisions as the expression of the personal right of freedom, self enhancement, and self determination (e.g., Deci and Ryan 2000; Snibbe and Markus 2005). Moreover, it is assumed that human behavior and experiences are triggered by mental states that are intrinsic, autonomous, and independent. This conception of autonomy has consequences for the definition of relatedness as another universal human need (see Keller 2016). Relatedness in this cultural model means that separate, self-determined individuals form relationships with other separate, self-determined individuals on a voluntary basis. The patterns and structure of social relationships are thus defined through the psychological autonomy of the individuals.

Children's Play Patterns

It can be assumed that focusing on the individual child during socialization processes has effects on the ability to cooperate with others. Accordingly, studies on cooperative behavior of Western children in group settings have demonstrated a distinct bias to solitary and dyadic behavior. Ishikawa and Hay (2006) invited triads of 24 months old children into a laboratory playroom where they could play whatever they wanted. Children spent most of the time in solitary or dyadic play, although they were able to interact triadically. Although some (Western) scholars argue that children younger than 24 months do not yet have the capability to interact with more than one partner (e.g., Viernickel 2000), other (Western) scholars emphasize that already by 3–6 months of age children can perceive and orient to triadic situations, at least with mother and father (i.e., the primary triangle, Fivaz-Depeusinge and Corboz-Warnry 1999). Also, older Western middle class children have difficulties in cooperating in groups. Peters and Torrance (1973) instructed 5-year-old European American children to build "big houses" from Lego bricks under two conditions: alone or in triads. In the latter condition cooperation was not particularly stressed. The results demonstrated that children in triads spent significantly less time with the task compared to working alone by themselves. Rogoff and collaborators have done extensive research on children's cooperation and learning in different cultural groups (Mejia-Arauz et al. 2007). They have found differences in the social organization of groups: European American children act primarily dyadically even when they are in larger groups. Children from rural Mayan families in Guatemala acted primarily as communal social ensembles (Chavajay and Rogoff 2002; Lipka 1991; Martini 1996; Rogoff 2003).

Culture and Mothers' Level of Education

In the same vein Meija-Arauz et al. (2007) examined how triads of 6 to 10-year-old children from 3 cultural backgrounds organized their interactions while folding

Origami figures. Two groups of Mexican-heritage children (differing in the degree of mother's formal education, seven grades of schooling or high school and more) whose families had migrated to the USA and European American children from middle class families observed a woman folding Origami figures and later were allowed to fold their own Origami figures. Children were grouped in triads and did not get any special instruction concerning their method of operation. Triads of children whose mothers had lower degrees of formal schooling acted more often as a coordinated ensemble, i.e., cooperated smoothly together and communicated mainly nonverbally. Triads from European American families whose mothers had extensive schooling more often engaged dyadically or individually. The Mexican-heritage children whose mothers had extensive schooling showed an intermediate pattern or resembled the European American children. The children also differed in their attentional strategies. Children with mothers of lower formal educational backgrounds showed more keen observation of the teacher whereas children from mothers of higher levels of formal schooling posed more questions and acted more verbally. When the European American children did engage as an ensemble, this often involved chatting rather than nonverbal actions regarding folding, which was more common among the Mexican-heritage children (Meija-Arauz et al. 2007). These results demonstrate that the degree of mother's formal education is powerful in shaping children's cultural educational agendas and children's behavioral development. Since higher levels of parents' formal education can be related to the cultural model of psychological autonomy, as we have argued before, implications for children's cooperative and collaborative behavior can be expected.

Other Variables that Affect Cooperation

Although culturally scripted socialization experiences can be regarded as powerful in shaping children's attitudes and behavioral strategies concerning cooperation, there are other dimensions that have proven to also influence the social organization of children's play (i.e., age, gender, and the stimulating nature of the play material). McLoyd et al. (1984) asked 3½- and 5-year-old same gender triads to play with toys in a laboratory. The 5-year-olds interacted triadically 67% of the time, whereas 3½-year-olds only acted triadically 28% of the time. Girl groups tended toward more triadic behavior than boy groups. When playing with unspecific material (e.g., pipe cleaners), more triadic behavior occurred than when playing with specific toys (e.g., dolls).

Observations in German daycare institutions alerted us to the relevance of the composition of children's social environment. A typical day in high quality institutions consists mainly of two settings: dyadic interactions between one teacher/care provider and one child on the one hand and free play situations on the other (Keller 2019). During free play situations children play more than 40% of the time singularly, they watch what other children are doing between 25 and 30% of the time, they play parallel between 4 and 8% of the time, and interact with other children, mainly dyadically, between 21 and 25% of the time (Gernhardt 2017). Group behavior and group-based activities are an exception.

A Study of Children's Cooperation

Since the studies reported so far did not instruct children specifically to cooperate, it remains open whether a particular cooperation necessitating set-up and the specific instruction to cooperate would increase triadic behavior. We therefore conducted a study to test cooperation among German children from middle class families who were specifically instructed to cooperate. We assessed 4- to 5-year-old children from middle class families who can be assumed to have been exposed to psychologically autonomous socialization and educational strategies in home and institution. In order to verify this assumption, the mothers answered a socialization goals questionnaire. We were further interested to see if triadic behavior occurred during the same age range as had been seen in other Western children. We also examined possible gender differences.

We assessed same gender children in dyads and triads with a cooperation task consisting of jointly copying a tangram figure which allowed variable solutions (rather than a fixed strategy (Schmidt et al. 2015). We decided against an Origami task because the children might differ in their manual dexterity, which could influence the cooperation.

We assumed that dyads would cooperate more dyadically than triads would triadically. We also assumed that the triads would cooperate less dyadically than the dyads. Further, we assumed that in the triadic condition more singular/isolated behavior would occur than in the dyads. Based on studies demonstrating age effects for triadic behavior we expected older children to act more triadically than younger children.

In the study, 106 preschool children participated, 23 dyads and 20 triads. There were 40 children in 20 same gender dyads (10 female) and 60 children in same gender triads (9 female). The assessments took place in different cities in two German states, Lower Saxonia in the north west and Rhineland-Palatinate in the south west. The cities were small to mid-size. The assessments took place in daycare institutions that volunteered to host the research team, and parents gave written consent. Children in the dyads (mean age 60.31 months, $SD = 7.56$) and triads (mean age 61.98 months, $SD = 6.16$) had a similar number of siblings (dyads mean 1.4, $SD = 1.54$, 31.4% single children; triads mean 1.17, $SD = 0.96$, 20.7% single children). The differences are not statistically significant (all $ps > 0.05$). The mothers' formal educational level was also similar (dyads, 10.23 years, $SD = 1.77$, 12.5% no data; triads, 11.45 years, $SD = 1.61$, 8.3% no data). Previous studies have demonstrated that 10 years of formal education is a valid cut off point between higher and lower formal education, with concomitant differences in socialization goals and practices (Keller 2007). Thus, both groups of mothers can be regarded as having higher formal educational levels. Mothers provided sociodemographic information and completed a socialization goals scale that assessed autonomy and relatedness in three subscales (cf. Döge and Keller 2014). Mean maternal ratings for *Psychological Autonomy* (4.78, $SD = 0.71$) were significantly higher than their ratings for *Prosocial Orientation* (4.67, $SD = 0.81$) and for *Hierarchical Relatedness* (4.43, $SD = 1.02$). These results are consistent with the mothers' higher degree of formal education and confirm that the children came from German middle class families and experienced an educational orientation towards Psychological Autonomy.

Teachers selected children for the dyads and triads who liked each other and they were seated next to each other at one side of a table. In three consecutive trials the children were asked to copy three different Tangram figures, first an ant, then a bunny, and last a cat. Prior to each trial, the Experimenter demonstrated the solution of the respective figure in front of the children with one set of wooden Tangram shapes. The children were asked what the figure would be. What they answered, even if it was wrong (e.g., a boat) was used in the following conversations to address the tangram figure. The first two trials served to familiarize the children with the task and the third trial was the critical one for cooperation. Children were instructed to copy the last task jointly (dyadic or triadic).

Videos of the sessions were coded along two dimensions: *task orientation* and *social organization,* and whether the tangram figure was successfully copied. The codes assessed whether the children were *task oriented* or *task avoidant* following McLoyd et al. (1984) and Mejía-Arauz et al. (2007). The social organization was coded as *singular, dyadic,* or *triadic,* and the dominant *social organization* during the cooperation task for each child was assessed. Interrater reliability was high (intra class correlations were between 0.72 and 0.99).

Looking at task solutions, 25% of the dyads and 50% of the triads solved the tangram figure successfully, a non-significant difference, but the solutions in both settings were not always found cooperatively. Individual children might have solved the task on their own in dyads and triads. These constellations will be discussed below.

Dyads and triads did not differ with respect to *Task Orientation* time (dyads 75.27% of time, triads 79.83%). However, differences appeared when social organization was examined. Although the children were explicitly instructed to work together (collaboratively) in both conditions, they spent about half of the time *in singular activities*, dyads 48.13% and triads 56.72%. Children in dyads acted dyadically 51.87% of the time. Children in triads acted triadically only 9.82% of the time and acted dyadically 33.46% of the time. There were no gender related differences. However, dyads/triads who were on average younger than 60 months spent more time in singular activities than dyads/triads older than 60 months (68.72% vs. 42.17%, $p < 0.05$).

Interestingly, when looking at children individually, 27.5% of the children in dyads and 18.3% of the children in triads did not participate in solving the Tangram task. Indeed, 27.5% of children in dyads and 58.3% of children in triads acted singularly most of the time, and 45% of the children in dyads and 18.3% of the children in triads acted predominantly dyadic. Only 5% of the children in triads acted predominantly triadically (three children, one triad). More children in dyads acted dyadically and fewer children acted singularly than in triads. Children younger than 60 months participated less in the task solution (37.5% vs. 11.9%) and acted less dyadically than children older than 60 months (15.0% vs. 39.0%).

Socialization Within Western Middle Class Families

Psychological Autonomy

The study described above is consistent with previous research that has demonstrated empirically that Western middle class families raise their children towards a cultural model of Psychological Autonomy (Keller and Kärtner 2013). This orientation implies that children learn from early on to communicate with others mainly in an exclusive dyadic format. Moreover, they also learn from early on to spend substantial parts of the day on their own, mostly surrounded by toys. We assume that these pervasive experiences influence their social behavior also in other social constellations, and that was shown with the triads in the above study.

In fact, the more educated middle class mothers of the participating children in our study preferred socialization goals that were predominantly oriented towards Psychological Autonomy. They least emphasized socialization goals that expressed the cultural model of Hierarchical Relatedness.

Children growing up in other sociodemographic contexts experience other learning environments. Particularly sociodemographic groups organized by lower degrees of formal education are oriented more to the cultural model of hierarchical relatedness with explicit socialization instruction of cooperation, harmony, sharing, and taking on joint responsibilities (Keller 2018). As the work of Rogoff and collaborators mentioned before has demonstrated, children living in families with lower degrees of formal education in Mayan villages demonstrate more cooperative behavior as coordinated ensembles than European American middle class children. Impressions of a pilot study with children from Palestinian middle class families living in East Jerusalem using the Tangram task paradigm with triads indicate a completely different mode of cooperation than observed in the German middle class children. The triads were in constant communication processes with each other (Issah 2019).

Cooperation

A review of the literature demonstrates a significant bias towards studies of cooperative behavior with adult-child or child-to-child dyads during children's early years. We assume that this reflects the emphasis put on dyadic communication in Western middle class families, where the bulk of existing studies is located. We also observed that children in daycare and kindergarten often play alone or communicate with an adult teacher during free play sessions. This is even the case for children who according to Western developmental timetables of social play would be able to play jointly or cooperatively, i.e., from 3 years of age on (see e.g., Parten's classic study of social play 1932). This is also reflected in Gernhardt's (2017) study which found that 3-year-old children in kindergarten play solitarily during about 41% of the day, were onlookers for about 24%, and interacted only for about 25%. We assume that this is a consequence of the experiences in the family.

Farver and Shin (1997) demonstrated that the thematic content and communicative strategies during pretend play are influenced by culture. They observed Anglo American and Korean American preschoolers during free play situations and found that Anglo American children were more self-centered, e.g., describing their own actions and rejecting other suggestions. Korean American children were more other-oriented, described the actions of others more than their own, were polite, and included more family role themes than the Anglo American children. The subjective focus on the individual is supported by the prevalent educational philosophy embodied in curricula and daily routines of daycare institutions (Bossong and Keller 2018). Children are supposed to engage their learning experiences on their own, during free play situations, alone or with a few others.

Our study clearly demonstrates that German children from middle class families preferred modes of interaction that were dyadic and singular, even when in dyads or triads. Interestingly and not unexpectedly, children acting in dyads were oriented more dyadically than children acting in triads. The children in the two social formats did not differ in their task orientation, which may indicate that there were no motivational differences to solve the task. There were also no differences in performance among the children when solving the tangram task individually. This may indicate that the children did not differ in their capability to solve the task. All children, independent of the dyadic or triadic test condition, could at least solve one task of two test trials. The results thus reflect social dimensions of children's preferred mode of action.

The reported findings are in line with other studies analyzing work and play modes and attitudes of Western middle class children (c.f., the results of highly schooled European American mothers in the Meija-Arauz et al. study 2007). Contrary to previous research children were not left to determine how to approach the task, but we instructed them explicitly to act cooperatively, dyadically in the dyads and triadically in the triads. Nevertheless, a large number of children, regardless of the group situation worked singularly. The children obviously did not know how to act cooperatively as many of their concomitant verbalizations indicate.

"*I can do this also on my own*" says one 5-year-old girl and takes the shapes away from another girl. "*It works.*"

Triads even seemed to hinder or prevent children's social interactional behavior, since acting singularly was most pronounced in triads. Joint activities were seen more in dyads (51.07% of the time), whereas triads acted jointly only 43.28% of the time, dyadically or triadically.

Acting triadically depends on social regulations between all three children, as the following example demonstrates:

Child A   Where does Rafael's pattern fit in?
             Rafael, now yours, it may fit in there.
Child B   No, that does not fit there, (removes a pattern that Child A had put down).
             This fits … this is an ear.
Child C   Ok, this is mine, we can put them together there, one from me and one
             from you. It looks like a chicken

A communal attitude is crucial for acting triadically, i.e., the solution of the task needs to be identified as a common problem. The individual perspective has to be subordinated to the joint perspective. Western middle class children often do not have those experiences during the early years because they are the center of the attention of their families. In line with other studies, our study confirms an age effect. Obviously Western middle class children learn a social communal perspective only gradually. They learn first about themselves before they learn about others. In cultural environments oriented towards Hierarchical Relatedness, children are geared to the community from birth on und learn first about others before they learn about themselves (Keller 2018). Accordingly, during the first months of life babies in these settings can interact triadically.

Gender Socialization

We could not confirm gender differences in children's behavior. Indeed, we also did not find gender differences between mothers of boys and mothers of girls regarding their socialization goal orientation (Keller 2007). This is in line with several studies addressing early socialization strategies in German middle class families where we could not find gender differences in socialization goals and early interactional strategies (for a summary see Keller and Kärtner 2013). This does not imply that mothers and fathers do not differentiate between their girl or boy children. We found that mothers were present more often with their three months old daughters than with three months old sons, whereas fathers were present more often with their boys than with their girls (Keller and Zach 2002). However, these differences do not seem to impact the general orientation towards psychological autonomy.

Implications

Although the design of our study does not allow for causal interpretation, the results have, nevertheless, important implications. German children from middle class families demonstrate amazingly low performance in cooperative tasks—with decreasing performance seen with increasing numbers of children. This seems to represent an alienation from the roots of socio-cognitive competences during the evolution of humankind. The emergence of these competences during human evolution has been linked to group experiences, especially multiparty behavior, starting with alloparenting (Burkart et al. 2009). The experience of multiple social encounters within the caregiving environment is conceptualized in the cooperative breeding hypothesis to be the origin of the emergence of prosocial psychology, affecting social regulations (cooperation, reciprocity) as well as cognition (for a discussion see van Schaik and Burkart 2010). The development of social coordination has been a crucial necessity that allows humans to live in larger groups and thus become more effective in defending against predators and exploiting resources. One theory about the origins of language development accordingly emphasizes language as a mean to communicate with several people at the same time. It is assumed that social cohesion was first maintained through dyadic reciprocity, e.g., expressed in mutual grooming. Since mutual grooming is too time consuming in larger groups, language as a means of social grooming evolved (Dunbar 1996). Neglecting multiparty behavior during human ontogeny in Western middle class families may have consequences for the development of this crucial capacity of cooperation and collaboration, which still is a vital part of human functioning in all cultures.

On the other hand, dense multiparty cooperative networks and multiple caregiving arrangements are still the reality in many parts of the world, particularly in non-Western rural farming environments. Many families who migrate to Western societies come from those cultures where cooperation in larger groups and communal acting are socialization goals for children (Keller 2011). The educational systems in many Western countries which emphasize psychological autonomy may therefore be rejected by many immigrant families (Bossong and Keller 2018; Tobin et al. 2013). Moreover, children cannot profit from educational opportunities that are extremely discrepant from their learning histories. This may create unequal educational opportunities which is contrary to most Western governmental curricula and societal educational goals (Bossong and Keller 2018).

Conclusions

The results of our study point to consequences of Western middle class educational agendas that may not be intended and also not wanted. The basic human capacity to cooperate, and especially in groups that are larger than dyads, seems to be affected by family and institutional curricula that are directed towards the cultural model of psychological autonomy. Unconditional centering on the individual child without systematic inclusion of the social context cannot be beneficial for children's healthy development. When considering early educational curricula, group-based activities with more than two children participating should become routine in day care and kindergarten daily life. Not only would children from hierarchically relational organized families benefit but also children from families that are geared towards psychological autonomy. The emphasis on individuality, uniqueness and separateness has beneficial effects but also potential negative consequences that are apparent also in other developmental domains, like e.g., "the terrible twos" which only occur in

Western contexts (Keller 2015). Future research should take the complexities of cultural emphases into account and try to assess all the consequences of parental and educational interventions.

References

Andres, B., & Laewen, H. J. (2016). Das infans-Konzept der Frühpädagogik (The infans conception of early pedagogics). *Kindergarten heute, 44–51.*

Arnett, J. J. (2008). The neglected 95%: Why American psychology needs to become less American. *American Psychologist, 63,* 602–614.

Bakeman, R., & Adamson, L. B. (1984). Coordinating attention to people and objects in mother-infant and peer-infant interaction. *Child Development, 55,* 1278–1289.

Bard, K., & Leavens, D. (2009). Socio-emotional factors in the development of joint attention in human and ape infants. In L. Roska-Hardy & E. Neumann-Held (Eds.), *Learning from animals? Examining the nature of human uniqueness* (pp. 89–104). London: Psychology Press.

Bossong, L., & Keller, H. (2018). Cross-cultural value mismatch in German day care institutions: Perspectives of migrant parents and day care teachers. *International Journal of Psychology, 53*(82), 72–80.

Brownell, C. (2011). Early developments in joint action. *Review of Philosophy and Psychology, 2*(2), 193–211.

Burkart, J. M., Hrdy, S. B., & van Schaik, C. P. (2009). Cooperative breeding and human cognitive evolution. *Evolutionary Anthropology, 18*(5), 175–186.

Chavajay, P., & Rogoff, B. (2002). Schooling and traditional collaborative social organization of problem solving by Mayan mothers and children. *Developmental Psychology, 38*(1), 55–66.

Corsaro, W. A. (1992). Interpretative reproduction in children' s peer culture. *Social Psychology Quarterly, 55,* 160–177.

Corsaro, W. A., & Eder, D. (1990). Children' s peer cultures. *Annual Review of Sociology, 16,* 197–220.

Darwin, C. (1871). *The descent of man, and selection in relation to sex.* London: John Murray.

Deci, E., & Ryan, R. (2000). The "what" and "why" of goal pursuits: Human needs and the self-determination of behavior. *Psychological Inquiry, 11*(4), 227–268.

Döge, P., & Keller, H. (2014). Factorial structure of a socialization goal questionnaire across non-migrant and migrant mothers in Germany. *European Journal of Developmental Psychology, 11*(4), 512–520.

Dunbar, R. (1996). *Grooming, gossip and the evolution of language.* Cambridge, MA: Harvard University Press.

Farver, J. A. A., & Shin, Y. L. (1997). Social pretend play in Korean- and Anglo-American preschoolers. *Child Development, 68*(3), 544–556.

Fivaz-Depeusinge, E., & Corboz-Warnry, A. (1999). *The primary triangle. A developmental systems view of mothers, fathers and infants.* New York, NY: Basic Books.

Gernhardt, A. (2017). Individuelle Freiheit oder Anpassung an die Gruppe? Zur Bedeutung von Kultur für die frühkindliche Bildung und Entwicklung (Individual freedom or adapting to the group. The importance of culture for early development and education). In C. Walter-Laager, M. Pfiffner, & K. Fasseing Heim (Eds.), *Beziehungen in der Kindheit. Soziales Lernen in frühpädagogischen Einrichtungen verstehen und unterstützen* (pp. 87–212). Bern, Switzerland: hep Verlag.

Haccou, P., Kruk, M. R., Meelis, E., Van Bavel, E. T., Wouterse, K. M., & Meelis, W. (1988). Markov models for social interactions: analysis of electrical stimulation in the hypothalamic aggression area of rats. *Animal Behaviour, 36,* 1145–1163. https://doi.org/10.1016/S0003-3472(88)80074-5.

Hamilton, W. D. (1964). The genetical evolution of social behaviour I and II. *Journal of Theoretical Biology, 7*(1–16), 17–52.

Hammes-Di Bernardo, E., & Speck-Hamdan, A. (2010). *Kinder brauchen Kinder* (Children need children). Kiliansroda: das netz.

Hartup, W. W. (1992). Friendships and their developmental significance. In H. McGurk (Ed.), *Childhood social development: Contemporary perspectives* (pp. 175–205). Hillsdale, NJ, US: Lawrence Erlbaum Associates, Inc.

Henrich, J., Heine, H. J., & Norenzayan, A. (2010). The weirdest people in the world. *Behavioural and Brain Sciences, 33*(2–3), 61–83.

Ishikawa, F., & Hay, D. (2006). Triadic interaction among newly acquainted 2-year-olds. *Social Development, 15*(1), 145–168.

Issah, S. (2019). Ongoing master thesis project, Hebrew University, Jerusalem, Nevet Greenhouse, School of Social Work

Keller, H. (2007). *Cultures of infancy*. Mahwah, NJ: Erlbaum.

Keller, H. (2011). *Kinderalltag. Kulturen der Kindheit und ihre Bedeutung für Bindung, Bildung und Erziehung* (Children's everyday life. Cultures of infancy and their importance for attachment, education and development). Berlin: Springer.

Keller, H. (2015). *Die Entwicklung der Generation Ich – Eine psychologische Analyse aktueller Entwicklungsleitbilder* (The development of the I generation. A psychological analysis on actual educational perspectives). Heidelberg: Springer Essentials.

Keller, H. (2016). Psychological autonomy and hierarchical relatedness as organizers of developmental pathways. *Philosophical Transactions of the Royal Society B, 371*, 20150070.

Keller, H. (2018). Universality claim of attachment theory: Children's socioemotional development across cultures. *PNAS, 115*(45), 11414–11419. https://doi.org/10.1073/pnas.1720325115.

Keller, H. (2019). *Der Mythos der universellen Gültigkeit. Kulturelle Perspektiven auf die Bindungstheorie und ihre Anwendung* (The myth of universality. Cultural perspectives on attachment theory and its application). Kiliansroda: das Netz.

Keller, H., & Kärtner, J. (2013). Development. The cultural solution of universal development tasks. In M. J. Gelfand, C. Y. Chiu, & Y. Y. Hong (Eds.), *Advances in culture and psychology* (Vol. 3, pp. 63–116). New York: Oxford University Press.

Keller, H., & Zach, U. (2002). Gender and birth order as determinants of parental behavior. *International Journal of Behavioral Development, 26*(2), 177–184.

Lipka, J. (1991). Towards a culturally based pedagogy: A case study of one Yup'ik Eskimo teacher. *Anthropology and Education Quarterly, 22,* 203–223.

Martini, M. (1996). "What's new?" at the dinner table: Family dynamics during mealtime in two cultural groups in Hawaii. *Early Development and Parenting, 5,* 23–34.

McLoyd, V., Thomas, E., & Warren, D. (1984). The short-term dynamics of social organization in preschool triads. *Child Development, 55,* 1051–1070.

Mejía-Arauz, R., Rogoff, B., Dexter, A., & Najafi, B. (2007). Cultural variation in children's social organization. *Child Development, 78,* 1001–1014.

Morelli, G., Chaudhary, N., Gottlieb, A., Keller, H., Murray, M., Quinn, N., et al. (2017). Taking culture seriously: A pluralistic approach to attachment. In H. Keller & K. A. Bard (Eds.), *Contextualizing attachment: the cultural nature of attachment* (pp. 139–170). Cambridge, MA: MIT.

Nielsen, M., Haun, D., Kärtner, J., & Legare, C. H. (2017). The persistent sampling bias in developmental psychology: A call to action. *Journal of Experimental Child Psychology, 162,* 31–38.

Ntwiga, D. B., & Ogutu. C. (2018). Interaction dynamics in a social network using hidden Markov model social networking. *Social networking, 7,* 147–155 https://doi.org/10.4236/sn.2018.73012

Olson, K. R., & Spelke, E. S. (2008). Foundations of cooperation in young children. *Cognition, 108*(1), 222–231.

Parten, M. (1932). Social participation among preschool children. *Journal of Abnormal Psychology, 27,* 309–314.

Peters, R., & Torrance, E. (1973). Effects of triadic interaction on performance of five-year-old disadvantaged children. *Psychological Reports, 32,* 755–758.

Rogoff, B. (2003). *The cultural nature of human development.* New York: Oxford University Press.

Schlack, R., Hölling, H., & Kurth, B.-M. (2007). Inanspruchnahme außerfamiliärer vorschulischer Kindertagesbetreuung und Einfluss auf Merkmale psychischer Gesundheit bei Kindern (Using extrafamilial early institutional care and its influence on children's health and well being). *Bundesgesundheitsblatt Gesundheitsforschung und Gesundheitsschutz, 50,* 1249–1258.

Schmidt, M., Hardecker, S., & Tomasello, M. (2015). Preschoolers understand the normativity of cooperatively structured competition. *Journal of Experimental Child Psychology, 143,* 34–47.

Snibbe, A. C., & Markus, H. R. (2005). You can't always get what you want: Educational attainment, agency, and choice. *Journal of Personality and Social Psychology, 88*(4), 703–720.

StatistischesBundesamt. (2018). https://www.destatis.de/DE/PresseService/Presse/Pressemitteilungen/2018/03/PD18_115_122.html;jsessionid=91DE0ADC14187A4196DDBD853551E0EC. InternetLive1. Retrieved 01.08.2018.

Tietze, W., Becker-Stoll, F., Bensel, J., Eckhardt, A. G., Haug-Schnabel, G., Kalicki, B., et al. (2013). NUBBEK. *Nationale Untersuchung zur Bildung, Betreuung und Erziehung in der frühen Kindheit* (NUBBEK. National Study of Education and Care in Early Childhood). Kiliansroda: das netz.

Tobin, J., Adair, J. K., & Arzubiaga, A. (2013). *Children crossing borders: Immigrant parent and teacher perspectives on preschool for children of immigrants.* New York: Russell Sage Foundation.

van Schaik, C. P., & Burkart, J. M. (2010). *Mind the gap: cooperative breeding and the evolution of our unique features.* In: P. M. Kappeler & J. Silk, (Eds.), *Mind the gap. Tracing the origins of human universals* (pp. 477–496). Berlin: Springer.

Viernickel, S. (2000). *Spiel, Streit, Gemeinsamkeit. Einblicke in die Soziale Kinderwelt der unter 2—jährigen* (Play, Fight, Community. Insights into the children s world of the under two years olds). Landau.

Warneken, F., & Tomasello, M. (2009). The roots of human altruism. *British Journal of Psychology, 100*(3), 455–471.

Part II
Socialization of Young Children

Chapter 10
Parenting: Talking with Children Across Cultural Contexts

Tiia Tulviste

Abstract Family is the initial and the primary setting for the socialization of children. This chapter deals with everyday family conversations with children in different cultural and interactional contexts. The focus is on variations in the amount and cultural meaning of the speech addressed to children, as well as on children's participation in family conversations and the content highlighted. I provide examples from our own comparative research as well as studies of other researchers about culturally-valued ways of talking with children. Theoretical conceptions about language acquisition and development stress the importance of a language-rich environment and child's conversational experiences in one-to-one dyadic interactions. However, dyadic interactions with children and child-adjusted language use are not that common in non-Western parts of the world. Moreover, the importance placed on talking versus silence, and cultural habits of talking also vary within Western cultures. The chapter closes with the conclusion that more investigations in diverse cultural contexts are needed to change our theoretical conceptions about the impact of family conversations on child development.

Emphasizing the centrality of family in studies of child development is a long tradition. The composition and size of families as well as children's, mothers', and fathers' roles have changed over time. Nowadays in many cultures toddlers and preschool age children spend most of their time in outside childcare rather than at home with their homemaker mothers. Families tend to be smaller and of many different structures. Despite tremendous changes, in most cultures parents still play the prominent role in child development regardless of the age of the child. The aim of the current chapter is to provide an overview of everyday family conversations with toddlers and preschoolers across cultures. A special focus is on how parents' culture-specific beliefs and values about child-rearing reflect and shape such conversations, and how children through participation in family conversations acquire language and its culture-specific use, as well as values deemed important in a specific culture.

T. Tulviste (✉)
University of Tartu, Tartu, Estonia
e-mail: tiia.tulviste@ut.ee

© Springer Nature Switzerland AG 2019
T. Tulviste et al. (eds.), *Children's Social Worlds in Cultural Context*,
https://doi.org/10.1007/978-3-030-27033-9_10

135

Cultural Variability in Social Context at Home

The number of family members children live with differs remarkably. A typical
Western middle-class family is small, averaging less than three persons per household
(United Nations, Department of Economic and Social Affairs, Population Division
2017). The child in such a family is usually an only child or a child with one or
two siblings (see Fig. 10.1). Children have few opportunities for spending time with
other family members. In typical Western families the child spends most of the time
at home with a single caregiver, usually the mother. However, in many non-Western
agrarian families which average five or more persons (United Nations, Department
of Economic and Social Affairs, Population Division 2017), distributed caretaking is

Fig. 10.1 A typical Western
middle class family (from
personal collection)

common. The child typically has five to ten siblings (Keller 2007) and daily contacts with a number of adults and children of different ages (Keller and Otto 2011).

Family Conversations and Learning to Talk

The social worlds of children differ greatly from birth on, and affect the way infants acquire language, and learn to communicate with others (see Demuth 2015 for an overview). Variability in the social environment is reflected in cultural differences in conversation partners (parents or other children), and the number of people in the conversation (two or more). For example, in many African cultures children primarily converse during play with siblings and other children of various ages (Geiger and Alant 2005). For a child from a typical Western family the most frequent conversational partners at home are their parents. From early on, Western children are accustomed to the dyadic model of interactions, mostly with mother or father. Dyadic turn-taking with one adult is not common for children from non-Western parts of the world, who are daily surrounded by a larger number of multi-age family members, peers, and adults.

Wide cultural variability exists as well in the kind of language (structure, vocabulary, intonation, grammar) children hear. Child-adjusted speech has been posited to play a key role in language acquisition and development (Snow and Ferguson 1977). Child-adjusted speech is that which is accommodated to the child's current level of language abilities; it can include, for example, simplified speech, changes in speed (i.e., slower), and pitch (i.e., higher and wider pitch; Broesch and Bryant 2018). According to studies conducted in Western English-speaking families, children's conversational participation is expected and encouraged from an early age on (Demuth 2015). Researchers have demonstrated that children learn language and conversational skills in back-and-forth dyadic interactions rather than through passive listening. The more children have been involved in face-to-face conversations, the better their language abilities are (Huttenlocher et al. 2007; Rowe 2012). Little is known about the mechanisms of language acquisition and development in non-English-speaking and non-Western parts of the world, where one-to-one dyadic conversation with children and child-centered language use are not so common as in Western cultures (Schieffelin and Ochs 1986).

Preschool age can be regarded as a period of rapid growth of skills that provide an important foundation for later cognitive and language development. Inequality in educational achievement of pupils has been traced back to the great variability in early language and communicative skills, especially to the size of the vocabulary in toddlerhood (Hart and Risley 1995). Poor early language and communicative abilities can have significant consequences for a child's later development: difficulties at school, poor interpersonal relationships as well as behavioral and psychological problems (Conti-Ramsden and Durkin 2012). Due to the central importance of early language and conversational skills in future development and adjustment, researchers seek ways to enhance these skills to better prepare children for school.

A great deal of theorizing and empirical research on language and communicative development has been done in the framework of a social-interactionist approach asserting that children acquire language and culture-specific ways of using it through conversational exchanges (Bruner 1978; Hoff 2006; Vygotsky 1978). Social disparities in children's early language experiences at home have been seen as the source of great individual differences in children's language skills. Studies show that the amount of speech addressed towards children (parental talkativeness) plays the leading role here, especially during the two first years of life (Huttenlocher et al. 2007; Rowe 2012). In the 3rd year of children's life, diversity of parental vocabulary is considered to have the most crucial impact on child language development, and the use of decontextualized language in the 4th year (Rowe 2012).

Ways of Talking with Children

Previous evidence indicates that children whose mothers talk more with them and expect more conversational participation from children have better linguistic and conversational skills (Hoff 2006; Rowe 2012). Researchers distinguish two parental conversational styles—directive versus conversation-eliciting styles—based on parents' conversational intents to control the child's attention and behavior versus eliciting his/her conversational participation (Hoff-Ginsberg 1991). The conversation-eliciting style is known to support language development, as parents who frequently ask questions make kids produce more talk. There is less clarity on the impact of directive conversational style on child development (see Flynn and Masur 2007).

Both the quantity and the quality of parents' conversations with children vary by socio-economic status (SES), especially the educational attainment of the parents, as well as by culture (Fernald et al. 2013; Hart and Risley 1995, 2003; Heath 1983). Typical Western middle-class parents tend to talk more and longer, use a greater variety of words, more complex syntax, more conversation-eliciting utterances, and fewer directives. Working-class parents tend to talk less and issue more directives; the educational achievement of their children is lower than that of children from higher SES groups (see Hoff et al. 2002 for an overview). The use of a directive style has been found to be typical of traditional African adult-child conversations: adults provide instructions and commands about how to behave, and do not encourage or expect verbal responses (Geiger and Alant 2005; Rogoff 2003; Sawadogo 1995).

Culturally-Valued Ways of Talking

A growing body of research from different cultural contexts indicates that children with non-Western backgrounds are expected to be silent in the presence of older people and to listen to others (Geiger and Alant 2005; Harkness and Super 1977; Schieffelin and Ochs 1986). Latino immigrant parents in the U.S. have been found to value children's listening skills more than their oral language skills (Greenfield et al. 2000). Japanese mothers themselves are more often silent and emphasize non-verbal communication with their children (Clancy 1986).

Moreover, in some Western cultures people generally are not so talkative as, for example, middle-class European Americans. For example, people from the Scandinavian and Northern European region, including Swedes (McCroskey et al. 1990), are stereotypically seen as less talkative than other Western people. Studies of national stereotypes indicate that Estonians and Finns perceive themselves as more quiet and tolerant of silence than people from other nations (Carbaugh et al. 2006; Daun et al. 2001; Kivik 1998; Mizera et al. 2013). Estonian teens have more negative and neutral attitudes toward talkative people than their Swedish counterparts (Tulviste et al. 2011). In Estonian and Finnish cultures the child is socialized to be a good listener (Smith and Bond 1999). Such culture-specific attitudes and traditions about silence and talking likely affect the language environment at home, especially the amount of speech produced during family conversations. A study in which we compared cultural patterns of mother-child interactions in Euro-American families with those of stereotypically silent regions—from Estonia and Sweden—demonstrated that Estonian mothers and two-year-old children indeed spoke significantly less than others. Very few conversation-eliciting utterances were used by Estonian mothers, indicating that little verbalization was expected from Estonian children (Junefelt and Tulviste 1997). This was not true in Swedish mother-child dyads, who proved to be as talkative as European American middle-class dyads. Moreover, Estonian mothers clearly preferred the directive conversational style, using more attentional (e.g., "look, there is a hole shaped like a pig") and behavioral directives (e.g., "turn the cow on its legs"), compared to European American and Swedish mothers. They uttered relatively fewer statements (e.g., "You have a nice moustache [from milk]") and questions (e.g., "Who is it who gives milk to a child") (Junefelt and Tulviste 1997; Tulviste 2004). A typical conversation is illustrated by the following example of an Estonian mother's mealtime interaction with her 2-year-old son.

*MOT   eat nicely!
*CHI   this is water.
*MOT   do not put your finger in it!
*MOT   eat nicely!
*CHI   [I] bite the bread.
*MOT   eat eat!

The reported differences in parental conversational styles are often interpreted as being related to the child's age (Pan et al. 1996). As children grow older, mothers' use of directives decreases. Studies carried out with Estonian families indicated that mothers of preschoolers and teens indeed used fewer directives than mothers of toddlers (Tulviste 2004). Despite this, a directive conversational style was still more prevalent among Estonian middle-class mothers of teenagers than among middle-class mothers from other Western countries, like Finland, Latvia, Sweden, and the U.S. (Tulviste 2004).

Family Conversations Across Interaction Contexts

Mealtimes, puzzle solving, book reading, toy play, and past event conversations are the most commonly represented contexts in studies about mother-child interactions. As our own research and that of others shows there are cultural differences with respect to the conversational style used in different contexts (Hoff-Ginsberg 1991; Junefelt and Tulviste 1997; Yont et al. 2003). For instance, cultural differences were more observed in mothers' interactions with two-year-old children during puzzle solving than at meals (Junefelt and Tulviste 1997). There are cultural norms for how much talk is socially acceptable in different contexts. Generally, mealtime has been considered by researchers as a language-rich context linking family members. At meals, the whole family is together, participating in intergenerational conversations, and people talk a lot at the dinner table. At the same time, many Estonian, Finnish, and Swedish mothers told us in interviews that when they were growing up, there was a stricture that one should not talk while eating (Junefelt and Tulviste 1997). The old social rule was still alive in some Estonian families as it was mentioned several times by mothers. For example, a mother told her 2-year-old boy "It's dinnertime now, don't talk". Some Estonian children also demonstrated that they have internalized this old cultural prescription ("You can't talk while you're eating. Nobody will understand a thing"; "You better eat. Don't talk at the table").

North Americans, however, expect speech to accompany all activities. Moreover, they like to talk for the sake of talking (Kim and Markus 2002). It was also observable in our study. North American mothers expected children to talk both while eating and while solving a puzzle (Junefelt and Tulviste 1997). Estonian mothers, in contrast, felt that talking prevented other ongoing activities. They wanted their children to concentrate on what they were doing: eating food ("Don't talk, eat") or solving the puzzle ("Don't talk, you are solving the puzzle").

Learning to Talk in Culture-Specific Ways

Through family conversations, children both acquire language and learn culturally-valued communication skills (Schieffelin and Ochs 1986). A comparative study of peer interaction during free play conducted in Estonian, Finnish, and Swedish kindergartens indicated that the language use of preschoolers mirrored that of parents (Tulviste et al. 2010). In peer groups, Estonian children were as talkative as Finnish and Swedish children. Their talk was not for the sake of talking but rather with the aim of regulating the playmate's ongoing activity, as seen in the following example from a conversation between two six-year-old boys. Here one boy was issuing directives, whereas his playmate was obeying them saying nothing himself.

*CHI: Wait, wait, find one more this [a block]!
        Find one this!
        One more this… for me.

I just need one [more].
See!
Do not bring any more!
Do not bring any more!

As illustrated above, the speech directed by Estonian children toward their play-mates contained significantly more directives than the speech of Finnish and Swedish preschoolers. This was especially obvious in socio-dramatic play when they were playing "house" and being a mother or father (Tulviste et al. 2010).

Cultural Meaning of Speech Addressed to Children

According to the contextual approach, children acquire knowledge about the culture they belong to through interaction with more competent members of their culture (Vygotsky 1978). Family conversations are important tools for transmitting norms, values, and beliefs that are important to pass on from one generation to another (Nelson and Fivush 2004). For the researcher, such conversations provide information about culture-specific socialization emphasis (Miller et al. 1997). A high frequency of Estonian mothers' behavioral and attentional directives seen in research (Junefelt and Tulviste 1997) that revolve around how to eat and solve the puzzle can have potential developmental benefits for children such as fostering children's learning to perform independently an ongoing activity. At the same time, parents' directiveness clearly restricts children's autonomy to make choices and to select what to do and what to say. It is likely that calling children's attention and keeping them on task by clear step-by-step instructions through directives does not grant a great deal of autonomy to the child or support children's initiatives. This could lead to children's low initiative in planning and carrying out activities on their own. The directive style is consistent with socialization toward relatedness or psychological relatedness, but not with autonomy socialization. In cultures oriented toward psychological relatedness, parental control serves the aim of developing cognitive abilities in children rather than exhibiting control over obedient kids. It is "order setting" rather than dominating (Kagitçibaşi 2005). Moreover, directive parenting has different cultural meaning, being perceived by children in some cultures as expression of parental love and care, but in most Western cultures as expression of parental hostility (Kagitçibaşi 2005).

Culturally-Valued Conversational Topics

The prevailing view in the literature is that cultural messages are embedded into daily family interactions. Parent-child joint conversations about past events, reminiscing, provide opportunities to understand the beliefs and values of parents from different socio-cultural contexts. These, in turn, influence how children construct the self, their views of others, and how relationships are derived from such conversations (Nelson and Fivush 2004). In discussing past events children practice how to talk about personal experiences, and they acquire the cultural meaning of personal experiences. Studies have found consistent differences in the topics highlighted across cultures during such conversations (Han et al. 1998). When providing recollections of past events, Chinese mothers tend to use more factual questions and focus more on other people relative to the child. Euro-American mothers are more interested in the child, and make more references to the child's inner states than do Chinese mothers (Wang et al. 2000). European American children, in turn, provide detailed memories and describe themselves in terms of inner states, such as feelings and preferences, whereas Chinese children's past event talk can be considered skeletal and focused on social interactions and daily routines (Wang et al. 2000).

In order to get a deeper understanding about cultural variability in the content of past event talk that is consistent with different emphases on autonomy and relatedness, we compared mothers reminiscing with their 4-year-old children in four cultural developmental contexts. The Autonomy-Relatedness Questionnaire (Keller 2007) was used to examine mothers' value orientation. The results indicated that mothers from three Western cultural contexts—Germany, Sweden, and Estonia—were similar in highly valuing autonomy of children, in contrast to rural Cameroonian Nso mothers. Mothers from all developmental contexts differed significantly from each other in terms of valuing relatedness (Tulviste et al. 2016). Cameroonian Nso mothers valued it most highly. Among Europeans, Estonian mothers valued relatedness the most, Swedish mothers the least, and German mothers' scores were in between. Our results showed that relatedness orientation was reflected in how much dyads spoke about other people, both within and across cultures. Past event conversations among Cameroonian Nso centered around other people. Among European dyads, Estonian mothers spoke about other people more than German and Swedish mothers, and German mothers more than Swedish mothers. Cultural differences between Western and non-Western dyads also emerged in what was said about other people. Mothers from European samples referred to what other people felt, wanted, thought, or preferred, whereas Cameroonian Nso mothers' talk contained a lot of information about other people's behaviors and actions (Tulviste et al. 2016). The following German mother-child dialog about the child's birthday illustrates typical past event talk in cultures supporting the development of psychological autonomy.

Mother This was a really beautiful day. And a really beautiful morning, too. Do you still remember, what we did after that? I still remember it. Pa came, he was in vesper (night watch) and you were already most impatient. You wanted to unpack your presents.
<M is laughing>

Mother You were so curious. You definitely wanted to know what was in the presents. But we had to wait for Pa first, and then he finally came and then we unpacked the presents. Do you still remember what your most beautiful present was? No? I don't believe it. Just say what it was.

Child A Barbie doll.

Mother The Barbie doll. Exactly. You had been crazy about getting one, hadn't
you?

On the other hand, among the rural Nso, children must develop action competence
and the ability to cooperate with other people (Keller and Otto 2011). It is likely that
besides mothers' stronger relatedness orientation the social context of family lives,
such as larger family size and close daily contacts with more people, are reflected in
the high frequency with which other people are mentioned in reminiscing.

A characteristic of Nso mothers' talk was also that it concentrated on human
beings—the child and other people—paying little attention to the non-social
attributes of the past experiences. European mothers, in contrast, described in detail
the place and time an event occurred as well as toys, clothes, pets and animals that
were present. The children in our study showed fewer cultural differences than their
mothers, possibly because 4-year-old children still contribute relatively little to the
dyadic conversations. The differences among children reflected those observed in
their mothers' talk. Nso children talked less than the other children, and incorporated fewer non-social topics into their past event talk (Tulviste et al. 2016).

Children's Contributions

Current developmental theories view the child as an active agent in her/his own
socialization. At the same time, studies in non-Western parts of the world illustrate
that there are cultural differences in what age the child is considered to be a conversational partner, when children have the right to speak, and in the extent parents
encourage children's conversational participation. For example, in African cultures
parents seldom interact verbally with small children "because children could not yet
speak". Parents start to converse with children more as they grow older (see Geiger
and Alant 2005). Children are taught quiet listening skills (see Geiger and Alant
2005). Children's initiative-taking in verbal communication is not appreciated in
African culture. Children are expected to learn that they are not supposed to initiate
talk and ask questions from adults (Kvalsig et al. 1991). Like African parents, Latinos
and families with Asian backgrounds tend to place more value on a child who listens
and observes than on a talkative child who initiates topics (Rogoff 2003). Similarly in
our study, Cameroonian Nso mothers typically served as the sole narrators of experienced events, and their 4-year-old children mainly listened to their mothers' talk,
seldom adding anything themselves. Estonian mothers, however, tended to engage
children in conversations by asking a lot of questions, and their children spoke when
asked by mothers. Swedish children, in contrast, took initiative, making contributions to conversations, and they did not need parental encouragement (Tulviste et al.
2016).

Changing Developmental Contexts

Today, parents may be raising their children in a changed socio-cultural context, facing child-rearing beliefs and practices that differ from those that were popular when they were children. In recent decades, the imprint of historical time on parenting, including the ways parents converse with their children, has attracted researchers' attention. Studies from China demonstrate how the one-child policy, rapid urbanization, and economic reforms have changed childhood, parental beliefs, and practices (Zhou et al. 2018). Today urban parents tend to encourage more independence, self-confidence, initiative-taking, and self-expression in children (Chen and Li 2012). Shyness in children has decreased, and is valued less by teachers, parents and peers than in past decades (Chen et al. 2009).

About 25 years have passed since Estonia regained its independence and returned to the Western world. The societal changes have altered the beliefs and values related to child-rearing in direction of stressing more autonomy and self-direction in children. At the same time, parents still assign importance to respect for others, kindness, politeness, and trustworthiness—qualities corresponding to the need for relatedness (Tulviste et al. 2012). A recent investigation indicates that the pattern of Estonian mothers' interactions with 2-year-olds has changed in terms of mothers becoming less directive, but societal changes over time have not made Estonian mothers and children more talkative (Tulviste 2019).

The research literature reveals changes in discussions about the culture-specific balance between silence and talk. Many Western researchers and educators worry about social disparities in children's language experiences and use intervention programs that teach parents and teachers how to engage children into conversations and make them more talkative, outspoken, and articulate. Some authors, in opposition, see the source of problems that people in Western world face in their tendency not to take silence and learning to listen seriously, as is illustrated in the popularity of international bestsellers like *Silence in the Age of Noise* (Kagge 2017).

Conclusions

In sum, this chapter illustrates the diversity in the ways parents converse with children in different socio-cultural contexts, and discusses the cultural assumptions behind those differences as well as the developmental consequences for children. The prevalent theories primarily describe Western patterns of parent-child conversations, and stress the importance of a language-rich environment that provides children with a lot of talking experiences in one-to-one dyadic interactions. At the same time, dyadic patterns and child-adjusted language do not adequately describe family conversations in non-Western cultures. Moreover, verbal self-expression is not highly valued in many cultures and children are expected to become good listeners of what older people say. The findings reported in this chapter support the importance of considering culture-specific ways of talking with children to change our theoretical conceptions. Research in diverse cultural contexts is still needed in order to better understand the nature of family conversations and their impact on child development.

Acknowledgements   The writing of this chapter was supported by the Estonian Research Council (grant no. PUT1359).

References

Broesch, T., & Bryant, G. A. (2018). Fathers' infant-directed speech in a small-scale society. *Child Development, 89,* 29–41.

Bruner, J. S. (1978). The role of dialogue in language acquisition. In A. Sinclair, R. J. Jarvella, & W. Levelt (Eds.), *The child's conception of language* (pp. 241–256). Berlin: Springer.

Carbaugh, D., Berry, M., & Nurmikari-Berry, M. (2006). Coding personhood through cultural terms and practices. *Journal of Language and Social Psychology, 25,* 203–220.

Chen, X., & Li, D. (2012). Parental encouragement of initiative-taking and adjustment in Chinese children from rural, urban, and urbanized families. *Journal of Family Psychology, 26,* 927–936.

Chen, X., Chen, H., Li, D., & Wang, L. (2009). Early childhood behavioral inhibition and social and school adjustment in Chinese children: A five-year longitudinal study. *Child Development, 80,* 1692–1704.

Clancy, P. (1986). The acquisition of communicative style in Japan. In B. Schieffelin & E. Ochs (Eds.), *Language socialization across cultures* (pp. 213–250). Cambridge: Cambridge University Press.

Conti-Ramsden, G., & Durkin, K. (2012). Language development and assessment in the preschool period. *Neuropsychology Review, 22,* 384–401.

Daun, Å., Verkasalo, M., & Tuomivaara, P. (2001). Stereotypes among Finns in Sweden. The character of Finns versus Swedes. *Ethnologia Europaea, 31,* 55–62.

Demuth, C. (2015). Mother-child communication: Cultural differences. In J. Wright (Ed.), *International encyclopedia of social and behavioral sciences* (pp. 874–880). Oxford: Elsevier.

Fernald, A., Marchman, V. A., & Weisleder, A. (2013). SES differences in language processing skill and vocabulary are evident at 18 months. *Developmental Science, 16,* 234–248.

Flynn, V., & Masur, E. F. (2007). Characteristics of maternal verbal style: Responsiveness and directiveness in two natural contexts. *Journal of Child Language, 34,* 519–543.

Geiger, M., & Alant, E. (2005). Child-rearing practices and children's communicative interactions in a village in Botswana. *Early Years: An International Research Journal, 25,* 183–191.

Greenfield, P. M., Quiroz, B., & Raeff, C. (2000). Cross-cultural conflict and harmony in the social construction of the child. In S. Harkness, C. Raeff, & C. R. Super (Eds.), *The social construction of the child, New Directions in Child Development* (pp. 93–108). San Francisco: Jossey-Bass.

Han, J. J., Leichtman, M., D., & Wang, Q. (1998). Autobiographical memory in Korean, Chinese and American children. *Developmental Psychology, 33,* 295–307.

Harkness, S., & Super, C. M. (1977). Why African children are so hard to test. *Annals of the New York Academy of Sciences, 285,* 326–331.

Hart, B., & Risley, T. R. (1995). *Meaningful differences in the everyday experience of young American children.* Baltimore, MD: Brookes.

Hart, B., & Risley, T. R. (2003). The early catastrophe. The 30 million word gap by age 3. *American Educator, 27,* 4–9.

Heath, S. B. (1983). *Ways with words: Language, life and work in communities and classrooms.* Cambridge: Cambridge University Press.

Hoff, E. (2006). How social contexts support and shape language development. *Developmental Review, 26,* 55–88.

Hoff, E., Laursen, B., & Tardif, T. (2002). Socioeconomic status and parenting. In M. H. Bornstein (Ed.), *Handbook of parenting* (2nd ed., pp. 231–252). Mahwah, NJ: Lawrence Erlbaum Associates.

Hoff-Ginsberg, E. (1991). Mother-child conversation in different social classes and communicative settings. *Child Development, 62,* 782–796.

Huttenlocher, J., Vasilyeva, M., Waterfall, H. R., Vevea, J. L., & Hedges, L. V. (2007). The varieties of speech to young children. *Developmental Psychology, 43*(4), 343–365.

Junefelt, K., & Tulviste, T. (1997). Regulation and praise in American, Estonian, and Swedish mother-child interaction. *Mind, Culture, and Activity: An International Journal, 4,* 24–33.

Kagge, E. (2017). *Silence: In the age of noise.* Pantheon Books.

Kagitçibaşi, Ç. (2005). Autonomy and relatedness in cultural context. Implications for self and family. *Journal of Cross-Cultural Psychology, 36,* 403–422.

Keller, H. (2007). *Cultures of infancy.* Mahwah, NJ: Erlbaum.

Keller, H., & Otto, H. (2011). Different faces of autonomy. In X. Chen & K. H. Rubin (Eds.), *Socioemotional development in cultural context* (pp. 164–185). New York: Guilford Press.

Kim, H. S., & Markus, H. R. (2002). Freedom of speech and freedom of silence: An analysis of talking as a cultural practice. In R. Shweder, M. Minow, & H. R. Markus (Eds.), *Engaging cultural differences: The multicultural challenge in liberal democracies* (pp. 432–452). New York: Russell-Sage Foundation.

Kivik, P.-K. (1998). What silence says: communicative style and identity. *Trames: A Journal of the Humanities and Social Sciences, 2,* 1, 66–90.

Kvalsig, J. D., Liddell, C., Reddy, A., Qotyana, P., & Shabalala, A. (1991). Communication and teaching at the home: A study of Zulu and Sotho preschoolers. *Early Child development and Care, 74*(1), 61–81.

McCroskey, J. C., Burroughs, N. F., Daun, Å., & Richmond, V. P. (1990). Correlates of quietness: Swedish and American perspectives. *Communication Quarterly, 2,* 127–137.

Miller, P. J., Wiley, A. R., Fung, H., & Liang, C. H. (1997). Personal storytelling as a medium of socialization in Chinese and American families. *Child Development, 68,* 557–568.

Mizera, L., Tulviste, T., Konstabel, K., & Lausa, E. (2013). Silent and slow Estonians, emotional and fast Russians: A comparative study of communication stereotypes in two neighboring countries. *Communication Quarterly, 61*(3), 268–283.

Nelson, K., & Fivush, R. (2004). The emergence of autobiographical memory: A social cultural developmental theory. *Psychological Review, 111,* 486–511.

Pan, B. A., Imbens-Bailey, A., Winner, K., & Snow, C. (1996). Communicative intents expressed by parents in interaction with young children. *Merrill-Palmer Quarterly, 42,* 248–267.

Rogoff, B. (2003). *The cultural nature of human development.* New York: Oxford University Press.

Rowe, M. L. (2012). A longitudinal investigation of the role of quantity and quality of child-directed speech in vocabulary development. *Child Development, 83,* 1762–1774.

Sawadogo, G. (1995). Training for the African mind. *International Journal of Intercultural Relations, 19,* 281–293.

Schieffelin, B. B., & Ochs, E. (Eds.). (1986). *Language socialization across cultures.* New York, NY: Cambridge University Press.

Smith, P. B., & Bond, M. H. (1999). *Social psychology across cultures.* Needham Heights, MA: Allyn and Bacon.

Snow, C. E., & Ferguson, C. A. (Eds.). (1977). *Talking to children: Language input & acquisition.* Cambridge: Cambridge University Press.

Tulviste, T. (2019). Mothers' conversational style in a changing developmental context. *Trames: A Journal of the Humanities and Social Sciences, 23,* 3, 277–286.

Tulviste, T. (2004). Socio-cultural variation in mothers' control over children's behavior. *Ethos, 32*(1), 34–50.

Tulviste, T., Mizera, L., & De Geer, B. (2012). Socialization values in stable and changing societies: A comparative study of Estonian, Swedish, and Russian Estonian mothers. *Journal of Cross-Cultural Psychology, 43*(3), 480–497.

Tulviste, T., Mizera, L., & De Geer, B. (2011). "There is nothing bad in being talkative". Meanings of talkativeness in Estonian and Swedish adolescents. *Journal of Pragmatics, 43*(6), 1603–1609.

Tulviste, T., Mizera, L., De Geer, B., & Tryggvason, M.-T. (2010). Cultural, contextual and gender differences in peer talk. *Scandinavian Journal of Psychology, 51*(4), 319–325.

Tulviste, T., Tõugu, P., Keller, H., Schröder, L., & De Geer, B. (2016). Children's and mothers' contribution to joint reminiscing in different sociocultural contexts: who speaks and what is said. *Infant and Child Development, 25*(1), 43–63.

United Nations, Department of Economic and Social Affairs, Population Division. (2017). *Household Size and Composition Around the World 2017 – Data Booklet*. Retrieved from http://www.un.org/en/development/desa/population/publications/pdf/ageing/household_size_and_composition_around_the_world_2017_data_booklet.pdf.

Vygotsky, L. S. (1978). *Mind in society: The development of higher psychological processes*. Cambridge, MA: Harvard University Press.

Wang, Q., Leichtman, M. D., & Davies, K. (2000). Sharing memories and telling stories: American and Chinese mothers and their three-year-olds. *Memory, 8*, 159–177.

Yont, K. M., Snow, C. E., & Vernon-Feagans, L. (2003). The role of context in mother–child interactions: an analysis of communicative intents expressed during toy play and book reading with 12-month-olds. *Journal of Pragmatics, 35*, 435–454.

Zhou, C., Yiu, W. Y. V., Wu, M. S., & Greenfield, P. M. (2018). Perception of cross-generational differences in child behavior and parent socialization: A mixed-method interview study with grandmothers in China. *Journal of Cross-Cultural Psychology, 49*(1), 62–81.

Chapter 11
The Sibling Relationship in Ecocultural Context

Ashley E. Maynard

Abstract For most people, the sibling relationship is the longest-standing relationship they will ever have, yet the sibling relationship cannot be taken for granted as being the same across cultural settings. The study of sibling relationships is an opportunity to examine socio-emotional and cognitive processes of development, as well as cultural values that shape the ways that siblings relate to one another and to their families and communities. Expectations for care, obedience, and helpfulness between or among siblings all vary across cultural groups. The level of emphasis on the sibling relationship is another part of a sociocultural complex of relationships. Rivalry develops out of competitiveness and a focus on independence. Sibling nurturance develops out of cooperation and a focus on interdependence and independence. Cultural expectations for the role of siblings after early childhood also vary, and these expectations are socialized in early childhood. The sibling relationship should be seen as culturally-embedded—shaped by and reflective of the cultural setting in which it develops.

Most children in the world grow up with one or more siblings. Interactions with siblings allow children to practice roles and to observe other children who are related and who have different skills. As children, siblings help each other with cultural activities involving cognitive and social skills. The sibling relationship is important in development through the lifespan, though the nature of sibling relationships varies across cultures. Who is a sibling? What kinds of relationships are siblings expected to have? What do siblings owe each other in childhood and in adulthood? Who manages the sibling relationship—parents or the children themselves? And what are the effects—cognitive, social, and linguistic—of having siblings? All of these questions have implications for how we understand siblings, development, and relationships that people share with one another.

A. E. Maynard (✉)
University of Hawai'i at Mānoa, Honolulu, USA
e-mail: amaynard@hawaii.edu

© Springer Nature Switzerland AG 2019
T. Tulviste et al. (eds.), *Children's Social Worlds in Cultural Context*,
https://doi.org/10.1007/978-3-030-27033-9_11

149

An Ecocultural Theory of Sibling Relationships

Sibling relationships are important in any cultural setting, though the degree of importance varies by cultural place and throughout the lifespan. Siblings are members of family networks and as such sibling interactions should be understood in the context of the family network. The ecocultural theory of the Whiting tradition (Whiting and Whiting 1975) is a useful framework for understanding the important influences that siblings have on one another. The major premise of ecocultural theory is that activities in the cultural setting influence the developing child: for example, each family member's role in the family subsistence, how much time the siblings spend together, and whether or not older siblings are responsible for the care of the younger ones, all affect sibling relationships and a child's ongoing development. There are various ecocultural influences on sibling interactions, including availability of caregivers to care for children, cultural beliefs about gender-roles and goals for child development, and whether or not a sibling group shares lifelong obligations to each other, such as economic reciprocity and arrangement of marriages (Weisner 1987). Siblings may play different roles in each other's lives depending on the local goals for development. We must examine cultural groups in their own right to see how siblings interact with each other and with other relatives and neighbors in order to figure out the role of sibling relationships in a given group. Examining sibling groups across cultures allows us to describe what resources, including both material and people, are available to individual children, what resources should be shared among them, and how they should work and sleep (Weisner 1989; Whiting and Edwards 1988). All of these aspects of interaction are influenced by cultural values pertaining to how children should relate to one another (Maynard and Tovote 2010).

Finding Out About Siblings

In some groups, siblings may be essential to caregiving, and the sibling relationship may be essential to what it means to be a member of that group (Maynard 2016). Thus, methodologically, it is imperative to know the role of siblings vis-à-vis each other and others in their lives. Whaley and colleagues (Whaley et al. 2002) explored infant-caregiver interaction in Kenya and the United States. Results showed that, when all caregivers, including siblings, were taken into account, similarities between Kenyan and American cultural groups in styles of interacting with young infants became more apparent. In the Kenyan group, infants' *en face* time with caregivers was distributed across adults and siblings; in the American group, parents (mostly mothers) provided the infant with *en face* interactions.

Who Is a Sibling?

Who are your siblings? It depends on the cultural place. In the United States, Europe, and other Western cultures, siblings can be genetic, adopted, or in a constellation called "step-siblings." Genetic siblings are those who share genetic parents, and therefore, approximately fifty percent of their genetic material. Step-sibling is a special term in English for a person who is the child of a spouse of one's parent, conceived from another union.

In many cultural groups, people with less genetic material in common, such as aunts, uncles, cousins, and siblings-by-baptism may be considered as important as genetic siblings. These "Classificatory siblings" indicate an important kinship category, where people have responsibilities to each other (Nuckolls 1993; Watson-Gegeo and Gegeo 1989). In some cultural groups, people who have these relations may be referred to as siblings and have the same obligations as blood-related siblings (Watson-Gegeo and Gegeo 1989; Zukow-Goldring 1995). For example, in many Asiatic, Native American, and Australian dialects there are kin terms that differentiate older and younger male and female siblings (Anthropological Institute of Great Britain and Ireland 1872). In Tzotzil Maya, an indigenous language of Mexico, all older sisters are referred to with one term, *vix*, which is something of a term of honor. Other younger and older siblings are given different referent terms depending on whether they are the younger or older brother of a boy or a girl, or whether they are a younger sister of a boy or a girl. This is an interesting problem for cognitive development, as a girl can be the *vix* of someone and also the *muk* of someone else. Greenfield and Childs (1977) found that children understood this simultaneous categorization problem by about seven years of age.

Translation does not always capture the important nuances of the sibling relationship. Katrin Tovote and I (Tovote and Maynard 2018) ran into a translation problem when asking indigenous Maya street children about their siblings. The Spanish word *hermanos* does not capture the complexity of the sibling relationship that Tzotzil speakers have, and, although the indigenous street vendors understood enough Spanish for their vending business transactions, they did not grasp that the researcher meant to ask them about all siblings, including whether they had older brothers, younger brothers, older sisters, or younger sisters, taking into account the target child's gender (see Table 11.1). Once we figured this out, we corrected the question by asking about all possible sibling categories the children might have.

Table 11.1 Tzotzil sibling terms

Older	*vix*	*bankil*	*xibnel*
	(girl's or boy's older sister)	(boy's older brother)	(girl's older brother)
Younger	*muk*	*itz'in*	*ixlel*
	(girl's younger sibling)	(boy's younger brother)	(boy's younger sister)

Although there are cultural definitions about who is a sibling, many people who grow up together in childhood treat each other as siblings and avoid incest taboos (Lieberman 2009), though there is some disagreement in the literature regarding these assertions because other sociological factors may play a role (Shor and Simchai 2009). In the Polynesian setting of Pukapuka, for example, siblings include the children of both parents' biological siblings, referred to as cousins in English (Hecht 1983). Furthermore, people from Pukapuka Atoll would refer to members of the same village or church as *taina* (sibling) and rely on each other for various kinds of material and social support. But in another cultural group in Oceania, the Malo people of the New Hebrides, cousins who are the same sex are considered siblings, as are a parent's siblings of the same sex, and grandparents of the same sex (Rubinstein 1983).

Who is responsible for helping children form relationships with other children? In the middle class European and Euro-American cultural groups, parents organize play dates and are often present when young children are playing together (Mellor 2012). This is not always the case. For the Kwara'ae of Micronesia, child caregivers introduce younger siblings to cousins and other children with whom they will have lifelong active social relationships (Watson-Gegeo and Gegeo 1989). On the other side of the world in Africa, the Giriama of Kenya count siblings as all children from the same village or tribe who are in the same age range (Wenger 1989); children in the same village grow up together, play together, form social and material bonds, and don't intermarry.

Influences on Sibling Interactions in Western Cultural Groups

Western parents tend to emphasize fairness in a family constellation where the parent-child relationship is more emphasized than the sibling relationship. In the United States, parents both foster and try to reduce sibling rivalry in an attempt to actively encourage positive sibling relationships (Mendelson 1990; Ross and Howe 2009). However, what is different in the US from many other cultural settings is that parents play a role in managing the sibling relationship through their treatment of the children. Siblings expect fair treatment from parents, and the model of relationships at home sets up children's expectations for relationships with others (Ross and Howe 2009). The emphasis is on the parents trying to influence siblings to get along in an environment characterized by fairness (Cicirelli 1995), which doesn't always work because fairness implies comparison.

Sibling rivalry is often an expectation in Western families, but it is not a universal phenomenon. Volling et al. (2010) reviewed sibling rivalry from a Western, lifespan perspective. Rivalry is socialized in many Euro-American families through comparison and competition among siblings. Recchia and Howe (2010) examined sibling conflict and resolution in the context of the family and found that children were more likely to compromise when conflicts involved physical harm and when children reported feeling sad during their fights.

How Do Siblings Relate in Non-western Cultural Groups?

In non-Western cultural settings siblings are typically expected to work out their own relationships, without intervention from adults (Whiting and Edwards 1988). And, the sibling relationship is often more influential across childhood and the lifespan than the parent-child relationship, and parents worry less about fostering positive sibling relationships (Whiting and Edwards 1988; Zukow-Goldring 1995). In the Polynesian islands of the Marguesas, Martini (1994) found that siblings helped each other learn to become competent at managing a stratified social situation respecting the complex social hierarchy of Marquesan cultural practices. Abaluyia children of Kenya automatically seek siblings or other peers for support as often as or more often than the mother (Weisner 1987). This may be because mothers are working and children are expected to rely on each other for social support more than their American counterparts. However, it is compelling that most American mothers are working, but their children tend to seek parental support and intervention, rather than rely on siblings.

Sibling Caretaking

While there have been a few studies of sibling caretaking in the United States (e.g., Heath 1983; Whiting and Whiting 1975), siblings are typically not expected to provide primary care for each other in most U.S. cultural groups. However, in many agrarian and traditional societies, sibling caretaking is a primary form of the social support of children (Weisner and Gallimore 1977; Whiting and Edwards 1988). In the practice of sibling caretaking, older siblings are responsible for the care of their younger siblings. This may mean that older siblings have to keep the child happy and entertained while an adult is within earshot, or it may mean feeding, bathing, and taking full responsibility for the child's safety and wellbeing while the adult is away. When older siblings can take responsibility for younger children, adults can perform their work, such as maintaining the household, working in fields or orchards, or engaging in other subsistence responsibilities and chores. Sibling caretakers do more than just provide basic biological needs of their charges; they socialize them to behave in culturally-appropriate ways (Rogoff 1991; Zukow-Goldring 1995). There are cognitive and social benefits that siblings gain in relying on each other (Hill 1991), even if they are not expected to provide independent care for each other. And, siblings can be effective at teaching their younger siblings everyday kinds of tasks (Maynard 2002). Thus, there are benefits for both the older siblings and the younger ones. Learning is reciprocal, with caregivers learning important skills for their future.

The cross-cultural study of sibling caretaking has revealed many similarities in the practice, probably because of the closer developmental status of children who serve as sibling caretakers (they are closer in age and developmental stage to each other than to their parents), but there are also cultural nuances (Rabain-Jamin et al. 2003). In their study of Wolof and Zinacantec Maya siblings, Rabain-Jamin et al. (2003) found that Wolof sibling caretakers engaged toddlers in many more verbal language exchanges than do Zinacantec children. Zinacantec children appeared to engage in observational learning—an expectation of the Zinacantec model of teaching and learning (Maynard and Greenfield 2005)—than did Wolof children.

Sibling caretaking is widely employed in Africa and in Latin America, and in more traditional, small scale, face-to-face groups in Asia. Rogoff et al. (1993) studied the ways that older siblings and caregivers guided the activities of younger children in the United States, Guatemala, India, and Turkey where children differentially are engaged in the care of each other: European American children were not expected to provide care for each other, while Guatemalan, Indian, and Turkish children were. Younger siblings pay close attention to the activities of the older siblings in order to learn how to be involved in daily activities. Gaskins (1999) described the ways that older Yucatec Maya siblings structured tasks for younger children in order to engage them in helping with chores. Working with another Maya group, Maynard (2002) found that older siblings teach younger ones everyday tasks in the context of sibling caretaking activities.

Influences of Sibling Interactions on Social and Emotional Development

As they mature, children must develop the ability to understand how people, including parents, siblings, and others outside the home, will behave and respond in social situations. The sibling group provides an arena for children to learn about social support and the social world more generally, including how to understand people's feelings and how to relate to others. Sibling interactions are associated with aspects of prosocial behavior, including perspective taking and helping behavior, in both the family and school contexts in the preschool period (Dunn 1989). Siblings can help each other understand other people's emotions, including internal mental states. Recchia and Howe (2009) found that siblings in high–quality relationships had more positive conflict resolution strategies. In the United States, maternal involvement in sibling interactions seems to help children develop social skills like perspective taking (Recchia and Howe 2008). Miskitu children in Nicaragua managed sibling groups as they learned how to negotiate hierarchies and to follow a dominant child (Minks 2008). Zinacantec Maya children learned to cooperate and respect authority in the context of sibling care (De León 2008). Guatemalan siblings socialize each other by teasing (Reynolds 2008). In the Marquesas Islands siblings shared with each other freely by age three years (Martini and Kirkpatrick 1992). These abilities to participate appropriately in hierarchies, cooperate with each other and respect authority, and share with one another all involve an understanding of one's self and the perspectives and needs of others. Learning these skills is important for both older children and younger children. Older children learn how to manage others, and younger children learn how to be managed. But older children are also managed by adults, and younger children eventually manage others younger than themselves, so children learn from the ever-changing developmental scaffold they participate in.

Interacting with siblings enhances children's social perspective taking and false belief understanding (Lewis et al. 1996; Perner et al 1994; Ruffman et al. 1998). In their studies in Japan and England, Perner et al. (1994) found that the more siblings a child has, the more likely he is to understand the classic false belief task, that others may hold beliefs that are actually false relative to the true state of the world, and that beliefs may change according to changes in the world. There are mixed results on the effects of having a younger sibling in the enhancement of the older child's ability to perform on the false belief tasks, with some studies finding that having a younger sibling leads to advanced theory of mind development (Peterson 2000) and some studies finding it does not (Perner et al. 1994; Ruffman et al. 1998).

Influences of Sibling Interactions on Cognitive Development

Interacting with siblings also has influences on a child's cognitive development. As with social development, most cognitive benefits of interacting with siblings are not unidirectional. Interacting with siblings increases cognitive functioning for both parties involved (Cicirelli 1995). Children may display cognitive capacities earlier with their siblings than with other peers or adults or when they are alone (Azmitia and Hesser 1993). Younger children were more likely to observe their older siblings, because of daily interactions, than they were to observe older peers. Younger children were also more likely to ask for help from their older siblings than from their older peers. And, older siblings were more likely to provide spontaneous instruction than older peers.

Sibling nurturance has been found to affect children's school behaviors and adjustment (Gallimore et al. 1978; Weisner et al. 1988). Gallimore et al. (1978) found that sibling caretaking in Hawaiian families was correlated with classroom attentiveness and chores at home (beyond sibling caretaking). Weisner et al. (1988) explored sibling relationships and found that children performed better in school when the learning environment more closely mirrored the environment for interactions at home, where children helped each other and collaborated on tasks. Positive sibling relations are related to perspective taking skills of the older child (Howe and Ross 1990). Early attention to distress may lead to the development of perspective taking abilities at a cognitive level as children try to meet the needs of their younger siblings more efficiently and sensitively.

Sibling Teaching

Siblings can be especially effective teachers of their younger siblings because they are related, they are emotionally close, they are close in age, and they spend a lot of time together. Teaching is a special kind of cognitive activity that involves taking the perspective of another in order to do it well (Strauss et al. 2002). Older siblings teach their younger siblings to do everyday kinds of things, especially in the context of sibling caretaking relationships (Maynard 2002). Older siblings may accrue advantages in cognitive functioning from teaching their younger siblings (Meisner and Fisher 1980) and younger siblings receive the benefits of guidance. Maynard (2004) found that sibling teaching at home may be affected by the models of teaching children are exposed to at school.

Most studies of sibling teaching have been conducted in laboratory settings (e.g., Cicirelli 1972, 1973; Stewart 1983), with protocols designed for experimental control, but perhaps lacking in ecological validity. Quasi-experimental or observational studies at home have indicated that children use their social and cognitive skills to teach each other. Sibling age spacing and the quality of sibling relationships affect teaching interactions (Howe and Recchia 2009; Recchia et al. 2009), and sibling teaching improves with age (Recchia et al. 2009).

Maynard (2002) used ethnographic video data to examine the development of sibling teaching in the context of caretaking interactions. Older siblings ages three to 11 years were recorded as they engaged their younger, two-year-old siblings in everyday activities. The oldest group of sibling caretakers, ages eight to 11 years, structured tasks for children, provided necessary materials, simplified tasks into doable parts, guided the bodies of learners, and provided both verbal and nonverbal feedback to help their youngest siblings do a task.

The Impact of Sibling Interactions on Language Development

Language is a powerful tool in the socialization of children. Parents and other socializing agents, such as sibling caretakers, express linguistic and cultural knowledge to indicate the appropriate behavior expected of children as they gain involvement in cultural practices (Ochs 1982). Interestingly, some cultural groups view babies as conversational partners while others do not. Ochs (1982) found that Samoan parents do not treat infants as conversational partners because they believe that infants don't understand and can't talk back. On the other hand, in most cultural groups in the United States, even very young children—two- and three-year-olds—adjust their speech to infants (Dunn and Kendrick 1982; Shatz and Gelman 1973). Zukow (1989) found that Euro-American and Latino adult and sibling caregivers use rich linguistic interactions to socialize children's language.

Both adult and sibling caregivers are adept at coordinating verbal and nonverbal discourse in order to help children understand what is happening. These interactions lead to close involvement in activities (Zukow 1989). In Africa, Melanesia, and Samoa, triadic conversations may also involve a present third party, where the mother, older sibling, and infant participate together in language socialization practices (Ochs 1988; Rabain-Jamin 1994; Schieffelin 1990; Watson-Gegeo and Gegeo 1989). In those interactions, mothers engage younger and older siblings to help the two understand others' perspectives emotionally and cognitively. Children also learn to take each others' perspective in the course of these triadic interactions.

Conclusions

Sibling relationships are important, lifelong bonds the characteristics of which vary across cultural settings. Children learn and practice social and cognitive skills as they relate to each other in childhood, including perspective taking, teaching, caretaking, and language socialization, but some cultural groups emphasize the importance and closeness of the sibling relationship more than others. Illuminating the sibling relationship in childhood can help explain why sibling relationships take the forms they do in adulthood. Understanding siblings can help us understand essential questions about culture and development because we can use this special relationship as a lens to focus on aspects of relationships and cultural activities that are part of the environment of the developing child.

References

Anthropological Institute of Great Britain and Ireland. (1872). *The Journal of the Anthropological Institute of Great Britain and Ireland*. London: Published for the Anthropological Institute of Great Britain and Ireland by Trübner.

Azmitia, M., & Hesser, J. (1993). Why siblings are important agents of cognitive development: A comparison of siblings and peers. *Child Development, 64,* 430–444.

Cicirelli, V. (1972). The effect of sibling relationship on concept learning of young children taught by child-teachers. *Child Development, 43,* 282–287.

Cicirelli, V. (1973). Effects of sibling structure and interaction on children's categorization style. *Developmental Psychology, 9,* 132–139.

Cicirelli, V. (1995). *Sibling relationships across the lifespan*. New York, NY, US: Plenum Press.

De León, L. (2008). *Authority, attention, and affect in directive/response sequences in Zinacantec Mayan siblings*. Paper presented at the 107th annual meeting of the American Anthropological Association, San Francisco, CA.

Dunn, J. (1989). Siblings and the development of social understanding in early childhood. In P. G. Zukow (Ed.), *Sibling interaction across cultures. Theoretical and methodological issues* (pp. 106–116). New York, NY: Springer-Verlag.

Dunn, J., & Kendrick, C. (1982). The speech of two- and three-year olds to infant siblings: "Baby Talk" and the context of communication. *Journal of Child Language, 9,* 579–597.

Gallimore, R., Tharp, R., & Speidel, G. (1978). The relationship of sibling caretaking and attentiveness to a peer tutor. *American Educational Research Journal, 15*(2), 267–273.

Gaskins, S. (1999). Children's daily lives in a Mayan village: A case study of culturally constructed roles and activities. In A. Göncü (Ed.), *Children's engagement in the world: Sociocultural perspectives* (pp. 25–61). New York: Cambridge University Press.

Greenfield, P. M., & Childs, C. P. (1977). Understanding sibling concepts: A developmental study of kin terms in Zinacantan. In P. Dasen (Ed.), *Piagetian psychology: Cross-cultural contributions* (pp. 335–358). New York: Gardner Press.

Heath, S. B. (1983). *Ways with words: Language, life, and work in communities and classrooms.* New York: McGraw-Hill; Oxford University Press.

Hecht, J. A. (1983). The cultural contexts of siblingship in Pukapuka. In M. Marshall (Ed.), *Siblingship in Oceania: Studies in the meaning of kin relations* (pp. 53–77). Lanham, MD: University Press of America.

Hill, M. (1991). The role of social networks in the care of young children. In M. Woodhead, P. Light, & R. Carr (Eds.), *Growing up in a changing society* (pp. 97–114). London: Routledge, in association with The Open University.

Howe, N., & Recchia, H. (2009). Individual differences in sibling teaching in early and middle childhood. *Early Education and Development, 20*(1), 174–197.

Howe, N., & Ross, H. S. (1990). Socialization, perspective-taking, and the sibling relationship. *Developmental Psychology, 26*(1), 160–165.

Lewis, C., Freeman, N. H., Kyriakidou, C., Maridaki-Kassotaki, K., & Berridge, D. (1996). Social influences on false belief access: Specific sibling influences or general apprenticeship? *Child Development, 67,* 2930–2947.

Lieberman, D. (2009). Rethinking the Taiwanese minor marriage data: Evidence the mind uses multiple kindship cues to regulate inbreeding avoidance. *Evolution and Human Behavior, 30*(3), 153–160.

Martini, M. (1994). Peer interactions in Polynesia: A view from the Marquesas. In J. L. Roopnarine, J. E. Johnson, & F. H. Hooper (Eds.), *Children's play in diverse cultures* (pp. 73–103). Albany: State University of New York Press.

Martini, M., & Kirkpatrick, J. (1992). Parenting in Polynesia: A view from the Marquesas. In J. L. Roopnarine & D. B. Carter (Eds.), *Parent-child socialization in diverse cultures* (pp. 199–223). Norwood, NJ: Ablex.

Maynard, A. E. (2002). Cultural teaching: The development of teaching skills in Zinacantec Maya sibling interactions. *Child Development, 73*(3), 969–982.

Maynard, A. E. (2004). Cultures of teaching in childhood: Formal schooling and Maya sibling teaching at home. *Cognitive Development, 19*(4), 517–536.

Maynard, A. E. (2016). How siblings matter in Zinancatec Maya child development. In M. C. Hay (Ed.), *Methods that matter* (pp. 249–267). Chicago, IL: University of Chicago Press.

Maynard, A. E., & Greenfield, P. M. (2005). An ethnomodel of teaching and learning: Apprenticeship of Zinacantec Maya women's tasks. In A. E. Maynard & M. I. Martini (Eds.), *Learning in cultural context: Family, peers, and school* (pp. 75–103). New York: Springer.

Maynard, A. E., & Tovote, K. E. (2010). Learning from other children. The anthropology of learning in childhood. In D. F. Lancy, J. Bock, & S. Gaskins (Eds.), *The anthropology of learning in childhood* (pp. 181–205). Walnut Creek, CA: AltaMira Press.

Meisner, J. S., & Fisher, V. L. (1980). Cognitive shifts of young children as a function of peer interaction and sibling status. *The Journal of Genetic Psychology, 136,* 247–253.

Mellor, C. (2012). *The three-martini playdate: A practical guide to happy parenting.* Chronicle Books.

Mendelson, M. J. (1990). *Becoming a brother: A child learns abut life, family, and self.* Cambridge, MA: MIT Press.

Minks, A. (2008). *Socializing rights and responsibilities: Domestic play among Miskitu siblings on the Atlantic coast of Nicaragua.* Paper presented at the 107th annual meeting of the American Anthropological Association, San Francisco, CA.

Nuckolls, C. W. (1993). *Siblings in South Asia: Brothers and sisters in cultural context*. New York: Guilford.

Ochs, E. (1982). Talking to children in Western Samoa. *Language in Society, 11*, 77–104.

Ochs, E. (1988). *Culture and language development: Language acquisition and socialization in a Samoan village*. Cambridge MA: Cambridge University PRess.

Perner, J., Ruffman, T., & Leekam, S. R. (1994). Theory of mind is contagious: You catch it from your sibs. *Child Development, 65*(4), 1228–1238.

Peterson, C. C. (2000). Influence of siblings' perspectives on theory of mind. *Cognitive Development, 15*(4), 435–455.

Rabain-Jamin, J. (1994). Language and socialization of the child in African families living in France. In P. M. Greenfield & R. R. Cocking (Eds.), *Cross-cultural roots of minority child development* (pp. 147–166). Hillsdale, NJ, US: Lawrence Erlbaum Associates Inc.

Rabain-Jamin, J., Maynard, A. E., & Greenfield, P. M. (2003). Implications of sibling caregiving for sibling relations and teaching interactions in two cultures. *Ethos, 31*(2), 204–231.

Recchia, H. E., & Howe, N. (2008). Family talk about internal states and children's relative appraisals of self and sibling. *Social Development, 17*(4), 776–794.

Recchia, H. E., & Howe, N. (2009). Associations between social understanding, sibling relationship quality, and siblings' conflict strategies and outcomes. *Child Development, 80*(5), 1564–1578.

Recchia, H. E., & Howe, N. (2010). When do siblings compromise? Associations with children's descriptions of conflict issues, culpability, and emotions. *Social Development, 19*(4), 838–857.

Recchia, H. E., Howe, N., & Alexander, S. (2009). "You didn't teach me, you showed me": Variations in sibling teaching strategies in early and middle childhood. *Merrill-Palmer Quarterly: Journal of Developmental Psychology, 55*(1), 55–78.

Reynolds, J. F. (2008). Socializing puros pericos (Little Parrots): The negotiation of respect and responsibility in Antonero Mayan sibling and peer networks. *Journal of Linguistic Anthropology, 18*, 82–107.

Rogoff, B. (1991). The joint socialization of development by young children and adults. In M. Lewis & S. Feinman (Eds.), *Social influences and socialization in infancy* (pp. 253–280). New York: Plenum Press.

Rogoff, B., Mistry, J., Göncü, A., & Mosier, C. (1993). Guided participation in cultural activity by toddlers and caregivers. *Monographs of the Society for Research in Child Development, 58*, (8, Serial No. 236).

Ross, H., & Howe, N. (2009). Family influences on children's peer relationships. In K. H. Rubin, W. M. Bukowski, & B. Laursen (Eds.), *Social, emotional, and personality development in context. Handbook of peer interactions, relationships, and groups* (pp. 508–527). New York: The Guilford Press.

Rubinstein, R. L. (1983). Siblings in Malo culture. In M. Marshall (Ed.), *Siblingship in Oceania: Studies in the meaning of kin relations* (pp. 307–334). Lanham, MD: University Press of America.

Ruffman, T., Perner, J., Naito, M., Parkin, L., & Clements, W. A. (1998). Older (but not younger) siblings facilitate false belief understanding. *Developmental Psychology, 34*(1), 161–174.

Schieffelin, B. B. (1990). *The give and take of everyday life: Language socialization of Kaluli children*. Cambridge, England: Cambridge University Press.

Shatz, M., & Gelman, R. (1973). The development of communication skills: Modifications in the speech of young children as a function of listener. *Monographs of the Society for Research in Child Development*. Chicago: University of Chicago Press.

Shor, E., & Simchai, D. (2009). Incest avoidance, the incest taboo, and social cohesion: Revisiting Westermarck and the case of the Israeli kibbutzim. *American Journal of Sociology, 114*(6), 1803–1842.

Stewart, R. B. (1983). Sibling interaction: The role of the older child as teacher for the younger. *Merrill Palmer Quarterly, 29*(1), 47–68.

Strauss, S., Ziv, M., & Stein, A. (2002). Teaching as a natural cognition and its relations to preschoolers' developing theory of mind. *Cognitive Development, 17*(3–4), 1473–1487.

Tovote, K. E., & Maynard, A. E. (2018). Maya children working in the streets: Value mismatches from the village to the street setting. *International Journal of Psychology, 53,* 34–43.

Volling, B. L., Kennedy, D. E., & Jackey, L. M. H. (2010). The development of sibling jealousy. In S. L. Hart & M. Legerstee (Eds.), *Handbook of jealousy: Theory, research, and multidisciplinary approaches* (pp. 387–417). New York: Wiley-Blackwell.

Watson-Gegeo, K. A., & Gegeo, D. W. (1989). The role of sibling interaction in child socialization. In P. G. Zukow (Ed.), *Sibling interaction across cultures: Theoretical and methodological issues* (pp. 54–76). New York: Springer Verlag.

Weisner, T. S., & Gallimore, R. (1977). My brother's keeper: Child and sibling caretaking. *Current Anthropology, 18*(2), 169–190.

Weisner, T. S. (1987). Socialization for parenthood in sibling caretaking societies. In J. B. Lancaster, J. Altmann, A. S. Rossi, & L. R. Sherrod (Eds.), *Parenting across the life span: Biosocial dimensions* (pp. 237–270). Hawthorne, NY: Aldine Publishing Co.

Weisner, T. S. (1989). Comparing sibling relationships across cultures. In P. G. Zukow (Ed.), *Sibling interaction across cultures. Theoretical and methodological issues* (pp. 11–25). New York, NY: Springer Verlag.

Weisner, T. S., Gallimore, R., & Jordan, C. (1988). Unpacking cultural effects on classroom learning: Native Hawaiian peer assistance and child-generated activity. *Anthropology and Education Quarterly, 19*(4), 327–353.

Wenger, M. (1989). Work, play, and social relationships among children in a Giriama community. In D. Belle (Ed.), *Children's social networks and social supports* (pp. 91–115). New York: Wiley Interscience.

Whaley, S. E., Sigman, M., Beckwith, L., Cohen, S., & Espinosa, M. (2002). Infant -caregiver interaction in Kenya and the United States: The Importance of multiple caregivers and adequate comparison samples. *Journal of Cross-Cultural Psychology, 33*(3), 236–247.

Whiting, B. B., & Edwards, C. P. (1988). *Children of different worlds: The formation of social behavior.* Cambridge, MA: Harvard University Press.

Whiting, B. B., & Whiting, J. W. M. (1975). *Children of six cultures: A psycho-cultural analysis.* Cambridge, MA: Harvard University Press.

Zukow, P. G. (1989). Siblings as effective socializing agents: Evidence from Central Mexico. In P. G. Zukow (Ed.), *Sibling interaction across cultures. Theoretical and methodological issues* (pp. 79–105). New York, NY: Springer-Verlag.

Zukow-Goldring, P. (1995). Sibling caregiving. In M. H. Bornstein (Ed.), *Handbook of parenting: Status and social conditions of parenting* (Vol. 3, pp. 177–208). Hillsdale, NJ: Lawrence Erlbaum Associates Inc.

Chapter 12
The Roles of Grandparents in Child Development: A Cultural Approach

David W. Shwalb, Ziarat Hossain and Giovanna Eisberg

Abstract Researchers in the field of child development have typically downplayed the influence of grandparents on their grandchildren and on their adult children, and most studies of grandparents have taken place in Western societies. This chapter focuses on three sets of research questions. First, how do grandparents influence their young or preschool age grandchildren, how are they influenced by their grandchildren, and how do grandparents influence their adult children? Second, what are some similarities and differences among grandparents, between and within cultural groups? Third, how do grandparents affect, and how are they affected by, cultural variations in children's social worlds and in social competencies valued by different cultures? As an assessment of the growing social science research literature on grandparenthood in cultural context, this chapter illustrates many contextual influences on grandparents and indicates that a multi-disciplinary and cultural approach is necessary to better understand and support grandparents worldwide.

Researchers in the field of child development have unfortunately ignored or underestimated the influence of grandparents on their young grandchildren and on their adult children (Shwalb and Hossain 2017, 2018). In addition, until recently research on grandparents was mainly on Western populations that value individualism, personal growth, emotional independence, and separateness (Hayslip and Fruhauf 2018; Szinovacz 1998). On the other hand, the collectivistic values of interconnectedness, emotional dependence, and togetherness are pertinent to the study of grandparents in non-Western families (Hossain et al. 2018). Indeed, societal values have significant implications for interactions among grandparents, their adult children and young grandchildren, and consequently for development across the lifespan. As a reassessment of the growing social science research literature on grandparenthood in cultural context, this chapter illustrates many contextual influences on grandparents and takes a multi-disciplinary and cultural approach.

D. W. Shwalb
Southern Utah University, Cedar City, USA

Z. Hossain (✉) · G. Eisberg
University of New Mexico, Albuquerque, NM, USA
e-mail: zhossain@unm.edu

© Springer Nature Switzerland AG 2019

T. Tulviste et al. (eds.), *Children's Social Worlds in Cultural Context*,
https://doi.org/10.1007/978-3-030-27033-9_12

Children around the world are usually studied based on a Western standard of child development, and historically- and culturally-biased value judgments have led to conclusions based on statistical averages. Yet we do not know if Western developmental norms apply to children who live in non-Western or developing societies. Although contemporary ethno-theories of child development (e.g., bioecological systems, cultural ecology, and developmental niche models) are widely accepted as applicable cross-culturally, studies based on other theories may apply cultural biases. Clearly, research and theories relevant to the roles of grandparents in child development is still nascent.

Grandparents engage in caregiver and educational activities that contribute to young children's healthy emotional and social development (Shwalb and Hossain 2018). For example, studies have demonstrated the importance of high quality early childhood education, and how those educational experiences correlate with children's healthy development and risk factors associated with adolescent and adult criminality (Jones et al. 2015).

This chapter addresses three research questions. First, how do grandparents influence preschool age grandchildren, how do their preschool age grandchildren influence them, and how do grandparents influence the parents of young children? Second, what are the similarities and differences among grandparents, between or within cultural groups? Third, how do grandparents affect, and how are they affected by, cultural variations in children's social worlds and in the social competencies valued by different cultures?

Grandparents' Influences on Young Grandchildren

In early childhood, children make significant strides in their motor, cognitive, and communication skills, including emotion regulation, culturally appropriate behaviors, and specific social skills that are necessary for the development of healthy friendships and relationships (Barnett et al. 2010). Although both parents and grandparents in developing societies are usually the primary socialization agents of young children, there is a paucity of data that explores the effects of grandparent interactions and learning in their grandchildren's lives, especially in early childhood (Coall and Hertwig 2010; Gregory et al. 2007; Hossain et al. 2018). Instead, most grandparenting research has focused on the grandparent-grandchild dyad, specifically on grandmothers in high-risk families and as caregivers (Barnett et al. 2010). Although many authors discuss grandparent roles in 'young childhood,' the majority of these studies focus on middle childhood (6–12 years of age) rather than on early childhood. This is striking given that Erik Erikson's psychosocial theory of development emphasized early childhood as a time when children are focused on their family life (Jones et al. 2015; Woody and Woody 2015). Grandparents foster intergenerational relationships as caregivers and socialization agents, and facilitate the learning of young grandchildren, and there is a need for more cultural research on grandparents' contributions to early childhood and children's emotional regulation.

Grandparents can influence young children both directly and indirectly (Pilka-uskas 2014; Shwalh and Hossain 2018). Studies on three-generational families with grandfathers who resided in the home with a young grandchild and with no other male present revealed two very important findings (Oyserman et al. 1993). First, evidence of grandfather involvement as a surrogate father to one-year-old grandchildren demonstrated that when grandfathers nurture their grandchild, affectionate interactions led to more compliance when their teen mothers made requests of them in their early developmental years. Second, young children showed less negative affect such as crying, fussing, or sadness when their grandfathers were involved in caregiving tasks. In addition, very young children lack the ability to regulate emotions that can lead to temper outbursts (Woody and Woody 2015), which frequently precipitates a parent's decision to harshly discipline a child. These findings show that grandparents can buffer the impact of harsh parenting (Barnett et al. 2010).

In many societies, especially in the West, high quality early childhood programs that include learning activities contribute to children's school readiness and improve academic success (Gorey 2001). A meta-analysis of thirty-five studies in preschools demonstrated how high quality early childhood education can positively increase intelligence scores and cognition and reduce relationship problems, 10–25 years later (Gorey 2001). Therefore, another way grandparents can influence their preschool age grandchildren is to provide rich experiences through learning activities such as telling stories and reading to them (Ruby 2012). Grandparents have the ability to provide many of the same rich experiences with additional benefits, such as personal historical familial knowledge, culture, and traditions. Yet research on the effects of quality early education is virtually non-existent among diverse groups especially in non-Western societies. Most young children first experience lessons in language and literacy at home. Strong familial interactions, especially with grandparents, may substitute for the same knowledge children in Western cultures gain from high quality preschool programs. Data on early child development suggest that non-Western grandparents contribute in similar ways as high quality educational programs do in Western societies (Nakazawa et al. 2018). These grandparents continue their care and teaching involvement with young grandchildren even after migration to a Western society. For example, Bangladeshi immigrant grandmothers in the U.K. frequently served as early educators teaching literacy, science, and environment to young grandchildren (Ruby 2012). Through interactions with their grandchildren, grandparents read and tell stories together, sing songs, and engage in various other activities (Gregory et al. 2007). These findings show that families must explore and tap into grandparental resources for child development when parents cannot afford high quality early childhood programs.

Grandparents in three-generation families in different societies also play a large role in transmission of language (Babu et al. 2018) and religious beliefs (Gutierrez et al. 2014). They also engage in socialization of culture (Ruby 2012), and serve as role models and sources of cultural identity (Gibbons and Fanjul de Marsicovetere 2018) for grandchildren. Spiritual and religious programs have been demonstrated to serve as a protective factor in early childhood (Woody and Woody 2015), and grandparents offer their grandchildren many opportunities to learn the importance of religion and cultural values (Gutierrez et al. 2014). For example, grandparents in South Asian families dress and escort their grandchildren to religious ceremonies and services (Babu et al. 2018). Clearly, grandparents in most societies are at the core of teaching young grandchildren about religious and spiritual values, cultural symbols, rituals, and environmental adaptation.

One is hard-pressed to find a grandparent that does not react with utter joy at the first mention of their grandchildren. Grandparents from diverse cultures describe their experience as a grandparent as significant in their lives, giving them fulfillment and overwhelming happiness, and making all of life's difficult trials worth it. Some grandparents report that grandchildren help keep them young (Smethers 2015), and that grandchildren help make their lives richer, while others state that grandchildren give them meaning and motivation to continue living (Nakazawa et al. 2018). Although studies have demonstrated negative mental and physical health effects in grandparents who have become primary caregivers for grandchildren (Coall and Hertwig 2010), some primary caregiving grandparents in Sub-Saharan Africa reported greater happiness and higher levels of life satisfaction (Mhaka-Mutepfa et al. 2018). Grandparents' caregiving involvement is beneficial overall to Chinese American grandparents' psychological well-being when the care was not overly burdensome (Xu et al. 2017).

In South African families, there are reciprocal expectations between grandparents who care for young grandchildren that when they need to be cared for someday, grandchildren will later step into fill the role of caregiver for their grandparents (Makiwane et al. 2018). Such reciprocal care interactions offer security to grandparents who know that the intra-familial transmission of responsibility through caregiving is shared by their grandchildren (Coall and Hertwig 2010), whom grandparents love deeply, and report that they receive unconditional love from their grandchildren, a feeling Central American grandparents say, is like *magic* (Gibbons and Fanjul de Marsicovetere 2018, p. 24). Evidence also suggests that altruistic acts of service such as those grandparents transmit to their grandchildren lead to higher levels of positive physical and mental well-being (Smethers 2015). These findings demonstrate support for the importance of the grandparent-grandchild relationship, especially in early childhood.

Grandparents' Influences on the Parents of Young Children

Life expectancy has dramatically increased over the last few decades across many nations (Smethers 2015). As a result, relationships between older generations and their children can last for over seven decades (Hagestad 2006). Therefore, the enduring relationship benefits all involved when these three-generational relationships work in synchrony. Parenting of children does not end when children become adults

(Hagestad 2006), and the quality of parent and adult children relationships often depends on the nature and frequency of contact (Tanskanen 2017). Relationships between grandparents and their grandchildren are in large part mediated by the relationship grandparents have with their adult children—the middle generation (Coall and Hertwig 2010). This middle generation as gatekeepers control the time and extent of the relationships their children have with their grandparents, especially in Western families.

Grandparents can indirectly have an impact on their grandchildren by having a direct effect on their grandchildren's parents. For example, grandparents are known to help their adult children by giving them emotional support, providing information as well as monetary support (Smith and Drew 2002). Grandparents also provide direct financial support and clothes for their grandchildren. Russian grandmothers, for example, often help their adult children by supporting them financially and providing care to young children (Utrata 2018). Monetary support can often relieve the financial stress parents face, and parents can enjoy higher levels of emotional and mental well-being, which usually translates to positive outcomes for children (Tanskanen 2017). Conversely, if grandparents interfere with their adult children's practices, they could increase stress levels in the home (Nakazawa et al. 2018). For example, one study of grandmothers in Singapore and Japan reported a strong over-arching premise of non-interference with the parents of young children, and it was very important to them to respect their adult children's form of child rearing (Onodera 2005).

Another way grandparents influence the parents of their grandchildren is through babysitting. In particular, adult children get a much needed break when grandparents offer respite care or more frequent caregiving of children with physical illness or disabilities. This involvement is significant as it helps adult children to reduce the stress associated with care for a child with a disability. Grandparents frequently help care for grandchildren with one or more disabilities, and often, there are multiple diagnoses, including intellectual deficits, speech and hearing deficits, and/or neurological problems (Hung et al. 2004; Janicki et al. 2000).

Comparisons of Grandparents Within and Between Cultural Groups

Multiple studies show that the role of primary caregiver of grandchildren often has negative effects, mentally and physically, on grandparents in the West (Coall and Hertwig 2010; Haylsip and Fruhauf 2018), sub-Sarahan Africa (Mhaka-Mutepfa et al. 2018), and East Asia (Shin 2015). These studies suggest that older individuals live a reduced quality of physical and mental health due to overload. 'Grandchild sickness,' a relatively new phenomenon, refers to physical exhaustion among grandparents in some Japanese families (Nakazawa et al. 2018), and the financial stress many grandparents experience has resulted from caring for grandchildren (An and Kim 2015). On the other hand, some South Korean grandparents reported heightened life satisfaction in caring for grandchildren because they were able to avoid the loneliness that frequently accompanies old age (Nakazawa et al. 2018).

Japanese mothers also reported a higher quality of life because of the availability of the grandmother who cared for young children. In Chinese families, grandparents assisted in educating their grandchildren and helping with child rearing, especially in caring for young children when their parents had to move to urban cities for better job opportunities (Nakazawa et al. 2018). When grandparents in these families chose not to care for their grandchildren due to family circumstances, the relationship between them and their adult children reportedly deteriorated (Cong and Silverstein 2012).

In sub-Saharan Africa, grandparents have by long tradition cared for grandchildren, and the need to care for young children has increased with urgency since the AIDS epidemic has claimed the lives of many of the young adults of childbearing age (Henderson and Cook 2005). In this region, 62% of the population is under the age of 24, and with a high mortality rate and life expectancy of only 56 years virtually every family in sub-Saharan Africa has had to provide care for grandchildren of all ages, while grandparents range in age between forty and eighty-five. This is striking because more than 80% of the poorest countries are in sub-Saharan countries (World Bank 2016). Many grandparents in South Africa also endure the tragic hardship of losing young adult children to the AIDS pandemic and therefore, grandparents take in their young grandchildren who are orphaned (Makiwane et al. 2018).

Similar to sub-Saharan and South African grandmothers, African American grandmothers in the U.S. have historically cared for young grandchildren and served as a mechanism for the survival of families. Regardless of their varied socioeconomic backgrounds, African American grandmothers, often within a co-parenting or co-residential multigenerational family unit, care, socialize, and provide shelter for grandchildren (Minkler and Fuller-Thomson 2005). According to a U.S. Census Bureau (Ellis and Simmons 2014), about 14% African American children below the age of 18 resided with their grandparents. A case in point is that former First Lady Michelle Obama invited her 71-year-old mother (Marian Robinson) to reside with them in the White House from 2009, and care for her two young granddaughters (Gibson 2014). The long-standing tradition of selflessness and obligation is rooted in African American grandparents' commitment to protect grandchildren from entrance into foster care. Their underlying foundational beliefs are that grandchildren are far safer when cared for by grandparents than by strangers, regardless of the health consequences such care might take on elderly grandparents (Gibson 2014). In addition to providing grandchildren with their basic needs, they continue to raise them with strong religious values and convictions (Copen and Silverstein 2012; Gutierrez et al. 2014).

While research about grandparents and their grandchildren during the early childhood years is scarce, studies of grandfathers are even more uncommon. Available research on grandfathers highlights that they make an important contribution to grandchildren's growth and development (Buchanan and Rotkirch 2016). One British study used the Foundation Stage Profile (FSP) to assess the influence of grandparents on grandchildren's personal, social, emotional, and creative development (Tanskanen and Danielsbacka 2016). Findings from Tanskanen and Danielsbacka's work and other longitudinal studies conducted in the U.K. demonstrate that grandchildren's positive early childhood experiences with their grandfathers and grandmothers were related to not only grandchildren's academic success, but also higher incomes in adulthood (Feinstein and Duckworth 2006).

Grandparenting research on Mexican and Central American families often underscores the role of grandfathers in the socialization of grandchildren for traditional values such as *machismo* (Gibbons and Fanjul de Marsicovetere 2018). Grandchildren learn the practice and contexts of male authority, patriarchy, and men's responsibility to run the family. As they move away from such a hegemonic gender ideology, many contemporary grandfathers teach their grandchildren about nurturance, commitment, and care for the family—a resilient view of *machismo* called *caballerismo*. A similar guardian or compensatory role is also very common in Asian cultures. However, compared to grandmothers, grandfathers typically participate less in active childcare of young grandchildren across cultural communities.

Variations in Children's Social Worlds, and Their Impact on Grandparental Roles

Social networks of young children vary across cultures and sometimes have sociopolitical implications. For example, an extended, interconnected, community-based network exists in families in India where grandparents play critical roles in helping to raise grandchildren to become socially adept, respectful, and conscientious citizens. These grandparents expect filial piety from their grandchildren, and to receive care when they become ill or elderly. During their grandchildren's early years of development, Bangladeshi immigrant grandmothers in the U.K. have been instrumental in raising their young grandchildren. These grandmothers spent time caring for their young grandchildren, as they read them stories, went on outings together, and taught them about family traditions (Ruby 2012).

Elsewhere, the Chinese practice of the One Child Policy (1979–2016) had a significant influence on children's social worlds. The policy made young children socially dependent on their parents and grandparents because children no longer had siblings to grow up with together. Grandparents in turn were more vulnerable because they had fewer family members to rely on in their old age, making it critically important that they get along with their adult child and grandchild. These types of political changes in some cultures have changed grandparental roles, and in turn have changed the way they interact with their grandchildren.

Variations in Social Competencies Valued Between Cultural Groups, and Their Impact on Grandparental Roles

Grandparents assume an important role in the inculcation of cultural values, and this has implications for young grandchildren's social and emotional competencies (Pilkauskas 2014). For example, grandparents' experiences with young grandchildren in Western societies (unlike practices of non-Western families) usually depend on their interactions with the parents of their grandchildren, and their influence in these early relationships often parallels the child's parents. This is mainly due to a rigid nuclear family boundary that determines roles and positions within the family system. However, this does not diminish their value or critical importance for young children's development (Haylsip and Fruhauf 2018).

Scholars have reported that the development of non-cognitive skills precedes the development of cognitive skills in young children (Jones et al. 2015). Scientific evidence lends indirect support to how grandparent-grandchild interactions play a role in early childhood development, e.g., in the landmark HighScope Perry Preschool program study. Cross-culturally, families include grandparental interactions both in Western non-resident (Tanskanen and Danielsbacka 2016) and in non-Western three-generation households (Pilkauskas 2014), and those interactions have powerful implications for child development.

The activities that grandparents engage in with their young grandchildren align with the active participation form of learning of the Perry program, and these grandparent-grandchild interactions occurred in the non-West long before this program existed. Play, as well as instrumental interactions between grandparents and their young grandchildren, has long been normative, especially in non-Western families. For example, proximal interactions between Indian grandparents and grandchildren provide the context of grandchildren's care and learning cultural values such as respect and harmony (Babu et al. 2018). Through caregiving, storytelling and cultural teachings that begin early on in a child's life, grandparents contribute to their young grandchildren's emotional regulation, positive behaviors, and social skill development. In most cases, non-Western grandparents, as family authority figures, function as primary socialization agents to instill values of respect, dependence, cooperation, and selflessness in grandchildren.

On the other hand, most Western cultures strongly emphasize children's personal growth, independence, and the implementation of technological skills. We may even argue that grandparents' role in Western child development is increasingly marginalized, because institutions and technological tools and gadgets teach children how to learn and behave in public. Unlike grandparents in non-Western societies, Western grandparents are less likely to exercise independent authority to teach grandchildren about social competencies. Because of rapid demographic shifts, e.g., increasing longevity, especially in Western societies, we need to reassess and recognize the social position of grandparents. In sum, the style of grandparents' involvement and types of social competences in children are not universal because of contextual (cultural and environmental) influences.

Conclusions

Research on the roles of grandparents in child development is profoundly limited especially for the preschool age group. Much of the available grandparental research focuses on grandmothers, and specifically maternal grandmothers (Buchanan 2018). This is astounding given that involved and nurturing fathers (most of whom will become grandfathers someday) have been shown to contribute to the cognitive and social development of their sons and daughters (Roopnarine 2015; Shwalb et al. 2013). The idea of 'new fathers' has become a catalyst for interest in 'new grandfathers' (Buchanan, 2018). Furthermore, research has demonstrated that men in Western societies became more nurturing as they aged (Oyserman et al. 1993), which has also been observed in Indian families. Although Indian fathers are less likely to show affectionate bonds with their own children, they become less reserved when they become grandfathers, and engage in more nurturing behaviors and play with their grandchildren (Babu et al. 2018; Chaudhary 2013). Future research can help capture the relationship dynamics between grandparents and grandchildren and how grandparents contribute to early child development.

Although limited, available research suggests that maternal grandparents, compared to paternal grandparents, may tend to contribute more and have closer ties to their grandchildren. Research is also needed to explore the nature of interactions between young children and mothers who lose their own mothers or fathers through early death. Just as adult children act as gatekeepers between their children and their own parents, maternal grandmothers may serve a similar role when they restrict paternal grandparents' contact and are readily available to their daughters' children. It is plausible that in these cases when a maternal grandmother is unavailable, paternal grandmothers and grandfathers play larger roles in the lives of their grandchildren. Future cross-cultural research can shed light maternal vs. paternal grandparenting.

We also need more research on grandparents as protective factors in high-risk families. In one relevant study, adolescent grandchildren who had greater closeness and connectedness with their grandparents did not exhibit symptoms of depression even when their mothers were clinically depressed (Silverstein and Ruiz 2006). This was important because infants, toddlers and preschool children are all susceptible to depressive symptoms when their mothers or primary caregivers are depressed. Further, although harsh parenting is often passed from generation to generation, grandmothers (Barnett et al. 2010) and grandfathers (Buchanan 2018) in some families counter the effects of harshness by being more sensitive and nurturant to their young grandchildren.

Although there have been many studies of grandparents as primary caregivers for their grandchildren because of parental absence (Makiwane et al. 2018), we have seen very few studies of grandparents' social roles and identities (Hossain et al. 2018). There is an urgent need for more cross-cultural and interdisciplinary empirical research on the reciprocal relationships between grandparents and young grandchildren, and the impact of grandparents on the psychological, intellectual, and physical development of young grandchildren.

Overall, grandparents across most cultures influence their adult children when they convey the importance of respect, family history, culture, values, and tradition as they share their knowledge and wisdom, so that parents can also transmit familial history to their grandchildren and great grandchildren (Hossain et al. 2018). However, the threat of the loss of cultural traditions and heritage has become more serious than ever before due to technological advances, economic changes, career goals, and both rural-to-urban and global migration. At the same time, future parents and grandchildren in each society may spend more time with one another because of increased life expectancies. In other words, grandparents are inseparable from family roots and grandchildren, and their adult children recognize this as important.

In answer to the three questions posed at the beginning of this article, the limited international literature supports the conclusion that reciprocal influences among grandparents, their adult children, and grandchildren exist across societies. Second, we can observe similarities and differences among grandparents, between and within cultural groups. Finally, we find that grandparental roles influence and are impacted by cultural variations in children's social worlds and in the social competencies different cultures value.

Acknowledgements We thank Barbara J. Shwalb, Tony Merz, Michael Ullery, Jonathan Berman, Andy Gorder, Allison Shwalb, Wendy Greenwald, Martin Greenwald, and Southern Utah University (SUU) Psychology Department chairs Grant Corser and Garrett Strosser. We also acknowledge the support of Hector Ochoa (University of New Mexico) and Daniella Elyse Pitzalis. This chapter is respectfully dedicated to our grandparents: Harry and Lena Shwalb, and Solomon and Martha Greenwald, of blessed memory; Adalat Bepari and Saleha Khatun, Alhaj Safatullah Khan and Shakhina Khatun; and Giovanna and Luciano Marchese, Mario and Letizia of blessed memory.

References

An, H. L., & Kim, S. M. (2015). A qualitative study of interpretations of grandmothers' childrearing experiences. *Journal of Korean Family Resource Management Association, 19,* 93–109.

Babu, N., Hossain, Z., Morales, J. E., & Vij, S. (2018). Grandparents in Bangladesh, India, and Pakistan. In D. W. Shwalb & Z. Hossain (Eds.), *Grandparents in cultural context* (pp. 159–186). New York: Routledge.

Barnett, M. A., Scaramella, L. V., Nepplyerer, T. K., Ontai, L. L., & Conger, R. D. (2010). Grandmother involvement as a protective factor for early childhood social adjustment. *Journal of Family Psychology, 24,* 635–645.

Buchanan, A. (2018). Changing roles of grandparents in the UK: Emergence of the "new" grandfather. In D. W. Shwalb & Z. Hossain (Eds.), *Grandparents in cultural context* (pp. 111–132). New York: Routledge.

Buchanan, A., & Rotkirch, A. (2016). *Grandfathers: Global perspectives.* London, UK: Palgrave Macmillan.

Chaudhary, N. (2013). The father's role in the Indian family: A story that must be told. In D. Shwalb, B. Shwalb, & M. Lamb (Eds.), *Fathers in cultural context* (pp. 68-94). New York: Routledge.

Coall, D. A., & Hertwig, R. (2010). Grandparental investment: Past, present, and future. *Behavioral and Brain Sciences, 33,* 1–59.

Cong, Z., & Silverstein, M. (2008). Intergenerational time-for-money exchanges in rural China: Does reciprocity reduce depressive symptoms of older grandparents? *Research in Human Development, 5*(1), 6–25.

Copen, C. E., & Silverstein, M. (2008). The transmission of religious beliefs across generations: Do grandparents matter? *Journal of Comparative Family Studies, 38,* 497–510.

Ellis, R., & Simmons, T. (2014). *Coresidential grandparents and their grandchildren: 2012.* United States Census Bureau: US Department of Commerce.

Feinstein, L., & Duckworth, K. (2006). *Development in the early years: Its importance for school performance and adult outcomes.* London: Centre for Research on the Wider Benefits of Learning.

Gibbons, J. L., & Fanjul de Marsicovetere, R. (2018). Grandparenting in Mexico and Central America: "Time and attention". In D. W. Shwalb & Z. Hossain (Eds.), *Grandparents in cultural context* (pp. 17–40). New York: Routledge.

Gibson, P. A. (2014). Grandmother caregiver-in-chief continues the tradition of African American families. *Journal of Women and Social Work, 29,* 298–309.

Gorey, K. M. (2001). Early childhood education: a meta-analytic affirmation of the short- and long-term benefits of educational opportunity. *School Psychology Quarterly, 16,* 9–30.

Gregory, E., Arju, T., Jessel, J., Kenner, C., & Ruby, M. (2007). Snow white in different guises: Interlingual and intercultural exchanges between grandparents and young children at home in East London. *Journal of Early Childhood Literacy, 7,* 5–25.

Gutierrez, I. A., Goodwin, L. J., Kirkinis, K., & Mattis, J. S. (2014). Religious socialization in African American families: the relative influence of parents, grandparents, and siblings. *Journal of Family Psychology, 28,* 779–789.

Hagestad, G. O. (2006). Transfers between grandparents and grandchildren: The importance of taking a three-generation perspective. *Zeitschrift fur Familienforschung, 18,* 315–332.

Haylsip, B., & Fruhauf, C. A. (2018). Grandparenting in the United States: Cultural and subcultural diversity. In D. W. Shwalb & Z. Hossain (Eds.), *Grandparents in cultural context* (pp. 41–49). New York: Routledge.

Henderson, T. L., & Cook, J. L. (2005). Grandma's hands: black grandmothers speak about their experiences rearing grandchildren on TANF. *International Journal of Aging and Human Development, 61,* 1–19.

Hossain, Z., Eisberg, G., & Shwalb, D. W. (2018). Grandparents' social identities in cultural context. *Contemporary Social Science, 13,* 275–287.

Hung, J. W., Wu, Y., & Yeh, C. (2004). Comparing stress levels of parents of children with cancer and parents of children with physical disabilities. *PsychoOncology, 13,* 898–903.

Janicki, M. P., McCallion, P., Grant-Griffin, L., & Kolomer, S. R. (2000). Grandparent caregivers I: characteristics of grandparents and the children with disabilities for whom they care for. *Journal of Gerontological Social Work, 33,* 35–55.

Jones, D. E., Greenberg, M., & Crowley, M. (2015). Early social-emotional functioning and public health: The relationship between kindergarten social competence and future wellness. *American Journal of Public Health, 105,* 2283–2290.

Makiwane, M., Gumede, N. A., & Makiwane, M. (2018). Grandparenting in Southern Africa: What the elders see while sitting on their toes won't see. In D. W. Shwalb & Z. Hossain (Eds.), *Grandparents in cultural context* (pp. 267–296). New York: Routledge.

Mhaka-Mutepfa, M., Mpofu, E., Moore, A., & Ingman, S. (2018). Carer grandparents of Sub-Saharan Africa: "Foster to be fostered". In D. W. Shwalb & Z. Hossain (Eds.), *Grandparents in cultural context* (pp. 245–268). New York: Routledge.

Minkler, M., & Fuller-Thomson, E. (2005). African American grandparents raising grandchildren: A national study using the census 2000 American Community Survey. *The Gerontology Journal: Series B, 60,* S82–S92.

Nakazawa, J., Hyun, J. H., Ko, P. C., & Shwalb, D. W. (2018). Grandparents in Japan, Korea, and China: From filial piety to grandparenthood. In D. W. Shwalb & Z. Hossain (Eds.), *Grandparents in cultural context* (pp. 187–219). New York: Routledge.

Onodera, R. (2005). Fluctuation of grandmother's view of gender division of labor derived from rearing grandchildren. *Journal of 21st Century Research Organization for Human Care, 10,* 95–106.

Oyserman, D., Radin, N., & Benn, R. (1993). Dynamics in a three-generational family: Teens, grandparents and babies. *Developmental Psychology, 29,* 564–572.

Pilkauskas, N. V. (2014). Living with a grandparent and parent in early childhood: Associations with school readiness and differences by demographic characteristics. *Developmental Psychology, 50,* 2587–2599.

Roopnarine, J. L. (Ed.). (2015). *Fathers across cultures: The importance, roles, and diverse practices of dads.* Santa Barbara, CA: Praeger.

Ruby, M. (2012). The role of the grandmother in maintaining Bangla with her granddaughter in East London. *Journal of Multilingual and Multicultural Development, 33,* 67–83.

Shin, Y. J. (2015). Grandparenthood revisited. *Andragogy Today: Interdisciplinary Journal of Adult & Continuing Education, 18,* 29–47.

Silverstein, M., & Ruiz, S. (2006). Breaking the chain: How grandparents moderate the transmission of maternal depression to children. *Family Relations, 55,* 601–612.

Shwalb, D. W., & Hossain, Z. (2017, December). Grandfathers: Uplifting the Western world's underestimated role. *50Plus Life.* (Columbia, PA).

Shwalb, D. W., & Hossain, Z. (Eds.). (2018). *Grandparents in cultural context.* New York: Routledge.

Shwalb, D. W., Shwalb, B. J., & Lamb, M. E. (Eds.). (2013). *Fathers in cultural context.* New York: Routledge.

Smethers, S. (2015). What are the issues affecting grandparents in Britain today? *Quality in Ageing and Older Adults, 16,* 37–43.

Smith, P. K., & Drew, L. M. (2002). Grandparenthood. In M. H. Bornstein (Ed.), *Handbook of parenting* (Vol. 3, pp. 141–169). Mahwah: Erlbaum.

Szinovacz, M. E. (1998). *Handbook on grandparenthood.* Westport, CT: Greenwood Press.

Tanskanen, A. O. (2017). Intergenerational relations and child development in England. *Anthropological Review, 80,* 127–139.

Tanskanen, A. O., & Danielsbacka, M. (2016). Maternal grandfathers and child development in England: Impact on the early years. In A. Buchanan & A. Rotkirch (Eds.), *Grandfathers: Global perspectives* (pp. 217–228). London, UK: Palgrave Macmillan.

Utrata, J. (2018). Grandmothers in Russia's matrifocal families: Shoring up family life. In D. W. Shwalb & Z. Hossain (Eds.), *Grandparents in cultural context* (pp. 133–156). New York: Routledge.

Woody, D. J., & Woody, D. (2015). Early childhood. In E. D. Hutchison (Ed.), *Dimensions of human behavior: The changing life course.* Thousand Oaks, CA: Sage.

World Bank. (2016). GNI atlas index. Retrieved from http://data.worldbank.org/about/countryand-lending-groups.

Xu, L., Tang, F., Li, L.W., & Dong, X. Q. (2017). Grandparent caregiving and psychological well-being among Chinese American older adults-the roles of caregiving burden and pressure. *Journals of Gerontology Series A: Biomedical Sciences and Medical Sciences, 1;72*(suppl_1), S56–S62. https://doi.org/10.1093/gerona/glw186.

Chapter 13
Japanese Preschool Approaches to Supporting Young Children's Social-Emotional Development

Akiko Hayashi

Abstract This chapter describes and analyzes a pedagogical practice that Japanese preschool teachers routinely use to support young children's social-emotional development. The central argument is that Japanese preschool teachers deal with children's disputes by employing pedagogical practices that work to scaffold the development of a *collective* rather than primarily *individual* locus of control. Japanese educators use the word "*mimamoru*" to describe a pedagogical strategy of low intervention in children's fights. *Mimamoru* refers to a practice of minimal intervention, based on watching and waiting. By holding back, Japanese preschool teachers provide opportunities not only for children involved in a conflict, but also the children around them, to experience strong emotions and experiment with conflict resolution strategies. The chapter closes with a discussion of the implications of Japanese preschool pedagogy for conceptions of self-regulation, prosocial behavior, and empathy-related responding. One implication is that more research is needed on how young children in Japan and elsewhere collectively handle misbehavior and emotions in group contexts.

For the past ten years, I have been conducting research on strategies Japanese preschool teachers use to scaffold their students social-emotional development, and more specifically on strategies Japanese teachers use to deal with children's classroom disputes. In this chapter I summarize findings from several of my research projects and draw from several of my published works on this topic (Hayashi 2011; Hayashi et al. 2009; Hayashi and Tobin 2011, 2015). I conclude with a discussion of implications of this research on Japanese preschool pedagogy for conceptions of self-regulation, prosocial behavior, and empathy-related responding.

A. Hayashi (✉)
Meiji University, Tokyo, Japan
e-mail: akiko_ha@meiji.ac.jp

© Springer Nature Switzerland AG 2019
T. Tulviste et al. (eds.), *Children's Social Worlds in Cultural Context*,
https://doi.org/10.1007/978-3-030-27033-9_13

Method

The research method used in each of these studies was video-cued ethnographic interviews (Tobin et al. 1989). The interview procedures included: (1) videotaping a typical day in a preschool classroom; (2) editing the video down to 20-min; and (3) using this video as a cue for in-depth interviews. Forty-five Japanese informants were asked to comment on videos made in Japanese preschools. Across these studies, we recorded and analyzed many scenes of Japanese teachers dealing with children having disputes. This chapter is focused on just one of these scenes, an interaction among a group of four-year-old girls we videotaped at Komatsudani Hoikuen (childcare center) in Kyoto in 2002.

The Teddy Bear Fight

During free play time before lunch, an argument breaks out among four girls. Nao, Seiko, and Reiko are pulling and tugging on a teddy bear, as Maki stands nearby watching their argument:

Seiko: Pull it this way.
Maki: Let go!
Seiko and Reiko: We got it! We got it!
Reiko: She is taking it back!
Seiko: We got it. We got it!

The three girls fall to the floor in a pile of twisting, pushing, and pulling bodies. Morita, the classroom teacher, calls from across the room: "*Kora, kora!*" (hey), but she doesn't approach the fighting girls. As Nao begins to cry, Reiko says to her: "Nao-chan, it's not yours. It's Seiko's." As Nao continues crying, Seiko, Reiko, Maki, and Yoko discuss what to do. Maki suggests that Seiko should give the bear to Nao. Nao, in tears, comes near to Seiko, who is holding the teddy bear close to her chest.

Seiko: Don't cry.
Maki: Seiko, give it to her.
Seiko: It's okay if you say, "Let me borrow it."
Nao: Give it to me!
Yoko: No!
Reiko: Stop it!
Nao: Give it to me.
Yoko: You shouldn't take it.
Reiko (to Yoko): You should scold her.
Yoko: That's bad! You can't grab the bear away like that!
Nao: But I had it first.
Maki: But then you put it down, so your turn was over.

Nao is led away to the other side of the room by Seiko, who links little fingers with Nao, the two girls swinging their hands as they sing, "Keep this promise or swallow a thousand needles!" Seiko then says to Nao, "Understand?" and as Nao nods in reply, Seiko puts her arm around Nao's shoulders and the girls walk off together.

Mimamoru: *The Logic of Watching and Waiting*

After showing the teddy bear fight scene to Japanese preschool teachers and directors, I asked them, "What do you think about this scene?" and "What would you do if you were in this situation?" One Japanese teacher explained to me:

> Japanese teachers wait until children solve their problems on their own. Children know what they are capable of handling. So, we wait. You could say that it is because we believe in children that we can wait. Otherwise, children become people who can't do things without permission. Of course, if they are in a situation where they don't know what to do, we talk it over with them, and then we wait and watch (*mimamoru*) to see what happens.

Mimamoru can be defined as "watching over," as in the song lyric, "someone to watch over me." *Mi* means to watch and *mamoru* means to protect. When put together, these two words make a phrase that has two meanings. One is to watch someone carefully in order to keep him or her from harm. The second meaning is to observe and reflect on someone's behavior. For example, *mimamoru* is used in such phrases as "*kodomo no seichyou o mimamoru*" (to track children's growing) and "*nariyuki o mimamoru*" (to follow the development of events). A related term used by Japanese educators is *machi no hoiku. Hoiku* means nurturing or childrearing. *Machi* is a form of the verb "to wait." *Machi no hoiku* is a pedagogical approach based on waiting, patience, taking a long perspective, and watching rather than acting.

In video-cued interviews, Japanese teachers frequently mentioned this strategy of watching and holding back to explain a range of pedagogical practices and developmental goals, including giving children opportunities to develop emotional, social, and intellectual skills. As a preschool teacher in Tokyo commented: "We think it's important to support children's emotional development. In order for this to happen, children need time to struggle by themselves. So, we watch over them (*mimamoru*)."

One of the meanings of *mimamoru* is to stand guard. The guard does her job not only or primarily by intervening when necessary, but also by letting people know that someone is on guard. In preschool classrooms, knowing that their teacher is watching over them gives the children the confidence and security they need to try to work things out on their own. She provides a sort of safety net or support for the children's social interaction.

In video-cued interviews, Japanese teachers often used the terms *mimamorareru* (to be watched) and *mimamorareteiru* (to be watched over) in such sentences as "Children need to know that they are being watched by their teacher," and "Being watched gives children confidence." These comments suggest a connection between *mimamoru* and the traditional Japanese concept of *seken no me. Seken* literally means "society"; *me* means "eyes." Together they mean literally "the eyes of society." When used outside of school settings, this concept sometimes has a negative meaning, as in suggestions that one is surrounded by nosey neighbors; but usually the phrase is used to refer to the positive role of social concern, especially in caring for children. Ethnographic descriptions of Japan in the pre–World War II era describe a culture in which in both rural villages and urban neighborhoods everyone knew each other and everyone took responsibility for watching and, when necessary, correcting children (Benedict 1946; Embree 1939; Lebra 1976; Smith and Wiswell 1982). If a child did something naughty or dangerous on the street, any adult who saw him would let him know he was being watched and that what he was doing was wrong. A lament often heard in contemporary Japan is that this sense of being watched and therefore protected and cared for by the eyes of the community has been lost with urbanization and the decline of traditional neighborhoods and villages. In contemporary Japan, preschool has come to replace the rural village and urban neighborhood as the key site where children can experience the feeling of being watched over.

There is a scene in the Komatsudani video that shows children from the five-year-old class spending time in the infant and toddler rooms and helping care for the younger children. These *toban* (daily monitors) help the little ones change clothes, eat, play, and even use the bathroom. When I asked, "Isn't this practice dangerous?" Nogami, the teacher of the five-year-old class, answered: "We keep a close watch over (*mimamoru*) the children." In another scene in the Komatsudani video, after the official day is over, we see children playing on the playground and four-year-old Maki is standing on top of a horizontal bar, nearly two meters off the ground. Samata-sensei, standing nearby, says, "Be careful," but she does not stop the girl from continuing her potentially dangerous play. Her watching and waiting here communicates both concern and confidence.

The central point here is not that teachers in Japanese preschools hesitate to intervene, but that while not intervening they let the children know that they are aware of what is going on. This is a complex dynamic. On the one hand, when children are doing something potentially dangerous or emotionally hurtful, the teacher needs to seem not to be watching in order to encourage the children to work things out on their own, without expecting the teacher to intervene. On the other hand, the teacher wants the children to know that she is aware of what they are doing, because this awareness helps prevent the situation from spinning out of control and gives the children confidence to take risks, knowing that their teacher will jump in if things fall apart. It is only in those moments when the teacher feels that children are on the edge of real danger that she makes her watching more explicit, as when Samata-sensei came over to caution Maki to be careful on the climbing bars but didn't tell her to stop. This is the art of Japanese teaching: the art of watching without being either too little or too much present. As one teacher explained to me:

> There is no one right version of *mimamoru*. It does not just mean watching children from a distance, or just letting them know we are watching and that we're ready to go to them if something happens. I believe that what it really means is that we simply exist in the classroom and create a mood that if something happens, the teacher will protect you. It is more like the air around us.

The *mi* in *mimamoru* literally means watching, but as this educator suggests, it also carries the feeling of a presence so all-encompassing and yet so subtle as to be no more noticeable than the atmosphere that surrounds us. Another teacher told us: "It is important that people experience the warmth of being watched over (*mimamorareteiru*). This is Japanese traditional childcare. From this big loving feeling of knowing one is being watched over and trusted, children figure out their independence."

Sympathetic Identification and Legitimate Peripheral Participation

By holding back, Japanese preschool teachers provide opportunities not only for the children directly involved in a conflict but also for the children around them to experience strong emotions and experiment with conflict resolution strategies. For instance, a small group of children is gathered around classmates who are fighting over a doll. The words Japanese preschool teachers use when discussing this scene suggest that the children watching are legitimate participants in the fights. As one preschool teacher commented on this scene: "Look—there is a *gyarari* (gallery). Fights are more important for the children who are not fighting. Teachers should pay attention to them and consider what they are learning."

The word gallery seems to suggest that those watching are passive, but this is not how the Japanese educators I interviewed described the *gyarari* that gathered around the fights in the videos. Several teachers emphasized the distinction between active and passive watching by making a distinction between being a member of a *gyarari*, on the one hand, and being a *yajiuma* (onlooker) or *boukansya* (bystander) on the other (Akiba 2004; Morita and Kiyonaga 1996).

The words "onlooker" and bystander" are derogatory, suggesting that those gathering around a distressing scene are motivated not by genuine concern but only by curiosity and a desire for vicarious thrills. One teacher said about the watching children in the video: "They look kind of like *yajiuma* (onlookers), but not really, because they are worried." This teacher suggests that it is the children's appearance of being worried, implying empathy, which leads her to see them as legitimate peripheral participants.

Like the audience at a play, the people in the galleries that gather around these fights are potentially both moved and edified by being present. Japanese educators emphasized that it is not only the children directly involved who learn from fights and their resolution, but also the children watching, through observational learning and sympathetic identification. Japanese preschool teachers often used the words *kimochi* (feelings), *doujou* (sympathy), and *omoiyari* (empathy) to describe children's experience of watching their classmates engaged in emotionally intense interactions. As one teacher said, "Sympathizing with others is important."

The experience of the *gyarari*, therefore, can be conceived as a form of vicarious participation, in which the observing children feel (or at least attempt to feel) what is being experienced by a classmate. The behavior of the *gyarari* children in the fighting scenes, as well as Japanese educators' reflections on these scenes, is largely consistent with Lave and Wenger's (1991) concept of "legitimate peripheral participation," and with the related concepts of "observational learning" and "intent participation." Rogoff et al. (2003) describe intent participation as "keenly observing and listening in anticipation of or in the process of engaging in an endeavor" (p. 176). Gaskins and Paradise (2009) write "Observational learning typically occurs in familiar contexts in which one person performs an activity while another person, who knows less, watches them do it" (p. 85).

The Japanese practices and beliefs I have presented here are unlike most descriptions in the literature of peripheral participation and observational learning in several key ways. First, the learning here is not, as in most of the studies of peripheral participation and observational learning, of a cognitive skill or a trade, but instead of social skills and emotional dispositions. The children are learning, through observation and sympathetic identification, how to feel, what to do with their feelings, and how to behave as a member of a caring community. Such learning in the domains of emotions and sociality is underdiscussed in the peripheral participation literature, which emphasizes the cognitive and skill domains, but well described in the psychological anthropological literature on acculturation (e.g., by Briggs 1999; Hayashi et al. 2009) and in some conceptualizations of observational learning. For example, Gaskins and Paradise (2009) suggest that children learn culturally structured rules about social behavior and social roles, in large part by observing the interactions that go on around them: "They can also observe the consequences of certain social acts in their particular social worlds—what Bandura (1977) called *vicarious reinforcement*—by observing others who share a social category with them and are seen therefore to be 'like me' (e.g., gender, age, race, or class)" (p. 108).

This points to a second key difference between the *gyarari* situations of peer learning I have presented here, and Lave and Wenger's notion of legitimate peripheral participation and Rogoff and her collaborators' notion of intent participation, which emphasize learning in hierarchical rather than peer contexts, and most often describing those observing and those being observed as "newcomers and old-timers" or as "masters and apprentices." I am not suggesting that such hierarchical forms of peripheral participation are not important in Japan, which is well known for its rich traditions of apprenticeship learning in the arts (Singleton 1998), or that hierarchical learning is a form of peripheral participation not found in Japanese preschools. Ethnographic studies have described the importance that Japanese preschools give to the benefits of mixed-age learning (*tate-wari kyōiku*) for both the younger and the older children (Tobin et al. 1989, 2009). But alongside the value placed on learning from old-timers, in Japanese preschools there is also a great emphasis placed on the value and importance of learning through peer relationships. "Peer" is a relative term. Even in classes of children of the same grade, there are differences of age and experience. Nao-chan is the youngest and newest child in her class, and her teacher suggested this played a role in the girls' behaviors during the teddy bear fight. But according to Morita and other Japanese teachers, the underlying value of allowing the children to experience fighting and emotions, both directly and vicariously, is that the children interact as a community of peers.

The third distinction I want to emphasize is that whereas most of Lave and Wenger's examples are of people learning as individuals, the *gyarari* situations emphasize group learning and group experience. None of these points are inherently inconsistent with Lave and Wenger's conceptualization of legitimate peripheral participation, Gaskin and Paradise's views of observational learning, and Rogoff and her colleagues' ideas about intent participation. Each of these theories is implicitly concerned with social as well as cognitive learning, in that peripheral participation and intent participation function not only to learn skills, but also to help individuals become full, appropriate, contributing members of a community (Singleton 1998). My argument is that the Japanese emic view can deepen the concepts of peripheral participation and intent participation, by adding more explicit emphasis on the acquisition of social-emotional skills, on learning with and from peers, and on peripherally participating as a group.

Collective Regulation

Most U.S. early childhood educational practices and beliefs, as well as Western theories of child development, conceptualize constraint on antisocial behavior as self-constraint. In contrast, Japanese early childhood educators' reflections on the two *gyarari* scenes emphasize the importance of children learning to function as a self-monitoring, self-controlling community. The locus of control on misbehavior is in the group, rather than in each child as an individual. Japanese early childhood educators conceive the *gyarari* not as a gaggle of busybodies, but rather as a collective, with the power to induce prosocial and limit antisocial behavior in others.

When I asked preschool teachers if they ever tell children who are watching fights to move away, most said no and emphasized that this sort of participation was beneficial not just for the watching children, but also for those being watched. For example, a teacher in Tokyo answered, "Most of the times, I tell the children who are directly involved that other children care about you and are worried about you." In addition to providing empathy and emotional support, the observing children are seen as a moderating influence on the fight protagonists. As Professor Hiroshi Usui said about the teddy bear fight scene: "The watching children function as one of the factors that control fighting. The observers don't let the stronger children take things away from the weaker ones. They provide some self-regulation to the fighters." Professor Usui's comment expresses the Japanese cultural belief in the collective ability of the group to self-regulate and in the importance of preschool as a site for this collective ability to be experienced, learned, practiced, and cultivated.

For most contemporary children, in Japan as in many other countries, preschool provides their first opportunity to learn to be a member of a community. Japanese preschools are sites for teaching young children to have a characteristically Japanese sense of self, which is to say a sense of self that is socially minded. Japanese educators' notions of peripheral participation in fights is a piece of this larger picture of how Japanese preschool classrooms function as sites for teaching young children to develop a collective as well as individual sense of self and of social responsibility.

The concept of collective self-regulation sounds oxymoronic to Western ears, but not so in Japan. The belief of Japanese educators that the locus of control for fighting and other antisocial behaviors is at the level of the group rather than the individual is a useful challenge to Western psychological theories of self-regulation and more generally of child development (Shimizu 2000). Most of the psychological work on the development of prosociality focuses on how individual children experience and express emotions and control or fail to control their behavior. Eisenberg and Spinrad (2004) make a useful distinction between self-regulation and externally imposed regulation, and "between being able to regulate emotion oneself and modulating emotion primarily through the efforts of others" (p. 336). A Japanese emic perspective would recast this distinction as that between a group regulated by its own emotions and behaviors and one regulated by others (e.g., by the teacher).

This Japanese perspective on behavioral regulation, while not discounting the importance of individual processes of emotion, cognition, and behavior, would expand the Western psychological literature by seeing the preschool classroom as controlled not just or primarily by the sum of the self-regulation abilities of each child, but also by the collective emotional and social skills of the class. The focus is on helping children learn to be members of the class as a community, and then on providing opportunities for this community to develop the capacity to self-regulate.

In arguing that the Japanese emic understanding of peripheral participation emphasizes the encouragement of a collective locus of control, I do not mean to suggest that peripherally participating Japanese children do not also have individual motives or that they lack the ability for self-control. As Raeff (2000, 2006) argues, it cannot be the case that children in some cultures are entirely independent and in some cultures interdependent, for all cultures require people to act both independently and interdependently. Therefore, the focus of my analysis is on explicating in which contexts in a culture children are expected to act independently and in which contexts interdependently. I am suggesting not that Japanese teachers always or consistently discourage independence, but that in the domain of dealing with children's fights in Japanese preschool classrooms, there is general encouragement from teachers for a collective solution.

Providing Opportunities for Peripheral Participation

This implicit cultural practice of not intervening in children's disputes does not mean never intervening, but instead having nonintervention in children's fights as an option, a strategy teachers can deploy. By pulling back our focus, and attending not to the children who were the protagonists in the fight, but instead to the children on the periphery, we can see how in these dissimilar interactions these teachers in different ways created an opportunity for a *gyarari* to form and for a group of children to experience vicarious emotion, empathize, and learn.

For a teacher to make a strategy of *mimamoru* effective, children need to know she is paying enough attention to give them confidence that someone will be there to keep things from getting totally out of control, but the teacher's presence, her watchfulness, has to be soft enough so children take responsibility and perform primarily not for her but rather for and in interaction with their classmates. In their review of observational learning Gaskins and Paradise (2009) emphasize that when children are allowed to follow their interests and are given only minimal feedback, "they take initiative in directing their attention and finding or creating activities to practice on their own skills they have not yet mastered" (p. 97). By avoiding being the primary audience for the children's performance, Morita allows for a child-oriented, childlike piece of drama to unfold.

I am not suggesting that it is at all unusual for preschool children to become peripheral participants in other children's fights. What I am suggesting is that the way Japanese teachers respond to such fights and to the role of those peripherally involved is characteristically Japanese. In this chapter I have emphasized that the Japanese teachers' goal is to encourage not just the protagonists at the center of the fight but also the wider group of children who gather around fights to explore, collectively, childlike solutions to disputes. Rather than telling the galleries of peripherally participating children "Move away" or "This is none of your business," Japanese teachers allow and quietly encourage children to get involved in everything that goes on in the classroom.

Although my focus in this chapter has been on the *gyarari* that forms around fights, Japanese early childhood educators are also supportive of peripheral participation of children in other emotion-laden events, such as experiencing sadness. Fights are dramatic, but they are far from the only dramas that take place every day in preschool classrooms.

Seeing Both Individuals and Groups

Morita's explanation for not intervening in the teddy bear fight emphasizes her knowledge of the children in her class both in terms of their individual personalities and the way they function collectively:

> Nao might have been having a tough day, but she is strong. She tried to get the teddy bear back even though she was crying…. I know that Yoko can be aggressive in that kind of situations because of her home environment. She sometimes behaves like an adult. The twins, Seiko and Reiko, always show a tight connection. But I could let them fight with Nao because I knew Maki was around.

Morita's thinking here is focused on the capacity of a group of children to handle a situation. Her focus is on this group of girls as a collective. This does not mean that she is not aware of their individual personalities. She mentions individual characteristics of each child. However, the individual differences are not her primary concern. As long as these children with very different personalities are interacting with each other, Morita-sensei is satisfied that there is an opportunity for their social-emotional development.

Childlike Children

In my interviews, I often heard teachers use the phrase "*kodomo-rashii kodomo*" (childlike children). An appreciation for the childishness of children is a core implicit pedagogical belief of Japanese early childhood educators. The logic goes: A baby can be a baby only when he is a baby and a four-year-old can be four years old only when she is four, so why rush things? When I asked Nogami-sensei at Komatsudani about children who are very dependent he replied: "I worry about children who are not dependent at this age." This is consistent with the comments of a teacher in Tokyo about children's fighting: "Children should fight at this age; otherwise, when can they fight? It's too late if they wait to start fighting when they get older. Then, it's dangerous." This long perspective underlies such practices of teachers as letting children fight, letting them express dependence, and letting them express emotions in immature, childlike ways.

Taking a Long Perspective

Japanese educators I interviewed used the term *nagai me* (long eyes) to refer to the value of teachers taking a "long perspective," a perspective that allows teachers to accept what they see as children's age-appropriate, childlike behaviors. This cultural notion of time underlies the logic of *mimamoru*. A long perspective allows and shapes the way Japanese teachers teach in their classroom and develop their teaching skills and knowledge. "It takes time" is one of the phrases that I most often heard from the teachers in the interviews. For example, teachers said, "It takes time to be able to create a gallery" and "It takes time to master *mimamoru*" (watching and waiting).

A long perspective underlies Japanese teachers' notions of child development and their role in scaffolding this development. Japanese teachers often explain their patience in dealing with children's disputes and emotional outbursts by saying, "I have three years with these children." Teachers often explained the thinking about an incident by pointing out when this incident occurred in the school year or at what age in a child's life or period since enrolling in school, in phrases such as "That fight happened in April," (the beginning of the school year), or "She was then the youngest child in the class," or "She was new to the school at that time." These comments suggest that teachers' approach how to deal with children not with a fixed set of practices but with a logic that depends on how they locate behaviors in a long flow of time.

Conclusion

I am not suggesting that children in Japan do not have individual executive function or that Japanese preschool teachers do not encourage individual self-regulation, prosocial behavior, and empathy-related responding. Rather, my research shows that in addition to individual self-regulation, prosocial behavior, and empathy-related responding, children in Japanese preschools are encouraged to develop collective self-regulation, prosocial behavior, and empathy-related responding. Even in countries such as the US, known to be individualistic/independent, children need to learn to regulate behavior collectively as well as individually. My research suggests that concepts of self-regulation, prosocial behavior, and empathy-related responding should be expanded and that more research is needed on young children's collective management of misbehavior and emotions. The collective emphasis found in Japanese early childhood education and backed up by Japanese philosophy (Kimura 1972; Hamaguchi 1988) and social psychology (Markus and Kitayama 1991) suggests that the emphasis Western psychology has given to self-regulation should be complemented by explorations of regulation as a collective process. This line of research can have important implications for both practitioners who work with young children and scholars who study them.

References

Akiba, M. (2004). Nature and correlates of Ijime—Bullying in Japanese middle school. *International Journal of Educational Research, 41*(3), 216–236.

Bandura, A. (1977). *Social learning theory*. Englewood Cliffs, NJ: Prentice Hall.

Benedict, R. (1946). *The chrysanthemum and The Sword: Patterns of Japanese culture*. Boston: Houghton Mifflin Company.

Briggs, J. (1999). *Inuit Morality Play: The emotional education of a three-year-old*. New Haven, CT: Yale University Press.

Eisenberg, N., & Spinrad, T. (2004). Emotion-related regulation: Sharpening the definition. *Child Development, 75*(2), 334–339.

Embree, J. F. (1939). *Suye Mura: A Japanese village*. Chicago: University of Chicago Press.

Gaskins, S., & Paradise, R. (2009). Learning through observation in daily life. In D. F. Lancy, J. Bock, & S. Gaskins (Eds.), *The anthropology of learning in childhood* (pp. 85–117). AltaMira Press.

Hamaguchi, E. (1988). *Nihon rashisa no saihaken (Re-discovering the Japaneseness)*. Tokyo: Koudansya.

Hayashi, A. (2011). The Japanese hands-off approach to curriculum guidelines for early childhood education as a form of cultural practice. *Asian-Pacific Journal of Research in Early Childhood Education, 5*(2), 107–123.

Hayashi, A., Karasawa, M., & Tobin, J. (2009). The Japanese preschool's pedagogy of feeling: Cultural strategies for supporting young children's emotional development. *Ethos, 37*(1), 32–49.

Hayashi, A., & Tobin, J. (2011). The Japanese preschool's pedagogy of peripheral participation. *Ethos, 39*(2), 139–164.

Hayashi, A., & Tobin, J. (2015). *Teaching embodied: Cultural practice in Japanese preschools*. Chicago: The University of Chicago Press.

Kimura, B. (1972). *Hito to hito tono aida (Among people)*. Tokyo: Koubundou.

Lave, J., & Wenger, E. (1991). *Situated learning: Legitimate peripheral participation*. Cambridge: Cambridge University Press.

Lebra, T. (1976). *Japanese patterns of behavior*. Honolulu: University of Hawaii Press.

Markus, H. R., & Kitayama, S. (1991). Culture and the self. Implications for cognition, emotion, and motivation. *Psychological Review, 98*(2), 224–253.

Morita, Y., & Kiyonaga, K. (1996). *Bullying—Pathology in classroom*. Tokyo: Kaneko Shobo.

Raeff, C. (2000). European-American parents' ideas about their toddlers' independence and interdependence. *Journal of Applied Developmental Psychology, 21*(2), 183–205.

Raeff, C. (2006). Individuals in relation to others: Independence and interdependence in a kindergarten classroom. *Ethos, 34*(4), 521–557.

Rogoff, B., Paradise, R., Arauz, M. R., Correa-Chavez, M., & Angelillo, C. (2003). First hand learning through intent participation. *Annual Review of Psychology, 54*(1), 175–203.

Shimizu, H. (2000). Japanese cultural psychology and empathic understanding: Implications for academic and cultural psychology. *Ethos, 28*(2), 224–247.

Singleton, J. (Ed.). (1998). *Learning in likely places*. New York: Cambridge University Press.

Smith, R. J., & Wiswell, E. L. (1982). *The women of Suye Mura*. Chicago: University of Chicago Press.

Tobin, J., Hsueh, Y., & Karasawa, M. (2009). *Preschool in three cultures revisited: China, Japan, and the United States*. Chicago: University of Chicago Press.

Tobin, J., Wu, D., & Davidson, D. (1989). *Preschool in three cultures: Japan, China and the United States*. New Haven, Conn: Yale University Press.

Part III
Children in Unique and Challenging Circumstances

Chapter 14
Socialization and Development of Refugee Children: Chances of Childcare

Julian Busch and Birgit Leyendecker

Abstract Europe has recently been experiencing one of the largest immigration movements of the past 70 years. In 2016, over 700,000 people were registered in Germany, mostly from war-affected Middle Eastern countries. Nearly 15% of these people are below the age of six. Contexts of flight pose challenges to child development and to the capacities of psychological and social adjustment. This chapter consolidates evidence on immigrant and refugee families from an integrated psychological, cultural, and educational perspective. In the first part, we review the situation of refugee families in Western countries. We then reflect on the diverse contexts of refugee children and the different influences on their socialization during early childhood. For this purpose, we make use of the developmental niche, an interactional framework by Super and Harkness. In the last section, we sketch an adapted childcare approach that considers the different influences on children from refugee families and deduce guidelines for adapted childcare. Childcare contributes to child development and family adjustment after immigration and sustainably shapes diversifying societies.

Motives for Migration

Global mobility has increased significantly over the past few years. When investigating immigrant groups, researchers have to be precise in distinguishing this heterogeneous population. Immigrants' backgrounds range with respect to their levels of education, socio-economic statuses, demography, motivations to relocate, and experiences of migration. Distinctions between immigration by choice and forced displacement are often fluid and, in some cases, the decision to immigrate is the result of consideration. People have different capacities for organizing and functionally adapting their ways of living in response to their life circumstances, personal objectives, and faced adversities. This capacity for adaptation is determined by the

J. Busch · B. Leyendecker (✉)
Ruhr University, Bochum, Germany
e-mail: birgit.leyendecker@rub.de

© Springer Nature Switzerland AG 2019
T. Tulviste et al. (eds.), *Children's Social Worlds in Cultural Context*,
https://doi.org/10.1007/978-3-030-27033-9_14

187

available resources, personal age and prospects, family constellations, level of education, and health.

Although not consistently used in literature, refugees are formally those immigrants or who have already been granted asylum in another country. In Germany, the refugee status can be granted for the following reasons: religious, racial, or political persecution; displacement as a consequence of war (but not civil-war); persecution due to gender and sexual orientation. Severe economic hardship and escape from environmental catastrophes are not yet included. In line with the scope of this chapter and beyond legal definitions, we use the term 'refugees' for all immigrants who reside in a foreign country in order to avoid adverse environments. Adversity includes increased levels of threat or deprivation or a combination of both.

Contexts of Refuge

International immigration to Western countries has by no means reached the numbers of refugees in non-Western countries. Likewise, internally displaced people in countries of humanitarian crises, i.e., those people relocating within national borders, recently exceeded the average numbers of people arriving in Western countries. Refugee status can be linked to very different experiences and living situations. Life in the world's largest refugee camps, such as Daabab in Kenya or Zataari in Jordan, is organized through specialized infrastructure and humanitarian agendas developed to serve refugee populations. Support is often limited to immediate human needs, i.e., security, nutrition, and medical care. Support to empower people and provide them with life prospects, i.e., education and resettlement objectives, is inconsistently available. However, the United Nations Health Commissioner for Refugees estimates that refugees stay in these camps for four years (median), and in some regions for more than 20 years (Devictor and Do 2016). In Western countries, refugees mostly settle in urban regions, where the post-migration period bears a risk for societal marginalization.

Before the recent influx of immigration to Germany began, more than 30% of all children below the age of five had at least one foreign born parent (Woellert and Klingholz 2014). Since 2015, approximately 1.2 million refugees have arrived in Germany, mainly from Middle Eastern countries. More than 15% of these are below the age of six years (105.000; Federal Agency for Migration and Refugees 2016). These children are often born shortly before, during, or after flight, and failure to meet their educational and developmental demands put them at risk for negative trajectories (Sirin and Rogers-Sirin 2015).

Childcare as a Complementing Context for the Development and Socialization of Refugee Children

Aims and Challenges in Childcare with Refugees

Sustainable humanitarian actions in Western countries encompass the extension and adaptation of education and care services for refugee families. Strengthening the sector of childcare is an effective strategy to address the needs of refugee families. In a recent survey of our research group (the Interdisciplinary Centre for Family Research, Ruhr-University Bochum), 28 teachers taking care of young refugee children stated their aims for the childcare of these children. Their objectives were (1) to prepare refugee children to transition into regular groups or into elementary school, (2) to bridge an increased demand for childcare enrolment opportunities, (3) to inform refugee families about the importance of childcare in Germany as well as the available social support services, and (4) to provide childcare in order to allow parents the opportunity to engage in other activities (e.g., language or integration courses). These goals demonstrate that childcare for refugee families serves additional purposes that are critical to their lives, a situation that places a greater strain on childcare providers.

Moreover, we asked the teachers about challenges in childcare with refugee children (Busch et al. 2018a). A mixed method approach yielded four domains of challenge: interpersonal stress (e.g., conflicts with the children and parents; children's behavioral problems), feasibility of operation of the facilities, and attendance of refugee families (e.g., unreliability, fluctuation, finding continuous funding for the specialized childcare), cultural and communication barriers (e.g., different expectations associated with childcare, language barriers), and structural features of a childcare group (e.g., providing adequate material and premises for the childcare of refugee children). Teachers perceived the language barrier as most difficult, followed by communication with parents, long-term feasibility of serving this community with specialized childcare group, and tardiness of children. In order to better adapt childcare to the needs of the newly arrived refugee population, we need to consider the diverse living contexts of refugee families, the rationales of childcare in Western societies, its foundations within a certain context, and potential differences from refugees' countries of origin.

Transitions of Refugee Children

Many countries from which refugees originate differ from Western countries in terms of demographic and social conditions (e.g., ethnic composition of a society, significance of religion, fertility rates), as well as educational (e.g., literacy rates, availability of tertiary sector), governmental (e.g., regimes, state security, welfare system), and economic conditions (e.g., lower GDPs per capita, higher unemployment rates). Thus, arriving in a country of resettlement is also a transition into a new context with social, economic, and cultural constraints as well as opportunities. We assume that studying the interplay between these children and the different contexts they encounter is the most appropriate approach to understand their development and socialization (cf., Super and Harkness 1986). Ideally, childcare of newly arrived refugee children should foster their development and prepare them for the specific socio-cultural environments of the country of resettlement. Therefore, adaptation of child-rearing practices and childcare is possibly needed to secure positive developmental trajectories within, but also adjusted to, the new living context.

Host countries' childcare practices are functionally embedded in the system of child-rearing and reflect the customs, attitudes, and also existential obligations (i.e., work, living conditions) of a local or national society (Greenfield et al. 2003). Childcare in Western societies is likely to promote adjustment to school-like settings and activities, and to encourage the development of self-regulation and independence. Moreover, children in childcare can acquire school-relevant skills and improve their social and communicative abilities. Refugee parents' decision to send a child to a childcare center or to keep the child at home is influenced by many factors such as their ethno-theories of parenting and child development, their personal experiences, level of education, and expectations towards society. Enrolling a child in childcare is likely to have a substantial influence on the socialization of a child and the child's family and to bring the home context and context of childcare into continuous exchanges.

Institutional Childcare Challenges Diverse Practices of Child-Rearing

Think about how the customs of child-rearing match practices in non-relative childcare. In childcare, are there different expectations towards boys and girls? What are regular activities and customs? What is the lingua franca? What is the diet? What is a child allowed to do, what kinds of behaviors are expected of him or her? Who disciplines a child, and what are the socially and legally legitimate measures? Thinking about these questions demonstrates that children's experiences of family and childcare can be far from consistent. Examining childcare as an additional context for the socialization of refugee children requires a theoretical framework. This framework needs to integrate theories of cultural community with theories of development as well as consider distinct perspectives on processes and mechanisms that are important to socialization and development within the different contexts of a child's life (Howes 2011).

Functional Embeddedness of Childcare in a Society

During childhood, children learn to predict reactions of caregivers in response to their own behaviors. From these reactions, children build an internal framework of references on desirable, tolerated, and unacceptable behaviors. This framework constitutes a basic set of appreciated social norms, values, and practices, which we call socialization. If caregivers belong to the same nuclear or extended family as the child, socialization is most likely to be consistent. However, experiencing variations in child-rearing is normative for children in Western societies (e.g., parental care, informal care, public or private day care). From a global perspective, the early childhood experiences of young children differ enormously. Socio-cultural and economic determinants of a society shape the parental goals of socialization, determine who is responsible for caretaking (parents, siblings, relatives, professionals) and whether a professionalized setting for childcare is available (Greenfield et al. 2003; Whiting 1981).

Understanding the Influence of Diverse Contexts on Child Development and Socialization

Focusing on the child who is embedded within certain living contexts, the developmental niche seeks to understand the processes of development and socialization under certain socio-cultural as well as psychological circumstances and restraints (Super and Harkness 1986). Originally conceived to understand child development within a distinct environment, we apply this concept to describe child development and socialization within the diverse contexts refugee children are exposed to. The developmental niche distinguishes between a child's physical and social settings, the childcare customs a child is exposed to, and the psychology of the child's caretakers.

Physical and Social Settings

The first determinant of the developmental niche is concerned with the *physical and social settings* of a child's everyday life. The settings constitute how much time of a day a child spends with whom (on his or her own, with the mother, or in social situations) and who is in charge of supervision (a group of people or a designated caregiver). It furthermore encompasses where a child spends the day and what modalities for activities these locations provide (e.g., materials, premises, partners for interactions). Basically, the home setting provides a predictable and secure base for a child within the proximity of his or her closest relatives. Most experiences at home are arranged through the immediate caregivers, usually a parent. The settings of childcare in the receiving society are likely to differ from the home settings of refugee children. In institutions of childcare, a child comes in contact with peers and new adults as well as with a new language. These new companions provide different experiences outside of the immediate control of the parental caregivers. Nuclear families from non-Western countries are likely to rely on a large network of immediate and extended family. Refugee families, however, are likely not only to lose financial resources but their social resources as well in the migration process. In addition, the physical settings are likely to differ. In Western societies, middle-class parents are likely to provide special rooms such as nurseries equipped with many toys for their young children.

Customs of Childcare

The second domain of influence on children, *customs of childcare*, covers the practices and habits of child-rearing and childcare. It encompasses parenting styles, long-term academic aspirations, socialization goals, attachment behaviors, and routines of everyday life (e.g., sleeping behavior, authority and responsibility of older siblings, peer-contacts). Customs of childcare in Western countries are shaped by individualistic tendencies (Markus and Kitayama 1991) and child-centeredness. Early achievements in pre-academic skills, independence, autonomy, self-regulation, self-directed learning, and freedom of choice are particularly valued (National Association for the Education of Young Children 2009). Moreover, childcare in Western countries typically focuses less on alternative values, e.g., traditional knowledge, respect towards the elders, familial obligations, and on becoming an integrated part of the society.

Authoritative parenting (i.e., high responsiveness and high demands) is the most valued style in Western societies. However, societies in collectivistic communities may also value authoritarian orientations. Consistently, refugee parents from Congo report that child-rearing in their home country has a stronger focus on obedience and instruction with less freedom of choice (Mitchell and Ouko 2012). As of today, no specific set of parenting styles seems superior, but each is functionally embedded within its ecological context (Bornstein 2012). Ideally, parents provide a secure base for a child during infancy and early childhood. These early experiences influence the social expectations of the behaviors of others later in life (Ahnert et al. 2006). Building a sturdy internal working model of attachment is important in allowing non-maternal caregivers to become figures of attachment in childcare. Traditional societies more often involve non-parental caregivers through co-parenting. Relying more strongly on several family members or adult peers, child-rearing is a practice and responsibility shared within the community.

Psychology of the Caretakers

The third domain, *psychology of the caretakers*, describes the individual beliefs of parents and caregivers as well as the collectively shared ethno-theories about child behavior, development, and affective orientations. It subsumes the intentions and views of a society, which are deeply anchored and often practiced unconsciously. These beliefs provide the basis for decisions and actions related to child-rearing and childcare. In Western societies, the decision to send children to childcare reflects beliefs about the desired socialization of children (e.g., learning independence) and the assumptions about a specific theory of change. Decisions on child-rearing incorporate what the children are supposed to learn, from whom (e.g., some societies propose the need of a younger sibling for an adequate socialization), and what they are capable of doing at a certain age (e.g., cleanliness, to stay with an unfamiliar adult, to acquire pre-academic skills). Professionalizing childcare has to some extent led to a scientifically-guided approach that is based on concepts of normativity in child development.

Complex Developmental Niches for Refugee Children

The general population in Western countries has become ethno-culturally more heterogeneous through recent immigration. Ideally, the developmental niche of children is coherent, i.e., different environments are not contradictory in the three domains described previously. However, mediating between the contexts of home and childcare can pose a potential challenge for refugee children. They are exposed to complexities and inconsistencies in their developmental niches. For successful adaptation, refugee children may need to develop the ability to detect a salient socio-cultural frame and act accordingly (frame switching, Benet-Martínez et al. 2002).

Childcare from ethno-culturally diverse groups can thereby follow two approaches. On the one hand, childcare can augment child-rearing of the home setting, e.g., enforcing parental socialization goals. This approach is based on Allport's (1954) hypothesis of contact. He proposed that positive exposure to members of an outgroup (e.g., refugees with another cultural heritage) reduces prejudice and negative stereotyping. Proponents suggest that continuous promotion of equality, inclusion, and egalitarianism in childcare fosters group cohesiveness. On the other hand, childcare can incorporate values and practices of the major societal group, independent of the values and practices of the home environment of refugee children (cf., Banks 1977). In recent years, the value of cultural pluralism and diversity as a resource has been increasingly acknowledged. Proponents argue that childcare needs to act as a facilitator for inclusion into the societal environment, in which the childcare is embedded. At the same time, children in culturally diverse contexts must be able to navigate and function successfully despite the differences in these contexts.

Ideally, both approaches are considered in childcare. Approaches to childcare according to Banks (1977) seem important for the socio-cultural adjustment of refugee children and their families. Childcare provides them with early access to the host community. There, they can meet peers and other parents, encounter the lingua franca of the host country, and learn about a set of social practices and activities of a (diverse) host community.

Adapting Childcare for Diverse Families

Effects of Childcare

In the Western countries, economic development and diverse family constellations have fostered the demand for childcare as a complement to home-based caregiving (Pearson and Degotardi 2009). Childcare helps parents to engage in work and in other activities. At the same time, childcare attendance can provide a unique contribution to child development and socialization. Effects of childcare are conveyed by teachers during caretaking as well as peer-interactions. Additionally, childcare has the potential to extend parenting skills through frequent exchanges. Understanding that migration represents drastic changes in the context of living and an increased risk for gaps in education, childcare can facilitate this transition and promote positive developmental trajectories for children. Beyond the necessary academic skills and socio-emotional development, adjustment to cultural pluralism and identity formation should be important developmental goals and therefore considered in childcare for refugee children.

Pre-academic Skills

Preparing children for positive trajectories in development and education within a specific socio-cultural context also requires learning about relevant competencies. In Western countries, most appreciated competencies focus mainly on cognitive development, skills of literacy and numeracy, and language acquisition. While children from immigrant families tend to lag behind in their pre-academic skills as they transition into elementary school, regular attendance of childcare reduces their achievement gap in the long run (Magnuson et al. 2006). Moreover, the Early Childhood Longitudinal Study shows long-term positive effects of childcare on a broad range of developmental and academic outcomes (e.g., socio-emotional skills, cognitive and language abilities; Han 2008).

Socio-Emotional Development

Considering the often-precarious situation of refugee children following migration, some relevant contributions of childcare are more salient. Since refugee children are at higher risk of psychological distress (Buchmüller et al. 2018), childcare services need to address socio-emotional domains. Essential aims of socio-emotional learning are to identify, label, and self-regulate one's own feelings, to familiarize oneself with the new environment, and to establish positive relationships with peers and teachers. In the long run, socio-emotional learning interventions in childcare are associated with lower school dropout rates, less substance abuse, and less youth delinquency (Webster-Stratton and Taylor 2001). Moreover, some evidence suggests that indicators of socio-emotional development predict later academic skills of children in at-risk families (De Feyter and Winsler 2009). Thus, stabilization of the early contexts of development seems important in supporting the positive academic trajectories of refugee children, e.g., via family-focused approaches.

Establishing Partnerships with Refugee Parents

Parents play a central role in fostering the development of their children. Therefore, fruitful cooperation between parents and other caregivers, also across different developmental contexts of children, is important (Galindo and Sheldon 2012). Parental involvement in childcare is associated with more positive socio-emotional and academic outcomes for children (Powell et al. 2010). Moreover, evidence from the Early Head Start data in the United States suggests that participation in childcare is associated with more positive parenting, i.e., heightened language and learning support, better supportiveness in play, a warm home, and more regularity related to bedtime (Harden et al. 2012). Effects of higher parental involvement are independent of the ethnic and socio-economic background of a family (Jeynes 2003). Frequent exchanges are more essential for refugee families because socio-cultural settings and practices between the home environment and childcare are likely to differ. However, a pending challenge is that immigrant mothers are less often involved in childcare (Hindman et al. 2012). The language barrier and feelings of alienation are potential explanations, and these are discussed below.

How Can Childcare for Recently Arrived Refugee Children Be Organized?

A child should not be the sole link between staff in childcare and the parental caregivers. Adapted childcare informs refugee families about their role as a partner in childcare and clearly communicates the expectations of the staff. Parent-teacher conferences and cooperation require more time and patience to foster effective communication if parents do not have previous experiences with childcare (Lunneblad 2017). Especially in ethno-culturally diverse contexts, thorough parent-teacher partnerships are essential in actively bridging potential discrepancies between the contexts. Therefore, staff needs to show interpersonal and knowledge-based cultural competence (Busch et al. 2018b). Regarding childcare, interpersonal cultural competence encompasses acknowledging the attitudes and parenting goals of the refugee families. Culturally responsive staff considers these as socio-culturally adaptive strategies to prepare the children for a specific environment, to avoid judgmental behavior, and to demonstrate interest in foreign perspectives. As distinct from interpersonal cultural competence, a certain extent of knowledge-based cultural competence about the socio-cultural practices (e.g., holidays, ethnic conflicts, significant social practices) of refugee children is additionally required by the staff.

Refugee families are linguistically diverse. This often requires the involvement of translators. Consultation of ethno-culturally diverse translators needs to consider potential conflicts between the translator and target persons (ethnic, personal, or regarding traditional attitudes). Besides verbal communication, some picture-based material is available to ensure basic communication.

During the post-migration period, refugees have an increased risk of feeling alienated and of experiencing discrimination (Lindencrona et al. 2008). Establishing an atmosphere that values plurality and cultural diversity is important for childcare with refugees. Activities which connect to the experiences and socially accepted habits of the participating families are especially suitable (e.g., cooking, singing). Within the first weeks of attendance, refugee parents might appreciate being involved at the childcare center in order to familiarize themselves with the childcare practices and to feel comfortable leaving their children in the care of someone else. Staff should therefore give consideration to parent-child activities within the curriculum as well.

A persistent challenge for organizers of childcare is to consider socio- and ethno-cultural diversity in practice. However, not all different socio-cultural contexts can be considered within a single childcare setting at once. Staff in childcare can therefore focus on broader key principles for a child's socialization. The general principles of sustainable societies are tolerance, empathy, and learning necessary skills to make relevant contributions to society. Additionally, socialization of children should reinforce coverage of cosmopolitan values (i.e., human rights, social justice, equality) and positive experiences of diversity.

Adapted Childcare for Refugees: "Bridging Projects" in Germany

Until 2015, the majority (69%) of newly arrived refugee children were enrolled in public childcare. This number is significantly lower than the enrollment rate of host-country children (90% for Germany; Gambaro et al. 2017). When a large number of refugees arrived in Germany in 2016, childcare centers were already stretched to capacity. In reaction to this influx, the federal state North-Rhine Westphalia funded a specialized childcare program for refugees. At a low-threshold, these Bridging Projects (BPs) are intended to approach recently arrived families and to prepare their young children for the transition to childcare or primary school. Therefore, organizers of BPs have the freedom to create locally embedded and need-oriented childcare groups.

Our research team conducted observations and semi-structured interviews in 42 BPs. We found evidence that the staff accentuates certain goals in childcare, depending on the setting (Busch et al. under revision). Some BPs are mobile and located in caravans on public playgrounds or in refugee accommodations. The staff in these BPs tries to establish first contact and to inform families about childcare options as well as introduce them to the German approach to childcare and its goals. Other BPs are located in daycare centers and primary schools. Their aim is to prepare children for their upcoming transition into regular childcare or even into first grade. Intensity of childcare varies across the settings. While contact-establishing BPs may consist of up to 30 children, group sizes of transition-oriented BPs are smaller.

Teachers of both subtypes reported that the parents repeatedly asked for additional support beyond the scope of caregiving. This suggests that isolated approaches with an exclusive focus on child development might disregard complex situations faced by refugee families during the post-migration period. Having arrived in a new country, refugee families often live in precarious situations at first. At the same time, they have to cope with a comprehensive set of various demands in unfamiliar contexts, e.g., application for asylum, residence permit, housing, finances. Therefore, newly arrived refugee families need focal points for orientation and support. BPs provide a vehicle for the holistic and need-oriented support of a family system. Anecdotal evidence suggested that those BPs focusing on child development and coping with post-migration living difficulties seemed most valued by the refugee families.

Conclusions

Diversity is neither a trend nor a temporary challenge in childcare. It reflects the demographic and societal changes of our times towards complexity and fragmentation, i.e., through increasing global mobility and connectedness. Adapting to these changes is essential. Therefore, principles of childcare should be reviewed to consider the increasingly diversified contexts of socialization of children in Western countries. Childcare can play a strategic role in the formation of diverse and pluralistic societies. Childcare provides a vehicle for family support services and, most importantly, contributes to the developmental contexts of a child's socialization towards functional adjustment, pluralism, and diversity. At the same time, childcare has to consider the heterogeneous and potentially contradictory physical and social settings of children, varying child-rearing practices, and the individual psychologies of different caregivers. We need to better understand the processes of enculturation and negotiation of cultural influences within diverse contexts. We should consider child development and socialization as socio-culturally entangled and most precisely studied in connection to its socio-cultural context. The developmental niche provides a useful framework to organize such investigations.

References

Ahnert, L., Pinquart, M., & Lamb, M. E. (2006). Security of children's relationships with nonparental care providers: A meta-analysis. *Child Development, 77*(3), 664–679. https://doi.org/10.1111/j. 1467-8624.2006.00896.x.

Allport, G. W. (1954). *The nature of prejudice.* Reading, MA: Addison-Wesley.

Banks, J. A. (1977). Pluralism and educational concepts: A clarification. *Peabody Journal of Education, 54*(2), 73–78. https://doi.org/10.1080/01619567709538109.

Benet-Martínez, V., Leu, J., Lee, F., & Morris, M. W. (2002). Negotiating biculturalism cultural frame switching in biculturals with oppositional versus compatible cultural identities. *Journal of Cross-Cultural Psychology, 33*(5), 492–516.

Bornstein, M. H. (2012). Cultural approaches to parenting. *Parenting, Science and Practice, 12*(2–3), 212–221. https://doi.org/10.1080/15295192.2012.683359.

Buchmüller, T., Lembcke, H., Busch, J., Kumsta, R., & Leyendecker, B. (2018). Exploring mental health status and syndrome patterns among young refugee children in Germany. *Frontiers in Psychiatry, 9.* https://doi.org/10.3389/fpsyt.2018.00212.

Busch, J., Bihler, L. M., Lembcke, H., Buchmüller, T., Diers, K., & Leyendecker, B. (2018a). Challenges and solutions perceived by educators in an early childcare program for refugee children. *Frontiers in Psychology, 9,* 1621.

Busch, J., Buchmüller, T., Lembcke, H., Bihler, L., & Leyendecker, B. (under revision). Early education and care for refugees: Implementation of a policy for transitional childcare in Germany. *Manuscript under revision.*

Busch, J., Leyendecker, B., & Siefen, R.G. (2018b). Clinical Assessment of Immigrant Children [Klinische Diagnostik bei Kindern und Jugendlichen]. In D. B. Maehler, A. Shajek, & Brinkmann, J.U. (Hrsg.), Handbook of Immigrant Assessment [*Diagnostik bei Migrantinnen und Migranten. Ein Handbuch*] (pp. 197–244). Göttingen: Hogrefe.

De Feyter, J. J., & Winsler, A. (2009). The early developmental competencies and school readiness of low-income, immigrant children: Influences of generation, race/ethnicity, and national origins. *Early Childhood Research Quarterly, 24*(4), 411–431. https://doi.org/10.1016/j.ecresq.2009.07. 004.

Devictor, X., & Do, Q.-T. (2016). *How many years have refugees been in exile?* Policy Research Working Paper No. 7810 (pp. 1–19). Washington, DC: World Bank.

Federal Agency for Migration and Refugees [Bundesamt für Migration und Flüchtlinge] (2016). *Report by the Federal Statistical Office [Bericht des Statistischen Bundesamts] No. 12 (pp. 1–12),* Berlin.

Galindo, C., & Sheldon, S. B. (2012). School and home connections and children's kindergarten achievement gains: The mediating role of family involvement. *Early Childhood Research Quarterly, 27,* 90–103. https://doi.org/10.1016/j.ecresq.2011.05.004.

Gambaro, L., Liebau, E., Peter, F. H., & Weinhardt, F. (2017). How many refugee children attend childcare or primary school? [Viele Kinder von Geflüchteten besuchen eine Kita oder Grundschule: Nachholbedarf bei den unter Dreijährigen und der Sprachförderung von Schulkindern]. *German Institute for Economic Research [Deutsches Institut für Wirtschaftsforschung – Wochenbericht], 84*(19), 379–386.

Greenfield, P. M., Keller, H., Fuligni, A., & Maynard, A. (2003). Cultural pathways through universal development. *Annual Review of Psychology, 54*(1), 461–490. https://doi.org/10.1146/annurev. psych.54.101601.145221.

Han, W.-J. (2008). The academic trajectories of children of immigrants and their school environments. *Developmental Psychology, 44*(6), 1572–1590.

Harden, B. J., Sandstrom, H., & Chazan-Cohen, R. (2012). Early Head Start and African American families: Impacts and mechanisms of child outcomes. *Early Childhood Research Quarterly, 27*(4), 572–581.

Hindman, A. H., Miller, A. L., Froyen, L. C., & Skibbe, L. E. (2012). A portrait of family involvement during Head Start: Nature, extent, and predictors. *Early Childhood Research Quarterly, 27*(4), 654–667.

Howes, C. (2011). Children's social development within the socialization context of child care and early childhood education. In P. K. Smith & C. H. Hart (Eds.), *The Wiley-Blackwell handbook of childhood social development* (pp. 246–262). Oxford, UK: Wiley-Blackwell. https://doi.org/10.1002/9781444390933.ch13.

Jeynes, W. H. (2003). A meta-analysis: The effects of parental involvement on minority children's academic achievement. *Education and Urban Society, 35*(2), 202–218.

Lindencrona, F., Ekblad, S., & Hauff, E. (2008). Mental health of recently resettled refugees from the Middle East in Sweden: the impact of pre-resettlement trauma, resettlement stress and capacity to handle stress. *Social Psychiatry and Psychiatric Epidemiology, 43*(2), 121–131. https://doi.org/10.1007/s00127-007-0280-2.

Lunneblad, J. (2017). Integration of refugee children and their families in the Swedish preschool: Strategies, objectives and standards. *European Early Childhood Education Research Journal, 25*(3), 359–369. https://doi.org/10.1080/1350293X.2017.1308162.

Magnuson, K., Lahaie, C., & Waldfogel, J. (2006). Preschool and school readiness of children of immigrants. *Social Science Quarterly, 87*(5), 1241–1262. https://doi.org/10.1111/j.1540-6237.2006.00426.x.

Markus, H. R., & Kitayama, S. (1991). Culture and the self: Implications for cognition, emotion, and motivation. *Psychological Review, 98*(2), 224–253. https://doi.org/10.1037/0033-295X.98.2.224.

Mitchell, L., & Ouko, A. (2012). Experiences of Congolese refugee families in New Zealand: Challenges and possibilities for early childhood provision. *Australasian Journal of Early Childhood, 37*(1), 99–107.

National Association for the Education of Young Children (2009) *Developmentally appropriate practice in early childhood programs serving children from birth through age 8* (Position Statement). National Association for the Education of Young Children. Retrieved from https://www.naeyc.org/sites/default/files/globally-shared/downloads/PDFs/resources/position-statements/PSDAP.pdf. Accessed on September 14, 2018.

Pearson, E., & Degotardi, S. (2009). Education for sustainable development in early childhood education: A global solution to local concerns? *International Journal of Early Childhood, 41*(2), 97–111. https://doi.org/10.1007/BF03168881.

Powell, D. R., Son, S.-H., File, N., & San Juan, R. R. (2010). Parent–school relationships and children's academic and social outcomes in public school pre-kindergarten. *Journal of School Psychology, 48*(4), 269–292. https://doi.org/10.1016/j.jsp.2010.03.002.

Sirin, S. R., & Rogers-Sirin, L. (2015). *The educational and mental health needs of Syrian refugee children. Young children in refugee families*. Washington, DC: Migration Policy Institute, 1–27.

Super, C. M., & Harkness, S. (1986). The developmental Niche: A conceptualization at the interface of child and culture. *International Journal of Behavioral Development, 9*(4), 545–569. https://doi.org/10.1177/016502548600900409.

Webster-Stratton, C., & Taylor, T. (2001). Nipping early risk factors in the bud: Preventing substance abuse, delinquency, and violence in adolescence through interventions targeted at young children (0–8 years). *Prevention Science, 2*(3), 165–192.

Whiting, J. M. W. (1981). Environmental constraints on infant care practices. In R. H. Munroe, R. L. Munroe, & B. B. Whiting (Eds.), *Handbook of cross-cultural human development* (pp. 155–180). New York, NY: Garland.

Woellert, F., & Klingholz, R. (2014). New Potentials: Immigration to Germany [*Neue Potenziale: Zur Lage der Integration in Deutschland*]. Berlin: German Institute for Economic Research [Institut für Bevölkerung und Entwicklung].

Chapter 15
Children's Perspectives of Risk and Protection

Yael (Julia) Ponizovsky-Bergelson, Dorit Roer-Strier, Yael Dayan
and Nira Wahle

Abstract Protection of children from risk is a major concern of scholars and practitioners in many countries. However, young children's perspectives on these issues
are rarely acknowledged. This chapter addresses Israeli children's perspectives on
what places children at risk and what makes them feel protected. The chapter adopts
a context-informed perspective that acknowledges hybridity and complexity, while
trying to avoid the assumption that cultures are uniform, monolithic, and static. The
chapter provides examples from the findings of a qualitative study conducted in
Israel. The study included children from diverse populations who differed in their
geographical place of living, their cultural background, their religious or secular style
of living, and their immigration or local experiences. Children were asked to take
photos and draw risk and protection and discuss their drawings and photos in small
groups. The analysis is based on children's explanations regarding their choice of
photos and drawings. Children's attitudes towards risk and protection indicate their
deep understanding of risk factors and, above all, their sense of agency, that is, their
ability to act and influence in order to prevent risk or to protect themselves from dangerous circumstances and to create situations of joy and pleasure that enhance their
sense of protection. The analysis showed that both perspectives of risk and protection
are shaped by the various contexts that form children's worlds. We therefore call for
the inclusion of children, their agency, and sense of protection in the discourse of
risk. We also highlight the importance of attention to the multiple contexts affecting
children's perceptions of risk and protection.

Much attention is given in Western psychological and developmental literature to
risks for children's development. However, the cross-cultural literature raises aware-

Y. (Julia) Ponizovsky-Bergelson (✉)
Faculty of Social & Community Sciences, Social Work Department, Ruppin Academic Center,
Hadera, Israel
e-mail: yael.ponizovsky@mail.huji.ac.il

Y. (Julia) Ponizovsky-Bergelson · D. Roer-Strier · Y. Dayan
Hebrew University of Jerusalem, Jerusalem, Israel

N. Wahle
Kibbutzim College of Education, Technology and the Arts, Tel Aviv-Yafo, Israel

© Springer Nature Switzerland AG 2019   201
T. Tulviste et al. (eds.), *Children's Social Worlds in Cultural Context*,
https://doi.org/10.1007/978-3-030-27033-9_15

ness to differences in risk definitions in diverse groups (Nadan et al. 2018). Children's voices are often missing from these debates. This chapter offers examples from a qualitative study conducted in Israel that aimed to document children's perspectives on what puts children at risk and what makes them feel protected. Due to its very unique human diversity, for years Israel has been a natural laboratory for cultural and contextual studies (Leshem and Roer-Strier 2003). The study included children from diverse groups. Children were asked to take photos and draw pictures of the above and discuss their drawings and photos in small groups. These discussions were analyzed. In this chapter, we discuss children's ability to affect their social worlds by actively preventing risk and promoting protection, a view that emerged from the children's perspectives.

Risk and Protection Discourse in Israel

According to the Statistical Report of the Israel National Council for the Child (2017), "Children in Israel 2017," the number of children in Israel was 2,768,700, and they comprised 33.0% of the population. The population of children in Israel is extremely diverse—about 70% are Jews, 23% Muslims, 1.5% Christians, 1.6% Druze, and 3% were not classified by religion. The aforementioned groups also present considerable diversity. There are Arabs and Jews, religious, ultra-Orthodox, secular, veteran Israelis, and immigrants from various countries living in cities, villages, and settlements, in the center, in the periphery, in the occupied territories, and in Bedouin recognized and unrecognized villages. According to the report, two out of three ultra-Orthodox children live below the poverty line, as do two out of three Arab children. In Jewish society, one in five children is defined as poor. The larger the number of children in a family, the greater the poverty of families. Fifty percent of families with more than four children and 64% of families with more than five children live below the poverty line.

According to the 2017 report, the number of children defined as being at risk was 367,440 children. According to the report, in addition to this group there are children in Israel whose legal status puts them at risk. Some 161,500 children (6% of the children of Israel) do not have full Israeli citizenship, of which (80%) are Arabs, residents of East Jerusalem. The rest are children of legal migrant workers, immigrant children and children of mixed marriages of Israeli citizens and non-citizens, especially Israeli Arabs and Palestinian residents of the occupied territories who have received a type of temporary status. A second group of 48,600 children are those without any legal status, not even residency status, and who have no rights, including the right to education, health and welfare services. These are the children of migrant workers, asylum seekers, infiltrators and those who reside in Israel after their tourist visa has expired.

Of the total number of children and youth at risk in Israel, 31% are in preschool age, 37% are elementary school age and 32% are youth (Navot et al. 2017). The increase in public awareness of the phenomenon of children at risk has led to significant development in many countries around the world and to an increase in welfare services, protection and treatment of the subject (Benvenisti and Schmidt 2010; Faber and Slutzky 2007). In Israel, the first law on youth care and supervision in 1960 recognizes that children and adolescents may be at risk in their parents' homes and that there are children in need of state protection. Alongside the recognition of providing protection for children, the Youth Law did not take into account the possibility of abuse or malice. The first law explicitly related to this in the context of children was the Penal Code in 1977, which defined the various offenses related to violence and defined the sanctions for them. The International Convention on the Rights of the Child, adopted in 1989 (Israel ratified it in 1991), presented a new conception of the child, which includes protection as well as risk. The child is perceived as an autonomous entity, carrying important and essential rights. "It is the obligation of the states to ensure the optimal development of children in all areas, and the primary responsibility for ensuring the development and protection of children rests with the parents, and the state has the duty to assist parents in this task by the means available to them" (Weisblay 2010, p. 5).

In 1991, the Law for the Prevention of Domestic Violence was enacted, and in 2000 the Harassment Law was established to protect children who are at constant risk of domestic violence and to restrict the offender. An amendment to the law required reporting to the authorities. In 2006 a special committee on children at risk was established. The Schmid Committee Report (2006) defines children at risk as "Children and adolescents who live in situations that endanger them in their family and environment, and as a result of their inability to realize their rights under the Convention on the Rights of the Child in the following areas: "physical existence, health and development; family affiliation; learning and acquiring life skills; welfare and emotional health; belonging and social participation and protection against others and their own dangerous behaviors" (Schmid Committee Report 2006, p. 67).

The Schmid Committee Report (2006) found that the majority of the services for children at risk in Israel are characterized by uniformity, with very few services tailored to diverse population groups. In 2007, the first stage of implementation of the National Program for Children and Youth at Risk began. This inter-ministerial program was led by the Ministry of Social Affairs and Social Services. The purpose of the program was to change perceptions and ways of dealing with adolescents and children at risk, by strengthening and expanding the services in the community designed for them and their cultural suitability (Sabo-Lal 2017).

Context-Informed Perspective on Risk and Protection

Risk, well-being, and protection of children are socially constructed and depend largely on the contexts in which families live. In Israel, despite more than 10 years of serious efforts for culture-competence training and cultural adaptation of intervention programs, the risk and protection field of knowledge is still largely rooted in universal developmental theories that were formulated based on empirical research and clinical experience conducted primarily in the West (Roer-Strier & Nadan in preparation). These universal theories are also the source from which professional definitions of risk and protection in Israel are derived. The Israeli risk discourse focuses on the parents and their ability to provide for the needs of the child. However, the perspectives of parents in general and children in particular are missing from the discourse. Although much effort is invested in the Israeli risk discourse, it suffers from a deficit-oriented perspective and context-blindness.

This chapter adopts a context-informed perspective. 'Context-informed perspective' is a term based on the view that human development and behavior and the theories humans form to explain their world are influenced by the many interlocked contexts that surround them: socio-political, historical, economic, cultural, gender, etc. (e.g., Shalhoub-Kevorkian and Roer-Strier 2016). Context-informed research consists of paradigms and methodologies that are applied to address the complexity of the studied phenomenon and include the perspectives of research participants.

The context-informed perspective adopts the views of critical theories that consider structural factors, power relations, and an understanding of socio-political context. This perspective acknowledges hybridity, complexity, and the dynamics of power and change, trying to avoid viewing cultures as uniformed, monolithic, and static. We propose that although our context-informed presentation will entail examples of separate contexts, in fact, these contexts are connected and interrelated. Therefore, while we will present six diverse communities we will not compare them as different cultural groups but highlight the contextual elements apparent in the children's reports such as the political, geographical, and religious contexts.

Other conceptual frameworks that inform this chapter are the notion of resilience (Harvey 2007), strengths perspective (Saleebey 2006), and salutogenic outlook (Braun-Lewensohn and Sagy 2011). These frameworks challenge the deficit nature of the risk discourse, claiming it should take into account protective factors, sense of coherence, and agency of children as well as families and communities. The salutogenic framework, for example, stresses that perceiving events as comprehensible and manageable (known as a sense of coherence) affects dealing with stress. Children with a strong sense of coherence manage stress effectively and show fewer risk-related poor outcomes. These abilities and resources are of great significance to those who plan and adapt interventions and prevention programs across different contexts.

Children's Perspectives

Children's active participation in families, communities, and neighborhoods is motivated by their desire to be participating members of these groups (Hedges and Cullen 2012). Scholars advocate for including children's perspectives in academic, practice and policy related discourses (Ben-Arieh 2005). Researchers also claim that very young children (ages 3–6) not only hold their own views and opinions, but also have the capability to express valuable perspectives regarding their contexts and world views (Clark and Statham 2005; Dayan and Ziv 2012). This "sociology of child-hood" conceives of children as capable and knowledgeable experts on their own lives (Clark 2004), possessing ideas, perspectives, and interests that are best learned through interactions with them (Clark and Moss 2001; Mayall 2002). This perspective represents a change from classical research with children; while children were previously regarded as dependent, incompetent, and acted upon by others, they are now perceived as social actors (Elden 2013), participants, and even co-researchers (Christensen and Prout 2002; Jones 2004; Lewis and Kellett 2004).

The Convention on the Rights of the Child (CRC), developed by the United Nations in 1989, emphasizes children's right to express their views and to influence their own lives (United Nations 1989). The CRC agenda shaped prevention and intervention programs by fostering a realization that children have a right to be consulted, heard, and to appropriately influence the services and facilities provided for them (Lansdown 1994; Woodhouse 2004).

Consequently, both Mayall (2002) and O'Kane (2000) refer to research as being with children instead of *about* or *on* children. Leonard et al. (2011) suggest the term "Child-focused research," pointing out that children have the ability to engage in the process of the construction of meaning in their own lives. Moreover, social scientists began to engage children in projects that explore their experiences, views, and understandings (e.g., Dayan 2007; Moore et al. 2008). In doing so, they were looking for and creating innovative ways to enter children's worlds (e.g., Curtis et al. 2004; Devine 2002; Lightfoot and Sloper 2002; Mulvihill et al. 2000; Shemmings 2000; Sloper and Lightfoot 2003).

Many scholars call attention to the need for the study of resilience and well-being to include the voices of children (Ben-Arieh 2002; Ben-Arieh et al. 2014). In this chapter, we aim to address both risk and protection resilience and agency as manifested in children's perspectives.

Purpose and Procedure of Current Study

Our study was conducted at the Hebrew University of Jerusalem's NEVET Green-house of Context-Informed Research and Training for Children in Need. NEVET's studies apply a context-informed approach to the study of perspectives of risk and protection among parents, children, and professionals from different communities in Israel, utilizing varied qualitative methodologies.

The main research question examined in this study was: What are the perspectives of risk and protection among young children in different neighborhoods in Israel? Data from 420 children aged 3–6 years were collected by twenty-nine graduate students in the school of Social Work and Social Welfare and the graduate program in Early Childhood Studies at the Hebrew University of Jerusalem.

In the current chapter we explored findings of six MA theses that documented the perspectives of risk and protection of one hundred and sixty-seven young children among very young children in six sub-samples listed below.

In the first group, the children came from immigrant families from Ethiopia (Group A: $n = 30$, 14 boys and 17 girls aged 3–6). The Ethiopian families resided in under-privileged and segregated neighborhoods located in two cities in central Israel. The Ethiopian population is among the poorest in the Jewish sector in Israel.

The second group contained children of immigrant families from the Former Soviet Union (FSU; Group B: FSU $n = 29$, 18 boys and 11 girls aged 3–6). The group included children to both religious and secular families who live in settlements in the occupied territories.

In the third group were children from Haredi Ultra-orthodox families from Jerusalem (Group C: $n = 30$, 18 boys and 13 girls aged 3–6). Haredi families adhere to strict religious laws and live in closed communities.

The fourth group consisted of children of Native Israelis who define themselves as "national- religious" residing in a village in central Israel (Group D: $n = 29$, 10 boys and 19 girls, aged 3–6).

The fifth group included children from four settlement communities residing in the southern Samarian hills of the occupied territories, close to Palestinian villages (Group E: $n = 31$, 17 boys and 14 girls aged 3–6).

In the sixth group were eighteen children from the "Bnei Menashe" community—living in the Negev desert (Group F: $n = 18$, 9 boys and 9 girls aged 4–8). The Bnei Menashe (son of "Menasseh" are an ethnolinguistic group from north-east India. This group claimed, since the late twentieth century, that they descend from one of the Lost Tribes of Israel and have adopted the practice of Judaism. The families regard themselves as religious.

All children interviewed had been born in Israel. The interviews took place in children's preschools and local playgrounds. The researchers contacted different preschools. Letters describing the goals and procedures of the study alongside with letters of consent were sent to parents by the preschool teachers. The teachers collected the signed consents and passed them over to the researchers. Informed consent was also obtained from the children. They were asked to help the researcher understand what places children at risk and what makes them feel protected and safe. After confirming that they understood the purpose and the process of the study, they recorded their agreement on an audiotape. Children's participation was voluntary, and they could withdraw from the study at any stage of the data collection. More-over, the researchers were instructed to ensure support and counseling for children if needed. In order to encourage the children to present their perspectives about risk and protection, three methods were used: photo elicitation, (Lal et al. 2012), drawings (Dockett et al. 2009; Fleer and Li 2016), and group discussion (Fleer and Li 2016).

The authors are four researchers from the Hebrew University, Jerusalem, Israel, specializing in research on children's perspectives, qualitative and mixed methods research, early childhood studies, and issues of multiculturalism. The study was supported by the Israel Science Foundation (ISF) and approved by the head researcher at the Ministry of Education and by the Hebrew University.

The trained interviewers collected the data in three steps: (1) Inside their preschools and in the outdoor yard, each child was asked to take two photos: first, of 'risk' ("What in your opinion places children at risk (danger)?") and later, of 'protection' ("What protects (defends) children, what makes children feel safe, secure, or protected?") (or vice versa). Risk and protection were alternated to prevent the order-bias. In the second step, children were asked to choose the best photograph describing 'risk' and the best describing 'protection' and to explain their choice. The explanation took place as part of a group discussion with two or three other children. Presenting to other children sparked a conversation between them and served as a trigger to elaborate and extend their arguments. For the third step, children were asked to draw a picture. The drawing provided the possibility to refer to the elements of risk and protection which were imaginary or to allow those children who could not take photograph at the location to participate. Each child received crayons and a sheet of paper divided into two parts (Einarsdottir 2007) and were asked to draw on one side 'What in your opinion protects children?' and on the other side 'What in your opinion places children at risk?' Sides were alternated. Upon finishing their drawings, children were asked to explain their pictures (e.g., Tay-Lim and Lim 2013). All comments and conversations were recorded and transcribed.

The interviews analyzed for this chapter were conducted in Hebrew. The authors served as the research team and together designed the procedure, guided the interviewers, and were closely involved in data analysis (Liebenberg 2018).

The data from the six groups described above were thematically analyzed. The thematic analysis was based on identifying key codes, categories, and themes (Shkedi 2003). In addition, coding pages were developed that included quotations from the interviewees.

Findings of Children's Perspectives on Risk and Protection

Our main finding in the six groups was that children are well aware of different types of risks. They explored various causes of risk in their environments. They were able not only to explain what puts children at risk and what protects them and prevents risk, but even when risk could not be prevented, children suggested ways to avoid harm. Their statements reflect a great sense of agency, which expresses their understanding and ability to control what is happening. The sense of agency reflected in the findings was the children's ability to act and influence in order to prevent risk or protect themselves from dangerous situations, and their ability to feel joy and pleasure that enhance their sense of protection.

Behavior that Prevents Danger (Risks)

One way to avoid danger is to follow a routine that prevents the possibility of harm. For example, in the context of warm weather of Israel and especially in areas close to the desert, children talked a lot about drinking water. Drinking water in their opinion, prevents headaches, helps in recovery from illness, and prevents death. The following quotes are some examples:

> So that their head will not hurt, that … that … there will not be very severe situations, for example, as I have a headache now, so … then it is the same thing and … and … that they drink a lot, so won't be bad and painful situations. (Group B, Boy, 5y)
>
> When you get sick, you drink water and then become healthy. (Group B, Girl, 5y)
>
> If a person lives without water, then he can die … If you live without water, then he needs at least a bit … a person can live for about two days without water … and if he goes … when you drink water, it helps your body and the body works well. (Group B, Girl, 6y)

Food is also an important part of life's routine that can prevent danger: "If you do not eat food then you will die, and food helps". (Group B, Boy, 6y). Interestingly, many references regarding health and prevention came from the FSU group (Group B). These results coincide with our studies of risk and protection among immigrant parents from FSU. The participating parents also expressed great concerns regarding children's health (Ulitsa et al. 2018). One girl suggested changing your place of residence in order to avoid injury. She said:

> Yesterday I went with my mother to take a book from the library and chose a book with large pictures that explains that there are infections which is very dangerous and unhealthy and I told my mother that maybe we should live in a village because there are no cars that make pollution which enters inside the body because it is a serious problem. (Group D, Girl, 6y)

Girls and boys frequently talked about the danger of falling, such as from a swing or ladder, and describe how to prevent it: "*When you swing, hold your hands, then you cannot fall.*" (Group C, Boy, 5.6y). "*If you do not hold the handlebars of the ladder then you just fall and if you hold them then they do not fall*" (Group D, Girl, 5y). Another way to avoid injury is to move away from the source of danger. For example, to keep away from fire, electricity or water: "*Fire … it is forbidden for children to approach … because fire is very dangerous for children*" (Group B, Girl, 5y), "*You must not touch the fire because then the hand will burn and you cannot touch the oven when mommy prepares [food] and she went for a little while…*" (Group A, Girl, 6y). "*It's dangerous that you should not put your hands in, into electricity, if … if it is a bit torn, the babies must not touch electricity because it can be electrocuted.*" (Group B, Boy, 6y) or to keep away from the sea: "*It's like … a sea … if they will not go there and they will not drown*" (Group B, Girl, 6y). Their awareness of risks and the ways to avoid them is also expressed in their attitude towards obstacles on the road. For example, crossing a road is dangerous and therefore:

> We need to be really small to be in a carriage and to cross only … only with mother … and when mother is not there, you give hand to father, father or mother. There are cars and they drive quickly, and if there is a little boy, they cannot see that he is really small, even when he is [age] three or four and five … so it is allowed to go only with mother or father, and cross the road cautiously. (Group B, Girl, 5y)

Another possible obstacle on the road is a pit. The following conversation between a boy and a girl emphasizes their own perceptions of their ability to choose whether or not they can prevent getting hurt:

Fig. 15.1 Being careful and conscious of danger (Girl, 5 years old, "national-religious" Israelis)

- *"Oh… my drawing is that a boy is keeping a hole ah … he falls into the hole and then he broke his leg. (Group B, Girl, 6y)*
- *Listen. It does not count, falling into pits is your choice… It's like you see a pit, so it's your choice whether you want to go into this pit or not … so it's not risky. They chose risk themselves. This is something that gives danger, but they give it to themselves".* (Group B, Boy, 6y)

Being careful and conscious of danger were also present in children's reports. While walking one may step on dangerous things and therefore must be careful:

"If the child does not go to the thorns, he will not be scratched and injured in his eyes" (Group A, Boy, 5.5y), *"If the child walks in a careful manner, he will not be injured by a stone"* (Group A, Boy, 5.5y), *"Do not walk barefoot … we can bleed."* (Group F, Girl, 5y). *"A bag on the ground because if you can, if you step on it and do not look, you can slip and break your head."* (Group D, Girl, 5y, see Fig. 15.1).

Children's knowledge of risk factors was also apparent as they listed actions that can cause danger. They often talk about the danger of falling and pointed out that climbing (on installations, windows, trees) is dangerous: A girl photographed a slide and said: *"that you can fall. Here…. There's blood. If you get on this side, and fall".* (Group C, Girl, 5.3y). *"What's dangerous is actually going up on trees because you can fall, and God forbid you break your head or something like that."* (Group B, Boy, 6y).

Protection from Danger

Children were aware of the dangers surrounding them; they took responsibility and offered active ways to defend themselves against peril. Some of the groups were interviewed during wartime where missile attacks were experienced by the interviewees. Children reported they felt safe in the shelters located at the preschools.

The following example illustrates how in her own home, a girl felt responsible to protect not only herself, but also her father, from incoming missiles:

"My father does not run to the shelter, he is not afraid, I tell him: 'Come, there's that Voice [siren], but he sits and does not get up" (Group A, Girl, 5.11y). A similar attempt to protect her father was manifested in another girl's report: *"I tell him [the father] you have to run to the shelter."* (Group A, Girl, 5.3y)

The house or home was also regarded as a safe place to protect oneself from bombs and other dangers: *"This is the house, and it has a strong wall ... If there is an alarm that means that there are bombs outside, then you can enter the house and wait"*. (Group B, Boy, 6y). The house was viewed as a safe place for protection from other risks as well. Interestingly, in most cases the children referred to the physical infrastructure of the house and much less frequently to family members who provide protection. If there is a danger of thieves or other strangers', one can hide or lock the door: *"What puts children at risk? If someone steals it [the child]... then he hides. in a safe place."* (Group B, Girl, 6y).

> It's a house with a door, because if someone wants to do something to the children then the children can go inside and then lock the house and nothing will happen to them, just close the door and lock it. (Group F, Girl, 8y)

A girl who lives in the Negev, a desert area with formidable and feared sandstorms, referred to stormy weather and the necessity to defend herself:

> If there is wind, we can close the door and close all windows. The house protects us because if there is a strong wind then we can close everything that is in the house and the wind will not be there, we won't feel the wind because it is too strong, A strong wind is not good as it swaps away little people. (Group F, Girl, 5y, see Fig. 15.2)

Children reported that joy and pleasant experiences created a sense of elevation and protection. Boys and girls often spoke about joy and fun as protective factors. Joy was derived from various activities and friendships: *"Can I also draw something that makes children happy? so I draw a computer in which we can watch a movie, that*

Fig. 15.2 House as a protective factor (Girl, 5 years old, "Bnei Menashe" community)

makes children happy" (Group E, Boy, 4.9y). *"It's really fun, I went to a swimming pool, every day we made braids like that ... and ... and we went to a lot to a theater and it was very happy*" (Group B, Girl, 4y). Interestingly, activities that involve movement and sensory stimulation, such as playing on a swing or slide, cause pleasure and are also related to sense of protection: *"I like to rock hard!*" (Group C, Girl, 4.3y). A girl explained why the slide is a protective factor: *"because we can touch it, it's fun and safe*" (Group C, Girl, 5.9 y). Another girl added: *"It is a safe thing, whoever wants to slide down from it, he feels it. He feels the slide. For me it is fun. Something tickles me, it is fun me, fun to me*" (Group C, Girl, 5.9 y) for this girl the fast movement and excitement were recognized as a feeling related to safety. Another sensation that was noted by one child was a pleasant smell. He drew a flower and said: *"to pick and sniff*" (Group C, Boy, 4y).

Some of the children's explanations included symbolic or metaphorical descriptions of what causes elevation of spirit and soul. One girl drew a butterfly and explained: *"When you see the butterfly flying in the sky and feel it, it helps children feel safe. It makes you feel happy*" (Group C, Girl 4y).

Another interesting finding was that in some groups children were more present than adults in the child's sense of safety. When taking a photo, one girl asked some children to hug each other because *"when the friends hug it helps to feel safe*" (Group C, Girl 4y). *"When they play, the children, it protects them and make them happy, it is very happy*" (Group B, Girl, 4y).

Children's sense of agency is also expressed by the presentation of good deeds as a protective factor. An Ultra-Orthodox girl drew a child wearing glasses inside a house and explained: *"I drew glasses ... I wanted to draw a child who makes Returning Lost Objects*". She was referring to the mitzvah (one of the commandments in Judaism) of returning a lost object to its owners, a protective act from her prospective: *"But I returned a lost object...the glasses... this is what I want to tell*" (Group C, Girl, 5.6y). Another child reported about feeling safe when doing something good: *"If you do something good to yourself, your heart feels safe*", and elsewhere noted that *"the playground [protects children], there are slides here, here you do good things here, when you do something good, you are safe.*" (Group F, Boy, 6.2y).

When reviewing the above examples our analysis shows that regardless of the contexts, the participating children demonstrated their profound understanding and knowledge of risk and protection as well as their ability to consider the means to prevent risk or maintain a sense of protection. Above all, children seemed to understand their sense of agency; that is, their ability to act and influence in order to prevent risk or protect themselves from dangerous situations and their ability to create feelings of joy and pleasure that enhance their sense of protection. The results reflect children's ability to make an impact, to influence, and have some sort of control, as well as their ability to know the world and change the world as a result of their knowledge (Giddens as cited in Oswell 2013).

In this chapter, framed by theoretical frameworks of resilience (Harvey 2007), strength perspectives, and salutogenic outlooks (Braun-Lewensohn and Sagy 2011; Saleebey 2006), we embraced the notion that risk discourse should take into account protective factors and a sense of coherence and agency of children, as well as of families and communities. The results illuminate the diverse perspectives that can offer a better understanding of their social worlds.

Influences of Context

In light of the above communalities one should ask what did we learn concerning the influence of the diverse contexts of the six groups that differ in their geographical place of living, their cultural background, their religious or secular style of living, and their immigration or native experiences? Oswell (2013) claims that it makes no sense to frame children's agency in terms of a simple binary, having or not having agency. He argues that children's agency should refer to complex situations in the context of family, health, playgrounds, culture, and politics. Agency is not only about individual experiences, but also the social, cultural, and historical contexts in which the experiences of individuals are formed. Agency is not a fixed trait, property, or capability that resides in the individual, but an action that shifts in relation to the social context. Agentive actions gain their meaning, their consequences, and their continuity from the interplay between individuals and social context (Sairanen and Kumpulainen 2014).

Our results support this argument: Children explored and discussed the opportunities and resources in their social worlds. Those opportunities and resources were external and internal. From children's sense of agency and their understanding of risk and protective factors, we can sketch their divergent contexts that construct their social and mental worlds. Agency may take different forms in different contexts and take into account contextual and cultural differences in meaning-making as well as political and socioeconomic contexts (Vandenbroeck and Bouverne-De Bie 2006).

According to their stories, the participants of this study who live in war zones are familiar with the meaning of missiles, bombs, and shelters. A girl's report of her attempt to protect her father by making him go to a shelter is an example for the importance of considering the political context of Israel. During missile attacks, children sit in shelters in the preschool. The effect of war is felt differently in different areas of Israel and is thus related to the geographic area where it occurs.

Contexts may interact. This interaction may be related to social class, economic ability and geographical context as well as to other resources. This is apparent in the examples of going every day to a swimming pool or to the theater, or even having a computer to watch films. The ecological context is also apparent in some of the groups. Children are affected by the warm weather in Israel, which influences the risk of dehydration if you do not drink water. Both parents and children from FSU (Group B) stressed issues of health and prevention of disease. The cultural literature has related this concern to the hygiene, health, nutrition, and protection against cold weather in the FSU, where the weather is very cold and accompanied by dangers of disease. In the FSU there was constant concern for the health and safety of children in light of the high morbidity (Ispa 1995, 2002).

Another example of contextual influences on children's perceptions comes from the context of religion. Belief in a protective God and adherence to religious laws was seen by the religious participants as a protective factor (Lanzkron 2015). The Ultra-Orthodox girl who tried to return the lost glasses to the owner adheres to religious law as a pathway to promote protection and prevent risk.

Neighborhoods, cities, and rural areas present different environment conditions for risk and protection. We found that children related to flowers, butterflies, the sea, or strong winds as sources of risk or protection. Children also referred to the difference between a village and a city and were very conscious of the dangers of the city, especially cars, busy roads, and pits in the road.

Conclusions

The findings stress the importance of children's voice. They demonstrate the importance of perceiving young children not as simply beings, but more significantly, as doers (Oswell 2013). In addition to the importance of young children's right to participate in society and to express their opinions in matters that affect their lives (Rajala et al. 2016), we call for the inclusion of children in the discourse of risk and protection. This is particularly relevant for the Israeli context but may be of relevance to other countries where the discourse ignores the views of children as well. We argue for the importance of including agency and protection in risk discourse and for recognizing children's sense of agency. We highlight the importance of attention to the multiple contexts affecting the children's perceptions of risk and protection.

References

Ben-Arieh, A. (2002). Evaluating the outcomes of programs vs. monitoring wellbeing: A child centered perspective. In T. Vecchiato, A. N. Maluccio, & C. Canali (Eds.), *Evaluation in child and family services: Comparative client and program perspective* (pp. 150–160). New-York: Aldine de Gruyter.

Ben-Arieh, A. (2005). Where are the children? Children's role in measuring and monitoring their wellbeing. *Social Indicators Research, 74*(3), 573–596.

Ben-Arieh, A., Casas, F., Frønes, I., Korbin, J. E. (2014). *Handbook of child well-being: Theories, methods and policies in global perspective*. Springer.

Benvenisti, R., & Schmidt, H. (2010). *Public survey on attitudes towards harming children and reporting to the authorities*. Jerusalem: Haruv Institute. [Hebrew]. http://haruv.org.il/_Uploads/dbsAttachedFiles/articlesemail.pdf. Accessed February 20, 2019.

Braun-Lewensohn, O., & Sagy, S. (2011). Salutogenesis and culture: Personal and community sense of coherence among adolescents belonging to three different cultural groups. *International Review of Psychiatry, 23*(6), 533–541.

Christensen, P., & Prout, A. (2002). Working with ethical symmetry in social research with children. *Childhood, 9*(4), 477–497.

Clark, A. (2004). The Mosaic approach and research with young children. In A. Lewis, M. Kellett, C. Robinson, S. Fraser, & S. Ding (Eds.), *The reality of research with children and young people* (pp. 142–161). London: Sage.

Clark, A., & Moss, P. (2001). *Listening to young children*. London: National Children's Bureau and Rowntree Foundation.

Clark, A., & Statham, J. (2005). Listening to young children: Experts in their own lives. *Adoption and Fostering, 29*, 45–56.

Curtis, K., Liabo, K., Roberts, H., & Barker, M. (2004). Consulted but not heard: A qualitative study of young people's views of their local health service. *Health Expectations, 7*(2), 149–156.

Dayan, Y. (2007). *Training teachers and early childhood educators: Children perspectives in kindergarten*. Jerusalem: Hebrew University of Jerusalem, Dr. Joseph J. Schwartz Graduate Program in Early Childhood Studies. [Hebrew].

Dayan, Y., & Ziv, M. (2012). Children's perspective research in pre-service early childhood student education. *International Journal of Early Years Education, 20*(3), 280–289.

Devine, D. (2002). Children's citizenship and the structuring of adult-child relations in the primary school. *Childhood, 9*(3), 303–321.

Dockett, S., Einarsdottir, J., & Perry, B. (2009). Balancing methodologies and methods in researching with young children. In D. Harcourt, B. Perry, & T. Waller (Eds.), *Researching young children's perspectives* (pp. 68–81). London: Routledge.

Einarsdottir, J. (2007). Research with children: Methodological and ethical challenges. *European Early Childhood Education Research Journal, 15*(2), 197–211.

Elden, S. (2013). Inviting the messy: Drawing methods and 'children's voices'. *Childhood, 20*, 66–81.

Faber, M., & Slutzky, H. (2007). Between protection and treatment of at-risk minors: The role of the child protective service workers. In D. Horowitz & M. Hovav (Eds.), *Abuse and neglect of children in Israel*. Jerusalem: Bialik. [Hebrew].

Fleer, M., & Li, L. (2016). A child-centered evaluation model: Gaining the children's perspective in evaluation studies in china. *European Early Childhood Education Research Journal, 24*(3), 342–356. https://doi.org/10.1080/1350293X.2016.1163934.

Harvey, M. R. (2007). Towards an ecological understanding of resilience in trauma survivors: Implications for theory, research, and practice. *Journal of Aggression, Maltreatment & Trauma, 14*(1–2), 9–32.

Hedges, H., & Cullen, J. (2012). Participatory learning theories: A framework for early childhood pedagogy. *Early Child Development and Care, 82*(7), 921–940.

Ispa, J. M. (1995). Ideas about infant and toddler care among Russian child care teachers, mothers and university students. *Early Childhood Research Quarterly, 10*(3), 359–379. https://doi.org/10.1016/0885-2006(95)90012-8.

Ispa, J. M. (2002). Russian Child care goals and values: From perestroika to 2001. *Early Childhood Research Quarterly, 17*(3), 393–414. https://doi.org/10.1016/s0885-2006(02)00171-0.

Israel National Council for the Child (2017). Statistical Report of the Council for the Child in Israel. [Hebrew]. https://www.children.org.il/wp-content/uploads/2018/10/%D7%99%D7%9C%D7%93%D7%99%D7%9D-%D7%91%D7%99%D7%A9%D7%A8%D7%90%D7%9C-%D7%A9%D7%A0%D7%AA%D7%95%D7%9F-2017.pdf. Accessed February 20, 2019.

Jones, A. (2004). Children and young people as researchers. In S. Fraser, V. Lewis, S. Ding, M. Kellett, & C. Robinson (Eds.), *Doing research with children and young people* (pp. 113–130). London: Sage.

Lal, S., Jarus, T., & Suto, M. J. (2012). A scoping review of photovoice method: Implications for occupational research. *Canadian Journal of Occupational Therapy, 79*(3), 181–190.

Lansdown, G. (1994). Children's rights. In B. Mayall (Ed.), *Children's childhoods, observed and experienced* (pp. 33–44). London: Falmer Press.

Lanzkron, Y. (2015). *Perceptions of risk and protection in children aged three to six living in a religious village*. Master dissertation submitted to the School of Social Work and Social Welfare, Hebrew University of Jerusalem.

Leonard, M., McKnight, M., & Spyrou, S. (2011). Growing up in divided societies: Confronting continuity and change. *International Journal of Sociology and Social policy, 31,* 520–530.

Leshem, E., & Roer-Strier, D. (Eds.) (2003). *Cultural diversity: A challenge to human services.* Jerusalem: Magnes Press.]Hebrew].

Lewis, V., & Kellett, M. (2004). Disability. In S. Fraser, V. Lewis, S. Ding, M. Kellett, & C. Robinson (Eds.), *Doing research with children and young people* (pp. 191–205). London: Sage.

Liebenberg, L. (2018). Thinking critically about photovoice: Achieving empowerment and social change. *International Journal of Qualitative Methods, 17,* 1–9.

Lightfoot, J., & Sloper, P. (2002). *Involving young people in health service development, research works, 2002–01* (p. 4). York: Social Policy Research Unit, University of York.

Mayall, B. (2002). *Towards a sociology for childhood: Thinking from children's lives.* Maidenhead: Open University Press.

Moore, T., McArthur, M., & Noble-Carr, D. (2008). Little voices and big ideas: Lessons learned from children about research. *International Journal of Qualitative Methods, 7*(2), 77–91.

Mulvihill, C., Rivers, K., & Aggleton, P. (2000). A qualitative study investigating the views of primary-age children and parents on physical activity. *Health Education Journal, 59*(2), 166–179.

Nadan, Y., Roer-Strier, D., Gemara, N., Engdou-Vanda, S., & Tener, D. (2018). In the eyes of the beholder: Parental and professional value mismatch in child risk and protection in two communities in Israel. *International Journal of Psychology, 53*(2), 23–33.

Navot, M., Shorek, Y., Sabo-Lal, R., & Ben Rabi, D. (2017). *System services for children at risk and their families: achievements and challenges according to Brookdale institute.* Jerusalem: Ministry of Social Affairs and Social Services. [Hebrew]. http://brookdaleheb.jdc.org.il/_Uploads/PublicationsFiles/heb_report_737_17.pdf. Accessed February 20, 2019.

O'Kane, C. (2000). The development of participatory techniques: Facilitating children's views about decisions which affect them. In P. Christensen & A. James (Eds.), *Research with children: Perspectives and practices* (pp. 136–159). London: Falmer Press.

Oswell, D. (2013). *The agency of children: From family to global human rights.* New York: Cambridge University Press.

Rajala, A., Martin, J., & Kumpulainen, K. (2016). Agency and learning: Researching agency in educational interactions. *Learning, Culture and Social Interaction, 10,* 1–3. https://doi.org/10.1016/j.lcsi.2016.07.001.

Roer-Strier, D., & Nadan, Y. (Eds.). (in preparation). *Context-informed perspectives of child risk and protection: Diverse populations in Israel.* New York: Springer's Child Maltreatment Series, Springer Publishing.

Sabo-Lal, R. (2017). *Children and youth at risk in Israel.* [Hebrew]. https://brookdale.jdc.org.il/wp-content/uploads/2017/12/RR-748-17_Hebrew_summary.pdf. Accessed February 20, 2019.

Sairanen, H., & Kumpulainen, K. (2014). A visual narrative inquiry into children's sense of agency in preschool and first grade. *International Journal of Educational Psychology, 3*(2), 141–174. https://doi.org/10.4471/ijep.2014.09.

Saleebey, D. (2006). *The strengths perspective in social work practice* (4th ed.). Boston: Allyn and Bacon.

Shalhoub-Kevorkian, N., & Roer-Strier, D. (2016). Context-informed, counter-hegemonic qualitative research: Insights from an Israeli/Palestinian research team studying loss. *Qualitative Social Work, 15*(4), 552–569.

Shemmings, D. (2000). Professionals' attitudes to children's participation in decision-making: dichotomous accounts and doctrinal contests. *Child and Family Social Work, 5,* 235–243.

Shkedi, A. (2003). *Words which try to Touch: Qualitative research-theory and practice.* Tel-Aviv: Ramot. [Hebrew].

Schmid Committee Report. (2006). *Report of the public committee to examine the situation of children and youth at risk and in distress.* [Hebrew]. https://www.molsa.gov.il/About/OfficePolicy/Documents/shmidreport2006newweb2.pdf. Accessed February 20, 2019.

Sloper, P., & Lightfoot, J. (2003). Involving disabled and chronically ill children and young people in health service development. *Child: Care, Health and Development, 29*(1), 15–20.

Tay-Lim, J., & Lim, S. (2013). Privileging younger children's voices in research: Use of drawing and a co-construction process. *International Journal of Qualitative Methods, 12,* 65–83.

Ulitsa, N., Yonna, L., & Roer-Strier, D. (2018). Children at risk in the eyes of parents of "One and a half generation" from the Former Soviet Union *MifGash (Incounter-Social Work in Education), 26,* 101–134. [Hebrew].

United Nations. (1989). *Convention on the rights of the child.* New York: United Nations.

Vandenbroeck, M., & Bouverne-De Bie, M. (2006). Children's agency and educational norms a tensed negotiation. *Childhood, 13*(1), 127–143. https://doi.org/10.1177/0907568206059977.

Weisblay, A. (2010). *Israel's actions in the implementation of the International Convention on the Rights of the Child.* The Knesset Research and Information Center. [Hebrew]. https://www.knesset.gov.il/mmm/data/pdf/m02734.pdf. Accessed February 20, 2019.

Woodhouse, B. (2004). Re-visioning rights for children. In P. Pufall & R. Unsworth (Eds.), *Rethinking childhood* (pp. 229–243). New Jersey: Rutgers University Press.

Chapter 16
Young Children in Institutional Care: Characteristics of Institutions, Children's Development, and Interventions in Institutions

**Megan M. Julian, Junlei Li, Annie Wright
and Pamela A. Jimenez-Etcheverria**

Abstract Worldwide, up to 8 million children reside in institutional care. While some characteristics are common to most institutional settings (e.g., group rearing, non-related caregivers), the social environments of institutions are highly variable. Institutions in Russia, China, Ghana, and Chile are described with reference to the circumstances that lead to children's institutionalization, resident children's social-emotional relationships, and unique characteristics of each country's institutional care (e.g., volunteer tourism in Ghana, and shifting demographics of institutionalized children in China). Children who have experienced extended and severely depriving institutional care are at higher risk of later social, emotional, and behavioral difficulties. Several intervention approaches have improved social-emotional care within institutional settings, with positive effects on resident children's development and caregivers' skill and wellbeing. Developing and implementing interventions that are both effective and locally sustainable is particularly crucial as institutions in many countries begin to shift from caring for mostly healthy children bound for adoption to higher proportions of children with disabilities who are likely to remain in residence for the longer-term.

Worldwide, up to 8 million children reside in institutions (Human Rights Watch 1996). While family care is considered the most appropriate setting for young children without permanent parents (UNAIDS et al. 2004), institutions continue to be necessary alongside these alternatives due to limited resources to devote to family

M. M. Julian (✉)
University of Michigan, Ann Arbor, MI, USA
e-mail: mmjulian@med.umich.edu

J. Li
Harvard University, Cambridge, MA, USA

A. Wright
Virginia Commonwealth University, Richmond, VA, USA

P. A. Jimenez-Etcheverria
Universidad de La Frontera, Temuco, Chile

© Springer Nature Switzerland AG 2019   217
T. Tulviste et al. (eds.), *Children's Social Worlds in Cultural Context*,
https://doi.org/10.1007/978-3-030-27033-9_16

care, and factors including war, HIV/AIDS, and poverty. Characteristics of institutions vary between countries, but several commonalities can be observed. Institutionalized children are typically raised in groups of unrelated children, and their caregivers, also unrelated, are generally paid to take this role. While family-reared children typically see the same caregivers every day, institutionalized children often have a larger number of different caregivers, with considerably less day-to-day stability. Further, children generally enter institutional care due to some kind of risk—whether it is parental illness or death, poverty or lack of resources, abuse or neglect, or a child's own disability or disease.

Institutionalized children have long captured the interest of both humanitarian activists and child development researchers who recognized that atypical social environments in institutions have serious implications for children's development. Institutionalization allows us to study how development is affected when certain expected early experiences—sensitive and responsive care from a few committed caregivers—fail to occur. Uniquely, many institutionalized children are adopted into families, resulting in a distinct end-point to their deprivation and allowing researchers to examine effects of the timing and duration of social-emotional deprivation. While some characteristics of institutions are nearly universal, institutions vary substantially in the quality of social-emotional care provided to resident children, the size and make-up of the resident children's social groups, daily schedules and activities, and material resources.

Social Environments of Institutions Around the World

Below, we describe the institutional environment for young children in four countries: Russia, China, Ghana, and Chile.

Russia

In the Russian Federation, 194 Baby Homes (BHs; institutions for children aged 0–4 years) house 14,000 children (www.gks.ru as cited in Solodunova et al. 2017). Most children enter institutional care within their first year of life due to poverty, family disintegration, domestic violence, or illness or disability, and have preexisting risk factors such as no prenatal care, prenatal exposure to alcohol or tobacco, medical problems during pregnancy, low birthweight, and/or delayed developmental status at intake (Russian Federation Ministry of Labor and Social Welfare 2012, as cited in Muhamedrahimov et al. 2016). The Russian Federation's child welfare system has recently prioritized supporting family care (e.g., kinship, adoptive, foster), resulting in fewer children entering BHs, and a greater proportion of BH residents having siblings (40%) or special needs (33%; Muhamedrahimov and Grigorenko 2015).

Russian institutions are generally "socially-emotionally depriving"; medical care, nutrition, toys, and equipment are adequate, but caregiver-child relationships are deficient (The St. Petersburg-USA Orphanage Research Team 2005). Children are housed in wards of 9–14 same-aged children, with disabled children in a separate ward. Children transition to new wards (and caregivers, peers) as they reach new developmental milestones. Wards follow set schedules of sleeping, feeding, and indoor and outdoor play times. Children are periodically pulled out for supplementary services including physical education, sensory stimulation, music, or massage. Generally, each ward has two caregivers during daytime and one at night, but due to caregivers' schedules (often long shifts, once every few days), pull-out services, vacation days, and staff turnover, institutionalized children usually see no common caregivers from one day to the next, and can see 50–100+ different caregivers by age 2.

Russian BHs typically prioritize medical care, and attend less to the quality of caregiver-child relationships. Caregiving is perfunctory, business-like, and adult-directed. Specifically, during a 3 hour observation period, an individual child interacted with a caregiver for 12.4 minutes, infants' bottles were propped up on pillows, and toddlers were fed 30 spoonfuls per minute with virtually no social interaction (Muhamedrahimov 2000). Caregivers attribute their lack of interaction with resident children to the priority of medical care and education or their unwillingness to form attachment relationships (The St. Petersburg-USA Orphanage Research Team 2005).

This institutional behavioral culture is associated with a unique constellation of behavior and affect among resident children (The St. Petersburg-USA Orphanage Research Team 2005). Whether children are alone or with other children in cribs or play pens, their activity level is generally low and affective expression is rare. Children play with toys in simplistic and repetitive ways, and stereotypic behaviors (e.g., rocking, head banging) are common. When approached by caregivers, children don't show any notable excitement or anticipation of interaction. Most play is adult-directed, and cooperative and imaginative play are exceedingly rare. While many toys and learning materials are available, toys are placed neatly on shelves and once a child is done with a toy, the toy is put away. When strangers enter a ward, older children often approach strangers with great excitement, and lack appropriate skills to relate to the stranger. On the wards where young children with special needs reside, children show even lower levels of activity and emotional expression, and often spend extended periods of time sitting or lying in awkward or uncomfortable positions and engaging in self-stimulation behaviors. Thus, while young children in Russian institutions are surrounded by peers and caregivers, they lead socially isolated lives.

Recently, many Russian BHs began adopting changes to enhance caregiver-child relationships, based primarily on the St. Petersburg-USA Project intervention (see below; Solodunova et al. 2017). Most children who transition out of BHs are adopted internationally or reunified with their biological family, but a small number transition on to institutions for older children or children with disabilities (The St. Petersburg-USA Orphanage Research Team 2005).

China

Beginning in the mid-1990s, reports by foreign NGOs (e.g., Human Rights Watch 1996) described Chinese institutions as lacking in both human care and nutritional and health care, and international adoptions soon began. Gender was then the deciding factor in illegal child abandonment; institutionalized children had typical prenatal care, and adoptees had favorable developmental outcomes (Cohen and Farnia 2011). From the 2010s forward, sustained international adoptions removed most healthy children from institutions, and cultural changes drastically reduced gender-based child abandonment, driving a shift in institutional demographics from predominantly healthy girls to overwhelmingly (about 95%) children with disabilities and medical conditions. Whereas "regular" caregivers (below high school education) had been sufficient to care for a mostly healthy female child population, the same caregivers lacked confidence and competence to care for a shrinking population overwhelmed with both physical and developmental disabilities.

Field observations (by JL and colleagues) suggest that children are grouped by age, often in infant wards (up to age 2), preschool wards (up to ages 5-6), and school-age wards (up to age 18), with a separate ward for children with moderate to severe disabilities. Typical infant and preschool wards have 15–25 children, with two daytime staff per ward and one nighttime staff for multiple wards. Staff tend to work in long shifts (12–16 hours) 3–4 days per week (most often on a regular schedule like 3 days on, 3 days off, 1 day back on). Staff assignments per ward tend to be stable and children switch wards when they mature in age.

Though primary caregivers are present 24 hours a day, daily routines during waking hours are constrained by the 8 hour working day of support staff (medical, kitchen, janitorial). Typically, children rise and feed early (6–7:30 a.m.), with a mid-morning snack between 9:30 and 10 a.m., lunch at 11 a.m., and nap starting between 11:30 a.m. and noon. They rise again by mid-afternoon, and have supper at 4:30–5:30 p.m., and then to bed. Time spent per child is limited and highly standardized because of the high number of children to be fed or changed within a rigid schedule. During in-between time, children are left alone because caregivers are needed to assist in other preparation or cleanup duties. Children have access to toys, but absent adult scaffolding and participation, play tends to be repetitive and self-soothing, rather than progressive and learning oriented. The official caregiver-to-child ratios, averaging between 3:1 and 4:1 (National Statistics Bureau 2006), do not align with field observations where one finds very unequal distributions of staff by ward, favoring wards with typically developing children over special needs wards. Some innovative local and NGO-supported programs have expanded and integrated foster care with special needs children, and greatly increased caregiver-to-child ratios as well as improved social-emotional care (Wang et al. 2017). Ratios are typically one child per family in community settings, or 3–4 per family within institutions (foster parents move into apartments within the institutional campus). Foster care placements are remarkably stable, terminating either with adoption or aging out at 18. Children who are capable of independent living are provided with apartments and jobs, while the rest are then transferred to adult institutions.

Ghana

Institutional care was brought to Ghana by European missionaries in the mid-1990s, and has increased rapidly due in part due to HIV/AIDS and poverty rates (Ansah-Koi 2006). Most children enter care due to poverty, child HIV status, parental death (i.e., belief that a child whose mother dies in childbirth is cursed and may be relinquished), or hope of better education and accommodations in institutional care (Frimpong-Manso 2014). Ghana's Department of Social Welfare (DSW) dictates that care should be family-like with a consistent primary caregiver providing sensitive and responsive care (Ministry of Employment and Social Welfare 2010). About 4500 institutionalized children in Ghana live in groups of up to 30 per home with siblings remaining together, and caregiver-to-child ratios expected to be 1:7; each home determines the ages and disabilities they will accommodate (Quartey 2013; E. Kponyoh and H. Yawson, personal communication May 17, 2018). Unfortunately, 96% of institutions are operating illegally and are not routinely monitored (Quartey 2013), resulting in much higher caregiver-to-child ratios, and older children caring for younger ones (Lemons 2010).

Institution caregivers report feeling overworked and inadequately trained and supervised, and state that children lack continuity of care across shift changes (Castillo et al. 2012). However, many children feel supported by friends inside and outside the home, feel part of a family within the institution, and 90% report feeling they received adequate affection from caregivers (Lemons 2010).

Volunteer tourism within institutional care is a large, active, but controversial industry in Ghana (Rotabi et al. 2016). Private institutions receive payments from volunteer organizations and donations from volunteers, providing incentives to maintain high populations and open new facilities (Rotabi et al. 2016). DSW permits volunteers to work within institutional homes, but mandates that they never serve as a primary caregiver or attachment figure (Ministry of Employment and Social Welfare 2010). Volunteers work for several weeks to many months, having the most direct contact with younger children (e.g., before school-age; E. Kponyoh and H. Yawson, personal communication May 17, 2018). Children's needs are more quickly met while there is a higher caregiver-to-child ratio, yet they experience rapid bonding and subsequent abandonment by temporary volunteers (Rotabi et al. 2016; Voyk 2011).

Institutionalized children often attend school and extra-mural activities within the community, and institution-based schools are open to local non-institutionalized children (Ministry of Employment and Social Welfare 2010). While a child is institutionalized, their biological relatives are encouraged to maintain contact in an effort to preserve connections to their community and local traditions (Ministry of Employment and Social Welfare 2010). At the time of placement, parents are encouraged to give children permission to bond with their new caregivers. Children are allowed to spend weekends, holidays and vacations with families, friends, and mentors who have been approved by DSW. However, some children are mistreated when they interact with teachers and peers at school or in the community due to jealousy of the resources they are perceived to have, or due to stigma of being an orphan (Voyk

2011). As foster care and adoption are rare in Ghana, youth who are not reunited with family typically remain institutionalized until adulthood (Frimpong-Manso 2014). Fortunately, many youth leaving care have built supportive relationships with their caregivers and feel able to turn to them in times of need (Frimpong-Manso 2017). They also often rely on older peers from their institution for guidance on navigating the transition to independence. The maintenance of these bonds suggests that the social ties developed within care benefit institutionalized children into adulthood.

Chile

Despite recent efforts in Chile toward family alternatives, institutionalization remains the primary placement option for children removed from their parents due to abuse or neglect. Currently 250 institutions house 14,000 children and adolescents, most from poorer families; 22% of resident children are under age 7 (average age at entry = 8.4 years), and 7% have a disability (Martínez 2010; Muñoz-Guzmán et al. 2015; SENAME 2015). Most enter institutional care due to parental neglect, abandonment, or abuse, though some (2%) enter because of child labor (Martínez 2010). Chile lacks comprehensive child welfare legislation, so the child welfare system, the National Service for Minors (SENAME), follows the *UN Convention on the Rights of the Child*, and instructions from Courts of Justice (Morlachetti 2015). Unfortunately, nearly half of school-aged children in institutions report violations of their rights including neglect, physical abuse, psychological abuse, sexual abuse, or exploitation (INDH 2018a; Muñoz-Guzmán et al. 2015).

While SENAME standards recommend a maximum of 20 children per institution, this standard is expensive and not enforced (de Iruarrizaga 2015); some infant institutions host over 90 children (Muñoz-Guzmán et al. 2015), and 21.2% of residences are over capacity (INDH 2018b). Chile has separate institutions and/or wards for children of different ages (infants, preschool, and 6 years and over) or special populations (i.e., children with disabilities, pregnant adolescents), and children are sometimes also separated by gender. SENAME (2007) stipulates that institutions for preschool-aged children should have one caregiver per 8–10 children during the day.

The technical team at each institution determines daily schedules of sleeping, feeding, and indoor and outdoor leisure activities (P. Mitterstainer, personal communication May 15, 2018). Some directors create daily schedules similar to a "traditional" Chilean house, with routines that include playing, painting, watching movies and walking outside the institution, but this is not universally true (J. P. Rubio, personal communication January 18, 2018). School-aged children attend school in the local community. Although most centers have green areas, they are often not suitable for play. Anecdotal evidence from institutional staff suggests that the institutions do not have many toys and most toys were donated by private benefactors.

With no regulations regarding the quality of caregiver-child social interaction, quality of care varies widely across institutions (P. Mitterstainer, personal communication May 15, 2018). Institutions often struggle to recruit and retain specialized professionals, and are unable to sufficiently train staff, hindering their ability to provide a high level of care to these vulnerable children with complex needs (Muñoz-Guzmán et al. 2015). Caregiving in Chilean institutions is "business-like", and punishment of children by the staff members is common (INDH 2018a). While many institutionalized children reunify with their biological families, the existing child protection system facilitates the severance of family bonds. Most institutions are far from the child's hometown, and many institutions impose restrictions on family visits (INDH 2018a). While little is known about outcomes of children residing in Chilean institutions, recent reports suggest that at least half of institutionalized children experience clinical levels of behavioral and emotional problems (Jiménez 2018; SENAME 2018).

On average, children remain in Chilean institutions for about 3 years (Martínez 2010). Following institutional care, 82% return to their biological families, 11% enter other SENAME programs, and about 2–3% are adopted, most domestically (SENAME 2015). In sum, while formal studies of children residing in Chilean institutions are limited, there is evidence that their social-emotional needs are not being met due to caregivers with insufficient training and resources, limited resources like toys and play spaces, restricted contact with family members, and frequent reports of abuse and neglect.

Development of Children Who Have Experienced Institutional Care

Although institutions vary widely in their characteristics, most represent a rearing environment that is far different from a typical family environment. Institutionalized children have a greater risk for problems including stunted physical growth, attachment difficulties, delayed cognitive development, and atypical hypothalamic-pituitary-adrenal axis activity (van IJzendoorn et al. 2011). Studies of post-institutionalized adopted children allow us to examine effects of time-limited social-emotional deprivation. Surprisingly, most post-institutionalized adopted children have behavioral and cognitive functioning within the normal range (Brodzinsky 1993). However, rates of problems are higher than parent-reared never-institutionalized children, especially in domains including internalizing and externalizing problems; attention, executive function, and emotion regulation problems; attachment difficulties and indiscriminate friendliness; and stunted physical growth (Rutter et al. 2010).

Quality of care in institutions varies widely from the globally deficient institutions of 1990s Romania to institutions of adequate quality in parts of Asia; post-institutionalized children's developmental outcomes generally correspond to the severity of institutional deprivation (Julian 2013). Children who are adopted at a relatively later age tend to have more problems than those adopted earlier; in many cases, the effect of age at adoption is not linear but instead step-like, with a certain

"Cut-off" age at adoption above which children are at a higher risk of experiencing problems (Julian 2013). Interestingly, the cut-off age at adoption appears to relate to the severity of institutional deprivation. For instance, children adopted from 1990s Romanian institutions have elevated rates of problems after as little as 6 months of age at adoption (Colvert et al. 2008); for children adopted from socially-emotionally depriving Russian institutions, this increased risk of problems only emerges after around 18 months of age at adoption (Julian and McCall 2016). Thus, institution-alized children's early social environment has a strong and lasting impact on their later social, behavioral, cognitive, and physical development, even when they later transition to better quality care in an adoptive home.

Interventions to Improve Social-Emotional Care Within Institutions

Institutions have long been the target of intervention programs that aim to improve resident children's development (reviewed in The St. Petersburg-USA Orphanage Research Team 2008). The nature of institutional interventions ranges broadly from simple sensory stimulation to comprehensive overhauls in the daily operations and staff behavior. Even simple sensory stimulation interventions produced small gains or prevented declines, but effects faded quickly after the interventions terminated. Short-term interventions focused on improving caregiver-child relationships have produced modest improvements in children's cognitive, motor, and social develop-ment. But these interventions typically use special staff, not regular caregivers, mak-ing longer-term maintenance difficult. A few institutional interventions have made more sustainable and systematic improvements to the quality of social-emotional care. Below, we highlight two programs that changed caregiver–child interactions during routine daily activities within institutions.

The St. Petersburg-USA Project

The St. Petersburg-USA Project implemented Training and Structural Changes to cre-ate a family-like environment within Russian Federation institutions, using existing BH staff. Training helped caregivers engage with children sensitively and respon-sively; be more child-directed and emotionally available; and foster children's inde-pendence and creativity. Structural Changes created an environment conducive to the development of attachment relationships. Stable, family-like groups were created by eliminating periodic graduations to new groups, integrating wards by age and dis-ability status, reducing group size from about 12 to 6, and assigning 2 primary and 4 secondary caregivers to each group. During a twice-daily "family hour," caregivers and children spent quality time together without any children pulled out or visitors coming in. Training and Structural Changes (T+SC) were implemented in one BH, Training Only in a second BH, and a third BH provided Care as Usual (CAU; control group).

The T+SC intervention allowed children to consistently interact with familiar caregivers and peers, facilitating their development of social awareness and understanding. During times when children had been largely ignored in traditional BHs, they were now engaging in reciprocal dyadic interactions with familiar caregivers who were attuned to their needs. With mixed-age groups of children, intervention caregivers were better able to distribute their attention. During meals, for example, instead of quickly feeding many infants, a T+SC caregiver feeds 2–3 infants while older children feed themselves. Instead of having nothing to do while all the children sleep, T+SC caregivers engage with older children while younger children sleep.

Relative to CAU children, T+SC children's developmental quotients increased from about 57 to 92 (The St. Petersburg-USA Orphanage Research Team 2008). Whereas CAU wards were quiet with minimal activity and children confined to cribs or playpens, T+SC wards were noisy, with children actively engaged with both caregivers and toys. While CAU caregivers prioritized order and obedience, T+SC caregivers followed children's lead, conversed with children during caregiving tasks and play periods, and showed affection to and interest in resident children. The indiscriminately friendly and stereotypic behaviors that were common among CAU children were replaced by appropriate wariness of strangers and use of caregivers as a secure base among T+SC children. While disorganized attachment styles were most common for CAU graduates, the T+SC graduates had more insecure-resistant and securely attached attachment styles. During dyadic play sessions, T+SC children showed improved quality of play, alertness, self-regulation, positive affect, social initiative, and communication, and T+SC caregivers showed more positive social-emotional engagement, responsiveness, and child-directed behaviors relative to CAU children and caregivers. Thus, both members of the dyad were showing more positive and attuned behaviors, creating a positive feedback cycle that facilitated the kind of mutually engaged, reciprocal interactions that promote attachment relationships.

Thus, while T+SC children were still institutionalized, their daily interactions were dramatically changed, resulting in improvements in developmental outcomes ($d = 1.05$) that were comparable in magnitude to the effect of adoption (Bakermans-Kranenburg et al. 2008). The intervention-related improvements to the BHs have been maintained for at least 7 years (McCall et al. 2013), and core intervention components are being disseminated among BHs across the Russian Federation (Solodunova et al. 2017). T+SC children who have gone on to be adopted into families continue to show better developmental outcomes, though group differences are small in magnitude (Julian et al. 2018).

Simple Interactions

The Simple Interactions approach rests on the ideas that "developmental relationships" are the indispensable active ingredients of children's development, and interventions should grow the local community's capacity to provide exemplary care to be sustainable (Li and Julian 2012). Simple Interactions conveys two interwoven messages to front-line staff: (1) How they relate to children matters, even in brief moments of routine care; and (2) They are *already* doing that well. The field team videotapes naturalistic staff practices, and then pre-selects overwhelmingly positive/teachable moments. Videos are replayed in staff workshops where staff discuss and reflect on their practices. Facilitators guide discussion around key aspects of relationships (i.e., Connection, Reciprocity, Inclusion, Opportunity to Grow) with the aid of a simple observational tool (see www.simpleinteractions.org). Staff are not being explicitly asked to do more, but simply to consider being intentional in doing what they *already* do. Participants report feeling uplifted by these workshops, and administrators consistently provide positive feedback. This approach has also been implemented in out-of-school time programs for non-institutionalized youth, with positive reviews from participating staff and beneficial effects on the quality of adult-child interactions (Akiva et al. 2017).

Conclusions

While support for family-based care for young children without permanent parents is expanding, institutional care continues to be a practically necessary placement option in many countries. Institutionalized children experience social-emotional care that is vastly different than family care, but the nature of their relationships while in residence is highly variable ranging from business-like (e.g., Russian Federation, Chile) to supportive of lasting social ties (e.g., Ghana). Even so, institutionalization offers species-atypical socialization experience, and a wide body of work suggests that children who have experienced severely depriving and lasting institutional care are at greater risk for a host of social, behavioral, and emotional difficulties as they grow older.

Improving the quality of care within institutions can have dramatic effects on resident children's development, particularly when caregivers regularly work with the same children, and increase their sensitivity and responsiveness during day-to-day activities. Many institutions are shifting from housing mostly healthy children bound for adoption to mostly disabled children who are likely to remain institutionalized. In this context of more vulnerable children remaining in residence for longer, it is even more vital to ensure that institutionalized children receive high-quality social-emotional care. While many institutional intervention programs have historically been funded by foreign NGOs, the changing climate of international adoption (e.g., Russian government terminating U.S. adoptions, rapid declines in international adoption from China) and increased availability of family care alternatives in many countries means that greater reliance on domestic resources to improve institutions may be more sustainable. Further, given the unique challenges and social climates within institutions in various regions of the world, the nature of the most effective and sustainable intervention in one region may be very different than that of another region, and approaches that seek to identify and support effective and locally sustainable practices may be most advantageous.

Acknowledgements T32 postdoctoral fellowship funding (HD079350; PI: J. Lumeng) supported the primary author.

References

Akiva, T., Li, J., Martin, K. M., Horner, C. G., & McNamara, A. R. (2017). Simple interactions: Piloting a strengths-based and interaction-based professional development intervention for out-of-school time programs. *Child & Youth Care Forum, 46*(3), 285–305. https://doi.org/10.1007/s10566-016-9375-9.

Ansah-Koi, A. (2006). Care of orphans: Fostering interventions for children whose parents die of AIDS in Ghana. *Families in Society: The Journal of Contemporary Social Services, 87*(4), 555–564. https://doi.org/10.1606/1044-3894.3571.

Bakermans-Kranenburg, M., van IJzendoorn, M., & Juffer, F. (2008). Earlier is better: A meta-analysis of 70 years of intervention improving cognitive development in institutionalized children. *Monographs of the Society for Research in Child Development, 73*(3), 279–293. https://doi.org/10.1111/j.1540-5834.2008.00498.x.

Brodzinsky, D. (1993). Long-term outcomes in adoption. *The Future of Children, 3*(1), 153–166. https://doi.org/10.2307/1602410.

Castillo, J., Sarver, C., Bettmann, J., Mortensen, J., & Akuoko, K. (2012). Orphanage caregivers' perceptions: The impact of organizational factors on the provision of services to orphans in the Ashanti region of Ghana. *Journal of Children and Poverty, 18*(2), 141–160. https://doi.org/10.1080/10796126.2012.710484.

Cohen, N., & Farnia, F. (2011). Social-emotional adjustment and attachment in children adopted from China: Processes and predictors of change. *International Journal of Behavioral Development, 35*(1), 67–77. https://doi.org/10.1177/0165025410371602.

Colvert, E., Rutter, M., Beckett, C., Castle, J., Groothues, C., Hawkins, A., et al. (2008). Emotional difficulties in early adolescence following severe early deprivation: Findings from the English and Romanian adoptees study. *Development and Psychopathology, 20*(2), 547–567. https://doi.org/10.1017/S0954579408000278.

de Iruarrizaga, F. (2015). *Redesigning the Chilean child protection system: Understanding the problem to propose alternative care models and help family reunification.* Retrieved from https://www.sociedadpoliticaspublicas.cl/archivos/septimo/Politicas_Publicas_y_Desarrollo_Regional/Redisenando_el_sistema_de_proteccion_a_la_infancia.pdf.

Frimpong-Manso, K. (2014). Child welfare in Ghana: The past, present and future. *Journal of Educational and Social Research.* https://doi.org/10.5901/jesr.2014.v4n6p411.

Frimpong-Manso, K. (2017). The social support networks of care leavers from a children's village in Ghana: Formal and informal supports. *Child and Family Social Work, 22*(1), 195–202. https://doi.org/10.1111/cfs.12218.

Human Rights Watch. (1996). *Death by default: A policy of fatal neglect in China's state orphanages.* Retrieved from http://www.refworld.org/docid/3ae6a85a0.html.

INDH. (2018a). *Misión de observación a centros residenciales de protección de la red SENAME 2017: Resumen ejecutivo [Observation mission to residential centers of protection of SENAME Network 2017: Executive summary].* Retrieved from https://www.indh.cl/destacados/mision-de-observacion-sename-2017/.

INDH. (2018b). *Misión observación SENAME: Condiciones de vida y de cuidados [Observation mission SENAME: Living conditions and care].* Retrieved from https://www.indh.cl/destacados/mision-de-observacion-sename-2017/.

Jiménez, P. (2018). *A comparison of psychological adjustment and cognitive functioning between adopted and institution-reared children in Chile* (Unpublished master's thesis). University of Cambridge, Cambridge, UK.

Julian, M. (2013). Age at adoption from institutional care as a window into the lasting effects of early experiences. *Clinical Child and Family Psychology Review, 16*(2), 101–145. https://doi.org/10.1007/s10567-013-0130-6.

Julian, M., & McCall, R. (2016). Social skills in children adopted from socially-emotionally depriving institutions. *Adoption Quarterly, 19*(1), 44–62. https://doi.org/10.1080/10926755.2015.1088106.

Julian, M., McCall, R., Groark, C., Muhamedrahimov, R., Palmov, O., & Nikiforova, N. (2018). Development of children adopted to the United States following a social–emotional intervention in St. Petersburg (Russian Federation) institutions. *Applied Developmental Science.* Advance online publication. https://doi.org/10.1080/10888691.2017.1420480.

Lemons, E. (2010). *The experience of the AIDS orphan in the central and eastern regions of Ghana: Communication between caregivers and orphans regarding HIV/AIDS* (Unpublished master's thesis). Ohio State University, Columbus, OH.

Li, J., & Julian, M. (2012). Developmental relationships as the active ingredient: A unifying working hypothesis of "what works" across intervention settings. *The American Journal of Orthopsychiatry, 82*(2), 157–166. https://doi.org/10.1111/j.1939-0025.2012.01151.x.

Martínez, V. (2010). *Resumen ejecutivo: Caracterización del perfil de niños, niñas y adolescentes, atendidos por los centros residenciales de SENAME [Executive summary: Profile of children and adolescents cared for SENAME residential care centers].* Retrieved from @@http://www.sename.cl/wsename/otros/INFORME_FINAL_SENAME_UNICEF.pdf.

McCall, R., Groark, C., Fish, L., Muhamedrahimov, R., Palmov, O., & Nikiforova, N. (2013). Maintaining a social-emotional intervention and its benefits for institutionalized children. *Child Development, 84*(5), 1734–1749. https://doi.org/10.1111/cdev.12098.

Ministry of Employment and Social Welfare. (2010). *National Standards for residential homes for orphans and vulnerable children in Ghana.* Retrieved from http://www.ovcghana.org/docs/Standards.pdf.

Morlachetti, A. (2015). *Comprehensive national child protection systems: Legal basis and current practice in Latin America and the Caribbean.* Retrieved from https://repositorio.cepal.org/bitstream/handle/11362/35884/1/S2013594_en.pdf.

Muhamedrahimov, R. (2000). New attitudes: Infant care facilities in St. Petersburg, Russia. In J. Osofsky & H. Fitzgerald (Eds.), *WAIMH handbook of infant mental health* (Vol. 1, Perspectives on Infant Mental Health, pp. 245–294). New York, NY: Wiley.

Muhamedrahimov, R., Arintcina, I., Solodunova, M., Anikina, V., Vasilyeva, M., Chernego, D., et al. (2016). Structural characteristics of the institutional environment for young children. *Psychology in Russia: State of the Art, 9*(3), 103–112. https://doi.org/10.11621/pir.2016.0307.

Muhamedrahimov, R., & Grigorenko, E. (2015). Seeing the trees within the forest: Addressing the needs of children without parental care in the Russian Federation. *New Directions for Child and Adolescent Development, 2015*(147), 101–108. https://doi.org/10.1002/cad.20080.

Muñoz-Guzmán, C., Fischer, C., Chia, E., & LaBrenz, C. (2015). Child welfare in Chile: Learning from international experiences to improve family interventions. *Social Sciences, 4*(1), 219–238. https://doi.org/10.3390/socsci4010219.

National Statistics Bureau. (2006). *Yearbook of China statistics 2000–2005.* Beijing, China: China Statistics Press.

Quartey, R. (2013). *Performance audit report of the auditor general on the regulation of residential homes for children (orphanages) by the Department of Social Welfare (DSW)*. Retrieved from https://bettercarenetwork.org/sites/default/files/attachments/Performance%20Audit%20Report%20of%20the%20Auditor%20General%20on%20the%20Regulation%20of%20Residential%20Homes%20for%20Children.pdf.

Rotabi, K., Roby, J., & McCreery Bunkers, K. (2016). Altruistic exploitation: Orphan tourism and global social work. *British Journal of Social Work, 47,* 648–665. https://doi.org/10.1093/bjsw/bcv147.

Rutter, M., Sonuga-Barke, E., Beckett, C., Castle, J., Kreppner, J., Kumsta, R., et al. (2010). Deprivation-specific psychological patterns: Effects of institutional deprivation. *Monographs of the Society for Research in Child Development, 75*(1), vii–ix, 1–252.

SENAME. (2007). *Lineamientos técnicos específicas: Modalidad residencias de protección para lactantes y pre-escolares [Specific technical guidelines: Residential protection for infants and pre-schoolers]*. Retrieved from http://www.sename.cl/wsename/otros/proteccion/lineamientos/bases_residencia.pdf.

SENAME. (2015). *Anuario estadístico SENAME 2015.* Retrieved from http://www.sename.cl/wsename/images/anuario_2015_final_200616.pdf.

SENAME. (2018). *Informe auditoria social [Social audit report]*. Retrieved from http://www.sename.cl/web/wp-content/uploads/2018/05/Informe-Auditoria-Social-Centros-Sename.pdf.

Solodunova, M., Palmov, O., & Muhamedrahimov, R. (2017). Family environment in institutions for young children in Russia: Mental health and development versus medical care. In A. V. Rus, S. R. Parris, & S. R. Stativa (Eds.), *Child maltreatment in residential care: History, research, and current practice* (pp. 199–218). Cham: Springer International Publishing. https://doi.org/10.1007/978-3-319-57990-0_10.

The St. Petersburg-USA Orphanage Research Team. (2005). Characteristics of children, caregivers, and orphanages for young children in St. Petersburg, Russian Federation. *Journal of Applied Developmental Psychology, 26*(5), 477–506. https://doi.org/10.1016/j.appdev.2005.06.002.

The St. Petersburg-USA Orphanage Research Team. (2008). The effects of early social-emotional and relationship experience on the development of young orphanage children. *Monographs of the Society for Research in Child Development, 73*(3), vii–viii, 1–297.

UNAIDS, UNICEF, & USAID. (2004). *Children on the brink 2004: A joint report of new orphan estimates and a framework for action*. New York, NY.

van IJzendoorn, M., Palacios, J., Sonuga-Barke, E., Gunnar, M., Vorria, P., McCall, R., et al. (2011). I. Children in institutional care: Delayed development and resilience. *Monographs of the Society for Research in Child Development, 76*(4), 8–30. https://doi.org/10.1111/j.1540-5834.2011.00626.x.

Voyk, E. (2011). *Orphan vulnerability, NGOs and HIV/AIDS in Ghana* (Unpublished master's thesis). Ohio State University, Columbus, OH.

Wang, W., McCall, R., Li, J., Groark, C., Zeng, F., & Hu, X. (2017). Chinese collective foster care model: Description and evaluation. *International Social Work, 60*(2), 435–451. https://doi.org/10.1177/0020872815594863.

Part IV
Conclusions

Chapter 17
Children's Culturally Enriched Social Development

Tiia Tulviste, Deborah L. Best and Judith L. Gibbons

Abstract Around the world children grow up in a variety of different cultural settings that shape their social relationships in ways that are adaptive for the societies and the social worlds in which they live. The physical and social setting, the family configuration, parents' ethnotheories about appropriate childrearing practices and parenting styles, and the broader social, governmental, educational, and economic context influence the course of the child's social, emotional, and cognitive development. Children learn a great deal over the preschool years as they interact with people in their social networks who help shape various aspects of their social development. Understanding the role of culture is integral to having a more complete, deeper understanding of children's development in their everyday social worlds.

The book *Children's Social Worlds in Cultural Context* provides important information about the diversity of social settings where children are growing up, both within and across cultures. The focus is on changes in children's social worlds over the preschool years and their association with cognitive, emotional, and social development. Each chapter reviews the most recent research in the field as well as the authors' own empirical findings across different places around the world. The authors have carried out extensive studies in a number of research locations often comparing data gathered from seldom investigated regions with what is known about the extensively investigated U.S. middle-class. Much of the information reported in this book comes from observational studies performed in natural, everyday settings. Some authors have applied mixed-method approaches, using both interviews and questionnaires to obtain comprehensive information. The number of diverse socio-cultural contexts where research has been conducted is growing, reflecting an increasing interest in

T. Tulviste
Department of Psychology, University of Tartu, Tartu, Estonia

D. L. Best
Department of Psychology, Wake Forest University, Winston-Salem, NC, USA

J. L. Gibbons (✉)
Department of Psychology, Saint Louis University, Saint Louis, MO, USA
e-mail: judith.gibbons@slu.edu

© Springer Nature Switzerland AG 2019
T. Tulviste et al. (eds.), *Children's Social Worlds in Cultural Context*,
https://doi.org/10.1007/978-3-030-27033-9_17

theory and research regarding the contextual issues as well as the practical need for such knowledge.

Part I: What Children Learn

The everyday social world of a child who is growing up in an ordinary Western middle-class family involves fewer people than that of a typical non-Western family, where he/she is surrounded by many siblings, multiple-age peers, and adults (see Chaps. 10 and 11). During the preschool years, the social world of the Western child also expands, mainly by increased contact with other same-age children and adults, such as peers and teachers at kindergarten. Children from communities with extensive formal education live in a separate "Children's social world," managed by the adults (see Chap. 3). These children are not involved in mature cultural practices of the community as are the children living in indigenous communities. Those children learn by observing what others talk about and do, helping when needed (see Chaps. 3 and 7).

Social relationships in indigenous and other traditional societies tend to be intense and lifelong, whereas those of a Western middle-class child may be more transitory and sometimes less close. Children's social worlds can also differ in terms of the relative amount of exposure they have to adults and other children, as well as in how many boys and girls they interact with. During this age period, children prefer to spend time in the company of same-sex children—resulting in separate worlds for girls and boys (see Chaps. 2 and 6). Moreover, children's social worlds in many countries have become multicultural as a result of rapidly increased migration (see Chaps. 14 and 16). As a result of differences in children's social worlds, the types of social experience provided by agents of socialization can vary greatly. Those experiences reflect the values, norms, and behaviors that are appropriate within specific cultures. We can image what would happen if a Japanese strategy for teaching children how to resolve conflicts (Chap. 13) were used in a Western kindergarten. It is likely that Western children would perceive themselves to be helpless (not protected) with a non-intervening teacher. Teachers' behavior as a non-intervening bystander would most likely not be approved by himself/herself and others.

The preschool years are a time of important changes in children's social skills. There may be cultural similarities and differences in how much a specific social skill or behavior is valued and cultivated, as well as how it is manifested. For example, children learn how to act in emotional situations in a culturally appropriate way. They learn how to understand their own and others' emotions, how much to express their emotions, and which emotions (negative or positive) are appropriate to display and which are not. Within the family context, children see parents' emotional displays, they see how parents respond to others' emotional displays, and in some cultures, parents have conversations with children about emotions. These experiences shape children's understanding of emotions and their emotional behaviors to be appropriate within their specific cultural contexts. Middle-class families, in particular, highlight feelings and emotions in their conversations with children, helping them to become more skilled at recognizing and understanding the internal states that motivate their own and others' behaviors (see Chap. 4). Indeed, caregivers in non-English and non-Western families are less likely to talk about emotions and internal states with their children. Instead, they tend to talk about behavioral rules and explanations underlying behavior (Chaps. 4 and 5).

Chapter 7 deals with how children across cultures help others. Children's propensity to help emerges early; children as young as 18–24 months of age spontaneously help. In traditional or indigenous cultures, the help consists of trying to participate in the daily tasks of adults around them. Older preschoolers may even serve as caretakers of younger siblings. There is cultural variability, however, in what constitutes helping, the available opportunities for children to help, as well as the link of helping behavior with other aspects of development. More specifically, self-recognition has been found to serve as a prerequisite for prosocial behavior in Western countries, but not elsewhere.

An important aspect of young children's social development is their social identity. They learn the social roles and rules that are appropriate for their gender, age, and social status. That is, children learn how to dress, how to behave in social situations, and how to play with and talk with other children and adults (see Chap. 6). The emergence of children's gender-specific conversational styles indicate that it is typical for boys to talk more about themselves and non-social topics, whereas girls talk was more about other people. Indeed, boys and girls differ in the social rules they stress during play with boys commenting more about moral rules than girls (Chap. 2).

Almost universally, through culture-specific socialization, children acquire social skills that correspond with the life-style and cultural practices of the contexts in which they are growing up. However, the promotion of certain culture-specific aspects of social development may also bring some unexpected consequences. For instance, Western middle-class children whose parents foster their autonomy and independence may also display more tantrums and rivalry than non-Western families (see Chaps. 9 and 11). Moreover, some social skills that receive little attention from socialization agents may not develop or may dissipate. For example, German middle-class children face difficulties when asked to cooperate in triads. They prefer to solve a task alone or with one other child, activities that are familiar and usual in their cultural setting (see Chap. 9). Likewise, children in highly schooled communities tend to focus on a single event at a time or vary their attention from one event to another rather than attending simultaneously to multiple events (see Chap. 3). These findings highlight the importance of the acquisition of different strategies, including those not frequently emphasized in the child's own cultural context. Perhaps to be successful, children should be encouraged to focus upon strategies that correspond to the requirements of specific tasks, rather than those strategies that are familiar and common in their culture.

Part II: Socialization of Young Children

In the second section of the book, chapters describe the primary agents of socialization in young children's lives—parents, siblings, peers, and teachers—each supporting different aspects of children's social development. Family socialization plays a crucial role in the child's development and may differ across cultural settings (Best et al. 1994). Parents play a special role in children's learning to communicate, to recognize their own and others' emotions, and to understand the family's values and beliefs. Most studies of children's social development have investigated the role of mothers and, to a lesser extent, fathers (see Chap. 10), tending to overlook the significance of other family members. As a result, there is relatively little recognition of the role that many grandparents play in children's lives (Chap. 12). Indeed, the longest-standing relationships in children's lives are with siblings who can be mentors, pupils, supporters, competitors, and best friends (Chap. 11).

Several chapters examine the role of peer socialization in children's social development. Through interactions with their peers, children acquire social rules about how to interact with agemates. They learn appropriate behavior for girls and boys (Chaps. 2 and 6). They also learn to deal with emotionally challenging situations, such as when conflicts arise (Chap. 8). Indeed, in Japanese kindergartens children learn strategies for conflict resolution under the watchful eyes of teachers who do not intervene (Chap. 13). Children develop problem-solving skills that are consistent with their cultural experiences.

Other important means of socialization are the everyday conversations children have with mothers, peers, or kindergarten teachers, and other agents of socialization. For example, middle-class families in Western societies talk about internal mental states of people, sensitizing children to this culturally significant topic (Chaps. 4 and 5). Frequent conversations about other people in non-Western families, in turn, increase children's sensitivity to people around them (Chap. 10). In Western English-speaking parts of the world, children's dyadic conversations with more competent members of their culture help children develop language and emotional competence. Children from different socio-cultural backgrounds may acquire these culture-specific social skills by being attentive to conversations in which they do not participate, learning by observing what other people are doing and talking about (Silva et al. 2015).

Studies conducted in various societies across the world demonstrate that aspects of social development differ across cultures and correspond to culture-specific lifestyles and practices. Research is beginning to uncover what is responsible for the cultural differences that have been found. Cultural variability in what is expected from children, how children's behavior is interpreted, who socializes children and what they do to promote expected social skills reflect underlying cultural beliefs, values, and practices. For instance, the importance placed on children's play differs across cultures, affecting the extent to which children's play is supported as well as with whom children are supposed to play—with other children or also with adults (Chap. 2). Cultural variation in social development has been viewed as the reflection of the relative importance placed on autonomy versus relatedness in child social-ization (Kagitçibaşi 2005). Although both are considered to be basic needs that are emphasized to some extent in every culture, the relative importance of those dimensions varies within and across cultures. Value orientation is related to the educational attainment of parents; more highly educated parents tend to value autonomy more than relatedness and the reverse is seen with parents with lower levels of education. Parents who stress the child's autonomy tend to raise children to be unique, encouraging them to be talkative and to express their emotions and personal viewpoints. Parents who focus on children's relatedness emphasize familial cohesion and a sense of social belonging with the aim that children will fit into their social worlds (see Greenfield et al. 2003). These families provide more opportunities for children to help with daily activities than those with a stronger autonomy orientation (Köster et al. 2015). As a result of these sorts of culture-specific practices, children in indigenous communities learn to attend simultaneously to multiple events (Chap. 3).

For many years, research has shown that formal schooling brings about changes in cognitive abilities (Cole and Scribner, 1981; Tulviste 1991; Wagner 1978). In early cross-cultural studies, researchers concentrated on how education influenced cognitive processes, comparing children and adults in traditional societies who received some education with those in their societies who were illiterate. Studies in the US and Europe have shown that some school problems of minority children resulted from their parents' views that their children's social development, rather than cognitive skills, was the key to future success at school (Harkness et al. 2000). In contrast, more highly educated parents had a strong autonomy orientation and placed a lot of attention on supporting their children's cognitive abilities. Moreover, stressing either autonomy or relatedness in children's development can result in both gains and losses. Improving children's social and cognitive skills prepare them for developing positive social relationships and problem-solving abilities (Jukes et al. 2018; Kagitçibaşi 2005; see also Chaps. 3, 9, and 10).

Part III: Children in Unique and Challenging Circumstances

The last section of the book examines the socialization of children under special conditions. Immigrant and refugee children find themselves in the host culture in circumstances that may differ greatly from their culture of origin. The socialization patterns and the social skills expected from children in their new country may be foreign to them and to their families, making it difficult to adjust and to cope with life in their new social world (see Chap. 14). Indeed, the social world and socialization practices of institutionalized children in different countries is also unlike that of intact families and may be quite difficult for children who have experienced extended and severely depriving institutional care (Chap. 16). Those who work with children and families in these different situations need to be culturally-sensitive with regard to childrearing beliefs and practices that would help these children adapt to their new situations. Children's conceptions of safe and dangerous places—a topic especially important in Israel where many children are at risk due to poverty, lack of legal status of families, living in a war zone—shows how well children cope with challenging life circumstances (Chap. 15).

Conclusions and Future Directions

As should be evident across the chapters in the book, there is no universal pathway for optimal social development. Many existing theories do not encompass the cultural variability of the development of social skills. More specifically, developmental theories, assumed to be universal, often do not fit well into the non-English and non-Western world; interventions based on Western developmental models may recommend to parents and others practices that do not fit the child's social setting. For example, a recent intervention tried to reduce rural-living Senegalese mothers' reliance on non-verbal communication (Morelli et al. 2018). Mothers were trained to talk with their children, one-on-one, in play situations using Western-style discourse, which was contrary to standards of good caregiving in these communities, stigmatizing the mothers who followed the training. With increased immigration into many Western countries, clashes between migrant families with different non-Western life-styles and educational levels would be expected. It is important to recognize such variability and to understand its sources and consequences. Surprisingly little is known about specific aspects of social development in many cultures, but such knowledge is critical for expanding theoretical conceptions of human development.

Future research should examine the values, rationale, and mechanisms of social development across varying cultural contexts. Socialization agents have their own distinctive representations of their culture and the ways they choose to shape children to be successful in those settings. Research has shown how the child develops through interactions with more competent members of the society (Vygotsky 1978) and the dyadic interaction between mother and child became the benchmark. Left out of this common conception of socialization were children in traditional societies where co-parenting by several family members and others was typical, as well as the roles of fathers, non-parental adults, siblings, peers, and grandparents.

The variety found in children's contexts, their developmental niche (Super and Harkness 1986), points to the links between their physical and social setting, the culturally-determined childrearing practices of the society, and parents' psychological characteristics. All of these determine the contexts parents choose for their children (Whiting 1980). Bronfenbrenner's (Bronfenbrenner and Morris 2006) bioecological model recognized the broader cultural elements in children's worlds, such as their neighborhoods, their parents' workplace and social networks, as well as the governmental and economic conditions in which they live. Children learn a great deal over the preschool years, which can readily be seen in a classic study by Barker and Wright (1951, 1955). They observed a 7-year-old American boy from the time he woke up one morning to the time he went to bed that night. They recorded everything the boy did, everywhere he went, and all that happened to him during that one day.

They found he participated in 1300 distinct activities in a variety of settings involving hundreds of objects and dozens of people. It was amazing to see the wide range of his social interactions and the cognitive and social skills he demonstrated. Investigating a child within the child's social context, the child's social network, looking at the people with whom the child has everyday contacts and who influence the child's social development, would be an immense challenge for researchers. Moreover, it could potentially lead to a deeper understanding of children's social development.

References

Barker, R. G., & Wright, H. F. (1951). *One boy's day: A specimen record of behavior*. New York: Harper Brothers.

Barker, R. G., & Wright, H. F. (1955). *Midwest and its children*. New York: Harper & Row.

Best, D. L., House, A. S., Barnard, A. E., & Spicker, B. S. (1994). Parent-child interaction in France, Germany, and Italy: The effects of gender and culture. *Journal of Cross-Cultural Psychology, 25,* 181–193.

Bronfenbrenner, U., & Morris, P. A. (2006). The bioecological model of human development. In R. M. Lerner & W. Damon (Eds.), *Handbook of child psychology: Theoretical models of human development* (pp. 793–828). Hoboken, NJ, US: Wiley.

Cole, M., & Scribner, S. (1981). *The psychology of literacy*. Cambridge, MA and London, England: Harvard University Press.

Greenfield, P. M., Keller, H., Fuligni, A., & Maynard, A. (2003). Cultural development through universal developmental tasks. *Annual Review of Psychology, 54,* 1–23.

Harkness, S. Raeff, C., & Super, C. M. (Eds.) (2000). Variability in the social construction of the child. In *New directions in child and adolescent development* (p. 87). San Francisco, CA: Jossey-Bass.

Jukes, M. C. H., Zuilkowski, S. S., & Grigorenko, E. L. (2018). Do schooling and urban residence develop cognitive skills at the expense of social responsibility? A study of adolescents in The Gambia, West Africa. *Journal of Cross-Cultural Psychology, 49*(1), 82–98.

Kagitçibaşi, Ç. (2005). Autonomy and relatedness in cultural context: Implications for self and family. *Journal of Cross-Cultural Psychology, 36,* 403–422.

Köster, M., Schuhmacher, N., & Kärtner, J. (2015). A cultural perspective on prosocial development. *Human Ethology Bulletin, 30,* 71–82.

Morelli, G., Quinn, N., Chaudhary, N., Vicedo, M., Rosabal-Coto, M., Keller, H., et al. (2018). Ethical challenges of parenting interventions in low- to middle-income countries. *Journal of Cross-Cultural Psychology, 49,* 5–24. https://doi.org/10.1177/0022022117746241.

Silva, K. G., Shimpi, P. M., & Rogoff, B. (2015). Young children's attention to what's going on. *Advances in Child Development and Behavior, 49,* 207–227.

Super, C., & Harkness, S. (1986). The developmental niche: A conceptualization at the interface of society and the individual. *International Journal of Behavioral Development, 9,* 545–570.

Tulviste, P. (1991). *The cultural-historical development of verbal thinking*. Hauppauge, NY, US: Nova Science Publishers.

Vygotsky, L. S. (1978). *Mind in society: The development of higher psychological processes*. Cambridge, MA: Harvard University Press.

Wagner, D. A. (1978). The effects of formal schooling on cognitive style. *The Journal of Social Psychology, 106,* 145–151.

Whiting, B. B. (1980). Culture and social behavior: A model for the development of social behavior. *Ethos, 8,* 95–116.

Index

A

Agency, 16, 104, 188, 201, 204, 205, 207, 211–213
Aggression, 78, 82, 103, 106, 109
Autonomy, 3, 15, 49, 60, 68, 89, 99, 103–105, 107, 108, 110–112, 117, 120–125, 127, 128, 141, 142, 144, 192, 235, 237

B

Baby X, 77, 78

C

Challenging circumstances, 1, 2, 4, 237
Child development, 26, 63, 68, 135, 138, 145, 150, 161–163, 168, 169, 179, 180, 182, 187, 190, 191, 193, 194, 197, 198, 218
Child language development, 138
Children's Perspectives, 4, 201, 202, 204–207
Communicative development, 138
Context, 1, 3, 5, 9–12, 14–16, 18, 19, 28, 35, 42, 45, 46, 48, 49, 55, 56, 61, 63, 66, 68, 75, 76, 81, 84, 89, 90, 96, 98, 104, 105, 108, 109, 111, 118–120, 125, 128, 136, 138, 140–144, 150, 152, 154, 156, 161, 167, 168, 178, 180, 187, 189–197, 201, 203–205, 207, 211–213, 226, 233–235, 238, 239
Conversations, 4, 14, 15, 27, 34, 41, 46–48, 59, 63, 64, 66, 67, 92, 124, 135, 137–145, 157, 207, 208, 234–236

Cross-cultural psychology childhood, 15, 43, 45, 50, 80, 84, 89, 95, 103, 106–108, 154, 169, 201, 237
Cultural change, 35, 220
Cultural differences, 3, 9, 11, 25–27, 33, 41, 46, 50, 59, 63, 64, 89, 95, 97, 98, 103–105, 107, 108, 111, 112, 137, 140, 142, 143, 212, 236
Cultural practice, 2, 23–25, 33–35, 95, 98, 104, 117, 153, 156, 180, 196, 234, 235
Cultural psychology childhood, 84
Cultural variations, 27, 28, 34, 35, 43, 45, 56, 64, 161, 162, 170, 236
Culture, 1, 2, 4, 5, 10, 15, 19, 25, 33, 43–45, 48–51, 55–57, 59–61, 63–68, 78, 79, 81–83, 89, 90, 93, 94, 96, 97, 99, 103–112, 117, 118, 121, 126, 128, 135, 137–145, 149–151, 157, 161–164, 167, 168, 170, 176, 180, 201, 203, 204, 212, 219, 233–238
Customs of childcare, 98, 192

D

Deontic reasoning, 49
Developmental niche, 89, 98, 162, 187, 191, 193, 198, 238
Directives, 11, 110, 138–141, 144
Dyads, 3, 47, 63, 112, 117, 123–126, 128, 139, 142

E

Early childhood, 14, 41, 56, 94, 149, 162–164, 166–168, 179, 181–183, 187, 191, 192, 194, 205, 206

© Springer Nature Switzerland AG 2019
T. Tulviste et al. (eds.), *Children's Social Worlds in Cultural Context*,
https://doi.org/10.1007/978-3-030-27033-9

Ecocultural methods, 150
Ecocultural theory, 150
Emotional competence, 55, 56, 58–62, 65, 68, 236
Emotional development, 3, 15, 55, 56, 58, 62, 68, 154, 173, 175, 182, 194, 195
Emotional reminiscing, 63, 66
Emotion display rules, 58, 67
Emotion regulation, 3, 56, 58–61, 162, 223
Emotions, 2–4, 15, 17, 42, 43, 45, 47, 48, 55–63, 65–68, 82, 90, 92, 154, 163, 173, 177–180, 182, 183, 234–237

F
False-belief, 42, 43, 48–50
Free play, 11, 79, 107, 120, 122, 125, 126, 140, 174

G
Gender development, 75, 77, 80
Gender differences, 2, 11, 14, 16, 66, 67, 75, 81, 82, 93, 94, 123, 127
Gender non-conformity, 77, 83
Gender reveal, 75, 84
Gender schemes, 81
Gender segregation, 11, 79, 80
Gender socialization, 3, 75, 76, 78–80, 127
Gender stereotypes, 81–83
Grandparents, 4, 30, 152, 161–170, 238
Gyarari, 177–179, 181

H
Helping, 3, 34, 59, 63, 81, 82, 89–99, 108, 152, 154, 166, 167, 176, 180, 234, 235

I
Immigrant children, 48, 202
Immigrant families, 27, 30, 128, 194, 206
Indigenous American, 29
Interactions, 1–3, 9–11, 14, 15, 27, 31, 41, 44–47, 49, 51, 55, 58, 59, 61–64, 68, 75, 76, 94, 97, 99, 103, 104, 109, 111, 118–122, 126, 135, 137, 139–142, 144, 149, 150, 155–157, 161–164, 168, 169, 174, 175, 177, 178, 180, 191, 205, 212, 219, 222, 224–226, 236, 238, 239

J
Japan, 57, 65, 66, 108, 109, 155, 165, 173, 176, 178, 180, 183

L
LOPI, 23, 28, 29, 34, 95, 97

M
Mental states, 2, 41, 44–51, 121, 154, 236
Mimamoru, 173, 175–177, 181, 182
Moral rules, 12, 14, 235
Mother-child interaction, 139, 140
Multi-cultural teams, 49, 137, 161
Multitasking, 31, 32

N
Nurturance, 78, 79, 82, 96, 149, 155, 167

O
Observational learning, 154, 177–179, 181

P
Parents, 2–4, 14, 15, 23, 27–30, 35, 45, 47, 48, 55, 56, 58–68, 75–80, 83, 90, 92, 95–99, 104, 105, 108, 110, 111, 119, 120, 122, 123, 135, 137, 138, 140, 141, 143, 144, 149–154, 156, 162–170, 189–197, 203–206, 208, 212, 217, 220–222, 226, 233–238
Peer conflict, 3, 103–105, 107, 110–112
Peer socialization, 236
Peripheral Participation, 177–181
Perspectives on migration, 46, 190, 201, 202, 207
Positive parenting, 195
Preschool, 1, 2, 4, 9, 11, 14, 15, 18, 19, 45, 58, 59, 62, 64–66, 79, 81, 103, 106, 109, 111, 154, 163, 168, 173–181, 183, 206, 212, 220, 233, 234, 238
Preschool age, 4, 58, 62, 82, 111, 135, 137, 161–163, 169, 202, 222
Preschool children, 9–11, 46, 81, 103–109, 112, 123, 169, 181
Preschoolers, 11, 58, 59, 65, 67, 105, 126, 135, 139–141, 235
Prosocial behavior, 2, 3, 65, 89–94, 96–99, 154, 173, 183, 235
Protection, 201–213, 223

Psychological autonomy, 117, 120–125, 127, 128, 142
Psychology of caretaker, 98, 191, 193

R
Recollections, 14–19, 142
Refugee children, 4, 187, 189–196, 237
Refugee families, 4, 187, 189, 192, 195–197
Relatedness, 3, 15, 48, 49, 89, 97, 103–105, 107, 108, 110–112, 121, 123, 125, 127, 141–144, 237
Reminiscing, 14, 15, 18, 19, 45, 46, 49, 63, 64, 66, 67, 141–143
Risk, 4, 5, 33, 50, 67, 79, 82, 162, 169, 176, 188, 194–196, 201–213, 217, 218, 223, 224, 226, 238

S
Schooling, 2, 25–30, 32, 33, 35, 44, 121, 122, 237
Sharing, 50, 82, 89–94, 108, 117, 125
Sibling, 4, 9, 11, 26, 27, 45, 120, 149–157, 193
Sibling caregiving, 150
Sibling caretaking, 96, 153–156
Sibling interactions, 150, 152, 154–156
Simultaneous attention, 23, 25, 27–29, 31–34

Social cognition, 9, 14, 15, 17–19, 43, 45, 91
Social development, 1, 2, 4, 5, 19, 75, 96, 155, 162, 169, 224, 233, 235–239
Social identity, 9, 14, 15, 18, 19, 235
Socialization, 2–4, 9–12, 14, 18, 26, 55, 56, 59–61, 63–68, 77, 79, 80, 90, 92, 104, 108, 110, 111, 117, 120–123, 125, 127, 128, 135, 141, 143, 156, 157, 163, 167, 187, 189–194, 196–198, 226, 234–238
Socialization agents, 3, 9, 14, 19, 105, 162, 168, 235, 238
Social norms, 12, 14, 49, 90, 191
Social referencing, 62
Social relationships, 2, 49, 59, 89, 121, 152, 233, 234, 237
Socio-cultural context, 2, 5, 44, 104, 111, 141, 194, 196, 198, 233

T
Talkativeness, 12, 14, 138
Tangram, 123–126
ToM, 47, 48, 50, 51, 92
Triads, 3, 26, 31, 32, 117, 121–126, 235

W
Watching and waiting, 173, 175, 176, 182

Made in United States
Orlando, FL
13 June 2023

34098654R00148